Global Finance and Social Europe

NEW DIRECTIONS IN MODERN ECONOMICS

Series Editor: Malcolm C. Sawyer

Professor of Economics, University of Leeds, UK

New Directions in Modern Economics presents a challenge to orthodox economic thinking. It focuses on new ideas emanating from radical traditions including post-Keynesian, Kaleckian, neo-Ricardian and Marxian. The books in the series do not adhere rigidly to any single school of thought but attempt to present a positive alternative to the conventional wisdom.

A list of published titles in this series is printed at the end of this volume.

Global Finance and Social Europe

Edited by

John Grahl

Professor of European Integration
Middlesex University Business School, UK

NEW DIRECTIONS IN MODERN ECONOMICS

Edward Elgar
Cheltenham, UK • Northampton, MA, USA

Published by
Edward Elgar Publishing Limited
The Lypiatts
15 Lansdown Road
Cheltenham
Glos GL50 2JA
UK

Edward Elgar Publishing, Inc.
William Pratt House
9 Dewey Court
Northampton
Massachusetts 01060
USA

A catalogue record for this book
is available from the British Library

Library of Congress Control Number: 2009925916

PEFC
PEFC/16-33-111
CATG-PEFC-052
www.pefc.org

ISBN 978 1 84720 643 5 (cased)

Printed and bound by MPG Books Group, UK

Contents

v

Figures and boxes

FIGURES

BOXES

Tables

Contributors

Thorsten Block is currently teaching economics and mathematics at Schulzentrum Bördestraße in Bremen, Germany. He received his PhD in economics at the New School for Social Research. He has also worked as a consultant for the United Nations Development Programme and the World Bank and has conducted research on financial systems at the Maastricht Economic Research Institute on Innovation and Technology (MERIT) in the Netherlands.

Trevor Evans worked for many years at the Regional Centre for Economic and Social Research in Managua, Nicaragua. He is currently Professor of Economics at the Berlin School of Economics and is an active member of the European Economists for an Alternative Economic Policy in Europe (EuroMemorandum Group). His recent research has been concerned with economic and financial developments in the US, and their international impact.

Marica Frangakis is currently working for the National Bank of Greece Group. Her principal research areas include economic policy coordination, privatization, financial integration in the EU. Her recent publications include a co-edited book *Privatisation against the European Social Model* (Palgrave; forthcoming). She is a member of the board of the Nicos Poulantzas Institute, a non-profit making institution, promoting public debate in a variety of areas. She is also active in the EuroMemorandum Group.

John Grahl is Professor of European Integration at Middlesex University Business School. His main research interests are European economic policies, European employment relations and financial integration in Europe. Recent publications include (with Photis Lysandrou) 'Capital market trading volume: an overview and some preliminary conclusions', *Cambridge Journal of Economics*, 2006, and 'Global finance after the credit crisis', *Journal der Entwicklungspolitik* (Vienna), 2009. He is active in the EuroMemorandum Group.

Jörg Huffschmnid is a retired Professor of Political Economy and Economic Policy at the University of Bremen. He studied philosophy and economics in Freiburg, Paris and Berlin, and did research at the LSER in London, at the IMEMO in Moscow and at the INI in Madrid. He was Visiting

Professor at the New School for Social Research in New York and the Université de Paris 13. His special fields of interest are financial markets, European integration and alternative economic policy. He is co-founder of the EuroMemorandum Group.

Photis Lysandrou is Professor of Global Political Economy at London Metropolitan University. His current research focuses on the political economy of globalization, global finance and corporate governance. Recent publications include 'Globalisation as commodification', *Cambridge Journal of Economics*, 2005 and (with Denitsa Stoyanova) 'The anachronism of the voice-exit paradigm: institutional investors and UK corporate governance' in *Corporate Governance: International Review*, 2007.

Dominique Plihon is Professor at the Department of Economics of Paris-Nord University. He has worked for the Banque de France and the Commissariat du Plan and was a member of the Conseil Economique, which advises the French government. He is also chairman of the scientific committee of Attac France. He has published widely in the fields of banking, international finance and European economics. Recent publications edited with other economists are: *Crises Financières* (Documentation Française, 2004), and *The New Banking Economics* (Edward Elgar, 2007).

Jan Toporowski is Senior Lecturer in Economics at the School of Oriental and African Studies, University of London, and is a Research Associate of the Research Centre for the History and Methodology of Economics at the University of Amsterdam. He has worked in fund management, international banking and central banking. His most recent book, *Theories of Financial Disturbance* was published by Edward Elgar in 2005.

Acknowledgements

Much of the work leading to this book was carried out in a thematic network, 'Financial Integration and Social Cohesion' (FISC), sponsored by the European Commission (contract HPSE-CT-2002-50027). The authors are particularly grateful to Ronan O'Brien, who acted as scientific controller of the project for the Commission, for the diligence and care with which he supported their work.

Two members of the FISC network, Professor Geert Reuten and Dr Robert Went, both of the University of Amsterdam, although they did not write chapters for this book, made very great contributions to the research and the discussions on which it is based.

The authors are grateful to the following experts who contributed to the seminars and conferences of the FISC network. None of them is responsible for the views expressed in this book.

Dr Kern Alexander of the Endowment for Research in Finance, Cambridge University; Professor Riccardo Bellofiore of the University of Bergamo; Dr Hans-Juergen Bieling of the University of Marburg; Dr Christophe Boucher of the Université Paris-Nord; Professor Robert Boyer of CEPREMAP, Paris; Mr Paul Cockerell of the British Trade Union Amicus and Ford UK; Mr Bryn Davies, Director of Union Pension Services Ltd; Professor Wlodzimierz Dymarski of Poznan University; Professor Miren Etxezarreta of the Autonomous University, Barcelona; Professor Peter Gowan of London Metropolitan University; Dr Walter Heering of the University of Brighton; Dr Jens Hölscher of the University of Brighton; Ms Laura Horn of the University of Amsterdam; Professor Michel Husson of INSEE and IRES; Dr Gregory Jackson of King's College London; Professor Tadeusz Kowalik of the Institute of Economics, Academy of Sciences, Warsaw; Dr Christel Lane of Cambridge University; Dr Susanne Lütz of the University of Hagen; Dr Helios Mayer, of BP&Mayer Consultants' Research Department, Ljubljana; Professor David Mayes of the Central Bank of Finland; Professor José Mencinger of Ljubljana University; Dr Anastasia Nesvetailova, of the University of Sussex; Professor Henk Overbeek of the Free University of Amsterdam; Mr James Perry of the University of Amsterdam; Professor Malcolm Sawyer of Leeds University Business School; Professor Bruno Théret of IRIS-TS and the University of Paris-Dauphiné; Dr Euclid Tsakalotos of the Athens University of Economics and Business; Professor Martin Upchurch of Middlesex University Business School; Professor Kees van der Pijl of Sussex University; Dr George Vaphiades of the Agricultural Bank of Greece; Mr Kees Vendrik, Spokesman on Finance for the Dutch Green-Left in the Netherlands Parliament; Dr Sigurt Vitols, of the Wissenschaftszentrum Berlin für Sozialforschung; Mr Arjan Vliegenthart of the University of Amsterdam; Dr Diana Wehlau of Bremen University; Professor Karel Williams of the University of Manchester.

Introduction

John Grahl

FINANCIAL CHANGE IN EUROPE

The financial systems of European countries are undergoing rapid change. The forces involved can be divided into two main groups. On the one hand, the various developments covered by the term globalization, involving increasing interactions across state borders and increasing interdependence among national systems of all kinds, are particularly marked in the sphere of finance – indeed it is clear that liberalized finance is one of the main forces behind the globalization process as a whole. On the other hand, there is a well-defined response by political leaderships in the European Union who have adopted a strategy of deeper financial integration within Europe – the key element of this strategy in recent years has been the Financial Services Action Plan (FSAP).

The increasing importance of financial relations across national borders, indicated both by very large international capital flows and by closely correlated movements in interest rates and share prices across many economies, has made for significant changes in the character of financial systems and in how financial sectors interact with households, governments and corporations.

One of these changes is a widespread expansion of financial sectors, which nearly everywhere account for a larger fraction of economic activity. Another, very important, change is a general decline in the ability of governments to influence financial processes – the removal or attenuation of official constraints on financial transactions has been both a cause and a consequence of the increasing internationalization of finance. Although forms of supranational financial regulation have emerged in response to this decline, these are in an early stage of development and certainly do not re-establish the comprehensive control over finance which existed in many countries up to the 1970s. Thirdly there has been a marked shift in the way finance is provided: although the shift has been very uneven in its timing and across different countries, security markets of all kinds, for company shares and for bonds as well as for complex derivatives based on both of these, have been playing a wider role while bank credit has tended to account for a smaller fraction of total financial provision. (This does not mean that the banks as institutions are less important; in fact large banks are extremely important actors in the new financial landscape and are involved in most aspects of security-based finance.)

The financial integration strategy of the EU has tended to reinforce these changes because that strategy has, in recent years, centred on the development of big financial markets, similar to those found in the United States. The US in fact has been the key model for European policy-makers as they tried to promote a unified, continent-wide, financial system.

The general assessment of this strategy made by the authors of this book is that the European financial integration strategy is a rational response to global developments. To put it baldly, if the Europeans failed to build large, liquid capital markets they would simply drive every investor in and issuer of securities into the North American ones. Such an outcome would have two potential disadvantages for Europe: it might lose influence over the shape of the emerging global financial system; and it might fail to develop strategic advantages in the financial sector itself.

There is extensive literature (for example Hall and Soskice, 2001), which emphasizes the strengths of Europe's inherited financial systems. Typically these written works have given a very big role to relationship banking (bank deposits being the primary way in which retail customers participated in the financial system). Large inside investors have provided much corporate finance, which has therefore depended less on the security markets than in the US. Stable, long-term relations between the users and the providers of funds, often supported by other social relations between them, such as membership of the same regional community, have lowered some of the costs and risks of arranging finance.

On the other hand, the traditional financial systems in Europe were fragmented and under competitive pressure from the globalized systems which developed first in the US. These systems themselves have important strengths arising from their scale and the standardization of many types of financial transaction.

Thus the integration of Europe's financial systems logically implies a change in their nature, both to meet external challenges and to facilitate the development of continent-wide financial relations within Europe itself.

FINANCE AND EUROPEAN SOCIETY

However, these financial transformations may have significant social consequences. This follows from the close connections between financial systems and other, usually national or regional, social structures. The scale and pervasiveness of the financial changes taking place, which imply other transformations in the economic system, also suggest that social consequences need to be investigated.

Four major issues in this context arise from ongoing debates among European social scientists. They are very different in their nature but a consideration of each seems essential for any systematic consideration of the social developments in question.

Economic Stability

The first question arises within the economic sphere itself and concerns the possible instability of the new, more integrated financial system with its stronger orientation towards the security markets. The implications of the emerging system for stability by no means all run in the same direction. On the one hand the increased speed and fluidity of financial relations may allow more scope for disturbances, while denser connections among financial actors may propagate these disturbances on a wider scale. The critical developments in financial systems in 2007 illustrate these dangers in a very clear way. On the other hand security-market finance at least in principle permits a very wide dispersion of risks and a much more complete diversification of portfolios while avoiding the concentration of risks in the banking system. However, recent developments indicate that the apparent securitization of bank assets does not always effectively move the risks involved away from the banks involved.

The social consequences of financial instability are clear – increased insecurity in employment and income for much of the population. In welfare terms it is therefore justified to accept lower average returns on investments if this contributes to greater financial and therefore economic stability. The policy issues which arise concern in the first instance financial supervision and regulation, and in the event of major disturbances, crisis management. But these regulatory questions then connect with institutional ones because they concern the complex assignment of tasks and responsibilities among authorities at national EU and world levels.

Social Protection

A second series of questions concerns the relationship between financial change and the reform of social protection systems. Clearly, in this case, the outcomes do not arise from market processes alone but involve political decisions. Nevertheless, there are close connections between the two spheres of finance and social protection: these are focused on the activities of the institutional investors (Davis and Steil, 2001).

The expansion of these institutional investors, insurance companies and collective investment organizations is a key aspect of current financial change. They channel household savings into the security markets by permitting a much more comprehensive diversification of portfolios than would be possible for most households if they invested directly.

A series of policy questions concerns the ability of institutional investors to take over some of the functions presently carried out by social security systems. The two areas most affected are health care and pension provision – this book focuses on the latter merely in order to keep the discussion manageable. There have already been moves in several countries to give institutional investors a larger role in pension provision, and the EU itself has tended to support this type of change. The main motive is to meet budgetary constraints but there are other goals which include the promotion of financial change itself and the desire to reshape incentives around employment and savings.

There are several potential social problems with this policy direction. One important issue concerns equality. The pay-as-you-go public pension systems which are currently under pressure allocate benefits roughly in line with wages. The institutional schemes which are being substituted for them can hardly avoid allocating benefits in accordance with wealth which, as is well known, is much more unequally distributed than income.

Retail Financial Services

A third set of issues concerns the provision of retail financial services. The relationship between these and wholesale financial transactions among banks, big corporations and security markets which have so far been central to the process of integration is itself an important policy question. The integration of wholesale finance, it was suggested above, is a rational policy response to ongoing developments in the global economy. The logic of integration in the retail market is much less clear. Nor indeed have general initiatives been taken in this field: although a programme to integrate mortgage markets was recently under active discussion at the European Commission, the recent chaos in US mortgage markets has probably put paid to that initiative.

Two rather different questions can be mentioned. There is the emergence of web-based financial services which may lead to more cross-border provision of retail financial services. Problems of regulation and control follow from this, which suggest a greater role for the EU.

However, a second issue concerns the consequences for individuals and households of the general changes in financial systems now taking place. The quality of retail services, their cost and accessibility, the risks of financial exclusion, and the cost of credit to low-income households are all characteristics of retail finance which might be affected by the transformation of wholesale systems. The necessary investigations here concern market processes but also regulatory practices. There is an obvious link to the issue discussed above of the substitution of private for public pension provision; such substitution is useful only if retail financial services are of a high quality.

The strengths and weaknesses of retail finance in the United Kingdom seem to offer useful evidence here. The UK financial system is in general much closer to that in the US than are many other systems within the EU. To some extent it indicates the advantages and disadvantages of the kind of transformations which are taking place elsewhere.

Finance and Employment Relations

Finally, financial change may have very important implications for the nature of European employment relations. This can be indicated briefly by pointing to the well-known contrast between a 'shareholder' and a 'stakeholder' concept of the business enterprise. Clearly this is not a hard and fast distinction – opinions on the matter have developed rapidly.[1]

However, the two concepts or models of the enterprise do still imply a different status for employees within it. The shareholder model makes the leadership of the enterprise into the agents of the legal owners as principals, and commits them to formulate strategies only in the interests of these principals. In a stakeholder conception, on the other hand, managerial strategies are determined by a coalition of interests that include labour.

Of course there are many difficulties in assessing whether corporate behaviour in Europe is actually moving from a stakeholder towards a shareholder model. It is certainly not the case that the increased salience of security markets in corporate finance must lead to such a result. The most closely studied case is probably that of Germany, and here there are disagreements about how far corporate behaviour is changing and what the implications for employees will be.

Nevertheless, there can be no doubt that these questions of employment relations are central to the European social models because they relate to the future nature of the social partnerships and the social dialogues which are, almost by definition, key components of the models.

PLAN OF THE BOOK

This book is based on the work of a European network (FISC) which discussed these issues intensively with a wide range of specialists over a period of three years. The network did not adopt any narrowly specified methodology – given the range of issues and their very different character, it was important to adopt a multi-disciplinary approach and to make use of all studies that helped to clarify the key questions. Nor did the authors attempt to reach unanimous conclusions – at the end of the work there were still some significant divergences among the authors on both theoretical and policy questions.

Nevertheless, the authors, all of whom are active in the Euromemorandum Group,[2] were broadly agreed on two key aspects of the work. In regard to financial processes themselves, they made eclectic use of work in each of the mainstream paradigms: the very abstract efficient markets approach; the asymmetric information approach which makes a major contribution to the understanding of economic institutions; as well as recent critical work within the mainstream, such as behavioural finance and the study of market microstructure. The only question asked was whether a particular study was useful for the research tasks of the network.

However, it is the case that all the members of the group have been influenced by heterodox, essentially neo-Marxist or post-Keynesian theories.[3] These schools of thought most certainly do not reject the insights referred to above but they share a common emphasis on the role of finance in disequilibrated economic systems. As Grahl (2007) points out, both the Marxian and Keynesian traditions call into question the tendency of markets to clear. In doing so they suggest firstly that only effective financial mechanisms permit a market economy to endure and secondly that the key adjustments in such economies are brought about by the pressure of surplus on deficit units rather than by the abstract responses to alterations in relative prices which are invoked in standard theories. Likewise both heterodox traditions, in spite of their differences, tend to regard finance as essentially the mobilization of monetary resources. The mainstream definition of a financial transaction as one which takes place over time is certainly not incorrect but tends to be seen as somewhat abstract.

This orientation does not automatically support any particular conclusions, positive or normative, about financial processes but it does suggest that these processes are extremely important and that changes in the financial sphere may be closely related to those in broader structures of production and exchange.

The second area of broad agreement among the authors concerns social justice. All the schools of thought in which the mainstream discussion of

European financial integration is rooted, have in common the belief that it is essentially market distortions which prevent financial markets from working in the most efficient way possible. In this view, inequalities of income and wealth are irrelevant to financial market efficiency. In contrast to this, the starting point of the authors represented in this volume is that banks and financial markets are chiefly influenced in the conduct of their business by the financing requirements of the wealthy and of the large corporations that have the widest access to and choice in banking and financial markets, and by the balance sheet requirements of the largest banks and financial institutions. The distribution of wealth and income is therefore a key conditioning factor in the functioning of those markets. In so far as an increasing proportion of wealth consists of financial assets, and because many ordinary households are increasingly debilitated by a lack of access to banking and financial services, the effects of financial intermediation on the distribution of wealth and income are a critical aspect of the efficiency of those services. The distributional conditions and consequences of European financial integration are the key links to social justice in the various spheres discussed in the following chapters.

Since these broad agreements were seen as more important than the differences of opinion among the authors, what they present in this book is not a simple collection of papers but rather a systematic and unified account of financial change in Europe and its social consequences. Because of the actual divergences, each chapter is signed by its main author, who assumes responsibility for the views expressed in it, but the sequence of chapters tries to achieve a logical and inclusive structure.

The first two chapters, by Trevor Evans, present a condensed account firstly of financial processes in general and then of international finance as they function in today's economies. These chapters specify, in some detail, the nature of the global financial processes which are developing and the same time explain the economic meaning of the main types of financial market and financial institution discussed throughout the book.

The third and fourth chapters, by Marica Frangakis, put European issues in the foreground: Chapter 3 analyses the pressures for change arising from globalized finance, while Chapter 4 gives a detailed account of the EU's financial integration policies.

The fifth chapter, by John Grahl, relates EU financial policies to the general framework of EU policy summed up in the Lisbon strategy. The sixth, by Grahl and Thorsten Block takes a highly critical look at some of the technical studies of financial integration sponsored by the Commission.

The focus then shifts to the four types of social impact discussed above. Jan Toporowski examines, in Chapter 7, the problems of stability associated with financial integration. The recent turbulence on financial markets clearly demonstrates the importance of the issue of stability, casually dismissed by the European Commission in its drive for financial market integration. In Chapter 8 Photis Lysandrou poses a key question: what are the implications of changing patterns of finance for European corporations?

In Chapters 9, 10 and 11, John Grahl continues the examination of the social impact of financial change, looking first at social security (especially pensions), then retail finance and finally employment relations. It is argued in each case that the EU drive for rapid integration is not accompanied by sufficient concern to prevent adverse social consequences.

The last four chapters, by Jörg Huffschmid and Dominique Plihon, continue the discussion of social impacts, but now with a specific view to making policy recommendations. In Chapter 12, Huffschmid proposes a range of interventions and controls designed to strengthen the position of ordinary citizens, both as employees and as consumers, against the power of the banks and financial corporations. In Chapter 13, he makes a strong case for the preservation and development of public pay-as-you-go pensions. Plihon discusses in Chapter 14 the measures needed to counter the acute financial instability of recent years. In the final chapter he widens the discussion to consider policy responses to the globalization process as a whole.

NOTES

1. See, as an interesting example, the evolving views of Michel Jensen (Jensen and Murphy, 2004), once regarded as a leading champion of the shareholder model
2. The Euromemorandum Group, 'Alternative Economic Policy for Europe', researches EU economic policies and publishes a critical assessment of them every year. See www.memo-europe.uni-bremen.de.
3. Indeed the FISC network included, in Professor Reuten and Dr Toporowski, two very distinguished historians of these schools of thought.

1. Money and finance today

Trevor Evans

1.1 INTRODUCTION

Money is such a pervasive feature of a capitalist economy that it is easy to take it for granted. Money, of course, did not arise with capitalism – the earliest surviving coins, found in Western Asia, date from the seventh century BC.[1] Nevertheless, in the ancient world, as for much of the Middle Ages, monetary transactions were relatively confined, and the lives of large parts of the population were not dependent on them. In a developed capitalist country, by contrast, money is omnipresent. Households depend on obtaining some type of monetary income, in most cases by means of paid work. The principal dynamic of the economy is determined by firms which invest money with the aim of making even more money. And while the state has come to play a major role in the economy, its scope is dependent on raising money, generally either through taxes or borrowing.

Although money is so widespread under capitalism, economists differ greatly on its economic significance. The mainstream or neoclassical approach to economics believes that money is like a veil in that it obscures what lies behind it. For this reason, it considers that it is helpful to separate economic analysis into a real and a monetary sphere. According to this view, by first focusing on the real sphere, where money is left out, it is easier to grasp the most important processes that take place in an economy. Neoclassical economists consider that money can then be added at a later stage of the analysis, and that it does not change anything fundamental about how the economy works. In this approach, money is said to be neutral, by which it is meant that developments in the monetary sphere do not have any impact on real variables, such as the level of output or employment. Many neoclassical economists do accept that, in the short run, money might have some effect on the real economy, but they are united in the view that, in the long run, money is neutral.

Heterodox economists, by contrast, insist that money is not neutral, even in the long run, and that it is not possible to understand how a capitalist economy works unless money is taken into account from the

1

very outset of the analysis.[2] According to this view, advancing money with the aim of making even more money is the central motivating force in a capitalist economic system. Heterodox economists also stress that in a monetary economy, the sale of one product does not necessarily imply the simultaneous purchase of another product, as it would in a moneyless economy. Consequently, it is possible for some producers to refrain from reinvesting the proceeds of their sales, and simply to accumulate money. If this happens, other producers will suffer from a lack of demand, and it will lead to a downturn in output and employment. In the worst of cases, if a significant number of firms are then unable to meet payment commitments (for instance for goods that have already been delivered, or for a bank loan), it can set off a financial crisis, a chain reaction that disrupts the economy at great social cost in a way that is difficult to envisage in a theoretical model without money.

1.2 FINANCE

The main feature of finance is that it is concerned with the mobilization of monetary resources. Businesses generally meet their regular payments for wages and other inputs using the money they receive from selling their products. But, if a firm's own resources are not sufficient to cover its spending, in particular when investment projects are being planned, it has to consider what other sources of money might be available. Similarly, although households generally cover most of their expenditures out of current income, they usually borrow in order to buy a house or to meet some exceptional needs.

The financial system is also concerned with managing risk, a feature that is particularly stressed by mainstream economists.[3] For firms with a financial surplus, or for wealthy households, the financial system provides a means of investing in various different types of assets, so as to reduce the risk of a big loss if one of the assets should fail. The financial system also provides various forms of insurance. In the simplest of cases, it offers protection against the risk of theft or fire or some other type of loss. In recent years there has also been an extraordinary growth of much more complex forms of insurance against financial risks, such as an adverse change in interest rates, or a credit default, through what are known as 'derivatives'.

Since the 1970s, the financial systems of the developed capitalist countries have all experienced a major increase in size and complexity as a result of an extensive process of innovation, deregulation and internationalization. Most mainstream economists take the view that this has been highly beneficial, that monetary resources have thereby been channelled to those that can employ them most efficiently, and that modern global networks have made it possible to diversify risks so as to strengthen the stability of the system as a whole. In this book we take a different view. We consider that the financial sector imposes excessive costs on the rest of the economy, that it does not ensure that capital is made available where it is most needed, and that it has been a key factor in leading to greater inequality and social insecurity. Although the financial system has succeeded in diversifying certain forms of risk, we believe that it has created new sources of potential instability that increase the risk of a major crisis for the system as a whole. This was demonstrated dramatically by the major financial crisis which erupted in the US in 2007, detonated by the failure of complex securities based on mortgages to low-income households.

1.3 THE DEVELOPMENT OF FINANCE

The development of the financial system in different countries has been strongly influenced by the state. One important factor has been the state's own need for finance. At the time when capitalism was emerging in Europe, monarchs often turned to wealthy merchants in order to meet their financial shortfalls, especially in times of war, providing an important impetus for the development of banking institutions. It was, for example, the British government's need for a large loan that led to the licensing of the Bank of England in 1694. To this day, government sales of bonds have played a key role in promoting and sustaining countries' capital markets, and government bond prices provide a benchmark for pricing bonds issued by private firms. The state has also played an important role through the impact of laws and regulations. Today financial institutions in the US and Britain are subject to far fewer constraints than those in countries such as Germany, where, despite some recent changes, banking is still subjected to a much more cautious ethos.

The most significant factor in the development of the financial system in most countries has been the financing of commerce and production. For many years, one of the main financial instruments was the bill of exchange, whose origin dates back to medieval trade fairs. A bill is a promise to pay a certain amount at a given date in the future. It was issued as a deferred form of paying for goods, but, once issued, it could circulate in payment for further goods, and the final holder would present it for redemption when it became due. In the nineteenth and early twentieth century, bills were an important source of financing for short-term commercial transactions, and a significant part of banks' business consisted in advancing money against such bills, a form of lending known as 'discounting'.[4] Today, firms are more likely to seek a short-term loan directly from their banks to finance such transactions.

For many businesses, obtaining external finance for longer-term fixed investment has usually been much more difficult than obtaining trade credit. At the time of the industrial revolution, most manufacturing enterprises in Britain were owned by a single person or family, and had to rely on their own financial resources. As the scale of businesses began to increase, the main form of raising larger sums of money was through a partnership, in which several individuals or households would pool their resources. The partners would share the profits, but they were also liable for any losses the partnership might incur. A crucial breakthrough occurred in the second half of the nineteenth century with the widespread introduction of the joint stock company and limited liability.[5] This enabled a company to raise much larger amounts of finance by issuing shares. The shareholders were the legal owners of the company, and, depending on how many shares they owned, they were entitled to a voice in the companies' policies and a share in any profits. Crucially, however, shareholders' liabilities were limited to the amount of capital they initially subscribed, so if a company went bankrupt, shareholders would lose their investment, but were not responsible for any debts the company might have run up. The joint stock company provided the basis for the emergence of large-scale firms in the late nineteenth and early twentieth century, notably in the US and Germany, which needed to establish large firms rapidly in order to compete with Britain, and to this day joint stock companies remain the predominant form of capitalist enterprise.[6]

While financial systems have long attended to the needs of the rich and powerful, it is only comparatively recently that they have begun to provide services for wider sectors of the population. As recently as 1980, one third of British households did not even have a bank account, although that had fallen to 6 per cent by 2006.[7] The situation is better in France, where there is a legal right to a bank account, and in Germany, where the savings banks are required to meet all requests for a bank account. In the US, however, 22 per cent of households, predominantly those with low incomes, did not have a bank account in 2002.[8] While long-term credits to finance the purchase of a home are generally available in most developed countries, the conditions often exclude low-income households, or drive them into more expensive mortgages, such as the so-called sub-prime market in the US. Furthermore, although consumer credit is widely available it is often exorbitantly expensive, with credit cards providing financial companies with one of their most profitable lines of business.

1.4 INTERNAL AND EXTERNAL FINANCE

The first issue facing a firm – or a household – when embarking on a large expenditure is whether it should be carried out using internal or external finance. For a business, the main sources of internal finance are accumulated profits, together with the depreciation funds that have been set aside to cover the cost of replacing fixed capital (equipment and infrastructure that last over many production cycles). Internal funds are by far the most important source of finance for businesses, and, according to one international study, account for at least two thirds of investment in the major capitalist economies (see Table 1.1).[9] Most businesses have a strong preference for internal finance, because it involves far fewer risks than external finance.[10]

A business might turn to external finance either because it does not have sufficient internal funds to finance a project, or because it wishes to keep at least some of its internal funds in reserve. There are two main channels through which a business can raise external finance. One is to approach a bank or some other financial intermediary for a loan; the other is to raise the money directly from the financial markets, by issuing a security, such as a bond or a share.

Drawing on external sources of finance can, however, pose risks for a company. If the company has borrowed the money, either through taking up a bank loan or by issuing a bond, then the money must be paid back with interest over a set period of time, and this could present a problem for the firm if its profits decline in the future, ultimately threatening it with bankruptcy. If, on the other hand, the firm has raised the external finance by issuing shares, it only has to pay shareholders a dividend in the event that it earns a profit; however, by increasing the number of shareholders in the company, it may tend to dilute control. In the extreme case, if poor returns should lead to a fall in the share price, another company might take over control completely by buying up a significant block of shares on the stock market.

As can be seen in Table 1.1, bank loans have been the most important form of external finance for companies in nearly all the main capitalist countries. Indeed for small and medium companies, this is generally the only source of external finance that is available to them. The US is the one country where bonds have accounted for a slightly larger share of external finance, although, in all the countries shown, bond financing has been increasing in importance since the 1990s. Share finance, by contrast, has – despite the publicity it receives – not been an important source of finance for the company sector as a whole, although it can be significant for some individual companies.[11]

Table 1.1   *Internal and external sources of company finance (per cent),*
1970–89

	Internal finance	External finance		
		Bank loans	Bonds	Shares
US	91.3	16.6	17.1	−8.8
Japan	69.3	30.5	4.7	3.7
West Germany	80.6	11.0	−0.6	0.9
France	66.3	47.7	0.7	−0.4
Britain	97.3	19.5	3.5	−10.4

Note: Rows do not sum to 100 as some other forms of finance are not listed.

Source: Corbett and Jenkinson (1996, p. 77).

1.5   THE BANKING SYSTEM

There are two main types of banks, commercial banks and investment banks. The distinctive feature of commercial banks is that they accept deposits and make loans. One of their primary functions is to run an economy's payments system. Today firms, and indeed most households, hold their money principally in the form of bank deposits. Most payments are then made by transferring a deposit from one account to another account, either with a cheque, a bank order or an electronic card.

A second and more striking function of the commercial banks is that they play a leading role in the process of creating money. When a commercial bank agrees to grant a loan to a firm or a household, it credits a deposit to their account at the bank, and the owner of the account can then draw on the deposit to make payments to other accounts. The deposits which banks create in this way result in money that did not exist before, and it is through this process that the total amount of money in an economy increases. Because bank deposits constitute the major part of the money supply in developed capitalist economies, the growth of the money supply is largely determined by the demand for loans and the commercial banks' willingness to fulfil this demand. The public authorities, through the central bank, only have an indirect impact on this process through the ability to influence interest rates.

Banks, of course, wish to be sure that their customers will repay their credits, and for this reason an important part of the business of banking consists in obtaining information about their customers' creditworthiness. However, as recent work by Joseph Stiglitz and others has stressed, banks always know less than their customers about how the money will actually be used, and how likely it is that the borrower will really be able to repay the loan.[12] For Stiglitz, this problem, known as information asymmetry, raises a major question mark about whether the optimistic mainstream view about the efficiency of the market system is applicable to finance, since it is based on the assumption that everyone has equal access to information.[13]

Banks have traditionally made most of their profits from the interest earned on making loans, or from investing in bonds or other financial instruments that pay interest. However, in recent years, banks have been subjected to regulations that require them to hold a certain amount of capital in proportion to the size of their loans.[14] This has encouraged banks to look for ways of earning money from activities for which they can charge fees, but which do not tie up their own capital. At its simplest this can involve selling other financial services, such as insurance, or access to investment funds, but it has also had an impact on the way that banks provide loans. In the US, banks earn fees by using their branch networks to grant loans, for example for house mortgages or to finance investments by small businesses, and they then package a large number of such loans together and sell them as a bond to some financial investor. In this way, the bank earns money, but does not finish up with a loan on its own books, against which it would be required to hold capital.

Commercial banks are today predominantly owned by private share-holders, and are concerned with maximizing their profits.[15] In Germany, however, around one third of bank deposits are held with savings banks that are owned by regional public authorities, and these have traditionally been the main source of loans for small and medium companies in their localities. In many countries there is also at least a small sector of coopera-tive banks which are owned by their customers.

The second main type of banks is investment banks. In contrast to com-mercial banks, the primary business of investment banks does not involve accepting deposits and making loans, but rather in advising and assisting firms that want to raise capital on the security markets. An investment bank will advise a firm on whether it is most advantageous to raise capital by issuing bonds or shares; on how to price the security; and on when, and perhaps where, to issue it. Once decided, the investment bank will then oversee the issue and sale of the securities. Investment banks also act as fund managers for pension funds and other institutions and, since the turn of the new century, there has been a marked growth of investing on their own account. However, when investment banks invest on their own account, this can lead to a conflict of interest when it comes to advising firms on how to raise capital.

In some countries, big banking institutions span both commercial and investment banking. This is the case in Germany, which has long had so-called universal banks. In the US, however, a law was passed in the aftermath of the 1929 financial crisis that required commercial and investment banking to be separated, and this remained in force until it was repealed by the Clinton government in 1999. Since then, large financial conglomerates, such as Citigroup and JPMorgan Stanley, which span both types of banking, have been re-established.

At the pinnacle of each banking system is a state-owned central bank – the European Central Bank in the eurozone, the Federal Reserve in the US, or the Bank of England in Britain. In most countries it is the central bank that issues the bank notes that serve as the national currency.[16] Historically, one of the functions of the central bank has been as banker to the government, but today a central bank's most significant economic functions involve managing and regulating the rest of the financial system, and in particular the commercial banks.

The central bank acts as banker to the commercial banks, and each commercial bank has an account at the central bank.[17] Through its lending to banks, the central bank seeks to influence the terms on which commercial banks lend to the rest of the economy, and in this way to shape the expansion of credit as a whole. central banks also impose rules and restrictions on the activities of commercial banks, both to facilitate their influence over the expansion of credit and to try and avoid bank failures.

The existence of the central bank is important for the functioning of an economy's payment system. Because commercial banks all have an account at the central bank, payments from an account at one commercial bank to an account at a different commercial bank can be cleared by transferring balances between the accounts of the two banks at the central bank.[18]

In order to participate in the clearing process, commercial banks need to keep some reserves in their account at the central bank. In fact, in most countries commercial banks are required by law to hold a certain percentage of their deposits as reserves at the central bank. Nevertheless, commercial banks generally resent being obliged to tie up money in this way, and, largely under pressure from the banks, reserve requirements have been reduced drastically in recent decades. Since the 1980s most deposits in the US have been subject to reserve requirements of 3 per cent, and when the European central bank started operating in 1999 it set the rate at just 2 per cent.[19]

The main way in which commercial banks obtain reserves is through loans from the central bank through a procedure known as open market operations.[20] The central bank sets the interest rate at which it lends the reserves, and this in turn has a decisive influence on the interest rates which the commercial banks set: they set their lending rates a few per cent above the central bank rate, and their deposit rate somewhat below it. There is a margin within which commercial banks can compete with each other for customers when setting their interest rates, but the overall result is that the rates set by the commercial banks normally move closely up and down in line with the interest rate set by the central bank.

Although it is individual commercial banks that must decide whether to extend a loan to a particular customer, the central bank, through its influence on the cost of credit, has a significant impact on companies' cash flows and, consequently, on their profitability and their desire to take up further loans. In this way the central bank can exert an important influence on the rhythm of investment and growth in a modern capitalist economy and, for this reason, their monetary policy decisions are followed closely. The key central bank interest rate is set by a policy-making committee that usually meets once a month in the eurozone and in Britain, and every six weeks in the US.

The priorities that guide a central bank's policy vary from one economy to another. The US Federal Reserve is, by law, supposed to direct monetary policy to maintaining both low unemployment and low inflation. However, there can be a conflict between these two aims, and at times it has given priority to one or the other: in the early 1980s it gave overriding priority to fighting inflation, but between 2001 and 2003 it lowered its main interest rate from 6.5 to 1.0 per cent in an attempt to stem the recession that followed the bursting of the stock market bubble. The European Central Bank, by contrast, has one overriding target, namely low inflation, and to date it has steadfastly rejected calls to use lower interest rates to strengthen growth and so reduce unemployment.

1.6 CAPITAL MARKETS

The main alternative to bank loans is to turn directly to the capital market, and issue a bond or a share. A bond, or fixed-interest security, is a form of borrowing that is employed by governments, by industrial and commercial enterprises, and by financial institutions themselves. The purchaser of a bond is, in effect, lending money, and is entitled to receive a regular interest payment, or coupon, which is set when the bond is first issued, and the full value of the bond is paid back when the life of the bond, known as its maturity, comes to an end. Generally, a maturity of less than one year is classified as short-term, up to ten years is considered medium-term, and ten years and more is characterized as long-term.[21]

An important point about a bond is that the rate of interest is determined by conditions in the financial markets. The rate on short-term bonds is generally influenced by the central bank's interest rate since bank loans can be a substitute for short-term bonds. But, as a rule, the interest rate is higher the longer the maturity of the bond. More significantly, the interest rate must also compensate investors for any risk – or perceived risk – that the issuer might default on their payments. For this reason, in the developed capitalist economies, bonds issued by the central government carry the lowest rate of interest, since it is most unlikely that they will default on their payments. Large, well-known companies might only have to pay slightly more than the government, but riskier ventures will have to pay substantially higher rates. The governments of developing countries that are perceived as risky also have to pay much higher rates.

Somewhat controversially, private credit rating agencies such as Standard and Poor's, Moody's and Fitch Ratings have come to occupy a very influential position in determining how much risk is attached to a particular borrower. For a fee, the agencies make an assessment of the financial viability of a company (or a country), and award a rating or grade, typically starting at AAA for the safest borrowers, and continuing through numerous steps to CCC, or something similar, for the most risky. These ratings effectively determine whether a company will be able to raise capital at all, and, if they can, the interest rate that they will have to pay.

Companies in the US have strongly increased their reliance on bond finance since the 1980s, and this has put pressure on banks to offer highly-rated companies more attractive interest rates.[22] European companies have generally relied less on bond finance, but this began to change in the 1990s, when larger companies in Germany and France also increased their borrowing in the bond market. There is, however, a drawback in relying on bond markets. Financial markets are strongly driven by herd instincts, and when market sentiment turns pessimistic – for instance at the onset of a recession – the supply of funds can completely dry up, even for large, established companies, and companies are then forced to turn back to the banking system if they need to borrow. Furthermore, small and medium companies are very rarely able to raise finance in the bond market.

The other way in which a company can raise finance from the capital market is by issuing shares. By buying a share, investors become part owners of the company, and, as such, are entitled to a share of the company's profits, which is paid out as a dividend, usually once or twice a year. They are also entitled (at least in theory) to a say in the policy of the company, usually through their right to vote at the company's Annual General Meeting.[23] The actual size of the dividend varies from year to year, depending on how profitable the year has been for the company. In a good year, the payout can be much higher than that on a bond, but, if the company has had an especially bad year, it could decide to pay no dividend. An important attraction of holding shares is that, if a company is expected to be successful, the demand for its shares might rise, pushing up the share's price and resulting in a capital gain for existing owners.[24] But, as many investors have learnt, for example after the stock-market bubble burst in 2000, share prices can also fall, and leave owners with a capital loss.

It has become quite common for newspapers and news programmes to carry daily reports on developments in financial markets, but most of this trading does not lead to raising new finance. The initial sale of bonds or shares, known as the primary market, does raise new capital, but accounts for only a small part of the business on the financial markets in most countries. The majority of transactions involve the so-called secondary market, where bonds and shares that have already been issued are resold. The secondary market is significant because, as the price at which bonds and shares are traded varies in response to market conditions, it provides an important indicator of the price that should be set for new issues. But it is important to note that the secondary market only involves a change in ownership of existing securities, and it doesn't generate any additional finance for companies.

During the information technology boom in the late 1990s, many new companies were showered with publicity when they initially issued shares on the stock market. In reality, however, for the US business sector in aggregate, shares are not an important source of finance; on the contrary, companies in the US have spent large sums buying back their own shares, and in recent years the sum spent in this way has been considerably larger than the amount of finance raised through new issues. Companies have been buying back their own shares because this drives up the value of the remaining shares. This is welcomed by the remaining shareholders, in particular the big institutional investors, such as pension and investment funds, and also by the top managers of a company, who often own significant quantities of the company's shares themselves. High share prices also make a company less vulnerable to a takeover. Nevertheless, while shares are not a source of new finance for the business sector as a whole, some companies do raise capital by issuing shares and, in this way, the stock market provides a means of redistributing capital within the business sector.[25]

1.7   FINANCIAL DERIVATIVES

Since the 1970s there has been an enormous growth of another type of financial instrument, known as derivatives, which are not concerned with raising finance at all, but rather with unbundling the different characteristics of a security, such as the risk of a change in its price, or of a default. This makes it possible to trade these characteristics without having to trade the underlying security on which they are based. Selling derivatives has become a major source of business for investment banks, who have taken to employing physicists and other graduates with advanced degrees involving maths (so-called 'rocket scientists') to dream up ever more complicated instruments.[26] Despite the complexity of many derivatives, they involve three basic types of instrument: forward contracts, options and swaps.

A forward contract is an agreement to buy or sell a specified quantity of a commodity or asset on a date in the future at a price that is specified when the deal is agreed. If you have a forward contract to buy a bond for 10000 euros in one year's time and, when it becomes due, the market price of the bond is 11000 euros, you will save 1000 euros. If, however, the market price had fallen to 9000 euros you would still have to buy the bond for 10000 euros, and therefore pay more than the market price. Forward contracts are usually sold by banks 'over the counter' with the amount and maturity date suited to the individual customer. A futures contract is similar to a forward contract, but is issued in standardized amounts and is traded on organized markets, such as the Chicago Mercantile Exchange, or the London International Financial Futures Exchange.

An option is a contract that gives the purchaser the right either to buy or to sell something in the future at a specified price, but the purchaser is not obliged to exercise the option. For a fee of 200 euros, for example, you might purchase an option to buy a bond at a date in the future for 10000 euros. If, when the option became due, the market price of the bond was 11000 euros, you could exercise the option, buy the bond for 10000 euros, and thereby save 800 euros (1000 euros less the fee of 200 euros). If, on the other hand, the market price of the bond was 9000 euros, you do not have to exercise the option, and you would just lose the 200 euro fee you had paid for the option.

In a straightforward (or 'plain vanilla') interest-rate swap, two parties agree to take over each others' interest-rate payments. For example, one firm that has a variable rate loan, and is worried about interest rates rising, might swap its interest-rate payments for those of another institution that has a fixed interest-rate loan, but is more concerned about interest rates falling. In reality, most swaps are much more complex (or 'exotic'), and the counter-parties are usually banks, who themselves use derivatives extensively.

There has been an enormous growth of derivatives since the late 1990s, especially in those based on interest rates. The most appropriate way to measure the market is, however, not entirely clear. In the example of an option given above, is the appropriate value the notional amount of the option (10 000 euros), or the value of the fee (200 euros)? According to surveys conducted by the Bank for International Settlements, the notional value covered by derivatives increased from 99 trillion dollars in 2001 to a staggering 516 trillion dollars in 2007.[27] For comparison, the market value of world corporate debt and equity at the end of 2006 was estimated at 94 trillion dollars.[28] On the other hand, the market value of derivative contracts increased from a more modest, although still very substantial 3 trillion dollars in 2001 to 11 trillion dollars in 2007.

While derivatives provides firms and financial institutions with a means of insuring against risk, they also offer the possibility of high returns – or losses – to financial investors and, as yields on bonds and shares fell following the bursting of the stock market bubble in 2000, the demand for these riskier, but potentially high-yielding, alternatives increased enormously. However, to the great concern of financial regulators, many of the more complex derivatives are being purchased by investors who do not understand the risks that are involved, and some of them have made very large losses. In 1994, for example, Orange County, one of the richest districts in California made a loss of 1.7 billion dollars as a result of naive investments in derivatives by its treasurer. Perhaps the most salutary example of the dangers of derivative trading concerns the New York hedge fund, Long Term Capital Management (LTCM), which collapsed in 1998 having failed to allow correctly for the impact of Russia's debt default on its gigantic holdings of derivatives.[29] LTCM had assets of 125 billion dollars, of which all but 4.1 billion dollars were borrowed, and held derivatives with a notional value of over one trillion dollars. The full extent of its liabilities were unclear at the time and the US Federal Reserve felt obliged to organize a 3.6 billion dollar rescue in order to ensure that the collapse would not set off a chain of defaults and a full-blown crisis in the US financial system.

1.8   INSTITUTIONAL INVESTORS

The term institutional investors refers to non-bank financial institutions such as investment funds, pension funds and insurance companies, in which households deposit funds that are then invested collectively by professional financial managers.[30] They are generally subject to quite strict legal regulation, which is intended to ensure that funds are not invested in unduly risky ways. Although institutional investors are not new, as shown in Table 1.2, they have increased greatly in size and economic significance since the 1980s.

Table 1.2   Institutional investors' assets (as percentage of GDP)

	Pension funds		Insurance companies		Investment companies		Total assets	
	1980	2006	1980	2006	1980	2006	1980	2006
Canada	16	53	17	34	1	38	35	124
France	–	–	9	91	3	41	11	132
Germany	2	11	13	62	3	46	18	119
Italy	–	·2	–	37	–	22	–	61
Japan	4	23	17	51	16	68	37	143
United Kingdom	21	76	22	88	6	30	49	194
United States	28	74	23	46	5	77	56	197

Note: UK figures are for 2005, not 2006.

Source: Note: OECD, *Institutional Investors Statistical Yearbook*, 2003 and OECD. StatExtracts.

Pension funds have historically been the largest form of institutional investor in the US, Britain and Canada. They provide a means for individuals to save money regularly during their working lives, which is then paid out, either in a lump sum, or in regular payments when they retire. The growth of such funds in recent years has been linked to a decline in the value of pension schemes provided by the state or private employers, and conscious government policies, usually supported by tax benefits, to shift the responsibility for pensions onto private households.

Life insurance companies originated as a means of providing for dependants in the case of someone's death, but they also serve as a way of saving money during a person's working life that can be drawn on at the time of retirement. As can be seen in Table 1.2, they tend to be more developed in countries, such as Germany, where pension funds have been less developed.

Investment companies are institutions where deposits are pooled and invested in securities. They provide a means by which individuals can invest in a diversified range of securities with relatively low minimum holdings. The value of a deposit in such a fund varies according to the current market price of the assets the fund has selected to invest in. Investment funds have been the fastest growing form of institutional investor in recent years. This rapid growth began in the 1980s in the US, partly influenced by a steady rise in share prices which started in the early 1980s; it was also related to the increasingly unequal distribution of income, as GDP growth disproportionately benefited the best-off 20 per cent of the population, and investment funds (known as mutual funds in the US) provided a more attractive return than bank deposits. In Europe investment funds grew strongly in the 1990s, and although they suffered a setback after the stock-market bubble burst in 2000, since 2003 they have begun to grow again.

The growth of institutional investors since the 1980s has been accompanied by a significant increase in the influence which they wield over large companies. Because they hold large blocks of shares, companies are anxious to ensure that investment managers at the big institutions will not sell their holdings – something which could have a very negative impact on their share's price.[31] To this end, companies have become accustomed to making regular presentations for the managers of funds, and in the US many firms have come to publish profit forecasts as often as once a quarter.[32] The incessant pressure to sustain profitability has, in turn, contributed to companies introducing repeated rationalization programmes which usually result in layoffs and a weakening in the bargaining position of employees. The influence of institutional investors in the US is demonstrated by the fact that the share of corporate profits paid out as dividends has steadily risen since the late 1980s and, even when profits declined sharply, as during the recession in 2001, many firms chose to absorb the decline internally, rather than reduce dividend payments, as would have been more usual in the past.[33]

1.9 HEDGE FUNDS, PRIVATE EQUITY FUNDS AND SOVEREIGN WEALTH FUNDS

While pension funds, investment funds and insurance companies are subject to quite strict regulation which limits their ability to take high risks with the money that has been deposited with them, this is not true of hedge funds and private equity funds, both of which have gained considerable notoriety in recent years because of concern at the social impact of their activities.

Hedge funds are private funds that are open to people or institutions with a lot of money – usually at least one million dollars in the US – which seek out investments that offer high rates of return, but that consequently involve a high risk. Because they do not accept deposits from small savers, they are not closely regulated as is the case with pension and investment funds. Hedge funds generally seek quick returns and are drawn to volatile assets where the chance of a large return is highest. For this reason they have been particularly attracted to derivatives, although they have also invested in a wide range of other assets, including currencies and, more recently, primary commodities. One of the best known examples of a hedge fund is that of George Soros's Quantum Fund, which is reputed to have made almost one billion dollars in the space of a few weeks in 1992 by speculating that the British government would not be willing to defend the value of the pound in the European Monetary System. Since the 1990s, hedge funds have expanded enormously, and by 2007 it was estimated that there were over 11 000 funds managing around 2.2 trillion dollars of assets, although the largest 300 funds accounted for about 80 per cent of the assets.[34] Around half the funds are officially registered in off-shore tax havens, such as the Cayman Islands, but they are managed from the principal international financial centres, in particular New York and London.

Hedge funds' investments are usually highly leveraged. This means that when they undertake an investment, only a small part of the money is from the funds they manage while a large part is borrowed, usually from banks. Providing the investment is a success, even after paying interest, the hedge fund can achieve a much higher return on its own money. But borrowing very large amounts to invest in risky – and often very complex – investment strategies involves potential dangers for the financial system. It is difficult for the financial authorities to assess the risk involved because of the lack of transparency – as hedge funds are not closely regulated, they are not obliged to publish details of their activities.[35] However, the European Central Bank, for one, is worried about the possible dangers. In the restrained language employed by central bankers, it has drawn attention to the fact that hedge funds follow very similar investment strategies, and expressed concern at what might happen if some event should trigger a widespread sale of assets as each fund tried to withdraw its money.[36]

Private equity firms share a number of the features of hedge funds: they are loosely regulated private funds that are open to wealthy individuals and institutions, which aim to achieve a higher than average rate of return, and which operate with large amounts of borrowed money. Private equity firms achieve their return by investing in companies, usually for periods of around two to five years, with the aim of being able to then withdraw and realize a large profit. One variant of private equity firms are venture capitalist firms, which provide start-up capital for new firms, and which played an important role in providing the initial finance for many information technology companies in the 1990s. More recently, private equity firms have attracted most attention for their role in taking over existing firms. Much of this activity has focused on medium-sized, private companies. However, private equity firms – sometimes acting together – have also begun to buy up share-owned companies. The takeovers are usually accomplished through what are known as leveraged buyouts, where the fund might borrow as much as 75 per cent of the money necessary to purchase a controlling interest in a firm. After the takeover, the management is usually replaced, and the company is then subject to a process of rationalization. Assets are sold off, some units are closed down, and parts of the work are outsourced. The largest private equity firms stem from the US, although they have expanded their activities in Europe since the turn of the century, most notably in Britain and Germany. Private equity funds were estimated to have assets equal to 0.8 trillion dollars in 2007.[37]

The supporters of private equity firms argue that they are a valuable mechanism for shaking up inefficient companies and laying the basis for a more profitable future growth. However, they have been widely criticized for their essentially short-term focus on achieving a high return, which virtually always involves a significant loss of jobs. Perhaps most controversially, private equity firms have been attacked for running up a company's debt in order to pay out higher dividends to themselves.[38]

Sovereign wealth funds are rather different from hedge and private equity funds. They are owned by governments, and primarily concerned with obtaining a long-term return on their investments. Many older sovereign wealth funds emanate from countries with large energy reserves, such as the United Arab Emirates or Norway, and are motivated by providing for the time when such reserves are depleted. More recently, successful manufacturing exporters, most notably China, have used part of their very large foreign exchange reserves to set up sovereign wealth funds, with the aim of achieving a higher return than that obtained by purchasing government bonds. Sovereign wealth funds have generally invested in shares, although some capital has also been directed to hedge funds and private equity funds. Sovereign wealth funds grew rapidly in the first decade of the century as a result of the big rise in oil prices and in Asian countries' export surpluses, and by the end of 2007 their assets were estimated at some 3.3 trillion dollars.[39]

The rapid growth of sovereign wealth funds has prompted politicians in a number of developed countries to raise concerns about the transparency of such funds, and to claim that they might be driven by political rather than purely commercial factors. The German government, for example, has called for the EU to set up a common approach to vetting such investments, and the US government has pressed the IMF to establish a code of conduct for government-owned funds. In the US, Congressional opposition – supposedly motivated by concerns about security – actually prevented a Gulf-owned fund keeping five port terminals it had acquired as part of a takeover in 2006.[40] But no strategic concerns were raised a year later, when big US banks turned to sovereign wealth funds in the Middle East and Asia to help replenish their capital following huge losses in the sub-prime crisis.

1.10   BANK VS. CAPITAL MARKET FINANCE

There has been a long-standing debate about the relative merits of financial systems in which firms have obtained their external finance predominantly from banks, and those in which they have relied more on issuing bonds and shares. For many years, Japan, Germany and France had financial systems which were predominantly organized around bank-based finance, while others, notably Britain and the US, have had systems in which capital market-based finance has played a more significant role (see figures for 1995 in Table 1.3).[41]

After the Second World War, it was noticeable that in Japan, Germany and France, where banks provided long-term loans for investment and often sat on company supervisory boards, the economy grew much more rapidly than in Britain or the US, where banks tended to provide only short-term loans, and had a much more distant, arm's-length relation with firms. This impression was reinforced with the end of the post-war boom in the 1970s, when Japan and Germany for some time appeared to weather the international economic slowdown more successfully than the Anglo-Saxon countries. In the 1990s, however, the supporters of the capital market-based type of financial system gained in influence as the US economy registered rapid growth and falling unemployment on the back of the information technology boom. Indeed, the European

Table 1.3   Structure of business finance (percentage of GDP)

	1995			2004		
	Bank loans	Debt securities	Stock market capitalization	Bank loans	Debt securities	Stock market capitalization
France	89.2	87.7	32.8	92.3	78.5	69.7[a]
Germany	94.7	78.2	23.3	155.3[b]	122.0[b]	40.2[b]
Great Britain	58.3	52.9	119.8	140.6	94.0	120.7
EU-15	82.4	87.0	42.2	121.2	116.4	68.6
Japan	93.3	92.7	66.8	–	–	61.6
United States	45.5	142.0	91.7	41.5[c]	156.3[c]	115.4

Notes:
a. Euronext includes France, Belgium and the Netherlands.
b. Figures for 2003.
c. Figures for 2002.

Source: European Commission, *Financial Integration Monitor, 2005 Update, Annex to the Background document,* June 2005 and *Financial Integration Monitor, 2006 Update, Annex to the Background document,* July 2006.

Commission was so enthused by the apparent US success that in 2000 it adopted what is termed the Lisbon Agenda. This called for making the EU the most competitive economy in the world by 2010, and, as part of this, it advocated promoting the development of US-style capital markets in Europe.

One of the issues at stake concerns the cost of finance. According to its supporters, market-based finance avoids the intermediation charges that are levied by banks and this makes it possible both to offer financial investors a higher return than bank deposits and to provide firms with finance at a lower cost than bank loans. This idea underlies the European Commission's claim that the creation of a deeper, unified European capital market will lead to a lower cost of borrowing, and hence promote higher rates of investment and economic growth. In the US, the availability of short-term market loans through commercial paper has certainly forced banks to reduce the margin on loans to their most trusted ('blue chip') customers. However, critics point out that institutional investors have emerged as the major source of finance in the capital markets, and the fees which investment funds and pension funds levy on their members can be rather high. Furthermore, when there is a downturn in the business cycle, such as occurred in 2001, market financing can completely dry up, forcing even the most reputable firms to turn back to the banking system for loans.

A second issue concerns the way in which investment projects are selected. The supporters of market-based finance argue that financial markets provide an unrivalled mechanism for assembling information about a company's prospects. In the most extreme form, known as the efficient markets hypothesis, it is argued that markets embody all the available information about a company, about the product markets in which it operates, and about the overall macroeconomic outlook which it will have to face, and that a company's share price is therefore the best possible indicator of a company's prospects. It follows that capital markets consequently provide the best guide for signalling where additional capital should be directed.

This is challenged by the supporters of bank-based finance on two grounds. First, they claim that, in a market-based system where investors' information about a company is derived principally from market signals, the signals transmitted by share prices primarily reflect expectations about the immediate outlook for profits. Consequently, companies are under much greater pressure to focus on short-term profitability, which can mean being forced to cut jobs or other forms of spending, such as research and development, that could contribute to longer-term growth.[42]

The second, and perhaps more fundamental argument is that investors in financial markets are less concerned with assessing the underlying financial strength of companies than with trying to second-guess how the market will move in response to what other investors decide. In a famous passage of his *General Theory*, Keynes likened stock markets to a beauty parade, where the aim is not to select who you think is the most beautiful person, but rather who most other observers are likely to select as the most beautiful person.[43] The stock market, he said, was like trying to anticipate what average opinion thought average opinion would be. The result is that prices on capital markets are strongly driven by a herd instinct, and price movements can develop a strong dynamic – up or down – that has little relation to underlying economic reality. It is this that gives rise to periodic bubbles in financial markets and, even for investors who are aware that securities are over-priced, it can still be rational to buy – and so push the price up yet further – if they believe they will be able to sell again before the bubble bursts.[44] At the height of the boom in the US in the late 1990s, the stock market did provide new capital for some start-up companies in the US, but the signals which the market sent out led to a massive misallocation of capital. The most spectacular case occurred in the telecommunications sector. As share prices soared, rival companies borrowed hundreds of billions of dollars to invest in new global fibre-optic networks, much of which has since lain unused.

According to its supporters, a bank-based system provides a much sounder basis for selecting investment projects. They point out that banks acquire a great deal of information about companies, partly through managing their accounts, which provides them with extensive details about companies' previous financial history. In addition, a bank that has a long-term relation with a company is more likely to receive fuller information about a project, and, if it has a seat on a company's supervisory board, might even be involved in the decision making. As a result, it is argued, banks are better able to judge the viability of a new investment project and, furthermore, able to take a longer-term view of its prospects. In this way they might approve financing for projects that will not necessarily be so profitable in the short term but which could make a substantial contribution to long-term growth.

A third issue in the dispute about bank and market-based finance is about what is known as corporate governance. This refers to how top managers run their companies, and the possibility that, in a large-scale corporation, there may be a difference of interest between the managers of the company and the shareholders who own it. Particularly if shareholders are widely dispersed, it can be difficult for them to exert effective control over the managers, who might purse their own interests rather than those of the owners – for example by investing in projects that increase the size and influence of the company, but which lower the return on the shareholders' investment. One way of trying to align the interests of managers with those of owners is to encourage the managers to become shareholders by offering them shares at very attractive prices. Share options were a much publicized feature of management pay in the US in the 1990s, aided by a curious accounting loophole that did not require companies to count the cost of such options against their profits. Some larger European companies also began to offer share options to senior managers, although in both the US and Europe, this became less attractive after the stock market bubble burst in 2000.

The supporters of market-based finance argue that market finance provides the most effective sanction against poor management since dissatisfied shareholders can sell their shares. In this view, extensive selling will lead to a fall in the share price and make the firm vulnerable to a takeover by another firm, in which case the senior managers will be punished by losing their jobs. There have been significant waves of takeovers in the US and Britain since the 1980s, and these have invariably been followed by plant closures and a loss of jobs. Indeed, the resultant insecurity of employment has been an important reason for the virtual stagnation of industrial wages in the US over many years. Such takeovers have been comparatively rare in most European countries until recently although, as part of the Lisbon Agenda, the European Commission put forward a Takeover Bids Directive, aimed at creating a common legal framework that would remove obstacles to takeovers in many EU countries. Nevertheless, because of concern at the prospect of treating companies as commodities that can be bought and sold, and the consequent impact on jobs, the initial proposal failed to get through the European parliament in 2001, and key parts of a revised proposal were also rejected in 2004.

As already noted, the position of shareholders has strengthened considerably in recent years as a result of the increasing importance of institutional investors. The investment managers at such institutions play close attention to the short-term returns of the companies they invest in, and, because they often have very large holdings, the possibility that they might sell their shares exerts a powerful force on corporate managers to give priority to what has become known as 'shareholder value'. In this way, firms in the US have been obliged to give overriding priority to sustaining dividend payments to shareholders, and consequently to embark on never-ending rounds of cost cutting, the results of which can be observed in the steady stream of layoffs and stagnant or falling wages and benefits. Nevertheless, at the same time, highly preferential share deals for top managers have resulted in a major increase in their holdings and, perhaps ironically, top managers have emerged amongst the principal winners from the new arrangements.

The supporters of bank-based finance, on the other hand, argue that where banks have a major involvement in financing companies, either through share ownership, or the long-term provision of loans, they are more fully informed about how management is performing than external shareholders, and are therefore in a stronger position to monitor and influence management decisions, especially when they have a representative on the company's board. Furthermore, it is claimed, a bank-based system of finance does not meet the same pressure to focus exclusively on shareholder interests, and therefore makes it more possible to attend to a broader range of interests, including those of employees, customers and the broader community, as well as those of shareholders, reflecting what has been termed 'stakeholder value'.

A final issue in the controversy regarding market- versus bank-based financial systems concerns which is most conducive to promoting a more democratic and egalitarian economic policy. Critics of the market-based system point out that a market system will, by its nature, tend to strengthen the influence of those with greatest financial power. By contrast, although current banking systems involve highly undemocratic concentrations of power and privilege, bank-based systems are potentially more amenable to greater democratic control than market-based systems. In particular, banks offer a greater possibility of channelling finance towards socially-defined development goals than the indirect, impersonal mechanisms of the capital markets, which are solely driven by the search for the highest return.[45]

As this brief summary indicates, progressive economists have generally favoured bank-based systems of finance. In recent years, however, there has been a tendency for market-based finance to increase at the expense of bank-based finance, not only in the Anglo-Saxon countries, but also in the countries formerly associated with bank-based systems, including Japan and more recently France and Germany. This has led some commentators who are concerned that market-based systems are more prone to finance risky investment projects to argue that there is a need for new forms of state regulation.[46] Nevertheless, while the significance of market-based finance has increased, it is important to note that banks, and in particular the big banks, are amongst the major players in the financial markets. The big banks strongly pushed for the development of financial markets, both in the US and Europe, since this offered greater opportunities for generating profits from fee-based activities. They are, of course, also extensively involved in trading on the financial markets, not only as agents for other parties, but, especially in the US, also on their own account.[47]

1.11 FINANCIAL CRISES AND THE NEED FOR REGULATION

While the financial system plays a major role in promoting investment and growth in a capitalist economy, it can also lead to major disruption. In the nineteenth and early twentieth century, as first Britain and then the US and other European countries industrialized and built up their financial systems, major financial crises occurred about once a decade, culminating in the great crash of 1929.[48] Because such crises could have a devastating economic and social impact, at times threatening political stability, the state responded by introducing much tighter regulations for banks and other financial institutions than for non-financial firms.

Crises stem, in part, from the nature of credit. A credit involves a promise to pay, but if companies are unable to sell all their output, they might – despite the best of intentions – be unable to meet a promise to pay. Because banks are engaged in extensive networks of borrowing and lending, both amongst themselves and with firms and households, the impact of a default can be transmitted rapidly throughout the financial system. This danger is exacerbated by a widely noted tendency for banks to over-lend during periods of rapid business expansion, sometimes prompting a sharp contraction of lending – a 'credit crunch' – when they find themselves overstretched, or when they fear that the expansion is about to end, something that can then set off the downturn they feared.[49]

Such instability can be reinforced by the behaviour of financial markets. The price of financial assets is strongly influenced by expectations: if the price of an asset is expected to rise, then the demand for it will increase and its price will tend to rise. In the course of a business expansion, a rise in asset prices can set off a speculative bubble, and, as a bubble takes hold, investors might borrow in order to take advantage of the rising price of shares, or of property or raw materials. But, when a bubble bursts, this prompts widespread sales as investors seek to avoid a further loss, thereby exacerbating the fall in asset prices. Investors who borrowed money might now find themselves unable to repay their loans, thereby putting pressure on the banks.

A key measure to combat the outbreak of financial crises was the emergence of the role of the central bank as lender of last resort, developed by the Bank of England as it learnt how to respond to bank crises in the course of the nineteenth century.[50] The basis for this was the recognition that even a sound bank can be threatened if it should suffer from a run, when a wave of depositors all demand to withdraw their money at the same time. This can occur when there is a threat of a crisis, and can be detonated by little more than a rumour. In such a situation, prompt action by the central bank can prevent a panic breaking out and spreading to the rest of the banking system. The key is that the central bank stands ready to lend money to a bank against a sound security, such as a central government bond, although at a higher than usual rate of interest. If it is clear that a bank is able to obtain money in this way, then it is no longer necessary for depositors to rush to the bank and withdraw their money, and a panic can be averted.

After the 1929 stock market crash, which began in the US and then spread rapidly to much of Europe, extensive controls were introduced to regulate banks and other financial institutions. In the US this involved very tight restrictions, including the separation of commercial banking and investment banking mentioned above, a prohibition on inter-state banking, and government-set maximum interest rates. These restrictions continued in place from the 1930s until the 1960s, a period that was characterized by an unusual degree of financial stability compared with the periods either before or after.

In the second half of the 1960s, however, big banks in the US began to find ways of circumventing such regulations. For example, when interest rates hit their maximum permitted level, the banks developed something called Certificates of Deposit, which provided a legal way in which they could raise funds by offering a higher interest rate than was permitted on normal bank deposits. More significantly, when the US government attempted to regulate outflows of capital from the country, this encouraged big banks to open branches in London, where they could continue to lend to their big corporate customers outside of the control of the US authorities. Later, when the authorities began to introduce international standards for capital requirements, the banks began to develop ways of earning profits from fees, rather than bank loans, thereby providing an important impetus for the growth of securitization, and of market-based finance. In this way, the desire to overcome government-imposed regulation has been an important force in driving financial innovation and in promoting the internationalization of banking and finance, which is discussed in the next chapter.

Since the 1970s, there has been a wide-ranging liberalization of the financial system, particularly in the US, Britain and a number of other English-speaking countries, and many of the restrictions on banks and other financial institutions have been relaxed or eliminated. In important respects this has been a response to the process of financial innovation, but it is also the result of a marked political shift towards free-market policies, reflecting a greater accommodation to the interests of business in general and of the financial sector in particular. Financial liberalization received an important boost in the 1980s following the election of President Reagan in the US and Mrs Thatcher in Britain, but subsequent governments in both countries have continued to extend and deepen the process. In continental Europe liberalization has been less rapid, but even here there have been important changes as the banks and other financial institutions have argued that, without such changes, they would be at a disadvantage when competing internationally.

Despite these developments, the financial sector everywhere is still subject to far closer supervision than other parts of the economy, with responsibility borne by some combination of the central bank, and one or more financial supervisory agencies, such as the Securities and Exchange Commission in the US, or the Financial Services Authority in Britain. However, developments in the financial sector are so fast-moving and complex, that the supervisors are faced with a daunting task, and detailed information about the most recent innovations is often not available.[51]

Since the period of greater financial liberalization began in the 1970s, there has been a striking increase in financial instability. The most serious impact has been in developing countries, where banking and stock-market crises have been accompanied by currency crises, leading to a widespread collapse in living standards.[52] In the developed capitalist countries there has also been a series of major banking and stock-market crises, but the economic and social impact of these has, until now, largely been contained by prompt central-bank intervention.[53] In 2007–2008, however, developed countries were hit by the most serious financial crisis since the 1930s.

Following the bursting of the US stock-market bubble in early 2000, there was a collapse of investment in equipment and buildings which led to a recession in 2001. The Federal Reserve attempted to contain the impact of the crash by dramatically reducing interest rates, which were kept unusually low for several years, thereby provoking a major growth of borrowing and a search for high-yielding financial investments. For several years, big banks were able to reap unprecedented profits, but this came to a dramatic end in August 2007 as a result of a banking crisis detonated by the failure of highly complex bonds based on sub-prime mortgages – housing loans to households with poor credit records. The crisis rapidly spread to banks in Europe and the IMF estimated that the total cost would amount to around 945 billion dollars.[54]

The major central banks have not been sanguine about the risks of a major crisis, and have held internationally-coordinated exercises to rehearse their responses to a major financial breakdown. But the pressure to achieve higher returns has led banks and other financial institutions to adopt much riskier investment positions, fuelled by the massive growth of the derivatives market, and driven by the highly leveraged activities of hedge funds and private equity funds. Although crises have been successfully contained in developed countries, if such an event were to spin out of control, it would – as has occurred in developing countries – have a devastating economic and social impact.

NOTES

1. Cameron and Neal (2003), p. 36.
2. Heterodox economics is understood to include a range of positions that do not accept the foundations of the neoclassical approach, and in particular those that draw on the work of Marxian and Keynesian economics.
3. A recent book by a prominent US professor claims that this is the primary function of finance, and that the possibilities for improving the quality of life through wider applications of risk management have scarcely been applied yet. See Schiller (2003).
4. So-called because the amount of money advanced by the bank was equal to the face value of the bill discounted by (i.e. less) the interest due on the amount until the bill became due, when the bank could redeem the full face value from the original issuer. According to the real bills doctrine, money lent in this way could not be over-issued, and thereby contribute to inflation, since the amount corresponded to the real growth of the volume of goods being traded.
5. Joint stock companies were legalized in Britain in 1844. Some joint stock companies had been created previously, including the East India Trading Company and the Bank of England, but were the result of a Royal Charter or a special Act of Parliament.
6. There are some well-known firms, such as Wal-mart in the US or Porsche in Germany that are still privately owned, but these are not common.
7. APACS and British Bankers Association (2006).
8. McKean, Lessem and Bax (2006).
9. Although this study is not up to date, the authors noted that the importance of internal funds tended to rise during the period that they studied.
10. Some post-Keynesian economists argue that the availability of internal funds is the main determinant of investment, and that large corporations, which are less subject to price competition, try to set their prices so as to generate sufficient internal funds to finance forthcoming investment projects. For a discussion of this and related positions, see Lavoie (2001).
11. The negative figures for shares indicate that in several countries the company sector as a whole spent more money buying back shares than was raised through the issue of new shares.
12. See Stiglitz and Greenwald (2003).
13. Most famously, Stiglitz argues that, if interest rates are free to rise, beyond a certain point finance will only by sought for projects promising a very high return, but which involve a high risk of failure. He argues that controls that limit interest rates can enable banks to restrict credit to projects with lower, but less risky, returns.
14. The original regulations, known as the Basel Accord, were introduced in 1988, and required banks to hold capital equal to at least 8 per cent of their risk-adjusted assets. A more complex system of regulations, known as Basel II, has been the source of much international negotiation since being proposed in 1999. For fuller details, see Chapter 14 below.
15. Until a wave of privatization in the 1980s, a major part of the commercial banking system was publicly owned in many European countries, including France and Italy and several smaller states including Belgium, Greece and Portugal.
16. In the nineteenth century, commercial banks issued their own bank notes in a number of countries. In Britain, note issue was restricted to the Bank of England under the 1844 Bank Act. In the US, note issue was restricted to the Treasury Department in 1862, and it continued to issue notes until 1971; since its creation in 1913, the Federal Reserve has

issued notes. It is a historical anomaly that commercial banks in Scotland and Northern Ireland still issue their own bank notes.

17. In countries where there are a very large number of banks, such as the US or Germany, smaller banks have an account at a large commercial bank, which in turn has an account at the central bank.

18. In the US there is a private system (Clearing House Interbank Payments System, or CHIPS) owned and managed by the largest banks for settling the net balance on large-value payments. But even where banks run their own clearing system, net balances are settled using deposits at the central bank.

19. In both the US and the eurozone, there is some variation in the reserve requirement according to the type, or size of the deposit. Until the 1970s, reserve requirements were more usually of the order of 10 to 15 per cent.

20. Formally speaking the central bank buys a bond and pays for it with a deposit at the central bank; under a repurchase agreement the seller agrees to buy the bond back after a certain period – usually seven days under the ECB system – and the difference between the purchase and the sale price is determined by the interest rate that the bank has to pay for the use of the reserves during the period.

21. In the case of short-term bonds, instead of making an interest payment, the bonds are often sold at less than their face value, and the interest payment corresponds to the difference between the sale price and the face value of the bond, which is paid out in full when the bond reaches maturity.

22. This is particularly true for the market in commercial paper, which refers to very short-term bonds with maturities of as little as seven or 14 days, where both borrowers and lenders can obtain marginally better interest rates than they would from banks. As a result, so-called 'blue chip' companies can obtain bank loans for less than the quoted prime rate, which used to be the basic rate of lending to the safest companies.

23. Some companies have different classes of shares, with some shares having restricted (or even no) voting rights. There are also some cases of companies which have a 'golden share', whose owner's approval is required for any major decision.

24. In the 1990s, shares in rapidly growing information technology companies were in such demand that the expectation of a capital gain was sufficient to attract investors, and the companies did not pay any dividend for a number of years. Microsoft was probably the best-known example of this.

25. Even when recently-started firms first turn to the stock market (so-called 'initial public offerings'), this is not usually a means of raising additional capital, but rather a means of providing an exit strategy for the existing owners, such as venture capitalists who had provided risk financing at a previous, more-uncertain stage.

26. For an entertaining account of the high-pressured sales techniques used by derivatives salesmen at Morgan Stanley, one of the leading US investment banks, see Partnoy (1997).

27. BIS (2004) and BIS (2007).

28. Figures are taken from the IMF's *Global Financial Stability Report 2008,* Statistical Annex, Table 3 (IMF, 2008a).

29. The poignancy of the collapse was increased by the fact that LTCM's founders included Robert Merton and Myron Scholes, two US academics who, in the 1970s, developed the standard model for pricing options for which they were subsequently awarded a Nobel prize.

30. This section draws substantially on Davis and Steil (2001).

31. Investment companies maintain portfolios that seek to offset various types of risk, and this involves selling and buying blocks of shares in response to changing market conditions.

32. The continual pressure on firms to focus on high short-term returns is something that has begun to be questioned, and some well-known firms have ceased to publish quarterly projections. See Francesco Guerrera (2006).

33. See US Bureau of Economic Analysis (n.d.).

34. International Financial Services London, *Hedge Funds 2008,* July 2008.

35. Since February 2006, some categories of hedge fund manager have been required to register with the Securities and Exchange Commission in the US.
36. ECB (2006c, p. 135).
37. See International Financial Services London, *Sovereign Wealth Funds 2008*, (IFSL Research, 2008b).
38. See Francesco Guerrera and James Politi, 'Moody's slams private equity', *Financial Times,* 9 July 2007.
39. See International Financial Services London, *Sovereign Wealth Funds 2008,* (IFSL Research, 2008b).
40. See Willman (2007).
41. A seminal contribution to this debate was Alexander Gershenkron's (1962), *Economic Backwardness in Historical Development*. This influential comparison of Britain, Germany and Russia explained the types of financial institutions that emerged in each country in terms of their different experience of industrialization in the nineteenth century. More recently, the distinction between bank-based and market-based financial systems has been identified as one of the key factors which distinguishes Rhineland capitalism from Anglo-Saxon capitalism in Michel Albert's (1993) *Capitalism Against Capitalism*, and between 'coordinated market economies' and 'liberal market economies' in Hall and Soskice (2001).
42. The short-termism of market-based financial systems was stressed in the best seller by Will Hutton (1996).
43. Keynes (1936), chapter 12, 'The state of long-term expectation'.
44. The role of rational and irrational behaviour in driving financial markets is a central feature of the fashionable new field of behavioural finance, which seeks to marry economic and psychological analysis. See Schleifer (2000).
45. See Pollin (1995).
46. See for example Joseph Stiglitz (1992).
47. See Peter Thal Larsen (2006).
48. For a very readable history, see Kindleberger (2005).
49. This is the central idea of Hyman Minsky's much quoted financial instability hypothesis. For a brief summary, see Minsky (1993).
50. The role of lender of last resort was first analysed in Walter Bagehot, *Lombard Street. A Description of the Money Market*, originally published in 1873.
51. At the time of writing, regulators in the US and Europe have been pushing for the collection of greater information about hedge funds, private equity funds and the market in derivatives.
52. The most notable cases include Mexico (1994–5), South-East Asia (1997–8), Russia (1998), Turkey (2001) and Argentina (2001–02). For a comprehensive chronology of banking crises since the 1970s, see Caprio and Klingebiel (2003).
53. The biggest interventions have been in the US, and include an estimated 150 billion dollar bail-out of savings banks in the 1980s, and major central-bank interventions after the New York stock market fell by 20 per cent on a single day in October 1987, and after the bursting of the stock-market bubble in Spring 2000.
54. IMF (2008a).

2. International finance

Trevor Evans

INTRODUCTION

Finance has long had a strongly international dimension. Modern European banking emerged in the Italian city states in the twelfth to the fourteenth century and was linked to the financing of trade with the East and the great European fairs in medieval France. As the centre of commercial capitalism shifted to northern Europe in the sixteenth century, the Italian banks lent large sums to the new financial institutions which developed in Amsterdam and they, in turn, played a key role in providing both bankers and finance for the growth of banking in Britain in the years immediately after the so-called 'Glorious Revolution' of 1688–9. In the eighteenth century, as Britain superseded the Netherlands as the leading capitalist nation, London emerged as Europe's most important financial centre, character-ized from the outset by a strong international orientation.

Since the expansion of industrial capitalism in the nineteenth century, it is possible to identify four main periods in the development of inter-national finance:

- The international gold standard (1870–1914)
- Breakdown and fragmentation (1914–45)
- The Bretton Woods system (1945–71)
- The re-emergence of private international finance (since the 1970s).

This chapter will briefly summarize the main features of the first three periods, and then examine the period since the 1970s in more detail.

THE INTERNATIONAL GOLD STANDARD

The classic period of the international gold standard is usually dated from around 1870 up to the outbreak of the First World War in 1914. Britain had in fact adopted a gold-based monetary system much earlier, in 1821;

amongst the other major economies, Germany did so in 1871, followed by France in 1878 and the US in 1879. Because the value of each national currency was fixed in terms of a specific weight of gold, the exchange rates between currencies were effectively fixed, and the gold standard provided an extremely stable framework for international trade and capital flows, both of which grew strongly during this period. The largest capital flows involved British overseas investment which averaged 5 per cent of the country's GDP between 1880 and 1913.[1]

The gold standard is sometimes presented as the model of a self-regulating system, but in fact it depended on day-to-day management by central banks, in particular the Bank of England.[2] By using its control over the London short-term interest rate, the Bank of England attracted or discouraged short-term capital flows so as to ensure that any imbalance between trade flows (generally in surplus) and long-term capital flows (generally marked by outflows) was exactly offset. In this way it provided a stable hub for the international system as a whole. Other central banks were then obliged to adjust their interest rates in order to ensure that their countries' international payments were kept in balance. Countries were therefore required to subordinate their monetary policy to sustaining the fixed exchange rate system, and exchange rate stability was achieved at the price of substantial instability in output and employment. In this way, the gold standard was characterized by very marked business cycles, with alternating periods of boom and bust, typically generated in Britain and then transmitted to the other industrialized countries through the international financial system.[3]

Governments were able to give priority to exchange rate stability at the time of the gold standard because, with limited mass democracy, those who were most affected by the recurrent bouts of unemployment were unable to exercise much influence over economic policy.[4] There was also a notable asymmetry in the system. While Europe and the US were able to maintain exchange rate stability, this was not true of peripheral countries, notably in Latin America. There countries depended overwhelmingly on exports of primary commodities, which are subject to large fluctuations in world prices. A sharp fall in prices could make it exceptionally difficult to sustain exchange rate stability, and Argentina and Brazil both suspended their membership of the gold standard at certain times.

Under the gold standard Britain held its international reserves largely in gold, but many other countries found it convenient to hold much of their reserves in pounds in London, so that international payments could be cleared by making transfers from one London bank account to another. However, while this system served the main capitalist countries well for several decades, the predominant position of Britain – which ensured the smooth functioning of the system – was being eroded. The US overtook Britain as the largest economy around the turn of the century, and Germany's industrial output exceeded Britain's in key sectors by the time of the First World War. In fact, by the time of the war, Britain's international financial position had become increasingly dependent on the financial surpluses which accrued from its colonies, above all from India.[5]

FRAGMENTATION AND BREAKDOWN

The gold standard was suspended at the outbreak of the First World War, and the period between the two world wars was characteriszed by great financial instability. Britain was weakened financially, having liquidated much of its overseas investments to raise finance for the war effort; both Britain and France were heavily indebted to the US following extensive war-time borrowing; and the new German Republic was severely burdened by reparations payments which contributed to the country's hyperinflation in 1923. In the first half of the 1920s only the US remained on the gold standard, having substantially increased its reserves of the metal during the war, and, in the absence of official regulation, the exchange rates of the other major currencies were left to float, an experience that was widely seen as destabilizing.

A major international monetary conference in Genoa in 1922 attempted to lay the basis for the reintroduction of the gold standard but this failed, largely because the US did not participate due to the isolationist position of the Congress.[6] In 1925, the British government, still dreaming of its former grandeur, took the lead in re-establishing the gold standard. However, the value of the pound was fixed at an unrealistically high rate and during the world economic crisis in 1931 the British, followed by many other countries, once again abandoned the gold standard and devalued their currencies. In 1933, the US also abandoned the gold standard and allowed the dollar to depreciate until it was pegged at a new lower value in 1934. As each state attempted to promote the economic interests in its own country at the expense of those in other countries, the international economy fragmented into several large currency blocs. Britain, whose sterling area included its extensive colonial empire, was least affected by this fragmentation; by contrast Germany, which had been stripped of its few colonies at the end of the First World War, was especially hard hit.

The breakdown of the international monetary and financial system in the 1930s seriously disrupted international trade and investment and was an important factor in explaining the depth of the Depression.[7] According to Charles Kindleberger, the most influential historian of the period, the breakdown may be explained by the fact that Britain no longer enjoyed the financial and political supremacy necessary to manage the system, while the US, which had become the largest economic and financial power, was not yet in a position to take on the task.[8]

THE BRETTON WOODS SYSTEM

At the end of the Second World War, a new international monetary system was created that ensured a period of considerable financial stability until its demise in 1971. The system is known by the name of the holiday resort in the US state of New Hampshire where it was agreed at an international conference in 1944. The British delegation to the conference was led by John Maynard Keynes, and the proposals he elaborated for the conference remain one of the most progressive plans to date for an international monetary system.[9] The main features of this included (1) creating an international clearing union (in effect an international central bank) that would issue a truly international money; (2) obliging countries to adjust, not only if they had an international deficit, but also if they had a surplus (as the US had at the time); and (3) relatively liberal conditions for providing loans to deficit countries. However, the US delegation, which was led by the Treasury's chief monetary economist, Harry Dexter White, opposed the key features of Keynes's plan, and the system that emerged reflected the dominant position of the US. The US's priority was to create the basis for an open trading system that would give it access to international markets, including those of the extensive – but closed – British Empire.

Under the Bretton Woods system the value of the dollar was fixed in relation to gold, and the value of other currencies was pegged to the dollar. The International Monetary Fund (IMF) was created to oversee the exchange rate system, and to provide short-term loans to countries faced with an international deficit. In view of a widespread belief that international capital flows had been highly destabilizing in the inter-war period, the IMF rules allowed countries to control international capital flows. However, the IMF rules required countries to eliminate all controls on current account transactions.[10] In fact, the first attempt to implement this led to a currency crisis in Britain in 1947, and it was not until 1958 that the developed capitalist countries were able to establish full current account convertibility.

The system of pegged exchange rates provided a very stable international framework, and international trade grew more rapidly during the period of the Bretton Woods system than in any comparable period, either before or since. Furthermore, by allowing controls on capital flows, national governments were able to give priority to domestic policy objectives which, given the balance of political forces after the war, involved a commitment to full employment and high growth.[11] In the developed capitalist countries, the Bretton Woods system was, consequently, associated with an unprecedented period of rising living standards and an expansion of welfare provision.

International financial transactions during the Bretton Woods era were predominantly associated with governments or other official, multilateral organizations. The US Marshall Plan provided support for post-war reconstruction in Western Europe; the IMF provided short-term loans to countries facing balance of payments deficits; and the World Bank and the regional development banks in Africa, Asia and Latin America, together with national aid programmes, provided long-term financing for developing countries. However, in the course of the 1960s, private capital flows began to increase in importance once again, with US banks developing so-called 'off-shore' operations in London, and this contributed to undermining the stability of the system. Speculation by private investors developed against the British pound in the mid-1960s, leading to a devaluation of the pound in 1966, and speculation then became focused on the US dollar.

The US dollar stood at the centre of the Bretton Woods system and, while the US held its international reserves in gold, other countries held a significant part of their reserves in dollars. Since the US government had committed itself to converting dollars for gold at the official rate of 35 dollars per ounce, the dollar was considered to be 'as good as gold'. However, an important flaw in the system was that there was no mechanism to regulate the supply of dollars to other countries. This emerged simply as a by-product of the US balance of payments.[12]

Because of the international role of the dollar, the US, unlike any other country, could continually run a balance of payments deficit – indeed, this was necessary if other countries were to gain access to dollars. In the 1960s, the US ran an increasingly large balance of payments deficit, fuelled by increased military spending in South-East Asia, and a growth of foreign direct investment by US multinationals, predominantly in Europe. The ability of US firms to buy up companies in Europe, effectively by printing dollars, outraged the French President, Charles de Gaulle. He denounced what he referred to as the 'exorbitant privilege of the dollar', and in 1965 announced that France would exercise its right to convert its dollar reserves for gold. As the quantity of dollars held abroad now exceeded the value of the US gold reserves, this would have presented a major problem for the US government if other countries followed suit.

Financial investors expected that, at some stage, the US would be obliged to devalue the dollar against gold – something the US government wished to avoid as it would have greatly reduced the international influence of its currency. But in 1968, following extensive speculation against the dollar, the convertibility of the dollar was suspended for private investors. Then, in August 1971, the US President, Richard Nixon, unilaterally announced that the US would no longer convert dollars into gold for central banks, thereby effectively marking the end of the Bretton Woods era.

THE RE-EMERGENCE OF PRIVATE INTERNATIONAL FINANCE

Since the breakdown of the Bretton Woods system, international financial transactions have come to be dominated by private capital flows, and this has been associated with much greater instability than during the initial post-war years. The huge growth of private capital flows has been driven by two interlocking processes: the internationalization of capital, led by US multinationals; and the policies adopted by the major capitalist states, in particular by the US.

The main features of the re-emergence of private international finance since the 1970s include the following:

● The rise of international banking in the 1970s;
● The growth of the foreign exchange markets since 1973; and
● The deregulation and internationalization of capital markets since the 1980s.

INTERNATIONAL BANKING

Banking had an important international dimension in the nineteenth and early twentieth century, but this was sharply curtailed in the 1930s, and remained limited through into the 1950s. In the 1960s, however, the situation began to change. Big US companies, which had invested widely in Canada in the 1950s, extended their activities to Europe in the 1960s, and US banks followed their corporate customers abroad. The process received an important boost in the mid-1960s, when the US government introduced a number of measures designed to reduce capital outflows from the US, and which made US corporations even more reliant on funding their overseas activities by borrowing from US banks abroad.[13] Whereas only eight US banks had overseas branches in 1960, this had increased to 130 by 1980.[14] The main centre for this expansion of international banking was London, which had been eclipsed by New York in the 1920s, and which now eagerly sought to attract the new business, strongly aided by the British government's willingness to allow the unrestricted expansion of business denominated in dollars.

By the 1970s the inter-bank money market, where banks borrow and lend money to each other, often for periods as short as overnight, had become substantially internationalized. As a result, a bank in one financial centre could borrow funds from other banks, not just in its own country, but also from those in other centres, such as New York, London, Tokyo or Frankfurt. This gave rise to a significant increase in short-term capital flows between the main capitalist countries.[15]

The internationalization of banking also opened new challenges for bank regulators. In 1974, for the first time since the Second World War, a synchronized recession occurred in all the developed capitalist countries and, as companies faced problems in repaying their credits, major banks in several financial centres faced serious difficulties. The most significant case involved the Frankfurt-based Bank Herstatt, which declared bankruptcy after having borrowed large sums from banks in other financial centres earlier in the same day. The event made it clear that the banking authorities had no provision for dealing with a cross-border crisis of this type and it led to the setting up of what became known as the Basel Committee under the auspices of the Bank for International Settlements. The Basel Committee's proposals included a minimum capital requirement for banks involved in international business and have been widely adopted as an international standard.[16]

International banks played a major role in intermediating surplus capital in the mid-1970s. Following a sharp rise in oil prices in 1973, oil-producing countries found themselves with huge sums of money, which they initially deposited with the international banks. In addition, the large companies, which had been the banks' principal customers, sharply cut their investments – and hence their borrowing – due to the outbreak of the recession in 1974–5. In this context, the banks needed to find new customers for their loans, and they did so by turning to developing countries. From the mid-1970s, the international banks began to lend large sums to the governments of a small number of newly industrializing countries, above all in Latin America. This continued until 1982 when, following a sharp rise in US interest rates, first Mexico and then the other Latin American borrowers found they were unable to meet their debt-service payments, ushering in what became known as the Third World debt crisis. The threat of a major crisis for the big banks was averted thanks to the intervention of the International Monetary Fund. The IMF provided the debt-stricken countries with emergency loans, but these were conditional on countries agreeing to fulfil a range of commitments, one of which being that they give priority to meeting their foreign debt-service payments. In this way, the banks were effectively rescued by the IMF, but for the countries concerned, the IMF conditions were associated with a protracted period of stagnation and a sharp fall in living standards, and the 1980s have become known in Latin America as the lost decade.

International banking was initially dominated by the big US banks. However, in the 1980s, US banks were for a while eclipsed by Japanese banks, which at one point accounted for eight of the largest ten banks in the world. This was a time when, difficult as it is to believe today, many US policy-makers believed that the US economy was on the verge of being overtaken by that of Japan. The Japanese economy was generating a large current account surplus thanks to the success of its manufacturing exports, and this gave rise to extensive financial claims on the rest of the world. In the event, the international position of Japanese banks was curtailed sharply in the 1990s. This was partly because a financial bubble developed in Japan in the late 1980s, notably in property and share prices, and after the bubble burst in 1990 the country's banks were left saddled with huge non-performing loans, and in no position to expand their business. But another significant factor was that Japanese banks had operated with a much lower capital base than US (or European) banks, and the Basel Committee's recommendations on capital requirements, which were first adopted in 1988, obliged Japanese banks to cut back the growth of their activities until they had built up their capital base.

European banks, for their part, have been engaged in an extensive process of mergers and takeovers since the 1990s. This has largely been within their home countries, although since 2000 cross-border takeovers within Europe have also increased.[17] By 2006, European banks accounted for 14 of the world's largest 25 banks, as shown in Table 2.1. The big banks were also extremely profitable. In 2006, US banks recorded a rate of return on their capital of 28.9 per cent and those in Britain achieved 27.3 per cent. The return in the EU as a whole was 22.7 per cent, although the figure for Germany was somewhat lower at 13.6 per cent.

Since the 1980s, the main growth in international finance has shifted from bank loans to cross-border investments in bonds and shares, and this has been accompanied by the growing importance of institutional investors in international transactions. Nevertheless, the major banks played a significant role in promoting the growth of capital market transactions, since the fees they earn from these have become an increasingly important source of their income. Furthermore, the banks also invest on their own account in the international bond market. Indeed, Citygroup created a furore in 2004 when it sold 11 billion euros' worth of European government bonds in less than two minutes and then, 30 minutes later after prices

Table 2.1   *Largest 25 banks by capital, 2006*

Position	Bank	Country	$ billion
1	Bank of America Corp	USA	91.1
2	Citigroup	USA	90.9
3	HSBC Holdings	UK	87.8
4	Crédit Agricole Group	France	84.9
5	JP Morgan Chase & Co	USA	81.1
6	Mitsubishi UFJ Financial Group	Japan	68.4
7	ICBC	China	59.2
8	Royal Bank of Scotland	UK	59.0
9	Bank of China	China	52.5
10	Santander Central Hispano	Spain	46.8
11	BNP Paribas	France	45.3
12	Barclays Bank	UK	45.2
13	HBOS	UK	44.0
14	China Construction Bank Corporation	China	42.3
15	Mizuho Financial Group	Japan	41.9
16	Wachovia Corporation	USA	39.4
17	UniCredit	Italy	38.7
18	Wells Fargo & Co	USA	36.8
19	Rabobank Group	Netherlands	34.8
20	ING Bank	Netherlands	34.0
21	UBS	Switzerland	33.2
22	Sumitomo Mitsui Financial Group	Japan	33.2
23	Deutsche Bank	Germany	32.3
24	ABN AMRO Bank	Netherlands	31.2
25	Crédit Mutuel	France	29.8

Source: *The Banker*, 'The top one thousand world banks', July 2007.

had plummeted, it bought back 4 billion euros of the bonds, making a profit of 17 million euros.[18] In addition, banks have been the most important players in promoting the enormous growth of the foreign exchange markets since 1973.

FOREIGN EXCHANGE MARKETS

When the US government suspended the convertibility of the dollar for gold in 1971, it also put pressure on Japan and West Germany to revalue their currencies.[19] This was intended to improve the international competitiveness of the US economy in relation to its two main rivals. Following a period of increasing monetary tension between the main capitalist states, the system of fixed exchange rates collapsed in 1973. Since then, governments have ceased to intervene systematically to maintain the value of their currencies, and instead, exchange rates have been largely left to fluctuate in response to market forces.[20]

The shift to flexible exchange rates in 1973 was followed by an enormous expansion of the foreign exchange market. According to the results of a survey conducted every three years by the Bank for International Settlements, by 2007 the value of the average *daily* turnover had reached an extraordinary 3210 billion dollars.[21] To put this in context, on the basis of 250 working days per year, this would amount to some 800 trillion dollars per year, whereas world trade goods and services in 2007 was worth around only 17 trillion dollars.[22] A large part of the turnover in the foreign exchange markets involves transactions between banks, and the growth of the market has been closely linked to the development of the international inter-bank money market and, more recently, the international bond market.

The foreign exchange market is a very fast-moving market that operates from dealing rooms which are largely run by banks. The main centre of this market is London, which in 2007 accounted for 34.1 per cent of turnover, followed by New York with 16.6 per cent, and Tokyo with 6.0 per cent.[23] The market is very concentrated, with 75 per cent of turnover being accounted for by just 12 banks in London, and a mere ten banks in New York. The currency concentration is even more marked, with the dollar appearing as one party in 88 per cent of transactions, with much smaller shares for the euro (37 per cent), the yen (15 per cent) and the British pound (14 per cent). For transactions between many other currencies it is necessary first to buy dollars (or less frequently, euros), and then to buy the required currency.

The adoption of flexible exchange rates was strongly supported by neoclassical economists, who argued that exchange rates would adjust smoothly so as to automatically eliminate any balance of payments surpluses or deficits, thereby avoiding some of the problems that had emerged in the Bretton Woods system.[24] In practice, however, exchange rates have tended to fluctuate widely, largely because they are driven by capital flows, which are themselves strongly influenced by expectations about the future course of exchange rates. As a result, the key exchange rates between the dollar and the other main currencies have not only been very unstable, they have also registered large swings, sometimes lasting for several years, in which the dollar has increased or fallen in value. As can be seen in Figure 2.1, the swings in the value of the dollar have been as large as 50 per cent measured against the Deutschmark or the euro.

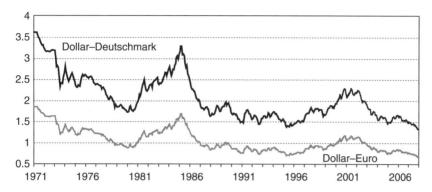

Figure 2.1   Exchange rate of the dollar, 1971–2007

The US government favoured a shift to flexible exchange rates because it believed that this would remove an important constraint on its economic policy. Indeed, one of the key channels by which US monetary policy has had an influence since the 1970s has been through its effect on the exchange rate, as changes in interest rates have made the country more (or less) attractive for foreign capital and, in turn, pushed the value of the dollar up (or down). In the 1970s, the US government was happy to see the value of the dollar decline, as this helped boost the country's exports (the country's finance minister was criticized at the time for 'talking the dollar down'). However, at the end of the decade the decline began to spin out of control and, in October 1979, the Federal Reserve was obliged to raise US interest rates sharply in order to attract capital back to the US and prevent an uncontrolled fall in the value of the dollar. Since the early 1980s, there have been two periods in which the dollar rose strongly (1981–5 and 1995–2000), and two periods in which the dollar weakened again (1985–94 and from 2002–08).

The US government has generally opposed any intervention to stabilize the foreign exchange markets, sometimes to the consternation of the European and Japanese authorities. In fact, the large swings in the value of the dollar have usually been welcomed by the US authorities since the dollar has tended to strengthen during booms, and thereby helped to attract foreign capital that could finance a growing trade deficit, while during recessions the dollar has tended to weaken, and this has helped to promote exports and growth. Nevertheless, in the mid-1980s when the dollar was faced with the possibility of an uncontrolled slide, the US government did turn to its major partners for support. By means of the Plaza Agreement in 1985, and the Louvre Agreement in 1987 it sought assistance, first in ensuring an orderly decline in the value of the dollar, and then in stabilizing its value within an agreed band. However, by the early

1990s when the crisis was over, the US authorities lost interest in further cooperation.[25]

The instability of exchange rates since the 1970s has meant greater uncertainty for firms involved in international transactions, since an unfavourable change in the exchange rate can wipe out the return that was expected on a trade deal, an investment project, or a loan. In response, the financial sector has developed a range of instruments designed to provide some protection against such fluctuations. One of the simplest of these is the forward contract, where the terms for a sale or purchase of a certain amount of foreign currency can be agreed for delivery at a date in the future. However, obtaining such insurance increases the cost of doing business; it is also difficult to obtain for more than one year into the future. For the banks, on the other hand, providing foreign exchange cover has been an important source of profitable expansion.[26]

INTERNATIONALIZATION OF THE CAPITAL MARKET

International portfolio investment in bonds was important prior to 1914, providing capital for financing the railways and other large investments, notably in North and South America. However, like international bank loans, these transactions were sharply curtailed in the 1930s, and remained limited for many years after the Second World War, when most countries maintained controls on international capital flows. Since the 1980s, however, international portfolio investment has increased strongly, leading to what is often referred to as the internationalization of capital markets. This has been facilitated by the widespread elimination of capital controls. The US lifted its capital controls in 1974, Britain followed in 1979, immediately after the election of Mrs Thatcher's government, and nearly all the other developed capitalist countries eliminated their controls in the course of the 1980s.

While the internationalization of capital markets was, of course, driven by financial institutions looking for ways to expand their business across borders, it was also a result of the policies adopted by the major capitalist countries, in particular those of the US government. In fact, in important respects, the international capital market is an extension of the US capital market, which has emerged as the hub for a very significant proportion of international flows of financial capital.

The internationalization of capital markets received an important impetus as a result of US policies after Ronald Reagan was elected president in 1980. The country's fiscal deficit rose sharply as military spending was increased and business taxes were cut. At the same time, the country's trade balance registered a rising deficit as high interest rates led to a marked rise in the strength of the dollar and, consequently, a loss in the competitiveness of US industry. In order to finance the fiscal deficit, the Reagan government sought to attract foreign finance to the US, a policy that also had the effect of providing capital inflows with which to offset the trade deficit. To this end, the government eliminated a withholding tax on interest payments to foreign holders of US bonds; it issued bonds specifically targeted at foreign investors; it pressured the Japanese government to eliminate controls on capital flows; and it sent senior Treasury officials to Japan and Western Europe to promote financial investment in the US.[27] Following these initiatives, the inflow of foreign capital into both government and corporate US bonds increased steadily, and this growth has continued broadly to this day.

The process of internationalization was also strengthened as a result of the growing importance of institutional investors. US institutional investors, especially investment funds (known as mutual funds in the US), have grown rapidly since the 1980s. This growth was initially channelled into shares and bonds in the US, but in the late 1980s the returns from the US market became less attractive. In October 1987 share prices on the New York stock exchange fell by over 20 per cent in a single day – the largest ever one-day fall; shortly after the Federal Reserve began to lower its main interest rate so as to relieve pressure on an overstretched banking system. Following the decline in returns in their home market, US institutional investors began to invest on a large scale in overseas markets in the 1990s. This investment was mainly directed at shares and bonds in Europe, especially Britain where the London stock exchange had been deregulated in 1986, and in Japan. In the 1990s, institutional investors from the US and the other developed countries also began to invest in so-called 'emerging markets' – middle-income developing countries in Latin America and Asia, whose stock markets were experiencing especially rapid growth – and in former Soviet bloc countries, where state-owned enterprises were being privatized by selling shares. Cross-border portfolio investment received a further boost from the stock market boom in the US and Europe in the late 1990s, although this declined somewhat immediately after the stock market bubble burst in 2000. However, growth has since resumed strongly, and the total value of outstanding cross-border portfolio investment increased from 14 trillion dollars in 2002 to 32.4 trillion dollars in 2006 (see Table 2.2).[28]

The growth of cross-border shareholdings by US institutional investors has contributed to transmitting the principle of 'shareholder value' – that companies should prioritize the return provided to shareholders above all

Table 2.2   Portfolio investment by top ten economies, 2006 ($ billions)

From	US	Britain	Lux.	France	Jap.	Ger.	Ire.	Neth.	Italy	Switz.	Other	Total
In												
US	–	817	417	254	798	179	397	306	104	119	2865	6254
Britain	1076	–	196	247	145	148	308	110	46	51	850	3178
Germany	288	144	304	239	174	–	115	192	141	101	844	2541
France	397	195	220	–	142	171	92	107	123	65	584	2096
Netherlands	60	87	–	124	89	300	39	61	325	131	437	1652
Japan	234	162	117	223	77	154	57	–	78	55	352	1509
Luxembourg	106	121	163	305	67	166	124	97	–	10	282	1441
Italy	586	231	104	86	–	28	57	37	14	19	273	1435
Cayman Is.	376	126	69	79	324	32	57	17	26	–	263	1368
Spain	111	101	98	223	33	216	76	63	33	8	158	1119
Other	2739	1085	743	651	494	544	272	274	251	322	2426	9801
Total	5972	3068	2431	2429	2343	1938	1594	1263	1141	881	9335	32394

Source: IMF (2008), Table 11.

other considerations – from the US, where it gained ascendancy in the 1980s, to continental Europe, where the dominant ethos had previously claimed to attend to a wider range of interests, including those of workers, consumers and the broader community as well as the interests of shareholders.

Another factor that has driven the growth of the international capital market has been the balance of payments current account surpluses generated by China, Japan and the other Asian countries, together with those of oil-exporting countries. These countries have invested their surpluses predominantly in US government bonds, and by 2007 foreign official institutions (usually central banks) held some 42 per cent of US government securities.[29] In fact, these holdings have generated a relatively low return for foreign central banks, and several countries have, or plan to, set up so-called 'sovereign investment funds', which will seek to invest in a range of higher-yielding financial assets. Countries such as the United Arab Emirates, Norway and Singapore have been doing this for some time, but after China announced in 2007 that it planned to assign 200 billion dollars from its official reserves to such a fund, senior politicians in a number of Western countries began to call for investments by such funds to be restricted. The usual argument is that the funds will not just be guided by commercial, profit-maximizing criteria, but might also seek to exert political influence.[30]

EUROPE AND THE INTERNATIONALIZATION OF FINANCE

While the US has emerged as the hub of the international financial system, some 80 per cent of international capital flows are between the US, the eurozone and Britain (see Figure 2.2)[31]. This, of course, reflects the fact that, with the exception of Japan, Europe includes most of the major developed capitalist countries outside the US. Since the Second World War, economic development in Western Europe has been closely linked with a process of European integration and this was extended to include much of Central and Eastern Europe after the collapse of the Soviet bloc.

One of the initial steps towards integration was the creation of the European Payments Union, which functioned from 1950 until 1958. At a time when most IMF member countries were not in a position to establish current-account convertibility, as envisioned by IMF rules, the European Payments Union established limited current account convertibility between Western European currencies, and provided credits for countries faced with a deficit. This facilitated a growth of trade between the member countries and, although it discriminated against trade with the US, it was accepted

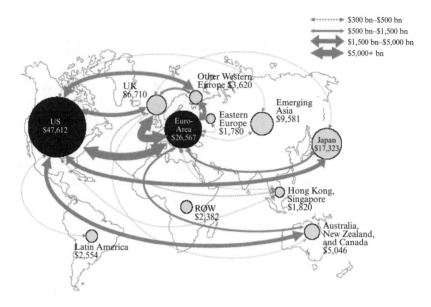

Notes
*Includes cross-border equity, debt, lending and foreign direct investment.
Figures in bubbles show size of total domestic financial assets 2005, $ billion.

Source: McKinsey Global Institute (2007).

Figure 2.2   Map of cross-border financial holdings, 2004*

by the US government because of its strategic interest in promoting the creation of a strong anti-Communist bloc in Western Europe.

The need for the Payments Union was superseded in 1958, when West European countries established full current-account convertibility. In the same year, the European Economic Community (EEC) was established, initially by six countries.[32] This abolished all tariffs on trade between members, and was followed by a major expansion of their trade with each other. Access to the larger market enabled firms to benefit from economies of scale and led to a significant deepening of the division of labour within Europe. In a context of widespread full employment, real wages rose steadily and the state was able to finance an expansion of its social provisions. Integration proceeded in 1967 when the EEC merged with two other European organizations to form the European Community (EC).[33] In the early 1970s, however, European economic integration was threatened by the exchange rate instability that emerged following the breakdown of the Bretton Woods' system of fixed exchange rates.

The members of the EC responded to the collapse of the Bretton Woods system by creating the so-called currency snake, which lasted from 1973 to 1979. This was a loose arrangement in which members tried to ensure that their currencies remained within a rough band so that they would move up and down together against the other major currencies. However, this proved difficult to sustain, and France was obliged to withdraw on several occasions.

The difficulties of sustaining the snake led to the creation of the European Monetary System (EMS) in 1979. This established a pegged exchange-rate system between its members, with countries required to keep the value of their currencies within 2.25 per cent against a central value defined in terms of the ecu (European Currency Unit), a unit of account whose value was determined by a basket made up of all the member states' currencies. Britain and Spain, which joined later, were allowed a wider margin of 6 per cent. The European Monetary Cooperation Fund was also set up to provide assistance to members with balance of payments difficulties. The EMS was very effective in achieving exchange rate stability within Europe during the 1980s, a period when the dollar registered very large swings in value. Nevertheless, the growth of private capital flows in the course of the 1980s made it more difficult to sustain a system of pegged exchange rates. The German mark was the strongest currency in the system, and after the German Bundesbank raised interest rates in 1992, the EMS experienced a serious crisis when massive speculation forced Britain and, temporarily, Italy to leave the system.

In fact, European heads of government meeting in the Dutch city of Maastricht at the end of 1991 had already agreed to move beyond the EMS and create a common European currency. The conditions for this were set out in the Maastricht Treaty, which was signed in early 1992, and which also led to the establishment of the European Union (EU) in 1993. Monetary unification was based on proposals elaborated by a high-level working group in the late 1980s, but its adoption was also linked to the new political situation created by German unification in 1990. Germany now had the largest population in Europe, and it sought to assuage any fears in France and other neighbouring countries about its future intentions by its willingness to give up the mark, the symbol of its post-war economic success, for a joint European currency.

Monetary unification, which occurred at the beginning of 1999, involved the creation of a new currency, the euro, and the European Central Bank, with headquarters in Frankfurt.[34] Eleven of the then 15 members of the EU participated, although it is envisioned that all EU members should eventually join.[35] Membership is, however, dependent on countries meeting a number of controversial conditions, most notably a budget deficit of below 3 per cent of GDP.[36] Only Britain and Denmark are not required to join the euro, having obtained opt-outs when the Maastricht Treaty was being negotiated. British reticence is partly based on economic concerns, particularly as regards the supposed loss of control over monetary policy, but it is also strongly influenced by political opposition to European integration, reflecting Britain's continued difficulty in coming to terms with its post-Imperial position in the world.

Once monetary union had been achieved, the EU then directed its attention to promoting the integration of financial markets in Europe. The Financial Services Action Plan, which was launched in 1999, set out 42 wide-ranging measures designed to establish common standards and regulatory approaches among the member countries, most of which were implemented on time.[37] The EU's Lisbon strategy – announced in 2000 with the aim of creating the most competitive knowledge-based economy in the world by 2010 – also envisaged a central role for an integrated European capital market which, it was claimed, would lead to a lower cost of finance, and hence to higher investment.

After the euro was introduced, cross-border financial investments between the eurozone countries increased strongly. The elimination of the risk of exchange rate changes resulted in eurozone financial institutions diversifying their holdings of government and corporate bonds. Monetary union also contributed to a significant increase in international capital transactions between the eurozone and other economies. In fact, in the very first year of the euro's existence, the issue of corporate bonds in the eurozone exceeded that in the US, boosted by US corporations raising capital in Europe, where interest rates were lower, and then transferring the funds to the US to finance the then ongoing investment boom. Nevertheless, although there has been a significant growth of the eurozone capital market, it is important to note that it is still smaller than the US capital market, as can be seen in Table 2.3. Furthermore, even though the total stock of government bonds in the eurozone is almost as large as that in the US, European bonds are issued by different governments and are more heterogeneous, and the market is therefore not as deep or as liquid as that in the US.[38]

Although Britain has remained outside the eurozone, London is by far the most important financial centre in Europe. Instead of losing business to Frankfurt or Paris, as some commentators anticipated if Britain did not join the euro, London has actually been closing the gap between itself and New York in terms of its significance as a global financial centre.[39] London has, of course, actively promoted this, instigating the so-called Big Bang in 1986, when the London Stock Exchange sought to promote its global role by abolishing fixed fees for conducting transactions. Figures for 2007 show that London was the leading international centre for cross-border

Table 2.3   Capital market indicators, 2006 ($ trillion)

	Stock market capitalization	Debt securities		
		Public	Private	Total
European Union	13.1	7.7	15.5	23.2
Euro area	8.4	6.6	12.2	18.8
Britain	3.8	0.8	2.5	3.3
United States	19.6	6.2	20.8	27.0
Japan	4.8	6.7	2.0	8.7

Source: International Monetary Fund (2008a, p. 147).

bank lending and foreign exchange dealing, and that it had overtaken New York as the leading centre for international share issues (see Table 2.4).[40] The leading role of London within Europe is demonstrated by the fact that around half of Europe's investment banking is conducted in the city, while 50 per cent of Europe's private equity assets and over three-quarters of Europe's hedge funds are managed from there.

THE DOLLAR AND THE EURO

One of the questions raised by the creation of the euro is whether the new currency could come to challenge the international role of the dollar.[41] Certainly the US has gained considerable advantages from the current position of the dollar: its companies benefit from conducting international business in their own currency, and are not exposed to the risk that the exchange rate will change before payments are received; more significantly, the US has been able to finance a large current-account deficit since the early 1980s; furthermore, because its foreign borrowing is denominated in dollars, the cost of servicing its external debt does not increase when the currency depreciates, as is the case for developing countries; finally, because oil and other key primary commodities are priced in dollars, the cost of importing these to the US does not automatically increase when the dollar declines in value.

European monetary union was motivated primarily by economic considerations: eliminating exchange rate risk between members, creating an integrated financial system, and – especially for smaller countries – gaining greater policy autonomy as part of a larger and stronger economic unit. However, in some countries – most notably France – monetary union was also motivated by the political desire to create an alternative to the dollar.

Table 2.4   Britain's share of global financial markets, 2007 (per cent)

	Britain	US	Japan	France	Germany	Others
Cross-border bank lending	21	9	7	8	11	44
Foreign equities turnover	46	43	–	–	4	7
Foreign exchange turnover	34	17	6	3	3	37
Derivative turnover						
Exchange traded	6	40	2	1	13	38
Over-the-counter	43	24	4	7	4	18
International bonds –						
secondary market	70	–	–	–	–	–
Fund management (end						
2006)	8	52	17	6	3	24
Hedge fund assets (2006)	21	66	2	1	–	10
Private equity (2006)	13	60	2	4	1	20
IPOs	18	16	–	–	–	66
Securitization issuance	6	76	2	–	1	15

Source: IFSL Research (2008c).

One of the factors that is important in determining which country's currency serves as international money is the size of its economy and its importance in international trade. Here the eurozone does represent a challenge: it is currently slightly smaller than the US economy but, if other EU members were to join, it would be larger, and the eurozone's exports already exceed those of the US. However, a further important require-ment is the existence of highly liquid capital markets, where a country's official reserves can be invested safely, or easily sold. Here the eurozone lags behind: the government bond market in the eurozone is fragmented along country lines, with different regulatory frameworks, and even dif-ferent credit ratings, and it does not provide such a large, liquid pool of bonds as the US market. There is also another important factor, known as 'network externalities': the international usefulness of a currency is enhanced by the number of other countries which use it. This leads to considerable inertia in the choice of international money – the British pound continued to be used for a considerable time after the US had overtaken Britain in economic output. Nevertheless, a corollary of this is that, when a change does occur, it can happen quite rapidly.

The last time the international role of the dollar suffered a serious threat was in the late 1970s, when the US government's attempts to boost exports by 'talking the dollar down' led to rising inflation and the value of the dollar threatened to plummet out of control. A threat by the Saudi

Arabian government to start pricing oil in special drawing rights, the IMF's unit of account, rather than dollars was only narrowly averted.[42] On this occasion, the US Federal Reserve re-established the value of the currency by raising interest rates to unprecedented levels in the early 1980s, making dollar assets highly attractive to international financial investors, but at the cost of a major international recession and the onset of the Third World debt crisis.

The early 1980s represented a turning point for the US. Since then, the financial sector has come to play a far greater role in driving the country's economy. There have been three phases of economic expansion, and each has been dependent on ever greater expansions of credit. In the 1980s, this was focused on a takeover and merger boom, where top management bought up their own companies by means of so-called leveraged buyouts; in the 1990s, the expansion was closely linked to the stock market boom associated with information technology; in the first decade of the new century, the expansion was linked to a boom in house prices, and an unprecedented growth of household indebtedness, which fuelled consumer spending. Internationally this has expressed itself in a huge current account deficit, which by 2007 stood at 731 billion dollars (5.3 per cent of GDP), something that could only be sustained because the US was able to attract a corresponding inflow of capital from the rest of the world.[43]

There is widespread agreement that the US current account deficit cannot be sustained indefinitely, and international organizations, such as the International Monetary Fund or the Bank for International Settlements, have regularly warned that one of the greatest dangers facing international financial markets is the possibility of what they call 'a disorderly adjustment of the dollar'.[44] The great fear is that a loss of confidence in the US currency could set off a massive sale of dollar assets. In such a situation, the value of the dollar would begin to fall precipitously and the euro would provide the most likely alternative.

China, which has the largest foreign exchange reserves in the world, together with a number of other developing countries, has already announced a policy of diversifying their official reserves so as to hold a more balanced amount of dollars and euros, although this seems likely to involve the acquisition of new assets, rather than the conversion of existing assets. But the large dollar holdings of China, Japan and other Asian countries means that they have a strong interest in avoiding a sudden collapse of the US currency.

The deregulation and internationalization of financial markets, together with the growth of ever more complex financial instruments, has made the international financial system more vulnerable to major crises in the last 35 years.[45] Most of the serious crises have occurred in developing or transition countries, where they have had a devastating social impact in Mexico (1994), South-East Asia (1997–8), Russia (1998), Brazil (1999), Turkey (2000), and Argentina (2003). But in August 2007 the US banking system was itself hit by the crisis detonated by the failure of complex securities based on sub-prime mortgages, and this crisis was rapidly transmitted to the European banking system.[46] Massive central bank intervention in both the US and Europe prevented a sudden decline of output and employment, as occurred during the crises in developing countries. However, if a major flight from the dollar were to develop, the US authorities would not be able to raise interest rates so as to attract capital back to the US – as they did in 1979 – without provoking a serious deepening of the crisis in the US financial system.

NOTES

1. These averaged 5 per cent of GDP between 1880 and 1913, with the figure rising to almost 10 per cent in 1913. (Bloomfield, 1968).
2. Bloomfield (1959).
3. The classic study is Morgenstern (1959).
4. This point is emphasized by Barry Eichengreen (1996), pp. 31 and 195.
5. De Cecco (1974).
6. According to Barry Eichengreen, Federal Reserve officials also resented the leading role of the Bank of England. See Eichengreen (1996, p. 63).
7. It also created a space in which many Latin American countries were able to begin developing their own industries.
8. Kindleberger (1973).
9. For a detailed discussion of Keynes's proposals and the negotiations at Bretton Woods, see Skidelsky (2000).
10. The main component of the current account is trade. It also includes international payments of profit and interest, and salaries. The rule implies that a central bank should provide foreign exchange on request, and without conditions, to any firm wishing to import goods.
11. Important factors affecting the political balance included (1) the discrediting of naked capitalism as a result of mass unemployment in the 1930s; (2) the role that working class organizations had played in the war against fascism; and (3) the need to demonstrate that capitalism could also maintain full employment in the face of systemic competition from the Soviet bloc.
12. This problem was highlighted by Robert Triffin (1960).
13. The main measures were the Interest Equalisation Tax, introduced in 1963 to discourage foreign corporations from raising capital in the US bond market, and the Voluntary Credit Restraint Programme, introduced in 1965 to discourage banks in the US from funding the overseas investments of US corporations.
14. Mizruchi and Davis (2003).
15. See Bank for International Settlements (1983). Between 1975 and 1981, the value of external claims of banks in Europe, Canada and Japan increased from 246 to 777 billion dollars.
16. Under what has since become known as Basel I, banks were required to hold capital

equal to 8 per cent of their (risk adjusted) assets. For fuller details of Basel I and its successor, Basel II, see Chapter 14 below.

17. For details, see ECB (2007a, p. 35).
18. The profits could have been much larger but other dealers were so outraged that – contrary to the rules of the market – many refused to deal with Citigroup any more. See Aline van Duyn and Päivi Munter (2004).
19. Parboni (1981).
20. This situation was formalized at a meeting of the IMF held in Jamaica in 1976, where it was agreed that governments might intervene to smooth out temporary disturbances, but not to influence the underlying value of their currency.
21. Bank for International Settlements (2007, Table 1).
22. World Trade Organisation (2008, Table 1).
23. All figures in this paragraph are from Bank for International Settlements (2007). The figures are for the UK, the US and Japan, but in each case, turnover is largely concentrated in the country's main financial centre.
24. Milton Friedman (1953).
25. Randal Henning argues that in the 1970s and 1980s, US policy towards the dollar was marked by cycles involving three stages: (1) a period of lack of attention, when misalignments developed; (2) a period when the US sought to pressure others into adjusting; and (3) a period when it sought cooperation. See Henning (1985, p. 306).
26. The corporate treasuries of some large multinationals, which act like banks in the foreign exchange markets, have on some occasions also earned more from such financial transactions than from their productive activities.
27. Henning (1985, pp. 273–4).
28. IMF (2008b, Table 11).
29. US Treasury Department, et al. (2008, tables 2 and 6).
30. John Willman (2007).
31. McKinsey Global Institute (2007).
32. The original six members were Germany, France, Italy, Belgium, Holland and Luxemburg. Britain, Ireland and Denmark joined in 1973, followed by Greece in 1981, Spain and Portugal in 1986, and the formerly neutral countries of Sweden, Finland and Austria in 1994 after the collapse of the Soviet bloc. Ten new members, predominantly from Eastern Europe, joined in 2004, with two more following in 2007.
33. The two other organizations were the European Coal and Steel Community, set up in 1952, and the European Atomic Energy Authority, set up in 1957.
34. National notes and coins continued to be used for retail transactions until 2002. The value of these was fixed irrevocably against the euro, which replaced the ecu, on the basis of exchange rates on the final day of trading in 1998.
35. The original 11 members were Austria, Belgium, Finland, France, Germany, Ireland, Italy, Luxembourg, the Netherlands, Portugal and Spain. Subsequent members include Greece (2001), Slovenia (2007), Cyprus and Malta (2008) with Slovakia due to join in 2009.
36. Other conditions concern inflation, long-term interest rates, government debt and stable exchange rates. Some wags have suggested that exceptionally stringent conditions were insisted on by the German Bundesbank in the hope that they would prove too onerous, and so prevent a European Central Bank from displacing them as Europe's *de facto* monetary authority.
37. For further details, see Chapter 4.
38. Depth and liquidity are important for ensuring a ready market where it is possible to buy or sell securities easily and without having a significant impact on prices.
39. This paragraph draws on Martin Dickson (2006).
40. This has been at least partly because the Sarbanes-Oxley Act introduced stringent and costly accounting rules for companies issuing shares in the US in 2002 in the aftermath of corporate scandals at Enron, WorldCom and other major US companies.
41. For a summary of recent academic debates, see Lim (2006).

42. See Spiro (1999, pp. 104–5 and 124–5).
43. This was slightly down on the figure for 2006, which was equal to 811 billion dollars, or 6.1 per cent of GDP.
44. See recent issues of the IMF's biannual *World Economic Outlook*, or the BIS's *Annual Report.*
45. See Aliber (2005).
46. For details see Evans (2008).

3. Europe's financial systems under pressure

Marica Frangakis

3.1 INTRODUCTION

Since the 1980s, the financial systems of the member states of the EU have come under increasing competitive pressure, as a result of developments both on the global and on the European level. On the global level, the collapse of the Bretton Woods agreement and of the system of fixed exchange rates, followed by the two oil crises in the 1970s, marks the end of the era during which governments stabilized their economies by fiscal and monetary policies and public sector activity, with limited or occasional interference from the financial markets.[1] This period is also known as the era of 'financial repression', denoting the fact that restrictions on international capital movement permitted many governments to maintain very low rates of interest, sometimes even negative in real terms (Toporowski, 2005).

Thus, the post-World War II dollar standard system of fixed exchange rates gave way to a liberalization and privatization thrust in economic policy both in the advanced and in the less developed countries in the late 1970s, introducing greater reliance on markets domestically and internationally.[2]

On the European level, developments were equally dramatic. As early as 1983, a White Paper on financial integration by the European Commission called for greater liberalization in the area of European finance.[3] Following the 1986 Single European Act, the 1988 Council directive on the liberalization of capital controls, the 1992 Treaty on the European Union, the introduction of the single currency in 1999 and the Financial Services Action Plan (1999–2005), various legal and economic barriers to an integrated financial market were progressively dismantled.[4]

More specifically, in most member states – with the exception of the UK, the Benelux countries and Germany – finance, and especially banking, had been subject to a wide range of regulations which now came under pressure. Table 3.1 portrays the range of financial regulations that were in place in 1980 in the member states of the EU.

Table 3.1   Financial regulations in EU member states in 1980

	B	DK	DE	E	F	GR	I	IRL	L	NL	P	UK
Control of interest rates	*	*	*	*	*	*	*	*	*		*	
Capital controls	*		*	*	*	*	*				*	
Stock exchange membership			*	*	*		*				*	*
Bank branch restrictions			*				*				*	
Foreign bank entry				*		*	*				*	
Credit ceilings			*	*	*	*	*				*	
Mandatory investment requirements				*	*	*			*	*		
Restrictions on insurance	*		*	*	*	*				*	*	
Leasing				*			*				*	

Notes: B: Belgium, DK: Denmark, DE: Germany, E: Spain, F: France, GR: Greece, I: Italy, IRL: Ireland, L: Luxembourg, NL: Netherlands, P: Portugal and UK: United Kingdom.

Source: Dermine (2002).

It is worth noting that capital controls co-existed with the European Monetary System (EMS), an early attempt to coordinate exchange rate policies in the EU. In fact, the existence of such capital controls is considered to have been instrumental in the long duration of the EMS, that is, spanning more than a decade (1979 to 1989 approximately). In particular, France and Italy maintained such controls during most of the 1980s, only eliminating them towards the end of the decade in conformity with the strategic EU policy decision to move towards a fully integrated internal market, whereby the free movement of capital was seen as an essential part of complete market integration.[5] In practice, capital mobility destabilized the EMS.

On a global level, financial market liberalization was virtually complete in the industrial countries by the early 1990s, while developing countries followed suit, making substantial progress in liberalizing their financial systems throughout the 1990s. As has been argued, by the end of the twentieth century, for all intents and purposes, the shift from a government-led to a market-led international financial system had been accomplished.[6]

In the case of the EU, these trends were intensified by the introduction of the single currency in 1999, as well as the preparation for it throughout the 1990s.[7] The direct effects of the European Monetary Union on financial markets, put forward by the European Commission (1990) report 'One market, one money', comprise standardization and transparency in pricing, the shrinking of the foreign exchange market, the elimination of currency risk, the elimination of currency-related investment regulations and the homogenization of the public bond market and of bank refinancing procedures. These are all drivers of financial market integration, the implications of which will be discussed below.

Although the indirect effects of the introduction of the euro are especially difficult to assess, it is believed to have further strengthened the tendency toward a more market-led financial system in the EU. For example, Danthine et al. (2000) found that the increased activity in the EU capital markets signified a 'shift from banks to markets', benefiting the more market-based asset management and investment banking activities, by comparison to the traditional deposit and lending business of commercial banks. Further, EMU had a major effect on bank restructuring in Europe, mainly through increased M&A activity. Pertinent though these results may be, they were recorded at a time of exuberance of the world financial markets, also known as the dotcom bubble, which burst in the early 2000s. How far these trends persist some years later is a key question to be examined here.

On the whole, both the direct and indirect changes induced by the introduction of the single currency in the EU signify a more competitive environment not only for the financial players, but also for the economy at large. What has been the response of European finance? More specifically, does the relationship or bank-based financial system, traditionally associated with Germany, or Rhenish Capitalism, converge towards the market-based, or arm's length one, generally associated with the UK and the USA, or Anglo-American Capitalism?[8]

At the height of the financial markets boom in 1999–2000, there were signs that such a shift was the case. So much so, that some analysts have claimed that a 'financial revolution' was in progress in the EU.[9] Some years later, as the effects of the protracted economic slowdown the EU entered, following the collapse of the stock markets, become clearer, can this be claimed to be the case?

Further, how have banks reacted to their changing environment? Does the increasing presence of market-based finance denote the deepening of financial integration, a central goal of policy under the Lisbon Agenda which set out the EU's strategy for the decade 2000–10?

Lastly, we must consider 12 new member states, of which ten were former transition countries, which joined the EU in May 2004, followed by two more in 2007, Romania and Bulgaria.[10] The financial systems of most of the transition countries were transformed from a mono-bank system at the end of the 1980s to the institution of market capitalism by the end of the 1990s. A defining characteristic of these systems is their lack of institutional maturity. The very large presence of foreign-owned financial concerns goes some way towards compensating for such a lack of experience.

At the same time, it gives rise to a different order of problems. Hence, the case of the transition countries needs to be especially considered.

In dealing with the questions raised above, this chapter is organized as follows. The next section (3.2) reviews the main tendencies in European finance, in terms of structural changes in relation to the USA and Japan. The so-called 'Continental' vs. the 'Anglo-Saxon' financing models are discussed. Also, the evolving structure of financial assets and liabilities by type of user and financial product in the euro area are examined, as are the particular characteristics of financial intermediation in the new EU member states. The following section (3.3) takes a closer look at the different segments of the EU financial services sector; developments therein, as well as actors. In particular, the banking sector and the response of the EU banks to the challenges of increasing competition are analysed, followed by an overview of developments in the EU capital markets, namely, the bond, equity and derivatives markets. There is then a review of the role of institutional investors and of the main features of the European security exchanges. The next section (3.4) is concerned with the degree and prospects of integration of the various EU financial services segments. Has the response of European finance led to a more integrated financial services sector, and in which areas? These are pertinent questions not only from an analytical point of view, but also from the point of view of policy, to the extent that financial integration is a core measure of the revised Lisbon Agenda. The final section (3.5) summarizes and concludes.

3.2   EU FINANCIAL TRENDS AND DEVELOPMENTS

Comparative Financial Structures

The financial system of the EU member states is generally regarded as bank-dominated, with the exception of the UK, which, together with the USA, represents the so-called 'Anglo-Saxon' model, where capital markets take up a considerable share of the financial services sector. This pattern has been gradually shifting in favour of the capital markets in a number of ways. Namely, the significance of capital markets has been increasing over time, albeit not necessarily in a consistent pattern from year to year; banks have developed their presence in capital markets both on their own account and on behalf of their customers, for example, by offering their services in security trading and underwriting; market participants tend to adopt a more market-type competitive behaviour under the perceived prospect or threat of increased competition (Grahl and Teague, 2003).

Table 3.2   Financial indicators (%)

Country	Bank loans to private sector/ GDP	Stock market capitali- zation/ GDP	Equity issues/ GFCF	Bank loans to private sector/ GDP	Stock market capitali- zation/ GDP	Equity issues/ GFCF
	1980			2000		
USA	35.4	46.0	4.0	49.3	154.9	20.7
UK	27.6	38.0	4.0	132.0	184.0	14.9
EU-14 average 'Continental'	60.1	7.8	2.0	93.7	104.6	32.2
France	73.1	9.0	6.0	86.4	108.7	14.5
Germany	86.4	9.0	1.0	120.7	66.8	6.5
Italy	55.5	7.0	4.0	77.0	70.3	4.1
Spain	n.a.	8.7	2.8	101.2	88.2	86.6

Source: Rajan and Zingales (2003).

The run-up to and the adoption of the single currency and of the common monetary policy by 12 out of 15 member states of the EU intensified these trends, so that at the turn of the century, a structural transformation was perceived to have taken place[11]. For example, Rajan and Zingales (2003) found that the main features of what they term the average 'Continental Europe' model came considerably closer to those of the average 'Anglo-Saxon' model over the space of 20 years (1980–2000), although there remained significant variations on a per country basis (see Table 3.2). Thus, Germany, a bank-dominated country, remained so, in spite of the increasing presence of the capital markets, while the UK, a market-oriented economy, also retained its main character, in spite of the great rise in bank loans.

On the other hand, the downturn of the world financial markets after the bursting of the dotcom bubble in the early 2000s hampered the rate of transformation in EU financial structures, while the unwinding of the financial imbalances induced an economic slowdown of varying duration and intensity across the member states, which further dampened activity on the financial markets. As a result, the trends of the late 1990s slowed down considerably, albeit not reversed entirely. Furthermore, by the mid-2000s, the growth of the financial markets had resumed on the global, as well as on the European level (Table 3.3).

As we can see, over the period under review, the size of the global

Table 3.3   Regional composition of global financial stock

		Global financial stock	USA	Europe	Japan	China	Rest of world
1993	US$ trillion	53					
	% Share	100	36	27	23	3	11
1996	US$ trillion	69					
	% Share	100	37	29	19	3	12
1999	US$ trillion	96					
	% Share	100	40	28	18	3	11
2003	US$ trillion	117					
	% Share	100	37	31	15	4	13
2006	US$ trillion	167					
	% Share	100	34	32	12	5	17

Notes: 'Financial Stock' includes amounts outstanding at year end of equities, private debt securities, government debt securities and band deposits; 'Europe' includes the following countries: UK, Austria, Belgium, Finland, France, Germany, Greece, Ireland, Italy, Luxembourg, Netherlands, Portugal, Spain, Switzerland, Sweden, Denmark, Norway and Eastern Europe.

Sources: McKinsey. (2005, 2008).

financial stock recorded the greatest rate of increase in 2006 (43 per cent over 2003) and 1999 (39 per cent over 1996).[12] Of course, the world financial turmoil of the late 2000s, which began as a credit crunch in the financially developed countries in 2007, is bound to influence negatively the rate of growth of world financial markets. It is, however, unlikely to reverse the long-run trends that appear to have been established since the 1980s.[13]

The size of the financial markets in relation to GDP – also known as 'financial depth' – and their structure by different products across different regions, as well as globally, is shown in Table 3.4.

As we can see, not only has the size of the financial markets been increasing in absolute terms, but also in relation to GDP across all regions. This was especially pronounced in the eurozone countries, where the relative size of financial markets increased more than fourfold between 1980 and 2006, although the rate of increase slowed down in the early 2000s and it is likely to do so again in the late 2000s, following the upheaval of the financial markets experienced in 2007–08. A high rate of increase was also recorded in the UK, in spite of its comparatively more developed financial system, more akin to the US, rather than to the 'Continental' Europe type. Lastly, the East European countries are steadily establishing their position in the global financial system.

In terms of structure, the eurozone countries' financial system is steadily

Table 3.4   Depth and structure of financial markets (% GDP)

	Globally	USA	Eurozone	UK	Japan	Eastern Europe
1980						
Equity securities	25	52	8	38	36	
Private debt securities	15	28	14	1	17	
Government debt securities	20	25	13	31	50	
Bank deposits	49	74	43	33	97	
Global financial stock:						
US$12 trillion						
% GDP	*109*	*179*	*78*	*103*	*200*	*N/A*
1993						
Equity securities	57	77	27	120	69	
Private debt securities	48	81	47	31	48	
Government debt securities	43	61	44	33	48	
Bank deposits	67	67	57	61	108	
Global financial stock:						
US$53 trillion						
% GDP	*215*	*286*	*175*	*245*	*273*	*N/A*
2003						
Equity securities	88	130	61	134	71	31
Private debt securities	85	143	92	115	49	3
Government debt securities	56	46	66	29	143	20
Bank deposits	96	78	95	107	148	45
Global financial stock:						
US$117 trillion						
% GDP	*325*	*397*	*314*	*385*	*411*	*99*
2006						
Equity securities	110	148	82	160	107	37
Private debt securities	89	153	114	106	45	4
Government debt securities	54	47	61	34	156	33
Bank deposits	93	76	99	122	138	56
Global financial stock:						
US$167 trillion						
% GDP	346	424	356	422	446	130

Notes: (a) Eurozone countries: Austria, Belgium, Finland, France, Germany, Greece, Ireland, Italy, Luxembourg, Netherlands, Portugal, Spain; (b) Eastern European countries: Bulgaria, Croatia, the Czech Republic, Estonia, Hungary, Latvia, Lithuania, Poland, Romania, the Slovak Republic and Ukraine.

Sources: McKinsey (2005) Taking stock of the world's capital markets (Exhibits 3, 10 and 15: own calculations) and McKinsey (2008) Mapping global capital markets – 4th Annual Report (Exhibits 1.1 and 1.2: own calculations).

Table 3.5   *Size and structure of financial markets in the eurozone countries, 2006*

	Total financial assets	Equities	Private debt securities	Government debt securities	Bank deposits
Germany	*US$ 9.5 trillion*				
	100	17	36	16	32
France	*US$ 8.2 trillion*				
	100	30	28	15	27
Italy	*US$ 5.9 trillion*				
	100	17	29	30	23
Spain	*US$ 4.9 trillion*				
	100	27	36	11	26
Netherlands	*US$ 3.1 trillion*				
	100	25	45	9	21
Belgium	*US$ 1.6 trillion*				
	100	25	25	26	24
Austria	*US$ 1.0 trillion*				
	100	19	33	18	30
Greece	*US$ 0.9 trillion*				
	100	23	11	41	25
Ireland	*US$ 0.8 trillion*				
	100	20	47	5	27
Finland	*US$ 0.7 trillion*				
	100	40	15	18	27
Portugal	*US$ 0.7 trillion*				
	100	16	31	23	30
Luxembourg	*US$ 0.3 trillion*				
	100	24	29	0	47

Source: McKinsey (2008).

becoming more market-oriented, although the emphasis appears to be on private debt securities, more than on equities. In fact, by the mid-2000s, securities as a whole represented a higher percentage of GDP in the eurozone countries than in Japan, thus reversing the situation of the previous years. The East European countries also appear to be going through a transformation process towards a more market-oriented system, albeit at a more gradual pace. The UK, on the other hand, maintains its position as the most market-oriented financial area within the EU.

As we can see in Table 3.5, within the eurozone, in 2006, the volume of financial assets was largest in Germany, followed by France and, at some distance, Italy and Spain. In terms of structure, the share of bank deposits in total financial assets was largest in Luxembourg, Europe's 'banker' along with Switzerland, followed by Germany, Portugal and Austria. On the other hand, the share of debt securities is prominent in all countries, accounting for approximately one half of all financial assets, with the exception of Luxembourg and Finland, where they account for about one third.

Overall, it would appear that the financial systems of the EU are in a state of flux, under the pressures of increased competition both on the global and on the European level. In spite of the periodic setbacks, the general trend towards a more market-based financial system is evident in Europe and especially in the euro area, which we shall now examine in greater detail.

Investment and Financing in the Euro Area

In the course of the 1990s, financial products and instruments accounted for an increasing share of investment and financing in the euro area, in spite of periodic setbacks. More specifically, the net acquisition of financial assets by the non-financial sector, including corporations and households, exceeded gross fixed capital formation in 2000 – the year of 'exuberance', to use the famous expression of Alan Greenspan, then Chairman of the Federal Reserve Bank – falling sharply in the next four years, only to bounce back to a level approaching that of the late 1990s by the mid-2000s (Table 3.6).[14]

A similar rise in the share of external financing both by non-financial corporations and by the households – other than their own savings – was recorded over the same period. Namely, the noticeable increase recorded in the late 1990s was followed by an equally noticeable drop over the following four years (2001–04), reversing and ascending again by the mid-2000s (Table 3.6).

The structure of the main liabilities of the non-financial sector in the euro area, reveals (i) the increasing indebtedness of households; (ii) the steadily high share of loans; (iii) the significance of debt securities; and (iv) the relatively smaller share of equities, which are back on the increase since 2002 (Table 3.7).

As we can see, the share of households in total liabilities increased between 1998 and 2004, remaining nearly constant after that, whereas that of the non-financial corporations increased, after an intermitent decline between 2002 and 2004. Lastly, the share of the general government declined, in spite of periodic upward shifts.

In terms of types of financial liabilities, much of the increase in loans, as well as in debt securities, has been directed towards long-term products, largely as a result of the low-inflation environment, encouraging long-term investment. The significance of equities, on the other hand, displayed a

Table 3.6   Investment, saving and external financing of the private non-financial sector* in the eurozone, 1993–2006 (%)

	Gross fixed capital formation as % GDP	Net acquisition of financial assets as % GDP	Gross saving as % GDP	External financing as % GDP
1992	18.8	13.5	21.0	10.2
1993	16.8	13.0	20.8	7.7
1994	16.9	13.7	20.7	9.6
1995	17.3	13.9	21.9	7.4
1996	17.1	12.9	21.4	8.8
1997	17.1	13.4	20.6	9.5
1998	17.4	15.8	19.9	12.2
1999	18.8	17.8	18.5	17.1
2000	19.4	21.1	18.1	22.7
2001	18.5	15.4	18.5	14.5
2002	17.1	12.5	18.8	10.0
2003	16.9	12.2	17.8	9.8
2004	17.1	11.2	19.1	8.8
2005	17.3	14.1	18.0	12.1
2006	17.9	14.1	15.9	15.2

Notes: * Includes the non-financial corporations and households.

Source: ECB, Monthly Bulletin, various issues; own calculations.[15]

strong increase in the late 1990s, falling sharply in 2001 and 2002, while it appears to be recovering since then.

Overall, financial developments in the euro area are indicative of the changes taking place in the EU financial services sector. In particular, bank loans retain their dominant position, even strengthening it, through the growth of 'leveraged' loans used to finance mergers and acquisitions as European corporations have restructured, as well as the increase in household credit. At the same time, capital markets are gaining in importance, although they only recovered in the mid-2000s from their severe setback after the boom years of 1999–2000. Bond market issues were much less affected by the crisis than issues in the equity markets.

Although relevant data are not available at the time of writing, it is to be expected that the financial turmoil experienced in 2007–08 will take its toll on both the total amount of financial liabilities in the euro area and their structure. It would, however, appear unlikely that the trends set in motion since the 1980s and especially since the 1990s will be reversed, although they may well be slowed down in the medium term.

Table 3.7   Main liabilities of non-financial sectors in the euro area (euro billions – outstanding amounts at end period, %)

	1998	1999	2000	2001	2002	2003	2004	2005	2006
Euro billion	13328	15132	15789	16063	15592	16567	17755	19525	21146
Structure by sector	*100.0*	*100.0*	*100.0*	*100.0*	*100.0*	*100.0*	*100.0*	*100.0*	*100.0*
Households	20.4	19.6	20.2	21.0	23.0	23.2	23.7	23.7	23.6
Non-financial corporations	44.8	50.1	50.2	48.3	43.6	43.9	43.4	44.5	47.3
General government	34.8	30.3	29.7	30.7	33.4	32.9	32.9	31.8	29.1
Structure by instrument	*100.0*	*100.0*	*100.0*	*100.0*	*100.0*	*100.0*	*100.0*	*100.0*	*100.0*
Loans	47.8	45.0	47.0	49.2	52.9	52.2	51.4	50.8	51.0
Short-term	9.9	9.5	10.4	10.7	11.0	10.3	10.0	10.1	10.1
Long-term	37.9	35.5	36.6	38.5	42.0	41.9	41.4	40.7	40.9
Securities other than shares	31.1	27.3	27.2	28.8	31.7	31.3	31.8	30.4	28.0
Short-term	3.9	3.3	3.2	3.5	4.0	4.2	4.5	4.2	3.9
Long-term	27.2	24.0	24.1	25.3	27.7	27.1	27.2	26.2	24.1
Shares	21.1	27.7	25.8	21.9	15.4	16.5	16.8	18.8	21.0

Source: ECB, Monthly Bulletin, various issues; own calculations.

On the whole, market-based finance appears to be contesting relationship finance. This is however best seen as a long-term trend, which evolves gradually and in a non-linear fashion. In this sense, claims that a 'financial revolution' took place in the EU after the 1980s are as misplaced as is the view that European finance remains anchored in the traditional bank products.

Financial Intermediation in the New Member States (NMS)

Of the 12 new member states that joined the EU on 1 April 2004, eight are transition economies, that is, they were formerly planned economies opening up to market competition in the early 1990s. Thus, a distinction needs to be made between Cyprus and Malta, the financial system of which was already close to that of the EU in terms of size and structure, and the central and eastern European countries and the Baltic states.

More specifically, the NMS rely more heavily on bank finance than on direct market finance, while stock markets are relatively small, by comparison to those in the older member states (Table 3.8; see also Table 3.4 above).

Generally, despite their different starting points and development trajectories, the NMS share a number of common characteristics. Financial intermediation is strongly dominated by banks, although retail banking

Table 3.8   Financial structure in new member states (% GDP)

	Domestic credit to the private sector		Stock market capitalization	
	2003	2006	2003	2006
Bulgaria	26.7	47.7	7.9	31.2
Czech Republic	30.7	39.9	17.6	31.5
Estonia	31.4	78.4	39.3	34.6
Hungary	41.0	54.6	18.3	34.1
Latvia	34.2	77.9	9.5	12.8
Lithuania	20.2	47.7	16.9	32.6
Poland	29.2	33.4	16.5	41.0
Romania	13.7	26.3	9.2	24.6
Slovak Republic	31.8	39.2	7.5	8.9
Slovenia	42.0	67.1	28.9	49.9

Notes: Domestic credit to private sector: total outstanding bank credit to private sector (households and enterprises) at end of year; Stock market capitalization: market value of all shares listed on the stock market at end of year.

Sources: EBRD, Transition Report 2007; Structural Indicators.

is still below the Western European levels of significance. Equity markets are weak, while stock market capitalization fluctuates greatly over time. As a result, firms tend to rely largely on internal finance and foreign direct investment, while banks are oriented towards funding government needs.

As these countries prepare for membership of the monetary union, the pressures leading to the convergence of their financial systems are expected to intensify. Thus, in the long run, the financial structures of the NMS will move closer to Western European standards. It is however hard to know how long this is going to take. Nor is it going to be a trouble-free process.

3.3 EU FINANCIAL MARKET STRUCTURES AND INSTITUTIONS

The Banking Sector

Many financial institutions, systems and techniques in today's markets have their roots in early Europe. The terms 'banks' or 'bankers' first appeared in the twelfth and thirteenth centuries; they are rooted in the benches or 'bancos' Italian merchants established at European trade fairs (Reszat, 2005). In 2006, there were 8441 banks in EU-25, of which 6130 (73 per cent) were in the 12 eurozone countries. They employed just over 3 million employees (approximately 2.2 million in EU-12), while their total assets amounted to 322 per cent of GDP (298 per cent in EU-12). As noted earlier, EU banks continue to play a dominant role in intermediating savings through the traditional means of collecting deposits and extending loans. Thus, in 2006 the total loans of EU-25 banks to the non-financial sector amounted to 132 per cent of GDP (129 per cent in EU-12), while bank deposits amounted to 109 per cent of GDP (108 per cent in EU-12) (ECB, 2007b).

EU banks are mostly commercial banks, although other types also exist, such as savings, cooperative or mutual and public banks (Table 3.9). In particular, savings banks mostly originated from local or regional banks supplying credit to farmers, artisans or other social groups, which were unable to obtain credit elsewhere. Nowadays, savings banks often focus on small and medium-sized enterprises, while they may be partly or entirely owned by state or local governments and municipalities. In fact, the most common type of public banks in Europe are savings banks. Cooperative banks, on the other hand, are typically owned by their depositors or creditors and their services are restricted to those who own them, although many now offer their services to others, as a result of liberalization. Other types of banks include specialized lending institutions, such

Table 3.9   Banking structure by type of institution in selected euro area countries

	% total assets (end 1998)	% total assets (end 2003)
France		
Commercial banks	54.1	68.4
Savings and coop banks	28.4	31.5
Others	17.5	0.5
Germany		
Commercial banks	47.9	46.9
Savings and coop banks	27.8	34.1
Others	24.2	19.0
Spain		
Commercial banks	55.7	47.4
Savings and coop banks	38.7	40.1
Others	5.6	12.5
Italy		
Commercial banks	81.1	80.9
Savings and coop banks	13.3	14.9
Others	5.6	4.2

Source: Belaisch et al., (2001); OECD (2005a).

as mortgage banks, agricultural banks, postal savings banks and banks servicing specific sectors of the economy.

It is worth noting that the size of the non-profit oriented segment of the financial services influences the interest rates charged by private profit-oriented institutions. For example, in Germany, France and Spain, public and cooperative banks tend to reduce such margins, although this situation could evolve, as these institutions change their legal status, a case observed in the UK, with large building societies becoming PLCs[16] (Dermine, 2002). In Britain, however, the remaining mutually owned building societies have proved to be very competitive and their market share has been growing.

The EU single banking market operates under a 'single passport', comprising a single banking licence, home country control, mutual recognition and common regulations. Furthermore, it goes beyond the member states of the EU, encompassing the countries of the European Free Trade Association – Iceland, Liechtenstein and Norway, with the exception of Switzerland. These constitute the European Economic Area (EEA) as of 1992.[17]

The corporate structure of EU banks today is a web of branches and subsidiaries. Although subsidiaries are considered to be domestic banks, as opposed to branches, which come under the single passport rules, there are nearly as many subsidiaries as branches. Thus, in 2006 there were 641 branches from other EEA countries in EU-25, the assets of which were equal to 8.5 per cent of the total bank assets and 499 subsidiaries, with a 10.5 per cent share of total bank assets (471 branches with a share of 2.6 per cent and 343 branches with a share of 8.2 per cent respectively in EU-12). Generally, in 2006 the presence of foreign banks (branches and subsidiaries from EEA and from third countries) as a percentage of the total assets of domestic credit institutions amounted to 27.1 per cent in EU-25 (12.1 per cent in EU-12).

The response of EU banks to the mounting pressures of the economic environment included disintermediation – selling on their claims on debtors in the form of securities, rather than holding them on their own books; consolidation; technological innovations, such as the setting up of new distribution channels, for example through ATMs and the Internet; and rationalization through cost-cutting measures.

In particular, banks diversified their income sources across both products and countries. On the liabilities side, they turned to the management of mutual funds, in which they have secured a prominent role. In fact, in several EU countries, most of the institutional investors are included in banking groups, operating under a common corporate strategy. On the assets side, EU banks developed trading activities and securitization operations, which significantly boosted their economic results, especially during the time capital markets were booming. However, in the case of securitization, when the tide turned, what served as an engine of growth became a source of concern.

More specifically, securitization enables a bank to convert a future stable cash flow arising from a financial asset, usually some form of loan, into a lump sum cash advance, by means of converting the future cash flows into tradable securities, which are then sold, thus raising capital. This is also known as the 'originate and distribute' model, which became popular in the EU banking sector towards the late-2000s, although it originated in the USA in the 1970s, and the US remains by far the largest market for securitizing assets. Within Europe – not just the EU member states – the UK, Spain and Netherlands hold a dominant position (Table 3.10).

Mortgage-backed securitization (MBS) accounts for the largest share of deals in the US and Europe. However, there are a range of other financial assets that are securitized, including home equity loans, credit card receivables, car finance, collateralized debt obligations (CDOs), student loans, equipment leases and manufactured housing contracts.[18] In 2007, 61.8 per cent of European securitization consisted of MBS and 26.5 per cent of CDOs.

While securitization has been viewed as a way to diversify risks for

Table 3.10   Securitization issuance based on originating country or region

	2003	2004	2005	2006	2007
World total $ billion	4094.00	3154.00	3780.00	4138.00	3826.00
Of which (%):					
USA	89.67	83.99	83.04	78.69	75.59
Europe	6.06	9.61	10.77	14.60	17.80
Of which (%):					
UK	2.10	4.12	4.15	5.85	6.19
Spain	1.07	1.30	1.32	1.33	2.20
Netherlands	0.59	0.73	1.30	0.87	1.46
Italy	0.93	1.36	1.08	0.92	0.94
Germany	0.20	0.32	0.50	1.14	0.68
Ireland	0.10	0.10	0.03	0.31	0.37
France	0.22	0.32	0.24	0.24	0.13
Portugal	0.29	0.32	0.26	0.17	0.39

Source: IFSL Research (2008a), Table 1 (own calculations).

the financial institutions which originate the securitized loans, allowing them to expand their lending activities, the credit crisis of 2007 led to the serious questioning of the 'originate and distribute' model. Although this resulted in the rapid expansion of activity within the financial sector itself, the redistribution of risk from the originator to other financial and non-financial institutions and the total lack of knowledge as to where risk is located has led to a loss of confidence in the creditworthiness of many financial institutions, including several 'too-big-to-fail' ones.

In the short to medium term, securitization issuance is likely to decrease. For example, it fell by 42 per cent from $432 billion in the first half of 2007 to $249 billion in the second half of 2007. In the long run, it is unlikely to disappear, although the relevant institutional and policy framework is expected to become tighter, benefiting the banks themselves, too.

Consolidation was another strategy the EU banks adopted, under the pressure of increasing competition. Such consolidation mostly took the form of mergers among relatively large private banks and among bank and non-bank financial institutions. A wave of mergers and acquisitions took place in the 1990s, especially in the run-up to the introduction of the single currency. Most of these deals were domestic ones. In the early 2000s, M&A activity declined considerably, picking up again after the mid-2000s.[19] Over the period 2003–07, there was a clear trend towards ever larger deals, while the previous dominance of domestic over cross-border deals was reversed. Banking dominated in terms of the value of deals (Table 3.11).

Table 3.11   Mergers and acquisitions deals in the EU financial services sector

	2003	2004	2005	2006	2007
Number of deals	154	170	198	175	281
Total value (euro million)	33526	44798	77537	136875	207743
Average value (euro million)	217.7	263.5	391.6	782.1	739.3
Cross-border deals as % of total value	32.18	61.99	66.80	44.44	64.44
Sector share in total deal value (%)	100.00	100.00	100.00	100.00	100.00
Banking	47.88	49.95	60.88	71.96	68.09
Insurance	33.93	32.20	24.51	18.57	21.57
Asset management	8.01	6.82	8.96	1.36	6.25
Other	10.17	11.03	5.65	8.11	4.10

Note: The above deals do not include those concerning minority stakes below 30 per cent.

Source: PricewaterhouseCoopers; Rupert Taylor Rea and Nick Page kindly provided the above data.

As a result of the consolidation process and organic growth of the sector, the size of the average bank in the EU-25 more than doubled between 1997 and 2006, reaching €4.4 billion of assets (€4.1 in the euro-zone). Furthermore, the degree of concentration is quite high so that a small number of banks dominate the banking sector, especially of the smaller member states.

As we can see in Table 3.12, the degree of concentration in the EU-25 on average is larger than in the eurozone. In fact, the market share of the five largest banks accounted for more than 60 per cent in 17 of the 25 member states, a percentage that was as high as 97 per cent in Estonia!

The EU banks further responded to the challenges of increased competition by taking measures in two areas – those of rationalization and of technological innovation. In particular, cost-cutting has in many cases entailed a restructuring of branch networks and a scaling down in the number of employees. For example, between 2002–06 the number of employees in the banking sector of the EU-25 fell by 96403 (of which 47877 in the euro-zone), that is by 3 per cent in relation to 2002 (2 per cent in the eurozone).

Other measures have included the centralization of services across institutions, especially in the area of credit risk management, settlement, invoicing and payment transactions, as well as outsourcing non-core activities, especially IT and back-office functions. In the area of technological

Table 3.12 Share of the five largest banks in total assets of sector (%;
unweighted average)

	2002	2003	2004	2005	2006
EU-25	59.3	58.9	58.8	59.6	59.2
Eurozone	52.7	53.1	53.3	54.3	53.7
Countries where the share of the 5 largest banks exceeded 50%					
Belgium	82.0	83.5	84.3	85.3	84.4
Czech Republic	65.7	65.8	64.0	65.5	64.1
Denmark	68.0	66.6	67.0	66.3	64.7
Estonia	99.1	99.2	98.6	98.1	97.1
Greece	67.4	66.9	65.0	65.6	66.3
France	44.6	46.7	49.2	52.3	52.3
Cyprus	57.8	57.2	57.3	59.8	63.9
Latvia	65.3	63.1	62.4	67.3	69.2
Lithuania	83.9	81.0	78.9	80.6	82.5
Hungary	54.5	52.1	52.7	53.2	53.5
Malta	82.4	77.7	78.5	75.3	71.4
Netherlands	82.7	84.2	84.0	84.5	85.1
Portugal	60.5	62.7	66.5	68.8	67.9
Slovenia	68.4	66.4	64.6	63.0	62.0
Slovakia	66.4	67.5	66.5	67.7	66.9
Finland	78.6	81.2	82.7	82.9	82.3
Sweden	56	53.8	54.4	57.3	57.8

Source: ECB (2007a).

innovation, the substantial growth in the number of ATMs in all EU countries must be noted, enhancing the distribution channels. More recently, telephone and Internet banking operations have also been introduced.

Internet banking is the fastest-growing electronic distribution channel for banks. The majority of large European banks offer Internet banking to their clients, while almost all banks offer Internet banking at least as a service channel, that is their clients can use Internet banking for information and transaction services. As we can see in Table 3.13, the percentage of individuals over 16 years of age who use the Internet is steadily, albeit slowly, increasing.

Overall, EU banks have been undergoing a process of transformation in the past decade or so, which is still not complete. In dealing with the challenges of an increasingly competitive environment, they have had to restructure and reposition themselves within the financial services sector,

Table 3.13   Use of Internet banking (%)

	2003	2004	2005	2006
EU-25	n/a	18	19	22
EU-15 ('old')	19	22	22	24

Note: The table shows the percentage of individuals over 16 years who used Internet banking at least once during the previous three months.

Source: ECB (2007a).

domestically, as well as internationally. This has allowed most of them to adjust successfully to the new challenges facing them. However, certain policy issues have emerged in the process.

More specifically, the diversification of risk through the 'originate and distribute' model of securitization has led to a dispersion of risk across the financial services sector, that is difficult, if not impossible, to control at a time of crisis. Furthermore, the high concentration of the banking sector gives rise to competition concerns. Similarly, the prevalence of large financial conglomerates gives rise to consumer and investor protection concerns. These are policy issues, which will be discussed in greater detail in the context of the EU financial services policy.

The Banking Sector in the New Member States

As mentioned earlier, the NMS, especially the former transition ones, rely mainly on bank finance, as opposed to direct market finance. Most banks are commercial ones, employing over 80 per cent of all staff and covering more than 90 per cent of all assets. In some countries – Cyprus, Hungary and Poland – there is also a significant number of small cooperative banks, while in some, specialized financial service providers are present.[19]

Foreign presence is very large in most NMS. Furthermore, with few exceptions, the largest banks are foreign. In 2006, the share of foreign-owned banks in total bank assets was greater than 80 per cent in seven of the 10 NMS (Table 3.14).

Largely, this situation is the result of the privatization of former state-owned banks. By the early 2000s, the privatization programmes in most NMS had been completed, so that state bank ownership was considerably reduced. In fact, in 2006 state bank ownership became completely extinct in Estonia and Lithuania, while it was minimal in Bulgaria, the Czech Republic, Latvia and the Slovak Republic (Table 3.14). During the same period, the presence of state banks declined in the other EU member

Table 3.14   Banks in the new member states

	Number of banks (foreign-owned)		Asset share of foreign-owned banks (%)		Asset share of state-owned banks (%)	
	2003	2006	2003	2006	2003	2006
Bulgaria	35(25)	32(23)	82.7	80.1	2.5	1.8
Czech-Republic	35(26)	37(28)	86.3	84.7	3.0	2.2
Estonia	7(4)	14(12)	97.5	99.1	0.0	0.0
Hungary	38(29)	40(28)	83.5	82.9	7.4	7.4
Lithuania	13(7)	11(6)	95.6	91.8	0.0	0.0
Latvia	23(10)	24(13)	53.0	62.9	4.1	4.4
Poland	58(46)	64(53)	71.5	74.3	25.8	21.1
Romania	30(21)	31(26)	54.8	87.9	40.6	5.9
Slovak Republic	21(16)	24(16)	96.3	97.0	1.5	1.1
Slovenia	22(6)	25(10)	18.9	29.5	12.8	12.6

Sources: EBRD, Transition Report 2007; Structural Indicators.

states, too. For example, in Italy, Spain and Belgium, it disappeared, while it was drastically reduced in all other EU member states.

Overall, the NMS face certain challenges arising out of the structure of their banking sectors. Namely, (i) financial intermediation is still low; (ii) technological change is ongoing, influencing risk measurement and management systems; (iii) the very high presence of foreign banks raises questions of stability, for example in relation to credit growth and/or balance sheet restructuring. The domination of external banks may also make the identification of opportunities and the measurement of risks less precise than if domestic actors were more involved. Another danger is that the NMS may be excluded from some of the most complex and valuable activities in the financial sector because the multinational banks will concentrate such activities in their home countries. These will be reviewed in relation to the EU financial services policy below.

Market-based Finance

Market-based financing in the EU has broadened in scope, as well as deepened in terms of liquidity, in parallel with the continuing predominance of bank financing. In particular, the range of financial instruments and techniques has broadened, as a result of financial innovation on a global level. In the case of the EU, the introduction of the single currency has had a major effect on capital markets, as it has expanded the investment opportunities on the supply side and the portfolio diversification possibilities on the demand side.

Money markets

A large part of the secured transactions taking place in the euro area money market involves transactions with counterparties of the same nationality, using collateral issued in that jurisdiction. In particular, the 2006 Money Market Study of the ECB notes that

> Despite the gradual increase in cross-border trading in recent years, the proportion of transactions carried out between national counterparties in the secured and short-term securities markets remained comparatively high. This shows that while the integration process of the repo and short-term securities markets across the euro area is continuing, it is still quite slow and complex (ECB, 2007a, p. 4).[21]

Problems associated with collateral assets – their heterogeneity across countries as well as technical difficulties in the custody and transfer of these assets – have tended to hold back integration of eurozone money markets and, therefore, to impair the liquidity of the European financial system as a whole and its security markets in particular. It is notable that European banks often use dollar deposits, rather than European debt instruments, to collateralize their lending to each other, a factor which swells the volume of foreign exchange swaps.

The unsecured market is driven largely by cash management and it is thus oriented more heavily towards short maturity transactions (of up to three months). Because problems with collateral do not arise, the definition of the product is fully standardized and all market participants (mostly banks) use the same products and market procedures. As a result, this is the most integrated financial market in the EU.

The global financial market turbulence during the second half of 2007 led to the emergence of liquidity problems in the short-term money markets, resulting in greater volatility of the overnight rates due to increased variability in credit risk among banks. Under extreme pressure, the EU money markets came close to freezing, so that the infusion of central bank liquidity became necessary for their operation. At the same time, they displayed enough resilience to allow them to continue functioning, albeit under stress.

Derivatives markets

Derivatives fall into two categories: (i) over-the-counter (OTC) derivatives, which refer to those traded directly between two parties and (ii) exchange derivatives, which are traded through a financial intermediary.

At the end of 2006, OTC derivatives accounted for 83 per cent of the world derivatives market.

The introduction of the single currency impacted especially on the derivatives markets, as it expanded the opportunities to hedge risk, thus giving rise to new instruments allowing for more sophisticated risk-mitigating techniques through interest rate-linked options and futures. It also boosted the growth of over-the-counter (OTC) interest rate swaps.

The EU-27 dominates the world OTC derivatives market, accounting for 65.9 per cent of the interest rate derivatives market and 60.4 per cent of the foreign exchange derivative market in 2007. Within the EU, London is the major OTC derivatives trading centre, accounting for 38.6 per cent and 44 per cent of global trade in foreign exchange and interest rate derivatives, respectively.

Bond markets

The increasing role of the European debt security markets, in terms of size and structure, was already discussed in section 3.2 above, in relation to

Table 3.15 Private and government debt securities in the eurozone and in the UK as percentage of GDP

	1980		1993		2003		2006	
	Eurozone	UK	Eurozone	UK	Eurozone	UK	Eurozone	UK
Private debt securities (% GDP)	14	1	47	31	92	115	114	106
Government debt securities (% GDP)	13	31	44	33	66	29	61	34
Total debt securities (% GDP)	27	32	91	64	158	144	175	140
Percentage share of debt securities in total financial stock (incl. equities and bank deposits)	34.62	31.07	52.00	26.12	50.32	37.40	49.16	33.18

Source: See Table 3.4 in section 3.2 above.

the comparative financial structures across regions. Table 3.15 extracts the relevant data from Table 3.4, in order to focus on the changes taking place in the area of debt securities between 1980–2006.

As we can see, the debt securities market in the eurozone increased from 27 per cent of GDP in 1980 to 175 per cent in 2006, while the greatest increase was recorded in the private debt market. The UK also recorded an increase over the same period, although in a more volatile fashion. Further, the predominance of government debt is seriously challenged both in the eurozone and in the UK.

In the East European countries, on the other hand, most of which have already acceded to the EU, the debt securities markets are not quite as dynamic, while they largely, if not exclusively, deal with government bonds (see Table 3.4).

Domestic debt securities remain the dominant source of debt finance, although the international debt market has been growing at a fast rate.[22] On the other hand, the EU is an important player in the international debt market. For example, in 2006, the amount outstanding of international debt securities of EU-27 amounted to €8.1 trillion, which accounted for 58.4 per cent of worldwide outstanding international debt securities. Within the EU-27, Germany, the UK, France, Spain, Italy and the Netherlands accounted for 81 per cent of total outstanding international debt securities and the largest source country was Germany (13.1 per cent).[23]

Generally, the size of the European bond market has grown significantly. As a result, the gap with other advanced financial systems and especially the USA, has narrowed considerably (see Table 3.4 above). Similar shifts can be perceived in relation to the market's structural characteristics, although, again, its initial structure directly influences its present one. As disintermediation gains ground, these tendencies will intensify, exerting pressure on the more traditional financial systems in the EU.

Equity Markets

As noted earlier, European stock markets grew strongly in the years to 2000 and then contracted, while they appear to be recovering as of 2002. During this period, the equity markets displayed a heightened degree of volatility, denoting their susceptibility to changing expectations. By 2006, the outstanding amounts of shares by euro area residents approached its boom level of 2000 (Table 3.16).

It should be noted that since equity market growth picked up in 2003, gains in developed countries have mainly reflected higher earnings, rather than higher P/E ratios. For example, the P/E ratio recorded in the eurozone was on average equal to 16 in 2003, 15 in 2004, 16 in 2005 and 15 in

Table 3.16   Quoted shares issued by euro area residents

	2000	2001	2002	2003	2004	2005	2006
Outstanding amounts (euro billion)	5431.7	4656.4	3132.4	3647.3	4033.8	5063.5	6139.4
% GDP	82.60	66.55	43.26	49.03	52.29	63.00	72.98
% by NFC	74.92	75.77	76.56	74.83	73.94	72.78	72.64

Sources: ECB, Monthly Bulletin, Jan 2003, T.3.7, p. 48, Sept 2004, T.4.4, p. S36, Jan 2006, T.4.4, p. S36, July 2007, T.4.4, p. S40.

2006. This is due to the slow recovery in stock market capitalization, following the burst of the dotcom bubble in the early 2000s. The same can be said of the USA, where the P/E ratio has in fact declined from 23 in 2003 to 18 in 2006, and of Japan, where it has been more volatile, although also on the decline.[24]

Institutional Investors

These include insurance companies, pension funds and investment funds. The relative importance of the different segments of the fund industry varies across the EU member states and in relation to the EU average. Thus, pension funds are more important in the UK and the Netherlands, investment funds in France and Germany, while the life insurance sector is an important repository of private savings in all member states and especially in the UK and in Germany (see Table 3.17).

On a world level, the USA is the dominant player, accounting for approximately one half of total fund industry assets. The EU, however, has been catching up fast, especially since the introduction of the single currency. On the other hand, assets under management in three out of the ten NMS – Poland, Hungary and the Czech Republic – accounted for just 0.74 per cent of total assets under management in EU-25 in 2006. These countries have relatively more developed bond and money market segments, but remain negligible by EU-15 standards.

Sovereign wealth funds (SWFs) have increased their influence on global financial markets in recent years. In particular, the profile of SWFs has risen considerably during 2007, as a result of sub-prime capital infusions into large financial groups in trouble, such as Citigroup, Merrill Lynch, Barclays, UBS, and so on. SWFs have also been active in cross-border M&A deals.

Although there is no universally accepted definition, SWFs are

*Table 3.17　Funds under management in EU-25, the eurozone and in
　　　　　　selected countries, 2006*

	Total	Pension funds	Insurance companies	Investment funds
UK (€ million)	6 133 617	2 351 452	3 173 492	608 673
% GDP	*321.75*			
Percentage distribution		38.34	51.74	9.92
France (€ million)	2 446 867	n/a	1 290 591	1 156 276
% GDP	*136.55*			
Percentage distribution			52.74	47.26
Germany (€ million)	2 062 446	510	1 033 295	1 028 641
% GDP	*89.32*			
Percentage distribution		0.02	50.10	49.87
Netherlands (€ million)	1 143 311	696 271	331 923	115 117
% GDP	*216.57*			
Percentage distribution		60.90	29.03	10.07
Italy (€ million)	916 155	21 016	554 448	340 691
% GDP	*62.10*			
Percentage distribution		2.29	60.52	37.19
EU-25 (€ million)	17 011 150	3 293 728	7 227 498	6 489 924
% GDP	*148.79*			
Percentage distribution		19.36	42.49	38.15
Eurozone (€ million)	10 229 544	834 812	3 846 401	5 548 331
% GDP	*122.09*	8.16	37.60	54.24

Source:　ECB (2007b), Tables 8, 9 and 14 (own calculations).

generally defined as large pools of capital controlled and owned by governments and invested in foreign assets for long-term purposes. SWFs fall into two major categories: commodity funds, funded predominantly from oil revenue and non-commodity funds, funded mainly from official foreign exchange reserves and, in some cases, from pension reserves. At the end of 2007, approximately 45 per cent of SWFs came from oil-rich countries in the Middle East, followed by Asia, with over a quarter of the total, and Europe, predominantly Norway (12 per cent) and Russia (13 per cent).[25]

Although SWFs are not new, their growing prominence is a recent phenomenon. The limited disclosure and transparency, as well as the multiplicity of objectives of many SWFs have given rise to concerns about their impact on global capital markets. Both the IMF and the OECD are working on a code of conduct for SWFs, while the European Commission is also working on its own proposals.

Overall, as market-based finance spreads across the EU financial services sector, both in terms of structure and in terms of market type of behaviour, the role of institutional investors is expected to increase, encompassing new regions and financial products. As with changes in the banking sector, this poses certain policy issues for the EU regulators, pertaining to the protection of investors and retail consumers more generally, as well as to the stability of the sector as a whole.

Securities Exchanges

Most of the European securities exchanges were founded as mutual associations by their users – mostly brokers and traders. However, an increasing number of exchanges are being transformed into corporations. Further, there have been a number of mergers and acquisitions between security exchanges, which is indicative of the cut-throat competition and of the pressures the financial sector is under.

One of the first such mergers was that between the German and the Swiss derivatives exchanges, which became known as EUREX. Similarly, the French, Belgian and Dutch exchanges merged into EURONEXT, while in 2007 the merger between the New York Stock Exchange (NYSE) and EURONEXT was finalized. Further, in 2007 the London Stock Exchange (LSE) bought Borsa Italiana, and Nasdaq became a major shareholder in OMX Nordic Exchange.

As can be observed in Table 3.18, in 2007, 90 per cent of all trading took place in six EU exchanges: London SE (34 per cent), Euronext (18.4 per cent), Deutsche Borse (14.2 per cent), the Spanish exchanges (9.7 per cent), Borsa Italiana (7.6 per cent) and OMX Nordic Exchange (6 per cent). If the SWX Swiss Exchange is included, then 96 per cent of all trading in Europe was carried out in six exchanges in 2007. Further, these six exchanges accounted for a 29 per cent share of world trading.[26]

Stock exchanges are serviced by settlement and payment systems, the most important of which are organized as corporations, often owned by a stock exchange which makes use of them. Two such systems are dominant: International Clearstream in Frankfurt, owned by Deutsche Borse (50 per cent) and CEDEL (50 per cent), a joint venture of 90 international banks; and Euroclear in Brussels. It is estimated that a process of concentration and consolidation in this area will take place, as capital markets recover more fully from their recent downturn (Huffschmid, 2002).

Financial Centres

There is no universally accepted definition of what constitutes a 'financial centre'. The IMF distinguishes three groups of financial centres:

Table 3.18   Stock exchanges in Europe, 2007

	Capitalization			Trading		
	Euro billion	2006/07 %	Share of EU %	Euro billion	2006/07 %	Share of EU %
Athens Exchange	181.2	19.1	1.5	122.4	43.9	0.6
Borsa Italiana	733.6	−5.8	6.2	1 680.2	33.6	7.6
Bratislava Stock Exchange	4.6	8.1	0.0	0.0	−69.3	0.0
Bucharest Stock Exchange	21.5	14.1	0.2	2.0	56.8	0.0
Budapest Stock Exchange	31.5	−0.5	0.3	34.6	40.5	0.2
Bulgarian Stock Exchange	14.8	89.3	0.1	4.6	227.5	0.0
Cyprus Stock Exchange	20.2	64.5	0.2	4.2	25.4	0.0
Deutsche Borse	1 440.0	15.9	12.3	3 144.2	45.2	14.2
Euronext	2 888.3	2.7	24.6	4 086.8	34.1	18.4
Irish Stock Exchange	98.4	−20.5	0.8	99.6	54.1	0.4
Lubljana Stock Exchange	19.7	71.1	0.2	3.1	113.0	0.0
London Stock Exchange	2 634.6	−8.4	22.4	7 545.0	25.9	34.0
Luxembourg Stock Exchange	113.6	88.4	1.0	0.2	−6.1	0.0
Malta Stock Exchange	3.9	12.8	0.0	0.1	−68.5	0.0
OMX Nordic Exchange	849.9	−0.2	7.2	1 321.8	27.5	6.0
Oslo Bors	241.7	13.9	2.1	399.1	24.3	1.8
Prague Stock Exchange	48.0	38.3	0.4	36.6	21.9	0.2
Spanish Exchanges (BME)	1 231.1	22.7	10.5	2 160.3	40.7	9.7
SWX Swiss Exchange	869.4	−5.4	7.4	1 368.8	24.1	6.2
Warsaw Stock Exchange	144.3	27.9	1.2	63.9	47.7	0.3
Wiener Borse	161.7	7.1	1.4	94.5	45.6	0.4

Source: London Economics (2008, Table 18).

- International financial centres offer the full range of financial services, are characterized by deep and liquid markets with diverse sources and uses of funds, supporting large domestic economies, hosting several internationally active banks. They have the regulatory and supervisory frameworks to safeguard the reliability of contractual relationships.

- Regional financial centres feature well-developed financial markets and infrastructure, associated with smaller domestic economies and more regionally focused banks.
- Offshore financial centres are much smaller and provide more limited specialist services. These refer to countries or territories where the financial sector is large as compared with domestic economy, moderately regulated, taxed at a low level and providing services mainly to non-residents.

According to the above categorization, Europe hosts 44 international financial centres, 12 regional ones and nine offshore centres, which is the highest concentration of financial centres in the world, at least in terms of numbers!

Further, in 2007 the City of London Corporation published for the first time the Global Financial Centres Index, which is a ranking of the competitiveness of financial centres based on 18878 total assessments (in 2008) from an online questionnaire together with over 60 indices, published twice a year. The ranking is based on an aggregate of indices from five key areas: people; business environment; market access; infrastructure and general competitiveness. Table 3.19 shows the financial centres in Europe, on the basis of the IMF categorization and the latest (March, 2008) GFCI ranking amongst the world top 50 financial centres (in brackets).

On the whole, the concept of a 'financial centre', albeit not new, explicitly introduces competition across regions as a strategy for the capture of financial business. Although this may be seen as the natural consequence of the expansion of the financial sphere in the economy, it internalizes the institutional and policy conditions that have led to the very state of financialization, namely: market deregulation and privatization. In this sense, while the concentration of a large number of financial centres in Europe is indicative of the deepening of its financial markets, it may also be a sign of possible regulatory and fiscal laxity on the part of governments, in an attempt to attract increasing amounts of financial business. This exposes the local economy to increased competitive pressures, while it may also entail increased risks.

3.4   THE STATE OF FINANCIAL INTEGRATION IN THE EU

Diagnosing the state of the EU financial integration is a complex task, due to the definitional and measurement problems involved, as well as the diversity of EU structures. An overview of the main financial segments

Table 3.19   Financial centres in Europe and GFCI ranking in global Top 50

International financial centres	Regional financial centres	Offshore financial centres
London (1)	Madrid (42)	Jersey (16)
Paris (14)	Milan (38)	Liechtenstein
Frankfurt (6)	Geneva (7)	Monaco (37)
Zurich (5)	Brussels (34)	Guernsey (19)
	Stockholm (32)	Gibraltar (26)
	Amsterdam (23)	Isle of Man (21)
	Munich (35)	Malta
	Luxembourg (17)	Cyprus
	Edinburgh (18)	Andorra
	Glasgow (22)	
	Dublin (13)	
	Vienna (43)	
	Copenhagen (44)	
	Oslo (45)	
	Helsinki (40)	
	Athens (46 in 2007)	

Source: Lannoo (2007, Table 1) adjusted with data from GFCI (City of London, 2008).

and their degree of integration in the eurozone is given in Table 3.20, provided by the European Central Bank.

As we can see, financial institutions operate in the most integrated environment, as opposed to households, which operate in the most fragmented one, reflecting the diversity in market structures arising from different borrower and product characteristics, business models, allocational practices, and so on. Non-financial corporations operate in a financial environment that is not yet fully integrated. We shall proceed to take a closer look at the extent of integration in each of the main financial markets in the EU.

Money Markets

These were directly affected by the introduction of the single currency. More specifically, spreads (between interest rates offered to lenders and rates required from borrowers) before and after 1999 were measured in basis points[27] and the corresponding German rate was used as a benchmark. Before 1999, the highest spreads existed in Greece, Italy and Portugal. After the launch of the euro, inter-bank rates in the 11 eurozone countries

Table 3.20　Financial integration in the euro area

Market	State of integration	Related infrastructure
Money Markets	'Near perfect'	Uncollateralized money
Unsecured money market	Advanced	market: fully integrated;
Collateralized money market		collateralized money market: cash leg fully integrated; collateral leg hampered by fragmentation
Bond markets	Very well	Fragmented
Government bond markets	advanced	Fragmented
Corporate bond markets	Fair	
Equity markets	Low	Highly fragmented
Banking markets	Well advanced	Fully integrated
Wholesale activities	Advanced	Fragmented
Capital-market related activities	Very low	Highly fragmented
Retail banking		

Source:　ECB, Monthly Bulletin, 10th Anniversary of the ECB, 2008, Section 6, Table 2.

(at that time, excluding Greece, which joined the EMU in January 2000) converged to a common Euribor rate and the spread became zero. In this sense, the euro area money market reached a stage of 'near perfect' integration almost immediately after the introduction of the euro.

The spreads of the countries not included in the euro area – Denmark, Sweden and the UK – decreased after the launch of the euro. Thus, the euro had a strong influence even on countries outside the EMU.

However, not all segments of the money market have reached the stage of 'near perfect' integration. More specifically, the euro area repo market segment is less integrated than the swap and the unsecured segments. This is explained by differences in practices, laws and regulations across member states, as well as remaining fragmentation of the market infrastructure (Baele et al., 2004).

Derivatives Markets

Derivatives markets in the EU have closely followed developments in the underlying financial markets. As a result, they are becoming more integrated and more liquid. For example, in the case of equity futures, the DJ Euro Stoxx 50 future index has become the benchmark as the most traded equity index future. Similarly, with regard to interest rate derivatives on organized exchanges, the number of Euribor and Eonia contracts has grown rapidly and they could soon become the world's most liquid exchange-traded derivatives contracts.[28] Lastly, most market participants have centralized business functions, organizing them by type of product, rather than by intra-European geographical area.

Bond Markets

Since the introduction of the euro, the degree of integration in the government bond market has been very high. Furthermore, it has been found that in the euro area, government bond yields have become increasingly driven by common news and less by purely local risk factors (Baele et al., 2004). This is especially true of the ten-year maturity segment, by comparison to the two and five-year ones.

In particular, convergence in long-term government bond yields – as measured by the coefficient of variation – decreased as of 1998, but has stayed at roughly the same levels since then. Such variation may reflect differences in perceived credit risks, as well as in liquidity, among individual countries. In other words, differentials in yields decreased but then stabilized, so that convergence first went ahead but then marked time. Hence, further integration is closely linked to the minimization of such differences.

The corporate bond market also displays a high level of integration. For example, it has been found that country premiums are low and only slightly above the country premiums reflected in the sovereign bond yields (European Commission, 2004a). In other words, investors' home bias is declining, although it would appear that a certain 'regional bias' is emerging. For example, in 2005 within the portfolio of long-term debt securities owned by foreign investors in the EU, on average 70 per cent was owned by investors from other member states. This 'regional bias' in the EU bond market is higher than in the equity market, reflecting the fact that the bond market has reached a relatively more advanced stage of integration.

Equity Markets

Equity markets have become more integrated to the extent that the 'equity home bias' – that is, the preference of investors for domestic stocks – appears to be waning. For example, the percentage of total foreign equity investments undertaken in another EU country has increased slightly between 2001 and 2005 (from 52 to 55 per cent), which suggests that the declining home bias has been matched by an increasing regional bias in the EU. In most EU countries such regional bias ranges from 50 to 70 per cent. However, in the Baltic states and Malta investors from other EU countries account for more than 90 per cent of all foreign investments.[29] It should be noted that the US is the largest external investor in EU equities, with an approximate market share of 30 per cent.

Further, local stock returns have become more sensitive to European market shocks, as compared with purely local ones. As Baele et al. (2004) have shown, the proportion of local return variance explained by aggregate European and US shocks rose from 20 per cent in the first half of the 1980s to more than 40 per cent in the post-euro period. Also, the ECB estimated that shocks from the eurozone explained more than 80 per cent of the variation of equity market returns over the period 1999–2007, more than twice as much as over the period 1973–85. However, it should be noted that return correlations have been shown to be considerably influenced by cyclical phenomena, so that their economic significance needs to be carefully considered in terms of disentangling cyclical from structural effects in the underlying economy and financial system (Adam et al., 2002).

Banking Markets

Since the late 1970s, EU banking markets have operated in an increasingly more harmonized regulatory and economic framework. In spite of this, however, integration is uneven in the different segments of the industry, while price differentials remain high, indicating that the local character of such segments is significant.

More specifically, the level of dispersion in national interest rates declined in the late 1990s in anticipation of the single currency, with the exception of consumer loans. As of 2001, the convergence process had slowed down for most credit markets with the exception of medium- to long-term loans to enterprises. Thus, in 2006 the coefficient of variation ranged from 20 per cent for loans to enterprises with a maturity of more than one year to 28.4 per cent for mortgage loans to households. In addition, fees for the most common banking products, such as current accounts, still differ substantially among member states (European Commission, 2007d).

The cross-border flow of inter-bank loans has increased in the wholesale segment of the euro area banking sector, reaching the level of approximately one third of total loans in 2006. On the other hand, the proportion of cross-border loans to non-bank clients is relatively small, at less than 5 per cent of total loans during the period 1999–2005. This is indicative of the significance of local presence in gaining and retaining customer trust, as well as of the existence of switching costs, which make customers reluctant to change banks.

Cross-border integration also takes place through the opening of branches and subsidiaries. As discussed above, in spite of the regulatory advantages of branches, the growth of subsidiaries in the EEA has rivalled that of branches. There are many reasons explaining such a tendency.[30] One such reason is the protection from risk-shifting, which is provided by a subsidiary structure and which weighs heavily in an uncertain environment.

Deepening integration has further led to increasing consolidation in the EU banking sector, while cross-border M&As constitute an internationalization strategy in the retail field. As we saw earlier, in the 1990s most M&As were mainly on a domestic basis, signifying the existence of barriers, such as different market practices, taxation systems, accounting procedures, legal issues, as well as varying cultural and political influences (Walkner and Raes, 2005). Since the mid-2000s however, cross-border M&As have been increasing in significance, pointing to the fact that the process of integration is gradually deepening.

Overall, integration in the banking markets of the EU is proceeding unevenly across its different segments. It is most advanced in the wholesale segment and least advanced in the retail one. This is due to the fact that retail financial services may be likened to non-traded goods, in so far as they contain a strong element of trust and confidence on the part of the customers, and asymmetric information on the part of the service providers. Where such elements are not significant, EU banking has been following a process of integration, which is, however, not as fast as that observed in most EU capital markets.

Related Infrastructures

As shown in Table 3.20 above, infrastructure can help deepen financial integration. Conversely, the lack of infrastructure is one of the reasons for the continuing fragmentation of various segments of the EU financial sector (Norman, 2007).

More specifically, the 'near perfect' integration of the EU money market has been greatly aided by the TARGET system for the EU-wide settlement of euro payments, established in 1999 and described as a 'system of systems'.[31] In May 2008, a second generation system, TARGET2, replaced its predecessor. In addition, the integration of the euro area money market has been facilitated by the cross-border transfer of collateral through the Correspondent Central Banking Model (CCBM). For example, in 2007, 81.5 per cent of cross-border collateral deliveries in the euro area were channelled through the CCBM.

In the case of bond and equity markets, progress in integrating securities infrastructures has not kept pace with that of large-value payment infrastructures. Since the TARGET system was launched in 1999, payments across national borders have represented approximately 20–25 per cent of total volumes and 35 per cent of total values. By contrast, the use of securities settlement systems has been scarce (less than 1 per cent of total volumes/sales).

While the post-trading infrastructure is fragmented for bonds, it is even more fragmented for equities. The cross-border settlement for bonds is largely concentrated within two international central securities depositories, whereas the cross-border settlement of equities relies heavily on national central securities depositories. A new initiative – TARGET2-Securities – was proposed by the ECB and the national central banks that are members of the European System of Central Banks (Eurosystem), in order to provide a single platform for making payments in central bank money. However, the TARGET system relates primarily to the 'cash leg' of financial transactions, that is payment by the purchaser of securities. The other side of the transaction – the transfer of the securities by the seller – still gives rise to significantly higher transactions costs than is the case in the US. Thus even when TARGET2-Securities becomes operational, securities will still be held on multiple platforms (central securities depositories), although it is proposed that they outsource their securities accounts to a neutral single platform (the single platform for payments), which would be operated by the Eurosystem. The expected launch date of T2S is in 2013.

Cross-border banking has also been hampered by the high level of the retail payments infrastructure. Each country has its own national payment instruments and different standards for payments made by credit transfers, direct debits and card payments. In early 2002 the banking industry founded the European Payments Council, which consequently formulated a strategy to create the Single Euro Payments Area (SEPA).[32] The Payment Services Directive, adopted at the end of 2007, forms the legal framework for payments in SEPA and is to be implemented by all EU member states by 1 November 2009.

3.5　SUMMARY AND CONCLUSION

Since the 1980s, the financial systems of the member states of the EU have come under increasing competitive pressure, as a result of developments both on the global and on the European level. On the global level, the substitution of floating exchange rates for the system of fixed rates in the late 1970s led to greater reliance on markets both domestically and internationally.

On the European level, the shift in emphasis from regulation to liberalization and privatization in the financial services sector became evident in the early 1980s. Following the 1986 Single European Act, the 1988 Council directive on the liberalization of capital controls, the 1992 Treaty on the European Union, the creation of the single currency and the Financial Services Action Plan, various legal barriers to an integrated financial market were progressively dismantled.

What has been the response of European finance? Further, how have banks reacted to their changing environment? Does the increasing presence of market-based finance denote the deepening of financial integration?

In dealing with the above issues, the following areas were reviewed in some detail: (i) the main tendencies in European finance, in terms of structural changes; (ii) developments in the different segments of the EU financial services sector, as well as among financial actors; (iii) the degree and prospects of integration of the various EU financial services segments.

(i) *In terms of financial structures*, the significance of EU capital markets has been increasing over time, albeit not necessarily in a consistent pattern from year to year. Overall, market-based finance appears to be contesting relationship-finance. This is however a long-term trend, which is not expected to evolve in a linear fashion. In this sense, claiming that a 'financial revolution' took place in the late 1990s in the EU overestimates the underlying trends, to the extent that what has been happening is both gradual and non-linear.

In the case of the new member states, despite their different starting points, policies and development trajectories, these share a number of common characteristics. Namely, financial intermediation is strongly dominated by banks, although retail banking is still below the Western European levels of significance. Equity markets are weak, while stock market capitalization is fluctuating greatly over time. As these countries prepare for membership of the monetary union, the pressures leading to the convergence of their financial systems are expected to intensify. Thus, in the long run, the financial structures of the NMS will move closer to Western European standards.

(ii) *In relation to developments in the banking sector*, EU banks have been undergoing a process of transformation, which is still not complete. In dealing with the challenges of an increasingly competitive environment, they have had to restructure and reposition themselves within the financial services sector, domestically, as well as internationally. This has allowed most of them to adjust successfully to the new challenges facing them. However, certain policy issues have emerged in the process. More specifically, the increasing concentration of the banking sector is giving rise to competition concerns. Similarly, the prevalence of large financial conglomerates is giving rise to the need for stronger and more comprehensive consumer and investor protection regimes. Lastly, the credit crisis of the late 2000s revealed the weaknesses of the 'originate and distribute' business model, implicit in securitization.

Banks in the NMS, on the other hand, face certain structural challenges bearing on future developments in the sector. Namely, (i) financial intermediation is still low; (ii) technological change is ongoing, influencing risk measurement and management systems; (iii) the very high presence of foreign banks raises questions of stability, for example in relation to credit growth and/or balance sheet restructuring.

With respect to security market-based financing, this has broadened in scope, as well as deepened in terms of liquidity, in parallel with the continuing predominance of bank financing. Furthermore, as market-based finance spread across the EU financial services sector, both in terms of structure and in terms of market type behaviour, the role of institutional investors is expected to increase. As with changes in the banking sector, this poses certain policy issues for the EU regulators, pertaining to the protection of investors and retail consumers more generally, as well as to the stability of the sector as a whole.

(iii) Lastly, *in terms of financial integration*, this is most advanced in the money markets and least advanced in retail financial markets, reflecting differences in practices, laws and regulations across member states, as well as in market infrastructure. As these differences recede, financial integration is expected to deepen. However, this is not necessarily going to benefit consumers, while it probably entails certain dangers to financial and economic stability, especially to the extent that policy does not cater for such eventualities. The financial crisis experienced in 2007–08 is a case in point.

Overall, the EU financial services sector is gradually being transformed, as new actors, products and practices are being introduced. As a result, it is becoming more market oriented than hitherto, although the EU banks continue to be major actors, adjusting to their new environment. This is a fast-changing sector, largely under the lead of the US. The competitive drive the EU financial services sector finds itself in entails potential benefits as well as costs, the distribution of which is going to be critical with respect to its future development.

NOTES

1. The demise of the Bretton Woods accord officially dates back to 1971. This was followed by the Smithsonian Agreement and the European Joint Float, both of which

failed in 1973. Governments then moved to pegged, semi-pegged or freely floating currencies. In 1978, the free-floating system was officially mandated by the IMF.

2. Around that time, the so-called 'Washington Consensus' – a term first used by John Williamson to describe the view that economies should increase their reliance on markets – prevailed in World Bank and IMF recommendations towards the less developed countries. The recommendations included privatization and deregulation and in terms of external policies, the opening of highly regulated domestic markets to cross-border transactions. Also, it was recommended that the current account be liberalized first, followed by rapid liberalization of the capital and financial accounts (ECB, 2003).

3. European Commission (1983).

4. *Dermine (2002).*

5. As De Grauwe (1994) has argued, the existence of capital controls tended to reduce the size of funds that could be mobilized for attacking a currency. In so doing, they gave the authorities some time to organize an orderly realignment of the foreign exchange rates.

6. Borio (2005).

7. The transition to a single currency area was divided into three phases. Stage I – 1 July 1990 to 31 December 1993 – provided for the freedom of capital flows and the coordination of national monetary policies. The European Monetary Institute was created in Stage II; this was the predecessor of the European Central Bank. Its mission was to prepare the monetary institutions and the European System of Central Banks (ESCB). Lastly, Stage III led to the European Economic and Monetary Union on 1 January 1999. Euro notes and coins were introduced in January 2002.

8. 'Arm's length' finance refers to market-based financial systems – where capital is raised from and returned to arm's length parties – as opposed to 'relationship' finance – where capital essentially circulates within a set of related firms and institutions (Rajan and Zingales, 2003).

9. Rajan and Zingales, 2003.

10. Bulgaria, Estonia, Hungary, Latvia, Lithuania, Poland, Romania, Slovakia, Slovenia and the Czech Republic. The two non-transition countries are Malta and Cyprus. For some purposes, it is necessary to distinguish Slovenia from the other 'transitional' financial systems because the Yugoslav system was different from, and more sophisticated than, those in the Soviet sphere.

11. Initially, the eurozone included Austria, Belgium, France, Finland, Germany, Greece, Ireland, Italy, Luxembourg, The Netherlands, Portugal and Spain. Slovenia joined in January 2007 and Cyprus and Malta in January 2008.

12. The measurement of financial depth by way of comparing a 'stock' concept (financial stock) to a 'flow' concept (GDP) is common because of the ease of conceptualization and of data availability (see McKinsey, 2005, p. 44).

13. According to London Economics, the prospects of the financial sector appear especially subdued in the short term (2008–09), highly uncertain in the medium term (2009), albeit sanguine in the long run. In particular, the size of the wholesale financial services – i.e., transactions conducted between financial institutions – is predicted to fall by 2.6 per cent–11.6 per cent below its 2007 level according to four different scenarios, ranging from the 'stressful' to the 'positive surprises' one ('The importance of wholesale financial services to the EU economy', 2008: 4)

14. Financial assets include bank loans, debt securities and equities.

15. ECB Monthly Bulletin issues and tables.

16. Public Limited Company – i.e., the shares of which are traded on a stock exchange.

17. Austria, Finland and Sweden joined the EU in 1995.

18. CDOs refer to a debt obligation whose underlining collateral and source of payments consist of existing bank loans and other forms of debt obligations, such as emerging market and high yield debt (IFSL Research, 2008a).

19. European Commission (2007d), chart 2.3.

20. In Cyprus, these are international banking units; in the Czech Republic and in Slovakia, building societies; in Hungary, building societies and mortgage banks.
21. A repo is a financial instrument which allows cash to be temporarily exchanged for securities for a predetermined period.
22. The BIS definition of international securities, as opposed to domestic securities, is based on three major characteristics of the securities: the location of the transaction, the currency of issuance and the residence of the issuer (Casey and Lannoo, 2005). However, in essence capital market liberalization has tended to reduce the importance of this distinction because the terms on which debt is issued in domestic and international markets have tended to converge.
23. London Economics (2008, Table 20).
24. McKinsey (2008) Exhibit 1.6, p. 24.
25. IFSL Research (2008b)
26. London Economics (2008, Table 5).
27. A basis point is one hundredth of a percentage point, 0.01 per cent.
28. Euribor – Euro Interbank Offered Rate – is the rate at which euro interbank term deposits within the eurozone are offered by one prime bank (of first class credit standing) to another prime bank and it is published daily at 11 am CET for spot value. It is the benchmark rate of the large euro money market. Eonia® – Euro OverNight Index Average – is the effective overnight reference rate for the euro. It is computed as a weighted average of all overnight unsecured lending transactions undertaken in the interbank market, initiated within the euro area by the contributing banks (same as those quoting for Euribor).
29. European Commission (2007d), ch. 2.1.
30. Dermine (2003) presents an exhaustive account of such reasons.
31. Trans-European Automated Real-time Gross settlement Express Transfer.
32. See the European Payments Council White Paper 'Euroland: Our Single Payment Area!' (May, 2002).

4. EU financial market integration policy

Marica Frangakis

4.1 INTRODUCTION AND OVERVIEW

The liberalization of financial markets that followed the collapse of the Bretton Woods agreement soon spread within and across national borders. Industrial countries typically began partial liberalizations in the mid-1970s, pushing such reforms considerably further in the 1980s, so that by the early 1990s financial liberalization was virtually complete. According to Padoa-Schioppa and Saccomanni's (1994) phrase, for all intents and purposes the shift from a government-led to a market-led international financial system had been accomplished.

As a result, striking changes have been taking place in relation to both the intermediation processes and the institutional design across time and space of the financial services sector. In particular, classic banking functionality has been in relative long-term decline more or less worldwide, while disintermediation, financial innovation and expanding global linkages have redirected financial flows through the financial markets. Such financial flow transformation has been especially evident in the USA, while changes in the EU have been less pronounced.

The ongoing disintermediation and the faster pace with which US financial structures are evolving – for example by comparison to the EU – have had an impact on global market-share patterns, as US financial firms have come to dominate various intermediation roles in the financial markets. For example, in the early 2000s, over 77 per cent of lead manager positions in wholesale lending, two-thirds of security issuance mandates in global debt and equity originations and almost 80 per cent of advisory mandates (by value of deal) in completed M&A transactions were handled by US financial firms (Walter, 2003). In fact, it is estimated that in 2000 US-based investment banks captured about 70 per cent of the fee income on European capital markets and corporate finance transactions (Smith and Walter, 2000).

The reasons behind this evolution include the size of the US domestic financial market, the early deregulation of US financial markets dating back to the mid-1970s and performance pressure bearing on institutional investors, as well as on corporate and public sector entities. One of the symptoms of this process is that small and medium-sized independent firms are being taken over by larger banking institutions, resulting in ever more complex financial institutions.

In Europe, this has led to the emergence of pan-European banking groups through cross-border mergers and acquisitions and the increasing provision of wholesale financial services across member states. It is estimated that there are around 40 major banking groups which, on average, are present in probably more than six of the 25 member states, with some having establishments almost across the whole EU (Schinasi and Teixeira, 2006).

As Robin Blackburn (2006) has pointed out, the growing and systemic power of finance and financial engineering – defined as 'financialization' – has come to permeate everyday life, as the increasing commodification of the life course leads to the proliferation of such financial products as student loans and pensions, credit cards and mortgages (Blackburn, 2006).[1]

Financial market integration has long been a declared policy objective of the EU. However, it was not until the late 1990s that it gathered pace, becoming a topical issue on the EU agenda. The primary driver was the introduction of the single currency, which eliminated foreign exchange risk. It was then realized by the EU political and financial elites that for the full benefits of the euro to be realized, a developed financial market was needed. Thus, a fast-track legislative and regulatory programme aimed at removing barriers to the cross-border flow of financial services, known as the Financial Services Action Plan (FSAP), came into existence in 1999.

The supranational legislative phase of the FSAP was largely completed by 2005, and the EU financial sector policy objectives for 2005–10 focus on the implementation, consolidation and improvement of the existing legislation at the national level. New EU legislative initiatives are contemplated in relation to retail financial services and asset management, areas which are considered to be highly fragmented.

At the same time, a new EU policy implementation and enforcement framework has been devised, known as the 'Lamfalussy process', aiming at achieving convergence of supervisory practices, consistent implementation of FSAP legislation and streamlined rule-making. The democratic accountability of the new process has been subject to criticism by the European Parliament.

While the new EU financial policy framework aims at increasing financial market integration, its provisions for stability and consumer protection are generally considered to be inadequate. In the case of financial stability, these rely on three basic principles: decentralization, segmentation and cooperation (Lastra, 2003). The adequacy of these arrangements has not so far been tested. As Lastra has argued: 'It will take the first pan-European crisis to cast some light on this issue' (Lastra, 2003, p. 7).

In the case of consumer protection, this remains a national concern. Although certain new bodies have been set up at the EU level, these are of a consultative nature.

The rest of this chapter is organized as follows:

- Section 4.2 looks at the evolution of financial regulation in the EU prior to the FSAP;
- Section 4.3 presents the main features of the current EU financial market integration strategy, and the following sections, 4.4 and 4.5, look at the two key parts of that strategy, the Financial Services Action Plan and the Risk Capital Action Plan, respectively;
- Section 4.6 considers EU financial policy after the completion of these two main legislative programmes;
- Section 4.7 examines the new committee structure of the EU financial sector, set up by the Lamfalussy Process;
- Section 4.8 is devoted to the crisis management arrangements of the EU financial services policy;
- Section 4.9 takes a closer look at the existing consumer protection provisions on the EU level.

4.2   EU FINANCIAL REGULATORY HARMONIZATION 1960s–1990s

The construction of an internal market consisting of the home markets of all member states constitutes a generic goal of the EU. Furthermore, the Treaty establishing the European Community prohibits all restrictions to the free movement of goods, services, capital and labour. However, it is the implementation of these in-built freedoms and the distribution of power between the central and the national levels of decision-making that have been shaping policy in the financial, as in other spheres of the EU over time.

The EU has been described as a 'polity sui generis', where the member states continue to play a dominant role, as opposed to the federal nature of the USA (Petschnigg, 2005, p. 4). This particular characteristic of the EU has been central in the evolution of financial regulation.

In particular, the early attempts at constructing an internal market concentrated on harmonizing those laws, regulations and provisions that affect its establishment and functioning through the issuing of directives (Art. 94 of the Treaty). These were aided by the establishment of a legal principle by the European Court of Justice in the Cassis de Dijon case in 1979, known as 'mutual recognition', aimed at enhancing market access across the EU.[2]

In actual practice, beginning in the late 1960s and continuing until the early 1980s, the European Commission produced approximately ten directives per year. While this rate was clearly inadequate for the economy at large, it was even more so for banking and the financial services, in view of the large differences across member states and the existence of exchange and capital controls.

The period of 'extensive harmonization', also known as the Classical Approach, came to an end in the mid-1980s, with the 1985 White Paper specifying that future legislative activity should be limited to harmonizing essential measures, beyond which mutual recognition should apply, as specified by the ECJ. Furthermore, the Single European Act introduced qualified majority voting instead of unanimity as the basis for adopting measures aimed at accomplishing the internal market (Arts. 95 and 251). This New or Minimal Harmonization Approach was seen to be a pragmatic response to the problems arising out of the previous extensive harmonization method.

The New or Minimal Harmonization Approach established the so-called 'single passport' for financial services in the EU, on the basis of two principles. Namely, the mutual recognition principle and that of the home country control. Thus, products or services that are lawfully produced and marketed in one member state are granted free access throughout the internal market, while the authorities of the member state in which the goods or service providers have their seat are responsible for carrying out regulation and supervision of the entity, mainly relating to risk monitoring. Host country authorities, on the other hand, retained responsibility in the area of liquidity and they may interrupt the provision of services by the branch of a financial institution if any legal provisions in this regard are violated (Walkner and Raes, 2005). However, with the introduction of the euro and the establishment of the ECB, control over liquidity passed to the ECB for those countries in the eurozone.

More specifically, the Single European Act gave rise to three groups of directives defining the main elements that were deemed necessary for mutual recognition to be operational.

- The 2nd Banking Directive (1989), the Investment Services Directive (ISD, 1993) and the 3rd Life and Non-Life Insurance Directives

(1992) established the right of financial institutions to provide their services across the EU on the basis of a single license.[3]

- The 1985 UCITS – undertakings for collective investment in transferable securities – Directive enables fund managers to provide investment funds across the EU, while the 1989 Prospectus and Initial Public Offerings Directives (IPO) harmonized the information that firms have to supply when offering securities to the public.
- The 1989 Solvency Ratios Directive harmonized the capital standards for banks in the EU, implementing the Basel Accord I, while the 1993 Capital Adequacy Directive set minimum standards for banks and investment firms.

Under the policy approach instituted in the late 1980s, the EU member states still retained a significant role in the process of decision-making, through the allocation of competencies and the preference for directives over regulations as the legal vehicle for the transposition of Community law into national law.

In particular, although the delegation of power under the minimal harmonization approach was more significant than in the past, this differed from one function to another. Thus, member states retained considerable control over the Commission's right to initiate policy, as well as over the execution of policy through the 'comitology system'.[4] On the other hand, member states cannot control the way the Commission monitors member state compliance in its role as the 'Guardian of the Treaties'. And they can only reverse decisions taken by the European Court of Justice in exceptional circumstances.[5]

In addition to the allocation of competencies, member states retained significant control through their preference for the issuing of directives rather than regulations. While both measures take precedence over member state laws, a regulation has direct effect, whereas a directive offers member states the ability to choose the particular implementation mode that best suits their particular circumstances.

Overall, the Minimal Harmonization Approach of the 1980s was more successful than its predecessor in establishing a single financial market in the EU, although the 'mutual recognition/home country control' left large areas of financial legislation in EU member states intact. One such area is that of taxation. In particular, the full liberalization of capital movements in 1988 and the adoption of the sectoral directives were not accompanied by any adjustments in the field of taxation.[6]

Furthermore, political deadlock was reached in several legislative areas, including the winding-up and liquidation of credit institutions and of insurance companies, takeover bids and the European Company Statute.

Lastly, the legislative process – adoption of legal measures and transposition into national law – proved to be slow by comparison to the ever-increasing pace of financial market developments.[7]

Thus, at the end of the 1990s, financial markets in the EU remained considerably fragmented, in spite of the ongoing process of internationalization, disintermediation and globalization of financial services.

4.3   EU FINANCIAL MARKET INTEGRATION POLICY SINCE THE LATE 1990s

The advent of the euro in 1999 produced a new sense of urgency, because it made many economies of scale feasible for the first time and EU policy-makers became aware of the importance of scale and scope for financial services and especially for the capital markets. This led to a new regulatory harmonization phase, beginning in the late 1990s and expected to have been implemented by 2010. This involves the further liberalization of financial services on the national level and their re-regulation along Community lines.

More specifically, financial integration was seen as a vital part of a broader economic reform package, the so-called Lisbon Strategy. The main objective of the Lisbon Strategy – adopted by the European Council meeting in Lisbon in March 2000 – is to increase the level of competitiveness of the EU economy and to close the gap with the USA, which is taken as a benchmark, by 2010 (see Chapter 5). In view of the fact that financial services cut across all other sectors of the economy, their reform has been placed high on the overall agenda.

The new EU financial integration policy consists of a number of initiatives, presented under two plans – the Financial Services Action Plan (FSAP) and the Risk Capital Action Plan (RCAP). Of these, the FSAP constitutes the 'centre piece of the Community's efforts to integrate Euro financial markets' (European Commission, 2003b,: p. 31).

4.4   THE FINANCIAL SERVICES ACTION PLAN

In June 1998, the Cardiff European Council invited the 'Commission to table a framework for action . . . to improve the single market in financial services' (European Commission, 1999, p. 3). In 1999, the European Council and the European Parliament endorsed the Financial Services Action Plan. The duration of the Plan was set at six years, 1999–2005.

The FSAP was structured on the basis of the principal objectives guiding policy and the relative order of priorities. It was designed to tackle three 'strategic' objectives. Namely, to ensure (i) a single market for wholesale financial services; (ii) open and secure retail markets; and (iii) state-of-the-art prudential rules and supervision. A fourth objective, headed 'wider conditions for an optimal single financial market', was also included. Under each of these objectives, a number of areas of action were outlined, while 42 legislative initiatives were proposed in total (Box 4.1).

Progress under the FSAP was impressive. Thus, by the 2005 deadline for its completion, 98 per cent of the measures had been completed. That is, 41 of the 42 measures have been adopted, with the exception of the proposed 14th Company Law Directive on the Cross-Border Transfer of Registered Office.[8]

Progress under the FSAP was also impressive in terms of breaking the previous political impasse reached in a number of areas. Thus, with few exceptions, long-standing differences of opinion either among national governments, or among the Council and the European Parliament were resolved, or a compromise was reached, due to the political commitment of the EU political elites to monetary and financial integration. On the other hand, various loose ends still remain, while political consensus has not been entirely uniform, as displayed by the Take Over Bids Directive. We shall go on to look briefly into three of the most important new pieces of EU legislation. Namely, the Capital Requirements Directive, the Markets in Financial Instruments Directive (or MiFID), and the Take Over Bids Directive.

- Following seven years of negotiations, the *Capital Requirements Directive* (CRD) got through the European Parliament in September 2005 and was formally approved by the Council of Ministers of the 25 member states in October 2005. This Directive transposes the Basel II framework on capital measurement and capital standards into EU law. All credit institutions and investment firms operating in the 25 member states will have to comply with the new Directive's provisions from January 2007 onwards for the simple approach, and from January 2008 for the more advanced approach to measuring credit and operational risks.

  There remain, however, certain problems in the implementation of the new Directive. These include the impact of the new approach on the minimum required capital level and the uneven implementation dates between the EU and the USA, which only plans to introduce the Basel II rules for its internationally active banking institutions.[9]

BOX 4.1   AREAS OF ACTION ENVISAGED BY THE FINANCIAL SERVICES ACTION PLAN 1999–2005

I.   Wholesale – securities and derivatives - markets

- Removing outstanding barriers to raising capital on an EU-wide basis
- Common legal framework for integrated securities and derivatives markets
- Moving towards a single set of financial statements for listed companies
- Providing legal security to underpin cross-border securities trade
- Promoting cross-border restructuring through mergers, takeovers, etc.
- Creating the necessary conditions for asset managers to optimize the performance of their portfolios

II.   Retail financial services

- Promoting information for cross-border provision of retail financial services
- Elimination of non-harmonized consumer-business rules
- Promoting the resolution of consumer disputes
- Creating a legal framework for new distribution channels and distance technologies on a pan-European scale

III.   Prudential rules and supervision

- Adjusting prudential legislation to international standards
- Regulating the prudential supervision of financial conglomerates
- Promoting cross-sectoral and regional cooperation amongst authorities on issues of common concern

IV.   Wider conditions

- Eliminating tax obstacles to financial market integration

Source: European Commission (1999).

The key question for regulators is whether it is safe for the financial system to replace the previous capital requirements, based on prescribed ratios for different types of exposure, by requirements based on risk assessments carried out by the banks themselves (see also Chapter 14). The outbreak of the sub-prime banking crisis in 2007 does not encourage confidence in the internal risk assessment procedures of the big banks.

- The *Markets in Financial Instruments Directive* (or MiFID) regulates the activities of brokers, exchanges and most financial corporations trading in securities, replacing the 1993 Investment Services Directive (ISD).[10] It consists of a 'framework' directive, adopted by the Council and the Parliament in April 2004 on the basis of the Lamfalussy Process – a new decision-making procedure, which we shall discuss in the next section – and a further implementing directive, which aims at securing a uniform, harmonized approach across the 25 member states. The aim of the Directive is to push forward the integration of the financial services sector by establishing homogeneous rules for the sale of securities across all member states. Key aspects of MiFID are: an obligation to secure the best terms when trading securities on behalf of a client; an obligation to avoid or to declare conflicts of interest which can work to the detriment of customers; and rules for the reporting of security transactions. In fact, the MiFID has been criticized for being 'far more onerous . . . than its predecessor'.[11] For example, the MiFID and its implementing measures contain 169 articles, numbering 67 192 words, as opposed to the principles-based approach of the ISD, which contained 32 articles and 14 381 words. In this sense, the MiFID is indicative of the shift of EU financial services policy from a principles-based approach to a rules-based one.

- An exception to the political consensus expressed by the FSAP was the Takeover Bids Directive.[12] The original proposals of the Commission were rejected by the European Parliament and the compromise version adopted in 2004 was very much weaker and allowed member governments much more scope to regulate takeovers (see Chapter 8). Thus, under the 'principle of reciprocity' member states may exempt domestic companies from the ban on anti-takeover devices when the bidding company comes from a jurisdiction permitting their use. This concerns restrictions on securities transfers and voting rights as well as the right of the board of the target company to issue shares without prior shareholder authorization ('poison pills').

The Commission, whose ambition was to establish a thoroughgoing 'market in corporate control' by blocking defences against hostile take-overs, is clearly dissatisfied with the Directive in its compromise form. A recent Commission report argued that member states were indeed blocking takeovers and that the situation should be closely monitored (European Commission, 2007c). As yet, however, there is no proposal for new legislation.

Generally, the FSAP expressed a clear political commitment to the liberalization of EU member states' financial markets and their re-regulation along EU lines, with special emphasis on the development of capital markets facilitating the cross-border flow of capital. Two significant policy areas were, however, underplayed; those of supervision and of the protection of consumers. In both areas, the Plan was especially lightweight, in so far as it introduced no new measures, commensurate with the degree of market integration it sought to promote. In sections 4.8 and 4.9 below we take a closer look into each of these two areas.

4.5   RISK CAPITAL ACTION PLAN

In parallel with the FSAP, the Risk Capital Action Plan was agreed upon. The rationale of this plan was the same as that of the FSAP, that is, creating the necessary conditions for the free circulation of capital across the EU. Furthermore, to the extent that the RCAP pertained to a new, relatively underdeveloped area of finance, that of venture capital, it also aimed at stimulating its establishment and growth in the EU member states.

More specifically, the RCAP was adopted in 1998 for a five-year period, which expired in 2003. The central objective of the RCAP was to develop an integrated market for equity financing – venture capital and buyouts – of SMEs by way of eliminating the existing regulatory and administrative barriers to competition at both the Community and the national level. It included a number of measures, which were in common with the FSAP, as well as certain measures beyond the FSAP, such as taxation, research and development, entrepreneurship and public funding, through state aid and the European Investment Fund (EIF), the 'equity' arm of the EIB.

The model of equity financing adopted by the RCAP was that of the US venture capital market, which in 2002 was nearly twice as large as that of the EU – 0.20 per cent of GDP as opposed to 0.11 per cent of GDP in the EU. The full involvement of pension funds was considered as one of the preconditions for the development of a mature venture capital market in the EU.

According to the 5th and final Progress Report on the RCAP:

> When taking the RCAP period as a whole (1998–2003) important progress can be reported. From the political point of view, risk capital issues are now at the top of the agenda in all regional, national and Community institutions. From the technical point of view most of the measures foreseen in the RCAP in 1998 have been completed (European Commission, 2003c:18).

The RCAP received less attention than the FSAP because it only related to a relatively small part of the financial sector. However, as the RCAP ended there was an explosion of investment in European venture capital: from 27 billion euros in 2004, this leapt to 72 billion euros in 2005 and 112 billion in 2006.[13] This surge was one aspect of a general move to highly leveraged positions by pension funds, banks and other financial corporations; the venture capital (also known as 'private equity') organizations use a lot of debt in order to raise the rate of return on their purchases of companies. In fact, the venture capital groups were unable to use all the money they were raising.

Although sometimes the activities of the venture capital groups are useful – for example in supporting company start-ups or in attempting to rescue otherwise insolvent companies – in many cases their activities have been strongly criticized, because they purchase companies with a view to selling them again quickly and can make their profit by asset-stripping or by loading the companies concerned with debt.[14] These aspects of venture capital, however, were not a concern of the European Commission in its drive for market-led integration.

4.6 WHITE PAPER ON FINANCIAL SERVICES POLICY (2005–10)

On the successful completion of the FSAP, the emphasis shifted to the implementation and enforcement of the new legislation by the member states, the development of EU financial sector infrastructure, such as clearing and settlement and payments, as well as the removal of the remaining barriers to cross-border activity in certain areas, such as retail finance and asset management. The central objectives of the EU financial services policy for the period 2005–10 were outlined in a White Paper published by the Commission in 2005.[15]

Overall, the White Paper follows the general argument and financial policy framework already set out by the Plans and especially by the FSAP, extending it to sectors left out by it and in particular to the retail financial services sector. Although it recognizes the dangers to stability that are inherent in financial integration – in terms of the possible spill-over effects of a system failure affecting several financial markets and/or groups on a EU-wide basis – it introduces no new measures. Similarly, while acknowledging the need for consumer protection, no new policy initiatives are presented in this respect.

Generally, the financial services policy of the EU remains heavily oriented towards serving the interest of markets and of the financial industry, even to the extent of offering vague protection from instability, so as to minimize the regulatory burden for firms, systems and markets. Furthermore, member states are asked to demonstrate 'renewed political commitment' to financial market integration, by pressing on with the transposition of new legislation. For example, member state actions are being monitored through a publicly available transposition matrix, showing which texts have been implemented by member states, when and how.

4.7 THE LAMFALUSSY PROCESS

Although the FSAP was concluded successfully, major problems arose with it. To begin with there were long delays in passing legislation and complaints, from the financial sector, about the quality of the legislation as it emerged from the European Parliament. It was becoming clear also that the FSAP would have to deal with some new issues, in particular the integration of clearing and settlement procedures related to trade in securities (see Norman, 2007). In addition there were problems in transposing the FSAP Directives into member state law: financial practitioners complained about 'gold-plating' or the fact that in some member states the FSAP financial regulation was more stringent than the Directives required. This was seen as a barrier to the integration of markets in financial services.[16]

It was felt that a new governance structure was needed, bearing on the allocation and exercise of power in the area of financial services policy. This should aim at increasing the speed and flexibility of rule-making in the EU, especially at the stage of the transposition of Community law into national law, as well as reducing the possibility for member states to 'gold-plate' such legislation.

It was not possible simply to transfer these problems to a European regulatory agency, analogous to the American Securities Exchange Commission (SEC). Because the EU is not a federal entity, such as the USA, the creation of agencies with discretionary regulatory powers needs to be explicitly authorized by the Treaty.[17] This is the Meroni Doctrine, developed by the European Court of Justice in the 1950s. It implies that EU institutions cannot delegate discretionary regulatory powers which have been conferred on them by the Treaty to outside bodies, as this would threaten the balance of powers between the institutions.[18]

A report was thus commissioned from the 'Committee of Wise Men' under the chairmanship of Alexander Lamfalussy, on the governance measures necessary for more complete and effective integration. This gave rise to a new policy formulation process, known as the Lamfalussy Process. Its main characteristic is that it distinguishes between 'framework' legislation, to be decided on the political level via the Council and the European Parliament and legislation concerning the 'technical details' of framework measures, to be decided by the Commission, which would be assisted for this purpose by a number of committees, the members of which include representatives of the Commission, the member states and the market participants. The users of financial services and the employees of the financial industry are not represented.

Accordingly, two new intermediary levels of policy formulation now intervene between the passing of framework legislation by the Council and the European Parliament on the basis of a proposal by the Commission under the co-decision procedure and its implementation by member-states. A schematic representation of how the four levels of decision-making are expected to work is shown in Box 4.2.

The Lamfalussy Process was put into effect in the securities sector in 2002, following a temporary agreement between the European Parliament, the Council and the Commission, known as the 'sunset clause', which is included in all Level 1 legislation. More specifically, this safeguards the Parliament's right to 'call-back', that is to look again at implementing legislation, in order to ensure that it corresponds to the intention of the primary legislation. Furthermore, in the event of disagreement, the Parliament expects the Commission to modify the draft measure by taking account of objections, to initiate a new legislative process, or withdraw it altogether.

The 'sunset clause' is a temporary agreement, aimed at safeguarding the Parliament's role as equal legislator under the co-decision procedure, given that the Council has the right to exercise its implementing powers directly in specific and exceptional cases. That is, the Council is both a delegating institution and one that can exercise the delegated competence. In order to redress the institutional balance in matters governed by the co-decision procedure, the Parliament demanded the reform of the relevant Treaty provisions (Article 202). The commitment by the Council and the Commission to such a reform was a precondition for the Parliament's support of the Lamfalussy Process.

BOX 4.2   THE LAMFALUSSY PROCESS

Level 1

Community legislation adopted under the co-decision procedure – Legislation should be only about framework principles and define implementing powers for the Commission.

Level 2

Community legislation adopted by the Commission to lay down the technical details for the principles agreed at Level 1. Particular features:

- Technical advice prepared by the Committee of European Securities Regulators (CESR) following mandates issued by the Commission and based on consultation with market users;
- Favourable vote of member states (qualified majority) as represented in the European Securities Committee (ESC).
- European Parliament may adopt resolutions (a) within 3 months on the draft implementing measure; (b) within one month after the vote of the ESC if level 2 measures go beyond implementing powers.

Level 3

The CESR, in which the national supervisory authorities are represented, to facilitate consistent day-to-day implementation of Community law. CESR may issue guidelines and common, non-binding standards.

Level 4

The Commission checks compliance of member state laws with the EU legislation. If necessary, it takes legal action against member states before the Court of Justice.

Source: First Interim Report Monitoring the New Process for Regulating Securities Markets in Europe, May 2003.

Thus, all legislation adopted under the Lamfalussy framework contains a 'sunset clause', which means that the delegation of implementing measures to the Commission will expire four years after their entry into force, unless renewed prior to the expiry date under the co-decision procedure

Table 4.1 *The EU organizational committee architecture of the EU financial services sector*

	Banking	Insurance and occupational pensions	Securities (incl. UCITS)
Regulatory Committee (Level 1)	European Banking Committee (EBC)	European Insurance and Occupational Pensions Committee (EIOPC)	European Securities Committee (ESC)
Committee of Supervisors (Level 3)	Committee of European Banking Supervisors (CEBS)	Committee of European Insurance and Occupational Pensions Supervisors (CEIOPS)	Committee of European Securities Regulators (CESR)

(Inter-Institutional Monitoring Group, 2004, p. 8). The failure of the Constitutional Treaty, which incorporated the new compromise, means that specific measures may be needed to ensure the continuity of the delegated legislation.

On the basis of the Lamfalussy Process, two new sets of committees have been set up, dealing with (a) regulatory matters and (b) operational matters in banking, insurance, including pensions, and securities (Table 4.1). The regulatory committees represent member state governments; the committees of supervisors represent the supervisory authorities of each member state.

Although the new committees operate within the political mandate given to them and the agreement reached by Council and the EP, they are to play a very significant role in the new phase the EU financial services sector is entering. In this sense, they are likely to acquire a significant autonomy vis-à-vis the other EU institutions. These structures seem likely to be very sensitive to the requirements of banks and financial corporations; the well-known danger of 'regulatory capture', where regulators respond to the needs of the regulated corporations rather than to those of the public, is amplified here because of the central role of the regulators in the legislative process.

At least in the short run, however, the Lamfalussy arrangements were successful. The legislative process was speeded up and the content of the legislation seemed better adapted to the functioning of the financial sector. It seems doubtful whether the FSAP could have been completed on time without this initiative.

Table 4.2   The institutional architecture of the EU single financial market

Levels	Functions	Decision-makers	Cooperation structures
EU 27 member states	● EU legislation (min. harmonization) ● Policy-coordination ● Policy shaping ● State aid control	● ECOFIN Council ● European Parliament ● European Commission: 1. Legislative proposals; 2. Competition authority	● Econ and Financial Committee ● Financial Services Committee ● Regulatory committees
EMU 14 member states	● Single monetary policy ● Payment systems oversight ● Contribution to financial stability and supervision	● ECB Governing Council	● Eurosystem committees
National		● 25 finance ministries ● 25 national parliaments	● At the EU level
	● Banking supervision ● Insurance supervision ● Securities regulation ● Supervision of financial conglomerates	● 13 national central banks ● 13 single (cross-sectoral) supervisory agencies ● 1 banking supervisor ● c. 12 insurance and pensions supervisors ● c. 12 securities regulators	● Home/host country relationships ● Consolidated supervision of banking groups ● Supplementary supervision of financial conglomerates ● Supervisory committees ● Bilateral, banking groups, regional and EU-wide Memoranda of Understanding ● (MoU)
	● Central banking functions (members outside euro area)	● 25 national central banks	● ECB Governing Council (euro area) and General Council (EU)

Table 4.2 (continued)

Levels	Functions	Decision-makers	Cooperation structures
	● Lender of last resort (emergency liquidity assistance)		● Eurosystem committees (euro area or EU) ● EU-wide and regional MoU
	● Deposit insurance	● C. 35 schemes (with diverse features)	● Informal

Legal framework: EU Treaty + directly applicable national laws and regulations (min. harmonization through EU legislation) enforced by national authorities and courts

Source: Schinasi and Teixeira (2006).

4.8 CRISIS MANAGEMENT ARRANGEMENTS UNDER THE EU FINANCIAL SERVICES POLICY

The integration strategies discussed in this chapter are essentially the responsibility of the European Commission, especially the Directorate-General for the Internal Market. However, the Commission takes no responsibility for the stability or otherwise of the market structures which emerge from the integration process. Crisis prevention and crisis management arrangements are based on three principles: decentralization, segmentation and cooperation.[19] That is, supervision is exercised by a multiplicity of bodies both at the EU and the member state level. Furthermore, in many instances, different segments of the financial industry are overseen by different bodies, while coherence across such a decentralized and segmented structure is sought through bilateral and multilateral cooperation. There are arrangements, largely under the auspices of the ECB, for the exchange of information and the possible coordination of policies relating to financial stability, but stability measures remain essentially the responsibility of the member states.[20]

Table 4.2 depicts the institutional architecture of the EU single financial market, reflecting the above three principles.

- As shown in the Table 4.2, the institutional architecture of the EU financial industry is *decentralized* to the extent that the financial stability functions are largely the responsibility of the national authorities – banking supervisors, central banks, finance ministries and deposit insurance schemes. Likewise, the performance of the lender of last resort function is a national responsibility, although its implications for the single monetary policy are closely followed by the ECB. Even in the euro area, the provision of emergency liquidity assistance is under the responsibility of national central banks.[21]

● Furthermore, it is *segmented* across sectors and member states. That is, supervision is exercised by single supervisory authorities and/or by the national central banks.[22] Prudential regulations are largely harmonized across the EU, although their implementation may vary in view of its decentralized nature. In the eurozone, banking supervision is the responsibility of the national authorities.

● The third principle of the supervisory arrangements of the EU single financial market is that of *cooperation*. This is conducted on the basis of a web of committees, largely set up under the Lamfalussy Process, reviewed above, as well as EU-wide cooperation agreements between authorities, known as Memoranda of Understanding (MoU), which are not public documents. Neither are they legally binding.

In 2001, the EU banking supervisors and central banks adopted the Memorandum of Understanding on cooperation between payment systems overseers and banking supervisors under the EMU, setting out arrangements for cooperation and information in relation to large-value payment systems. In addition, two MoUs on financial crisis management came into existence in 2003 and 2005 respectively, dealing with cooperation between EU banking supervisors, central banks and the EU Finance Ministries. They include provisions and procedures relating to the identification of the authorities responsible and the cross-border flow of information in the case of systemic crisis with spill-over effects in several countries.

While the above arrangements constitute a general framework for the supervision of the EU financial services sector, there are a number of challenges which may potentially raise problems. These include the role of the European Central Bank as a lender of last resort and the mismatch between home-country control of supervision and host-country operational conduct of financial market surveillance.

As we saw above, the lender of last resort function is primarily a national responsibility and liability. The issues that arise in this respect relate (a) to the role of the European Central Bank and (b) to the coordination between national central banks in the case of a pan-European banking group.

More specifically, the European System of Central Banks has only a limited role with regard to the safeguard of financial stability.[23] In particular, Art. 105.5 of the Treaty specifies that 'The ESCB shall contribute to the smooth conduct of policies pursued by the competent authorities relating to the prudential supervision of credit institutions and the stability of the financial system'. In this sense, prudential supervision is a 'non-basic' task of the ESCB.

On the other hand, according to Art. 105.2 of the Treaty, the ESCB is responsible for the 'smooth operation of payment systems'. That is, should there be an explicit *payment system failure*, the ECB has competence to act as lender of last resort (LOLR). For example, the Bank of England was asked to put up a substantial collateral with the ECB to take part in TARGET (Trans-European Automated Real-time Gross-settlement Express Transfer), whereas this is not the case for the central banks of the member states participating in the EMU.[24] Thus, although payment system supervision is difficult to dissociate from banking supervision, the Treaty does so. However, should a crisis occur outside the payment system, then the role of the ECB is at best ambiguous.

In particular, Art. 105.6 of the Treaty, also known as the 'enabling clause', allows for a possible expansion of an ECB supervisory rule on the basis of a unanimity rule, rather than the formal amendment of the Treaty:

> The Council may, acting unanimously on a proposal from the Commission and after consulting the ECB and receiving the assent of the European Parliament, confer upon the ECB specific tasks concerning the policies relating to the prudential supervision of credit and other financial institutions with the exception of insurance undertakings.

Therefore, in the case of an emergency the ECB may be enabled to intervene. Whether this will happen, how long it will take and how effective it may be is not clear. With now 27 member states the unanimity requirement could be an obstacle to prompt action. It has in fact been argued that such ambiguity is 'constructive', in so far as it does not reveal the predisposition of the authorities to intervene in case of difficulties and therefore it reduces moral hazard. However, ambiguity about the procedures and responsibilities in such an instance may well reduce public confidence, accountability and even the effectiveness of crisis management in the EU.[25] Hence, the role of the ECB in the case of a financial crisis with broader repercussions needs to be clarified. Furthermore, as Lastra (2003) has argued, the centralization of the LOLR function does not necessarily imply the centralization of other supervisory functions, which may appear premature at the present time.[26]

The exercise of the LOLR function may further give rise to problems of coordination between national central banks in the case of a pan-European banking group. In particular, a gap between micro and macro prudential controls may arise out of the mismatch between home country control of supervision and host country operational conduct of financial market surveillance.[27]

This is even more so in the case of a foreign financial institution that is especially large in relation to the size of the host economy, as is true of many of the new member states of the EU, the financial industry of which is dominated by a small number of foreign-owned concerns. Further, where the foreign-owned concern is small in relation to the parent institution or group, the home country authorities may not even have the incentive to intervene. That is, there arises a case of a possible conflict of incentives.

Overall, the existing EU crisis arrangements are both ambiguous and inadequate. As pointed out by Petschnigg (2005), regulatory agencies in the USA appear to have sprung out of political and/or economic crises. Should the same happen in the EU, then the tale told by Dermine (2003) is not completely unlikely:

> During a week-end, the Banking Supervisory Committee met in Frankfurt to consider the need to launch the bail out of a large international bank. As it was becoming rapidly clear that the ECB should not increase the money supply to restore the solvency of that bank, and that tax-payers' money would be needed to finance the bad debts, ECOFIN was invited to take the decision to bail it out. On the following Monday, due to a public outcry, that supervision of the problem bank had not been handled properly by the national supervisors, a decision was taken to transfer supervision to a European agency. (Dermine, 2003, p. 71)

Some light is thrown on EU stability arrangements by the events of the sub-prime banking crisis which broke out in 2007. In general, crisis management procedures seemed to work reasonably well. The European Central Bank undertook to provide exceptional liquidity to the eurozone banking system as a whole, while national central banks dealt with the specific problems of individual banks in difficulty, such as the British bank, Northern Rock, which was eventually taken over by the British government. There did not seem to be disputes over responsibilities between member states and the EU, although it might be a cause for concern that the ECB, responsible for monetary policy in most of the major European economies and the Bank of England, supervising the most important financial markets in Europe, adopted rather different approaches to crisis management.

On the other hand, crisis prevention policies and prudential supervision were clearly inadequate. In general the obvious move of the financial system as a whole to riskier positions and in particular the vast accumulation of US mortgage-backed securities by the banks and other financial corporations took place without any effective control or intervention by the authorities, who indeed were busy relaxing the existing regulatory regime by the introduction of the Basel II agreement which gives the big banks in particular increased scope to adopt speculative positions. The ECB, at the apex of Europe's financial system, was surely at fault in doing nothing to prevent or limit these threats to stability (see also Chapters 7 and 14).

4.9 CONSUMER PROTECTION PROVISIONS UNDER THE EU FINANCIAL SERVICES POLICY

Consumer protection is generally a national concern, governed by the 'general good' concept, as provided for by Article 153(5) of the Treaty on 'Consumer Protection'.[28] According to the rulings of the ECJ, the following are legitimate motives for invoking this concept:

- Depending on the risk level and the complexity of the financial service in relation to the degree of vulnerability of the recipient of the service. While professional clients are able to assess risks associated with specific services properly, this may not be the case for individual consumers (Case C-222/95 Parodi).
- Ensuring fairness in commercial transactions may necessitate restrictive rules on advertising and selling methods, as well as price transparency for financial services.
- Maintaining consumer confidence allows for measures aiming at the protection of financial market integrity at the firm level (Case C-204/90 Bachmann, Case C-80/94 Wielockx, Case C-484/93 Svensson and Gustavsson).
- Lastly, for the effectiveness of fiscal supervision member states may take measures restricting the cross-border trade in financial services (Case C-315/02 Lenz and Case C-319/02 Manninen).

Generally, EU legislation on retail consumer protection is limited in scope. Not surprisingly, its policy for financial integration pays little attention to this area.

More specifically, both the FSAP and the financial policy framework for 2005–10 put on consumers the onus of protecting their own interests, given that the provisions made in this respect are hardly adequate. These provisions include an out-of-court complaints network (FIN-NET), which aims at resolving cross-border legal disputes between consumers and financial service providers and a forum of financial services experts, advising the Commission from a user perspective (FIN-USE). This is a newly established group, which is to deliver opinions on legislative initiatives of concern to users of financial services and to identify key financial services issues affecting them.

Although both initiatives represent positive developments, they are inadequate by comparison to the multiplicity and complexity of financial developments. Also, they address computer-literate consumers – be they individuals or SMEs – a limitation which is of particular relevance for the less developed areas of the EU.

Generally, consumers of retail financial services are suspicious of enterprises in this sector. This suspicion is justified by the boom and bust pattern of financial developments in the late 1990s and early 2000s both in the EU and globally. Furthermore, the suspicions of consumers will impact not only on retail services but also on the financial markets and the general process of integration as their concerns for safety and liquidity will hold back the development of financial intermediation in general.

Therefore, if the EU objective of an integrated financial sector is to be achieved, consumer confidence needs to be reinforced. However, in the absence of a Europe-wide drive for substantively higher standards, the EU approach – involving market liberalization, minimal harmonization of regulatory standards, mutual recognition of supervisory regimes and home country control over financial enterprises – makes this difficult. As argued by Grahl and Teague (2003), the 'not obviously legitimate desire for rapid integration' impedes the pursuit of more complete and effective consumer protection (see also Chapters 10 and 12).

4.10 CONCLUSION

At one level the EU's strategy for financial integration, centred on the FSAP, has to be regarded as very successful. A very complex programme of legislation was enacted at both EU and member state levels. When serious difficulties arose, the Lamfalussy initiative made a realistic analysis of the problems and proposed major changes which were accepted and speedily implemented by the political actors, and this got the strategy back on track. Although the outcome will certainly not be the tightly integrated and highly efficient financial system which was promised by EU leaders, substantial progress was made towards large, liquid security markets in the EU, and this progress has contributed to Europe's current ability to challenge US hegemony in the financial sphere.

It is clear that the basis of these successes was political – European leaderships, at both member state and EU levels – believed in the project and were prepared to make the necessary adaptations in existing systems and procedures to ensure that it was carried out. If a similar measure of commitment could be achieved in other spheres the EU could become a very effective and dynamic force indeed.

The limitations of the financial integration strategy are just as clear. It has been a narrowly economic project, focused on the imitation of US models, with no wider social objectives. As the remarks above on financial stability and consumer protection indicate, market integration was driven through with insufficient concern for its social consequences. The challenge for the EU now is to mobilize the same kind of unity and determination in the pursuit of broader objectives more closely related to the well-being of its citizens.

NOTES

1. 'The individual is encouraged to think of himself or herself as a two-legged cost and profit centre, with financial concerns anxious to help them manage their income and outgoings, their debts and credit, by supplying their services and selling them their products' (Blackburn, 2006, p. 39).
2. This section builds on Lannoo and Levin (2004).
3. It should be noted that the 1st Banking Directive, already adopted in 1977, had stipulated that national bank supervisors should cooperate and that a banking licence could not be denied on the grounds of foreign identity, but it had not introduced a 'single passport' or asserted home country control.
4. According to the 'comitology system', the Commission presents draft proposals to committees composed of member state representatives before adopting them, whereby Management Committees have the right to block proposals and refer them to the Council of Ministers, while Regulatory Committees must approve the proposals put forward by the Commission by qualified majority or refer them to Council.
5. Where the Court interprets treaty rules, the member states have to abide by the decision of the Court. Where it interprets EU legislation, however, member states may re-legislate.
6. As the Commission has pointed out 'It would be technically unbalanced and politically difficult to boost the full realization of a Single Market for financial services unless the parallel process of tax coordination currently under way delivers the expected results' (Press Release, CEC, 11 May, 1999: 3).
7. On past experience, the adoption of directives in the field of financial regulation takes 2–3 years, followed by a 1–2 year period for national implementation.
8. Single Market in Financial Services Progress Report 2004–05, SEC(2006)17. The 14th Company Law Directive was abandoned by the Commission in 2008. The reasons are not altogether clear, but the Directive, which would have allowed, for example, a French company to become an Italian company without being liquidated in France and then established as a new company in Italy, was perhaps seen as undermining member state competence in the sphere of company law. The measure could thereby have affected employment rights where these are linked to the company status of the employer. The Commission could not disturb member state company law beyond a

certain point without assuming responsibility for the promulgation of company law at EU level and it may have been reluctant to do this. See the worker participation website of the ETUI: http://www.worker-participation.eu/company_law_and_cg/news/corporate_governance_and_company_law_news_march_2008.

9.   The rest of the US banking system, composed of approximately 8900 regional and community banks will operate a Basel IA set of rules, which is an improved version of Basel I.

10. Dir. 2004/39/EC.

11. Casey and Lannoo (2005, p. 2). For details of the legislation and the way it is being implemented in the British financial markets see the FSA website: http://www.fsa.gov.uk/pages/About/What/International/mifid/index.shtml.

12. Directive 2004/25/EC of the European Parliament and the Council of 21/4/2004.

13. See the website of EVCA, the European Venture Capital Association: http://www.evca.eu/knowledgecenter/statisticsdetail.aspx?id=414.

14. See for example the critical report on private equity by the House of Commons Treasury Committee (2007).

15. COM (2005) 629.

16. These objections to 'gold-plating' raise a serious political problem. It has always been the case that individual member states were entitled to impose higher regulatory standards than those promulgated by the EU, whether the regulation concerned the environment, worker protection or consumer protection. The resulting differences in regulation are certainly a barrier to trade among member states but they work to raise standards in general and it is always open to enterprises to penetrate the national markets concerned by meeting their stricter regulatory requirements. It is not clear that there is any good reason to adopt a different approach in financial regulation.

17. See Meroni Co., Industrie Metallurgiche, SpA v. High Authority, Cases 9 and 10/56, ECR 11-48, ECJ 1958, as quoted in Petschnigg (2005).

18. Such a delegation of powers to outside bodies should be seen as distinct from the delegation of implementing powers by the Council to the Commission under the 'comitology' system, which is explicitly authorized by the Treaty (Art. 202).

19. Lastra (2003) and Schinasi and Teixeira (2006).

20. See ECB (2006a) for an account of the coordination arrangements.

21. The 'lender of last resort' function and the 'emergency liquidity assistance' are used here interchangeably.

22. National central banks perform supervisory functions in 13 of the 25 member states: Austria, Cyprus, the Czech Republic, Germany, Greece, Italy, Lithuania, the Netherlands, Poland, Portugal, Slovakia, Slovenia and Spain.

23. The ESCB consists of the ECB and the national central banks of all EU member states. By contrast, the Eurosystem consists of the ECB and the national central banks of the states that participate in the EMU.

24. Lastra (2003).

25. Kremers et al. (2003).

26. On existing stability arrangements see also de Boissieu (2003).

27. Schinasi and Teixeira (2006).

28. The ECJ rulings are cited by Walkner and Raes (2005).

5. Lisbon, finance and the European social model

John Grahl

5.1 INTRODUCTION

The European Commission's (2000a) contribution to the Lisbon Council opened with a self-congratulatory account of economic progress in the EU. The 'best economic conditions for a generation' were signalled in terms of disinflation, the stabilization of public finance and lower interest rates. However, weaknesses, 'in spite of this positive outlook', were acknowledged in growth and employment, especially in comparison with the US. The expression, 'in spite of' might be considered tendentious in that the severe monetary and fiscal stabilization measures of the 1990s are regarded by many as, at least, the proximate cause of slow growth and high unemployment. But the relative lack of employment and output dynamism in the EU was traced not to any macroeconomic circumstances but to inadequate technological progress. The 'knowledge economy', centred on information and communication technologies (ICT) and the Internet, was seen as the sphere in which Europe needed to catch up.

Transformed *financial relations* were to be a key linkage in the catch-up strategy. Within a 'sound macro-economic environment', policies for social inclusion, investment in human capital, integrated research policies and so on were to promote a surge in innovation, while finance was essential to the successful introduction of innovation into the economic system. 'An integrated capital market and a dynamic financial services industry' would translate these more fertile and entrepreneurial conditions into success on EU and global markets by widening financial options for enterprises and driving down the cost of capital (Figure 5.1). Specific dimensions of this financial component in the strategy ran as follows:

- The relatively low capitalization of EU equity markets and their fragmentation were to be overcome by integration and the removal of administrative and legal obstacles.

INTEGRATING POLICY TO CREATE A DYNAMIC,
INCLUSIVE EUROPEAN ECONOMY

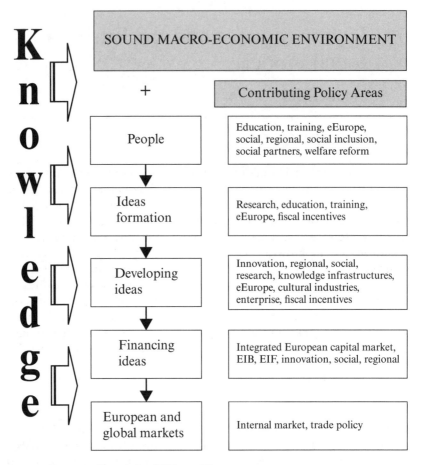

Source: European Commission (2000a, p. 10).

Figure 5.1 Finance and the Lisbon strategy

- The removal of portfolio restrictions on pension funds; if these funds in other member states were to reach the level achieved in the Netherlands, five trillion euro could be placed on EU capital markets.

These were the main considerations which made the already established financial integration policies (the general Financial Services Action Plan and the Risk Capital Action Plan) into indispensable components of the agenda.

As regards the first issue, the scale of security markets, a judgement was implied that the bank-based systems of many EU countries were inferior to the more equity-based US system in terms of both the general cost of capital and the finance of innovative start-ups. This judgement might well be questioned because, although there is a lot of evidence that financial deepening is necessary to economic development, the evidence on the importance of particular financial structures is much weaker.

The subsequent European Council (2000) completely endorsed these Commission proposals, adding the famously ambitious goal for the coming decade 'to become the most competitive and dynamic knowledge-based economy in the world, capable of sustainable economic growth with more and better jobs and greater social cohesion'. The only significant difference from the Commission document was a particularly heavy emphasis on the role of small and medium enterprises (SMEs) as bearers of the innovations leading to the knowledge economy. The financial paragraph began:

> Efficient and transparent financial markets foster growth and employment by better allocation of capital and reducing its cost. They therefore play an essential role in fuelling new ideas, supporting entrepreneurial culture and promoting access to and use of new technologies. It is essential to exploit the potential of the euro to push forward the integration of EU financial markets. Furthermore, efficient risk capital markets play a major role in innovative high-growth SMEs and the creation of new and sustainable jobs.

There followed a repetition of the need for rapid implementation of the Financial Services and Risk Capital Action Plans.

5.2 THE SOCIAL POLICY AGENDA

The Commission (2000b) developed its view of the social policy content of Lisbon a few months later in its *Social Policy Agenda*. It is interesting that the introduction to this document put forward two motives for social policy: social cohesion and 'fairness'. In the tradition of Rawls (1971), fairness is a term which can be given a clear meaning and as an objective it might imply a very ambitious policy indeed. However, this was the only such reference in the document, which subsequently spoke only of 'cohesion'.[1] But social policy was not only seen as serving social objectives; we also find the claim that social policy is to be seen as a productive factor. Thus it was asserted that the economic, social and employment strategies

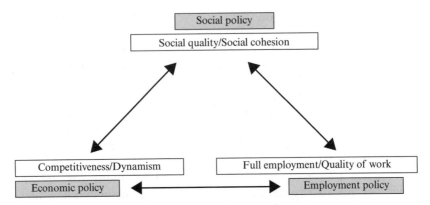

The policy mixes to be established to create a virtuous circle of economic and social progress should reflect the interdependence of these policies and aim to maximize their mutual positive reinforcement.

Source: European Commission (2000b, p. 6).

Figure 5.2   Social policy and the Lisbon strategy

reinforced each other through a virtuous cycle (in fact, in Figure 5.2, two such cycles – clockwise and anticlockwise).

One key concern was the anticipated difficulty in paying for social expenditures – especially pensions and age-related health care – in European countries. Another was that social protection regimes were not sufficiently supportive of employment. The social strategy as defined in this document in fact included employment policy (essentially the European Employment Strategy, EES) as its main content, on the grounds that 'raising the employment rate will underpin the sustainability of the financing of social protection systems' and that employment was the main route to social inclusion.

The EES as such is discussed below. Apart from a restatement of the Luxembourg process and its employment objectives, the *Social Policy Agenda* did recognize that other social policies were necessary because fuller employment could not in itself resolve such problems as poverty (Figure 5.3).

Thus, besides reiterating the Luxembourg employment targets, the *Social Policy Agenda* specified two further objectives:

● **Quality of social policy** implies a high level of social protection, good social services available to all people in Europe, real opportunities for all, and the guarantee of fundamental and social rights. Good employment and social

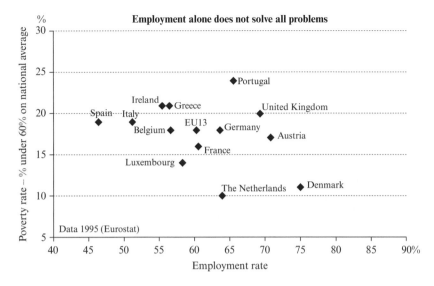

Source: European Commission (2000b, p.12).

Figure 5.3 Poverty and employment in the EU

policies are needed to underpin productivity and to facilitate the adaptation to change. They also will play an essential role towards the full transition to the knowledge-based economy.

- **Quality in industrial relations** is determined by the capacity to build consensus on both diagnosis and ways and means to take forward the adaptation and modernization agenda.

  This also includes coping successfully with industrial change and corporate restructuring. (European Commission, 2000a, pp. 13–14)

The gloss on the first of these objectives moved to a generally more defensive specification but with a very surprising exception. Improving the quality of social policy included: firstly, 'modernising' and 'improving' social protection (it being added that, in practice, this means 'making work pay', 'making pensions safe and pension systems sustainable'); secondly, 'preventing and eradicating poverty'; thirdly, promoting 'full participation of women in economic, scientific, social, political and civic life as a key component of democracy' (again the benefits of such participation for production are emphazised); finally, the 'development and respect of fundamental social rights' with emphasis falling on tackling discrimination and xenophobia.

We have here important objectives to counter discrimination but which, in themselves, are market-conformable. Few large enterprises today, for example, are without equal opportunities policies. The specification of 'safe pensions' and 'sustainable pension systems' conspicuously failed to add 'better pensions'. The notion of 'making work pay' is, of course, a classical EU ambiguity – which might and probably does connote completely opposed labour market interventions at one and the same time, that is, both higher minimum wages and reduced support for the unemployed.

The most far-reaching of the social objectives was therefore most certainly the second on the list – the 'eradication of poverty'. This wholly laudable target, which together with the near simultaneous commitment to 'full employment' gave the EU a surprisingly ambitious social policy, will be examined below.

The second objective, of 'quality in industrial relations' reminds us that the 'Cologne Process', involving improved employment relations was, in principle at least, part of the overall agenda, but the development of this theme was very sketchy. The Commission limited themselves to a call for 'social dialogue at all levels (to) contribute in an effective way to the challenges identified. To promote competitiveness and solidarity and the balance between flexibility and security'. But this early allusion to the holy grail of 'flexicurity' was not translated into any concrete policy orientations besides the ever-present need for 'dialogue'.[2]

5.3   CONSISTENCY: THE SAPIR REPORT

Almost from the launch of the Lisbon agenda both its main components and the strategy as a whole were subject to repeated review. Many specific anxieties lay behind these repeated reassessments, but the failure to close the gap in GDP growth between EU and US was always part of the picture.

The Sapir Report (Sapir, 2003), was an early attempt to address this core problem of slower growth. The report had the merit of emphasizing the possible inconsistencies of the agenda – indeed it offered a typology of such inconsistencies, which might impair:

1.   coherence at the level of instruments and objectives,
2.   coherence at the level of decision-makers and jurisdictions, and
3.   coherence over time for a given decision-maker and/or jurisdiction.

In general, however, the resolution of inconsistencies was to be sought by a strong emphasis on growth, since this was a necessary condition for the achievement of all the other objectives of the strategy. Growth might raise certain problems of cohesion (especially among regions) but the main notion was that a rising tide floats all ships. And growth was to be pursued essentially by way of structural reforms and further liberalization. (The Report began to problematize the EU's macroeconomic framework, but in the limited terms that have since become standard: the Growth and Stability Pact might indeed represent an obstacle to expansion, but if this was so it was because member state budgets had failed to build up sufficient surpluses during the boom to allow for fiscal relaxation in the downturn.)

According to the report, the European Social Model (ESM) was in deep trouble. In what was soon to become the new orthodoxy, both technological change and the rise of the Chinese economy were seen as lowering the relative demand for unqualified labour. In these circumstances, labour market regulation and social protection which raised the price of such labour would only generate unemployment and destabilize the public finances. Population ageing exacerbated these problems. It should be remarked, however, that the empirical support for these explanations of widening labour market inequalities is fragile. Glyn (2001) reported that increasing wage inequalities were by no means a simple question of declining fortunes for the less qualified – they pervaded the entire distribution and were in fact more marked *among* highly qualified workers than between them and the unskilled. At the same time, the high risks of unemployment faced by workers with low bargaining power were not a European phenomenon: although general rates of unemployment were often lower in the US than in the EU, the concentration of unemployment on the less skilled was just as marked across the Atlantic.

In considering finance, the Sapir Report stressed the issue of risk capital. Between 1995 and 2000 the growth of labour productivity in the US outstripped that in the EU for the first time since the Second World War, 'an extraordinary performance for a country at the leading edge of the production possibility frontier'. The previous catch-up in European productivity levels had been to a great extent based on imitation; in the 1990s, however, innovation became much more important. Among the conditions of research investment is 'good access to risk capital by new start-up firms'. Thus the lack of risk capital had become a serious obstacle to European growth (Figure 5.4). The report gave the following details:

> In 1999, total US expenditure on R&D at 2.6% of GDP was over a third higher than that of the EU. Nearly all of the difference can be attributed to a substantially higher investment in R&D by business (1.8% against 1.2%). Within the EU, the low level of business R&D reflects a general north–south divide. Finland and Sweden have both overall and business-financed R&D expenditures exceeding those of the US, while Germany is not far behind. At the

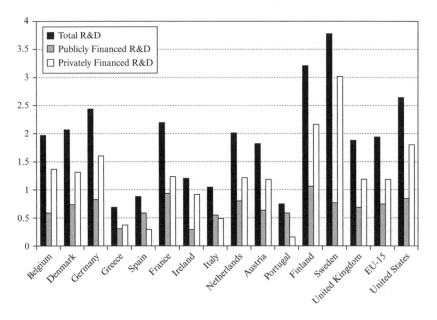

Source: Sapir (2003) High-level Group.

Figure 5.4 R&D finance by source, 1999, as percentage of GDP

other extreme, all EU Mediterranean countries have low overall and business-financed levels of R&D. Nor are trends in R&D expenditure favourable to Europe. The US increased its lead in R&D expenditure by €95 billion between 1996 and 2000, of which €20 billion was publicly financed. Between 1991 and 2000, public research budgets in Europe declined from 0.91% to 0.73% of GDP. (Sapir, 2003, p. 34)

The Sapir Report also gave a strong endorsement of the FSAP, while insisting that the integrated capital markets which should emerge be lightly regulated.

Given the crucial role of financial integration for growth, completing the Single Market for financial services is crucial. A number of specific proposals currently in the pipeline address issues identified in this Report. For example, credit markets and the financial system for innovation are the subject of the Risk Capital Action Plan and Financial Services Action Plans. We support the accelerated implementation of both these actions rather than bringing forward new recommendations in these areas. An effective regulatory system for financial services, such as that proposed by the Lamfalussy Report on securities markets, represents a requirement for the efficient functioning of the financial system. In general, the regulatory process needs to become much closer to, and more aware of, market developments in service sectors and utilities. Possibilities for self-regulation as a partial or complete substitute for statutory regulation need also to be explored. (Sapir Report, 2003, p. 130)

In its general orientation, the Sapir Report, having given detailed consideration to possible inconsistencies in the Lisbon agenda and to trade-offs among the various Lisbon targets, came down decisively in favour of growth: 'there is a need to give higher priority to growth, because it is the means to achieve the economic, social and environmental objectives of the enlarged Union. Growth is also crucial to help the Union fulfil its political objectives' (Sapir, 2003, p. 124). And the way to achieve that growth was essentially to learn from US experience:

> The main reason for disappointing growth in the EU is quite clear. During the past decades, the economy has been confronted by a series of long-lasting shocks – the information technology revolution, German re-unification, the opening up to the new market economies of central and eastern Europe, globalisation – which called for new organisational forms of production. The situation demanded less vertically integrated firms, greater mobility within and across firms, greater flexibility of labour markets, greater reliance on market finance and higher investment in both R&D and higher education. In other words, this required massive change in economic institutions and organisations, which has not yet occurred on a large scale in Europe. (Sapir, 2003, p. 123)

As will be seen below, the Sapir report could be taken as forecasting the actual evolution of the Lisbon strategy towards an essentially economic programme in the tradition of the EU since its inception. Other targets were to be made possible by achieving growth, while growth itself would follow from market-oriented integration. It was suggested therefore that some temporary sacrifice of other priorities, such as 'cohesion', would in the longer term be rewarded by more abundant resources to sustain the ESM. An appeal was made in this context to the experience of the post-war decades, when high growth rates went together with social progress. But, since the report also recognized that the nature of the growth process had changed and since it advocated economic policies very different from those of the *trente glorieuses*, it is not clear that such a comparison was relevant.

5.4 REASSESSING THE SOCIAL AGENDA

The Social Agenda was revisited by a group of experts (European Commission, 2004b). Following the Barcelona Council, the group defined the ESM thus: 'The European social model is based on good economic performance, a high level of social protection and education and social dialogue'. It was recognized that 'since the creation of the European Communities, social policy has always been lagging behind economic policy' and it was added that 'it is probably one of the major achievements of the Lisbon Strategy to try to put them on an equal footing'. This seems an optimistic judgement both because the constitutional structure of the EU privileges the economic and because the social content of the post-Lisbon epoch is still to be demonstrated.[3] The group endorsed the view that 'the social model functions as a productive factor':

> Three key compromises can be detected within the social model: between the state and the market; between labour and capital, requiring concerted action and a role for nationwide agreements; and between the welfare state and individual responsibility.
>
> In the 1960s, the conditions were excellent, with strong economic growth and low inflation. There is also a high level of training of the labour force. As a consequence, there was confidence in public affairs as well as in individual rights. Law and collective bargaining fulfilled a key role, the latter one through a truly credible commitment between employers' and workers' representatives. The strength of the European Social Model was determined by the way in which competitiveness, solidarity and mutual trust interacted.
>
> However, since the 1970s this model has become less effective. This is due to the fact that the appropriate conditions are not met anymore. The balance between economic efficiency and social progress has to be adapted to take account of changing economic environment and social context. European Commission, 2004b, (pp. 27–8)

Three challenges to the ESM were specified: enlargement, population ageing and globalization. These were said to necessitate a certain modification of the Lisbon agenda in the following ways:

- To put more emphasis on the employment possibilities of the service sector as a whole, rather than on the potential of the ICTs;
- To address demographic issues by longer working lifetimes (the target of five more years was adopted by the Barcelona Council in 2002), immigration and natalist measures ('to allow European couples to have the number of children they desire') centring on improved child-care facilities, parental leave and so on;
- Certain reforms to the Stability and Growth Pact, so that the constraints involved relate more to long-term conditions and less to short-run fluctuations in budgetary positions.

As regards social protection, the group called for this to be financed increasingly out of social income as a whole, rather than labour income;

it called for strengthened social dialogue at all levels; and it asserted that since globalization threatens certain groups in the developed world, "social inclusion must be developed as a policy in itself".

Of specific relevance to financial issues is the position that the group adopted on pensions. As a general framework, it suggested a new inter-generational pact which would address both pension problems and those of young people (insecurity, adverse distributional developments). This proposal was subsequently adopted, at least in principle, by the Commission, although it is still unclear what the content of such a pact would be. Besides the risks traditionally covered by European social protection regimes, the report identified new risks, resulting from globaliz-ation, and necessitating 'new securities' which include lifelong learning and 'capital ownership'. Although the latter point was not fully developed, it relates in part to funded market pension schemes. The report argues that the expansion of such schemes is necessary to preserve European owner-ship of European enterprises:

> Recent developments have proved the great vulnerability of companies whose capital is owned by Anglo-Saxon pension funds or hedge funds. If the EU wants to keep control of the economic centres of decision of its companies, it has to develop European pension funds as well as capital ownership by the workers themselves, which has already developed recently in many Member States in a very rapid and successful way. (European Commission, 2004b, p. 29)

This tied the social agenda very closely to financial integration and its consequences. The rapid growth of institutional investors became a way of limiting external ownership and at the same time of providing a new, asset-based, security for workers. The linkage calls for at least two comments. On the one hand, the transition from 'insider' to 'outsider' investment systems, together with privatizations financed by stock market flotations, has been so far the basis for a new heightened penetration of US pension funds into the ownership of European companies, for instance in France. On the other, if a 'new security' is to be based on the individual possession of financial assets, what needs to be said about the distribution of such assets among the insecure?

After this report, the Commission itself published a brief review of the Social Agenda in February 2005. For the most part this dealt with employment issues, and the expansion of employment was still seen as the main weapon against 'exclusion'. The issue of poverty was handled in a more cursory fashion – there was to be a 'European year of combating poverty and exclusion' in 2010. An attempt would be made to focus such EU-level instruments as did exist (above all the European Social Fund) on the priorities of the agenda, but in general the Union could only deploy the Open Method of Coordination (OMC) in the field of social policy, that is, it could only encourage, not determine, certain lines of policy because member states retained control in this field. Here, the aim was to stimulate improvements in the minimum income programmes of the member states, which was certainly the only logical approach within the existing constitutional and budgetary constraints, but it is extremely difficult to assess progress in counteracting poverty because few data are available since the launch of the Lisbon agenda. The Commission (2005b) noted that, 'at the start of the decade, the number of citizens of the enlarged EU who were at risk of poverty and persistent poverty was very high: 15 per cent and 9 per cent respectively'. (These data seem to refer to the 15 member states at the time – such data as are available suggest that the corresponding levels in many new member states are rather higher.) The document did make the judgement that 'many people are still in considerable difficulties and are obtaining neither employment nor the national minimum income protection'. In view of this, 'from 2005, the Commission will begin consultations on the reasons why the existing schemes are not effective enough'.

It should be noted in this context that, while the employment component of the Social Agenda was closely linked to the Lisbon growth objectives, this was not as true of the anti-poverty component since the measure of poverty applied is relative, some 60 per cent of median income. (This use of the median is perhaps significant – it means that measured poverty rates are not sensitive to widening inequalities in the upper half of the income distribution, such as might follow from higher rewards for highly qualified workers or for successful entrepreneurs.) The Commission vehemently denied that the goal of poverty eradication had been ditched, but, as yet, it is impossible to see what effect that goal has had on social outcomes.

5.5 THE KOK REPORT

The High Level Group chaired by Wim Kok (2004) was clearly responding to what was, by the time of its convocation, something of a crisis in the Lisbon agenda.

After a recapitulation of the original Lisbon programme, the High Level Group acknowledged that it had been framed in the climate of 'irrational exuberance' which had characterized stock markets around the time of its formulation: 'The Lisbon strategy is sometimes criticized for being a creature of the heady optimism of the late 1990s about the then trendy knowledge economy, neglecting the importance of the traditional industrial

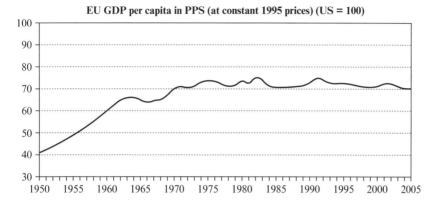

Source: Commission services, 2004–05: forecasts.

Figure 5.5   European productivity relative to the US

strengths of the European economy ... this is a fair criticism' (Kok, 2004, p. 9 with the omission of a quite unnecessary qualifying clause).

But things had gone wrong. Like most other commentators, the Group emphasized the failure to meet growth and employment targets, but they also mentioned failure to meet environmental objectives. To some extent these problems resulted from contingencies – the US downturn and so on – but the main factor had been 'a lack of commitment and political will', compounded by 'incoherence and inconsistency, both between participants and between policies' (Kok, 2004, pp. 39–40). Neither the OMC nor the Community Method has been working properly.

Were European macroeconomic policies in any way responsible for the failure of Lisbon? The Kok report asserted several times the need for 'a wider macroeconomic framework as supportive as possible of growth, demand and employment' and in this sense endorsed the planned revisions to the Stability and Growth Pact (SGP). The perhaps Aesopian reference to macroeconomic issues repeated that the problem was that insufficient surpluses were built up in periods of high economic activity; however, it is difficult to see which period could have been meant because the 1990s were not a period of boom but were in fact dominated by the struggle to meet the Maastricht criteria.

Lisbon, however, remained indispensable because of the deep and manifold challenges faced by the EU and the ESM. The Group insisted that 'The Lisbon strategy is not an attempt to become a copy-cat of the US – far from it; Lisbon is about achieving Europe's vision of what it wants to be'. However, the US remained the key external reference and provided the metric of success and failure, for example in terms of labour productivity (Figure 5.5).

Although, as with most recent assessments of Lisbon, the original agenda was seen as too complicated, the Group insisted that its revision should maintain the scope of the original version, including its social and environmental dimensions. Thus five priority areas were specified:

- Innovation and the knowledge society
- The internal market (including financial markets)
- The right climate for business (including risk capital)
- An inclusive labour market
- Sustainable development

It will be shown below that in practice the revised agenda was rather narrower than this but it can be noted already that the Group, although they listed the 'eradication of poverty' (together with the application of the OMC to social protection) as a component of the original agenda, did not address in their recommendations this most striking and ambitious goal of the Lisbon enterprise. This silence might be taken to imply that the goal was seen as unrealistic or the social agenda as too crowded. The Group repeated, very reasonably, that higher levels of employment would work to reduce poverty; their main recommendation on 'inclusion' was to reinforce the European Employment Strategy. But apart from labour market policy the only proposals in the 'social' sphere concerned 'life-long learning' and 'active ageing' – policies aimed, respectively, at improving employment outcomes and at containing pension costs.

On financial services, the Kok Group repeated that 'dynamic and highly competitive financial markets . . . are an essential driver of growth in all other sectors of the economy and must be a cornerstone of efforts to boost the EU's economic performance' (Kok, 2004, p. 26). This led to an endorsement of the FSAP, of its extension to integrate clearing and settlement systems and of a further drive for integration in the field of retail finance. The report was, of course, a stimulus to policy discussion rather than an academic treatise but the expression 'essential driver of growth' might require both some qualification and some evidential support.

On risk capital, the Group repeated the standard analysis that there is 'insufficient mobilization of capital' to sustain entrepreneurial activity, but added that 'investors in Europe should be more encouraged to commit to long-term involvement in start-ups'. This view marked a certain distance from the US model where it is, on the contrary, not long-term commitment but the prospect of early exit via an IPO which is often seen as an indispensable incentive.

The Group went on to endorse the general process of financial integration, but again with a slight change in emphasis:

> Equity markets and funds remain fragmented and below their critical size. As a consequence, the risk run by funds and private investors is unnecessarily increased as exit strategies are blocked. This in turn leads to lower investments and to Europe missing out on many opportunities. Therefore, the whole chain of creating worthwhile opportunities and assuring investment in them needs to be reinforced, linking funds, companies, industry and universities. (Kok, 2004, p. 30)

The suggestion here seems to be that financial integration would lead to more liquid markets and, because this would permit dealing on a larger scale, to bigger institutional investors better able to diversify risks and rebalance portfolios. Thus we see the benefits of the FSAP and the RCAP defined, in a very realistic way, in terms of scale benefits rather than in terms of more intense competition or enhanced allocative efficiency. (Note that the reference to 'exit' in the second quotation sits somewhat uneasily with the 'long-term involvement' of the previous one.) But the new stress on the innovation 'chain' as a whole and on communications among all the actors seemed to reduce the usual emphasis on finance and financial markets.

In a further shift, one subsequently endorsed by Commission President Barroso, the public sector and public finance appeared as key supporters of start-ups and innovations: 'Financial and public institutions offering different financing instruments supporting a specific policy objective, such as privileged loans, grants or subsidies, could cooperate better to make it easier for companies to locate the appropriate funding and to make use of the opportunities offered' (Kok, 2004, p 30). (If, *per impossibile*, these public participations gave rise to ownership rights, this would represent a somewhat surprising ideological departure; see Holland (1972) on 'the state as entrepreneur'.

Overall, the Kok Group went farther than other commentators in the attempt to rescue the Lisbon agenda as a strategy combining employment and growth objectives with ambitious ecological and social targets. They endorsed the intention 'to embed Europe's commitment to social cohesion and the environment in the core of the growth and jobs generation process so they are part of Europe's competitive advantage' (Kok, 2004, p. 16).

But their analysis went along with a general drift towards seeing growth and employment as the means to these other ends: these are the 'key priorities'.

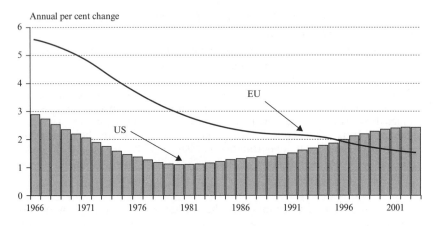

Source:	Kok (2004, p. 16).

*Figure 5.6	Productivity per hour in the US and the EU*

## 5.6	THE PRODUCTIVITY GAP

What is the exact nature of the emerging productivity gap between the EU and the US? The aggregate data often referred to in the Lisbon literature are illustrated in Figure 5.6, from the Kok report.

A study by O'Mahoney and van Ark (2003) permits an accurate disaggregation of the productivity gap. In country terms, three quarters of the productivity slowdown in the EU can be attributed to two countries: Germany and Italy, 'with Germany about twice as important as Italy'. Thus what is often presented as a Europe-wide problem is in fact dominated by events in this single member state, which might therefore be accorded a priority position in analysis.

In terms of sectors, the study used three interrelated classifications: in terms of technology, labour force skills and innovation. Results are summarized as follows:

— *US productivity growth acceleration, EU unchanged or declining.* Industries that are ICT producing manufacturers or intensive users of ICT, employ graduates or lower intermediate skilled labour, and where innovations arise through specialized suppliers, supplier based innovation and are provided through demands of clients.
— *EU productivity growth relatively high, little or no US acceleration.* Industries that are ICT-producing services, employ highly skilled craftsmen (higher intermediate skilled labour) and/or where innovations are largely process changes arising from in-house R&D.

— *Relatively low and declining productivity growth in both the US and EU.*
Industries that neither produce nor intensively use ICT and employ mostly
unskilled labour (pp. 12–13).

Of course, a sectoral analysis of the productivity gap is not the same
thing as a sectoral explanation. There may be, and most probably are,
economy-wide factors in the EU or in the US which have played a part
in the differential performance of various sectors. But the phenomenon
under study does seem to relate to a very specific aspect of technological
development and technology diffusion over a relatively short period of
time. The time period may even be too short to justify strong policy conclusions, but to the extent that it does we are confronted essentially with
an *investment* problem and responses might be sought in a close analysis
of the determinants of ICT investment.[4]

Connections between these investment issues and the broad themes of
European employment policy are complex. There are certainly education and training issues, but the pertinence of 'flexibility' in the sense of
atypical contracts is questionable. A recent sectoral study of productivity
growth and employment factors finds no connection whatsoever – the
high-performance sectors tend to employ full-time, prime-age male
workers on permanent contracts and could therefore be said to be as far
away from the 'flexible' labour market as it is possible to go (Anderson
et al., 2006).

In any case, the productivity gap, as the core phenomenon behind
much of Lisbon's economic prescriptions, does not seem to admit of a
detailed analysis which would support the key themes that were adopted.
In general, the drastic slowdown of the US economy in 2008 also calls
into question the supposed structural superiority of the American model,
while the massive disturbances in financial relations at the same time must
qualify, in particular, the enthusiasm for US financial practices which
inspired the Lisbon agenda.

5.7 BRITAIN AND THE INCLUSION INDICATORS

A simple point should be made about the various indicators of social
exclusion developed in the context of Lisbon. This is that the UK (often
accompanied by Ireland) displays particularly bad performance across
virtually all the measures available (see Table 5.1).

The general picture is that Britain (and Ireland) exhibit inequalities and
levels of social disadvantage similar to those of Spain and Portugal, in
spite of significantly higher levels of income, and that these two countries

Table 5.1   Social indicators for Britain and other EU countries

Indicator	EU-15 average	United Kingdom	Notes
Percentage of population at risk of poverty 2001	15	17	UK level exceeded by Ireland, Spain, Italy, Greece, Portugal
Percentage of children at risk of poverty 2001	19	24	UK level exceeded by Ireland, Italy, Spain, Portugal
Percentage of 65+ population at risk of poverty 2001	19	24	Higher figures only in Ireland, Portugal, Spain, Belgium
Income quintile ratio S_{80}/S_{20} 2001	4.4	4.9	Exceeded by Greece, Spain, Portugal
Gini coefficient 2001	n.a.	31.0	Exceeded by Portugal, Spain, Greece
Percentage of children in jobless households 2003	9.8	17.0	UK highest in EU-15
Long-term unemployment rate 2002	3.0	1.1	UK bettered only by Sweden, Austria, Netherlands, Luxembourg, Denmark
Early school leavers not in education or training (%) 2003	18.1	16.7	Figures higher only in Portugal, Spain, Italy

Source: European Commission (2003c).

therefore represent somewhat retrograde social systems among those of Northern Europe. This pattern occurs in spite of relatively low unemployment rates, which might be thought to be a counteracting influence.

In most discussions of financial reforms, on the other hand, Britain (with Ireland, which was historically a subordinated region of the British economy) is seen as a pioneer – approaching much more closely the US structures and practices which provide the model for the financial integration programmes than do other member states. This is hardly a coincidence – it is the actual functioning of the market mechanisms celebrated as the economic dimension of Lisbon which generates the 'exclusions', that is to say, the inequalities which are recorded in the Lisbon indicators.

It must be added that the New Labour government in Britain made strenuous efforts to square this circle, essentially by major programmes of tax credits aimed at children and low-paid workers. It is perhaps a little

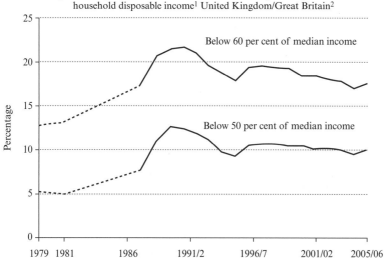

Figure 5.7 Poverty indicators for Britain

Notes:
1 Contemporary household disposable income before deduction of housing costs, using OCED equivalization scale.
2 Data for 1994/5 to 2001/02 for Great Britain only.

Source: Office for National Statistics (UK), *Social Trends*, 2008.

early to judge the success or otherwise of these programmes, but recent data suggest that, together with rising employment, they may have helped to stabilize the percentage of the population falling below the usual EU poverty threshold (60 per cent of median income) (see Figure 5.7).

However, to the extent that wealth becomes a factor of increasing importance in social and economic outcomes, the trend in Britain seems to be adverse (see Table 5.2).

Notice the continued deterioration under New Labour. As wealth inequalities are translated into socio-economic inequalities of all kinds the New Labour tax credit programmes may be running hard to stand still.

5.8   THE MOVE TO A NARROWER AGENDA

Commission President José Manuel Barroso (2005) offered a condensed account of the New Lisbon agenda. Firstly, the general failures of the

Table 5.2   Wealth inequalities in Britain

	Distribution of wealth in UK (%)				
	1976	1986	1991	1996	2001
Most wealthy 1%	21	18	17	20	23
Most wealthy 25%	71	73	71	74	75
Most wealthy 50%	92	90	92	93	95

Source: Office for National Statistics, *Social Trends*, 2003.[5]

first five years were acknowledged in a reasonably frank way. As the Kok report indicated, Europe had, if anything, moved further away from becoming 'the most competitive and dynamic knowledge-based economy in the world' in that it now confronted not only a continuing gap vis-à-vis the US but also the dramatic transformations in India and China. The main problem, however, was in implementation:

> While many of the fundamental conditions are in place for a European renaissance, there has simply not been enough delivery at European and national level. This is not just a question of difficult economic conditions since Lisbon was launched, it also results from a policy agenda which has become overloaded, failing co-ordination and sometimes conflicting priorities (Barroso, 2005, p. 5).

Yet the programme remained valid. 'We need a dynamic economy to fuel our wider social and environmental ambitions'. Failure to resurrect the strategy would involve 'the costs of non-Europe' which 'have been substantiated through a large volume of academic evidence'. (It was added immediately, and very correctly, that 'one can argue with the figures'.) (Barroso, 2005, p. 6).

The rebirth of Lisbon was sought through a sharper focus on central objectives, essentially on jobs and growth, and the strategy was given an alternative name, 'Partnership for Growth and Jobs'. Political obstacles were to be overcome by mobilizing 'support for change'. 'Everyone . . . and at every level must be involved in delivering these reforms' (Barroso, 2005, p.7). Procedures and reporting had to be streamlined. One measure that was taken was to simplify the policy guidelines issued by the Commission. These now cover several years, and the economic policy and employment policy guidelines have been compressed into a single document, although the latter move may only serve to further subordinate employment standards to economic imperatives.

Thus, the core economic and employment objectives were given complete priority. For example, completion of the internal market again moved centre stage. The ambition of the revised social agenda, to use the Open Method of Coordination to promote minimum income systems, although not repudiated, was absent from this document; the 'modernization' of social protection seemed only to signify improved employment incentives and pension schemes which encourage a longer working life. In this way, broader social (and environmental) objectives were in practice subordinated to the traditional economic programmes of the EU, with the reassurance that economic success would permit these wider objectives to be reached. One might question both the assumptions on which this reassurance rested: firstly, the assumption that the proposed economic reforms would indeed lead to more growth and employment; and secondly, the assumption that economic policies of the kind envisaged would be compatible with the values and outcomes required for the European Social Model.

In fact, economic performance in the EU improved a little after the midpoint of the Lisbon strategy in 2005, but it is by no means clear that this was due to the Lisbon measures. The report prepared by Iain Begg (2007) for the European Parliament, although generally sympathetic to the Lisbon agenda in its revised form, finds no link between the Lisbon measures and the limited economic upturn and warns of a serious imbalance among the EU economies, with German employment recovering via increased exports which put pressure on its neighbours.

On the specific issue of finance, however, the long reconsideration of Lisbon does seem to have led to a certain demotion. This can be seen in two fields. The optimism of Lisbon (and of the early FSAP) that the emergence of big European institutional investors would provide a solution to pension problems seems to have been silently abandoned. The key measure now is to extend working life with, as supporting policies, the promotion of both immigration and fertility. This shift has at least the merit of making declared policies somewhat more logical. The 'modernization' of pension systems is still called for, but, to the extent that the ambiguities of EU language can be penetrated, this term seems increasingly to refer to parametric changes to existing systems rather than to a rapid privatization of provision (see Chapters 9 and 13). Of course, it remains the case that serious reductions in public provision would in themselves drive people towards market-based pensions, but the latter are no longer painted in such rosy hues as in the past.

Secondly, there was a similar switch in emphasis as regards risk capital. The Lisbon target of much higher R&D spending (3 per cent of GDP) was repeated, but rather less was said about the organizational forms of risk capital. Instead we have a somewhat ironic reorientation as regards *state aid policy*. At the Stockholm Council, this was still anathema: '*State aid* in the European Union still accounts for more than 1 per cent of GDP. This must be further reduced and the system made more transparent' (European Commission 2000c – presumably the figure given excludes agriculture). Now it became clear that state aid was to have a new and more positive role in support of R&D and innovation, especially in the SMEs. The Barroso document asserted that, 'starting later this year, member states, regional and other public actors will have more scope to support research and innovation, particularly by the EU's small and medium-sized businesses' (2005, p. 9). Revisions to the code of conduct governing macroeconomic policy seem to support this new approach in that they suggest a slight relaxation of budgetary rules to encourage this type of expenditure. Like the implicit move in pension policy, this shift on R&D cannot be faulted on logical grounds, but it testifies to a certain disappointment with the promise of financial reform as such to dynamize the EU economy.

NOTES

1. The term 'social cohesion' suggests an absence of conflict, which may not be compatible with, for example, a strong movement for a fairer distribution of income or wealth. The other term in standard use in the EU, 'social exclusion', is also problematic. Originally, it had a precise meaning in the context of Bismarckian social protection systems based on labour market participation. Someone without an adequate record of such participation could find themselves excluded from the social protection regime. In other contexts, the term seems to be a euphemism for 'disadvantage' or 'poverty'.
2. Subsequent development of the 'flexicurity' theme permits a more precise interpretation of its meaning to the European Commission. On the one hand the 'security' referred to is *employment, not job* security. This is a dubious switch because someone who loses their job and then finds another often suffers substantial reductions in pay and conditions. On the other hand, the broad recognition of problems with the standard 'flexibility' agenda, that is with the multiplication of 'atypical' employment contracts – such as part-time and temporary contracts, 'zero hours' contracts, the use of agency labour, putative 'self-employment' is now used to justify not enhanced protections for the workers concerned but rather a general weakening of standard labour contracts. This kind of reasoning is also being used to support a decisive turn in EU employment policy towards deregulation. For the new official position see the Green Paper on 'Modernising' European Labour Law (European Commission, 2006c). For a critique, see Keune and Jepsen (2007).
3. Most commentators are of the view that this imbalance persists. For example, see Scharpf (1999).
4. It is interesting that O'Mahony and van Ark suggest (2003, p. 11) that the European slowdown is partly related to 'moderation in wage growth ... during the second half of the 1990s' which may have discouraged the rapid substitution of capital equipment for labour. On this issue see also Kleinknecht (1998).
5. Because of problems in data collection, this table has been dropped from subsequent editions of *Social Trends.*

6. The official case for financial integration

Thorsten Block and John Grahl

6.1 INTRODUCTION

This chapter looks at some of the studies of financial integration sponsored by the European Commission. It is argued that most of the claims they put forward on the benefits of financial integration are, to say the least, exaggerated.

The plan of the chapter is as follows: there is firstly a brief characterization of the general position of the Commission on markets and integration; then a look at the viewpoint taken by European leaderships on financial integration in particular; next there is a discussion of market liberalization in general; this discussion is then related to the financial sphere; there is then a critical assessment of three economic studies which make the case for financial market integration. It is not denied that a certain consolidation of European financial systems may be necessary as a response to the ongoing process of financial globalization; this latter argument for integration, however, which is developed throughout this book, depends on market integration being combined with effective measures for social control over the financial sphere. It is concluded that the use of technically sophisticated but in fact quite unrealistic studies to suggest that major economic gains can be achieved without such control amounts to a distortion of democratic debate.

6.2 THE COSTS OF 'NON-EUROPE'

It is well known that, in recent decades, the integration strategy adopted by the leadership of the EU has been strongly biased towards 'market creation' rather than 'market correction' (see Scharpf, 1999). For this reason, EU policies have tended to reinforce neoliberalism, in the sense of a political project which deliberately intensifies certain market pressures in order to block, or even reverse, forms of collective action and state intervention which were seen as threatening by dominant interest groups.

In some respects, however, decision makers in the Commission and the Council of Ministers have been more royalist than the king. Even those who are most committed to the market economy normally recognize that some markets do not exist simply because there is no need for them. The Commission on the other hand tends to regard the absence of any Europe-wide market as being necessarily the consequence of damaging 'barriers' which must be levelled to avoid 'the costs of non-Europe'.

This was the title given to the Cecchini Report, a series of studies commissioned by the EU in the late 1980s and purporting to show that the liberalization strategy launched by the Single European Act would lead to massive economic benefits. These, it is generally acknowledged, never materialized.[1]

However, the almost routine falsification of such claims never holds the Commission back from the next assault on 'non-Europe' or from the extravagant promises which are made to justify it.

6.3   THE GENERAL CASE FOR LIBERALIZATION

The standard argument for trade liberalization is that the removal of barriers or the reduction of tariffs will increase the scope for advantageous exchange: a country which imports more of the commodity concerned will do so because it is cheaper for it to import than to produce at home; a country which exports more will likewise find that the returns from so doing are higher than from using the same commodity at home. This standard case is sometimes referred to as the theory of comparative advantage but in fact it is no different from the usual argument for specialization: the case for free trade is simply the case for market exchange.

This case is subject to the usual caveats on markets. Three important qualifications of the case for free trade are:

- it is subject to the full use of resources; a country which reduces its home production of a product in favour of imports obtains no advantage from so doing unless and until the resources no longer used in that industry are redeployed more effectively;
- there must be no adverse developmental effects, as when specializing in a low productivity industry prevents a country from moving into more advantageous specialisms at a later date, or when a country, by importing a sophisticated product, makes it difficult for domestic firms to acquire expertise in its production;
- adverse distributional effects from trade liberalization must be avoided – an example might be when wealthy consumers benefit

from imported luxury goods while low-income producers suffer losses; to ensure that free trade is advantageous in such a case, the winners from liberalization must compensate the losers.

Many studies of trade liberalization neglect these important qualifications or assume them away. Even when such assumptions are made, however, standard studies usually indicate that the gains from liberalization are small, and this is especially the case in the EU.

There are two reasons for this. The first, which applies very generally, is that in market economies there are usually many substitutes for any given good or service; it may be damaging to suppress market interactions as a whole, but if only a single market is suppressed the impact on welfare is likely to be small. If one can't get apples, one eats pears; if one can't go by train, one takes a bus and so on. Thus GATT studies of substantial tariff reductions rarely showed very large benefits, even when very optimistic assumptions were made.[2]

The second reason relates specifically to the EU. This is already an extremely liberalized economic bloc, far more so than any other trading bloc, and the barriers to free exchange among member states are already very low. In particular, the Single European Act and further Treaties since enshrine the 'four freedoms', the right of all persons, corporations and other organizations legally present in the EU to move goods, services, capital and labour across member state borders. These are effective rights, upheld not simply by the European Court of Justice but also within national judicial systems. If, therefore, barriers between member states prevent a corporation from making money, it has an effective remedy, even against the government of its home country. This unique legal structure has led to a very high degree of integration. In spite of endless complaints from the Commission about 'non-Europe' it is probably already the case that in those areas where cross-border transactions are limited this is because there would not be much advantage in increasing them.

6.4 THE NEW INTERNATIONAL TRADE THEORY

In the last two decades a further rationale for trade liberalization has been developed on the basis of the linked phenomena of imperfect competition and scale economies. The two phenomena are linked because in a competitive industry enterprises can achieve the optimum level of output; where competition is limited, however, and enterprises have significant influence over prices, there may be unexploited economies of scale – countries may be too small to achieve the optimum scale of output.[3]

In a situation characterized by unexploited scale economies and imperfect competition, the gains from free trade may be much larger than in the standard argument because, firstly, trade may increase the level of competition and align prices more closely on costs and, more important, the creation of a larger market may permit the scale of production to increase and thus drive down costs. (Note that the same caveats as to full employment and so on apply as in the standard case.) However, the case becomes much more complex because the way the gains from trade are divided between the countries involved is now much more complex. The existence of monopoly revenues means that countries which specialize in the activities concerned may profit at the expense of their trade partners.[4]

It was this line of reasoning which was used or abused in the Cecchini Report to promise the huge gains mentioned above. The difficulty was that in most of the sectors where big scale economies are to be found, usually manufacturing sectors, the level of European integration was already very high prior to the Single European Act.

6.5   FINANCIAL LIBERALIZATION

Mutatis mutandis, the same kind of argument for free trade applies to the financial sector as to the rest of the economy. The standard case for financial liberalization is that it would lead to a better allocation of capital by inducing flows of capital from countries where interest rates and yields on financial assets are low, to countries where they are high. This kind of reasoning is hardly pertinent to the situation in the EU, however. Individuals and enterprises in EU countries have the legal right to invest in assets or to issue liabilities in any member state they choose; in principle, they have had this right since the Treaty of Rome, 50 years ago. In practice, some member states restricted access to foreign exchange into the 1980s, but these restrictions were removed between 1990 and 1992. There are no pools of excess capital trapped in individual member states nor are there member states suffering capital shortage. Fifteen member states, accounting for well over half EU output and employment, belong to a monetary union within which there are no longer any exchange rate risks attached to international finance.

Of course, just as with trade in goods and services, there may be situations where local solutions are superior to international ones. Some types of risky investment are difficult to assess without local knowledge – this may be the case not only for countries but also for regions, cities and smaller communities. Only the Commission, however, would find anything inefficient as such in the use of local knowledge to make a local investment rather than a cross-border one.[5]

In fact, contemporary financial systems are often marked by a hierarchical structure which combines an integrated, centralized allocation of standardized financial claims (bank deposits, government bonds, the shares of big multinational corporations) with decentralization of many decisions requiring local knowledge, such as investment in small businesses – the branch networks of efficient commercial banks may function in this way, as may also networks of independent local banks.

In any case it is impossible to claim that levelling barriers to capital movement would produce major benefits simply by evening out the supply of and the demand for capital across member states. The official case for financial integration is much more analogous with the 'new international trade theory' – it rests not on allocative efficiency but on competition and technical change.

All the caveats and qualifications to liberalization mentioned above continue to apply but now with a crucial addition – the problem of macroeconomic stability. Much more than the liberalization of exchange of goods and services, capital market liberalization can lead to acute problems in the foreign exchange market and the banking system (see also Chapters 7 and 14).

6.6 COMPETITION, EFFICIENCY AND FINANCIAL TRANSFORMATION

Thus the rationale put forward for the financial integration programmes in the EU has less to do with the allocation of capital than with the transformation of financial systems. The argument is made that regulatory barriers and differences in financial practice have allowed inefficient financial systems to survive. The integration process is seen as transforming the weaker and less efficient financial systems and bringing them up to the standards in those Northern European countries which are regarded as the most advanced.

One objection to this view is that the measures proposed – regulatory harmonization and so on – might simply be too weak to produce the postulated effects. In other sectors – manufacturing for example – there remain very large differences in productivity across member states after more than five decades of integration; it seems doubtful that much more rapid change can be obtained in the financial sector.

A second objection can be derived directly from the new international trade theory. The 'transformation' of the weaker financial systems may take the negative form of penetration by foreign financial enterprises, a centralization of financial activities in the stronger countries and a high level of dependence on external financial markets. In such a case, there might still be some growth of productivity in the domestic financial sector, but this sector would remain small and the main benefits from integration would accrue to the stronger countries.

This is not a hypothetical pattern of events: it is an accurate account of what has already happened in those member states which used to be in the Soviet bloc.[6] Their banking systems have been taken over by West European banks and their security markets seem likely to go the same way and become mere branch offices of the big Western markets. This would represent 'modernization' of a kind and many services might be provided in a more efficient way after the old domestic financial enterprises have been closed, but this kind of dependence will not contribute to economic development, since it confirms the exclusion of the country concerned from the most complex and profitable activities in the financial sector. As will be seen below, there is a considerable body of evidence linking financial *development* to economic development in general. There is no evidence, however, that mere financial *openness* has similar effects – in fact several researchers report the contrary.

6.7 FINANCIAL DEVELOPMENT, FINANCIAL INTEGRATION AND ECONOMIC GROWTH

The academic literature on the finance–growth link has so far mainly focused on the role that financial development, rather than financial integration, plays in the process of economic growth. In this literature, financial instruments, markets and institutions may arise to mitigate the effects of information asymmetries and transaction costs. By ameliorating market frictions, financial arrangements alter agents' incentives and constraints, thus influencing savings rates, investment decisions, technological innovation, and consequently long-run economic growth. In a recent survey of the role of finance in growth Levine (2005) identifies, *inter alia* (i) the generation of *ex ante* information about possible investments and the allocation of capital; (ii) the monitoring of investments and the reinforcement of corporate governance after funds have been provided; and (iii) the facilitation of the trading, diversification, and management of risk as important functions performed by the financial system and as mechanisms whereby finance can promote general economic development.[7]

Now, a key part of the Commission's case for the FSAP and other financial integration strategies is to suggest that financial *integration* and financial *development* are the same thing. The Commission's Economic and Financial Committee (EFC) in its report on financial integration nicely summarized the argument (European Commission, 2002, p. 10):

'Financial integration = a more efficient financial market'.

More precisely, increased competition among financial service providers will compress the margins levied by intermediaries and thus lead to a lower cost of capital for borrowers and higher rates of return for investors. A larger internal market allows financial service providers to exploit economies of scale and scope, and increases the liquidity and depth of capital markets which also drives down the cost of capital. A more efficient financial market thus translates directly into better economic performance.

A pervasive weakness in the studies to which the Commission appeals is that they all tend to make this very dubious assumption that integration and development are identical. In so doing they beg one of the key questions raised by the financial integration strategy.

6.8   IRRATIONAL EXUBERANCE AND THE LISBON STRATEGY

The financial transformations discussed so far relate to differences in the efficiency of Europe's own financial systems, to the gaps in financial development between North-West Europe on the one hand and Southern, Central and Eastern Europe on the other. In this context the main problems with the integration strategy are firstly that it may take very much longer to change systems than policy-makers suggest and secondly that integration may not lead to widespread financial development but to an increased dependency of the weaker systems on the stronger ones.

However, by the late 1990s a very different concept of financial transformation had come to dominate the thinking of EU leaderships – a concept based on the US financial system. The rapid growth of the US during the 1990s was perceived as resulting from its successful transition to a 'knowledge-based economy'.[8] The Lisbon Strategy, adopted in 2000, was essentially an attempt to replicate US success, based on the adoption of certain features of the US economic model, notably its financial system.

What was at stake now was no longer the level of financial development in Europe; by most indicators the financial systems of France, Germany and the US are roughly equivalent in their levels of development. Rather, European leaderships decided to promote a change in the nature of the financial system and to enhance the role of stock markets. It was thought that stock markets in the US were making a massive contribution to economic growth and to the knowledge-based economy, especially in the support of innovative new enterprises in high technology sectors.

It will be remembered that the year 2000 saw the peak of a stock market bubble, well described in the expression of Alan Greenspan, head of the US central bank, as due to 'irrational exuberance'.[9] There can be little doubt that EU leaderships were affected by the same euphoria.

Now, there has been a great deal of discussion and debate in recent years about different types of financial system, but it can be emphasized that comparisons are extremely difficult. A Commission economist ends his survey of the issue with a simple statement: 'Evidence that market-based systems are constantly superior to bank-based financial systems does not exist'. (Thiel, 2001, p. 45).

One of the many difficulties in making such an assessment is to decide on the appropriate criteria. Several commentators (for example, Dore, 2000) suggest that the financial systems traditionally found in continental Europe, with powerful inside investors and a heavy reliance on bank credit, may achieve a very precise and efficient matching of the interests of investors to those of the users of funds. On the other hand, this micro advantage may be associated with weakness on a larger scale – it is often thought that the immense security markets which have developed on an international scale are more effective in bringing about major reallocations of capital from region to region or sector to sector (Grahl, 2001).

There are also of course very important social questions, explored throughout this book, relating to these patterns of financial development.

None of these points implies that the attempt to build big integrated security markets in Europe was an irrational policy. The general shift from financial systems based on bank credit and powerful 'inside' investors to systems making much more use of security markets may prove to be irreversible. In that case, a failure to build big, open, liquid security markets in Europe would simply drive every investor and every issuer on the planet into the North American markets. This outcome might deprive Europe of influence over financial developments and of highly remunerative financial business.

Thus it is most certainly not claimed here that the financial integration strategy was irrational. But it is asserted that the benefits of integration were grossly exaggerated and that the potential problems of financial transformation, in both the social and the economic sphere, were understated.

This assertion can be supported by an examination of some of the most influential studies used by the Commission to justify its financial strategy.

6.9 THE LONDON ECONOMICS STUDY

The procedure adopted by London Economics (2002), in a study commissioned by the European Commission, is as follows:

- A relationship is estimated linking trading costs in equity markets to the size of the markets (measured by *capitalization*, that is the value, at prevailing prices, of the shares issued by corporations which are traded on the given market). As one would expect, trading costs are lower in bigger markets.
- This relationship is used to estimate the reduction in trading costs which would come about with complete integration, that is if all the equity markets in Europe were replaced by a single, aggregated, market.
- A relationship is then estimated between trading costs and the cost of capital to corporations – the latter being measured by the returns received by shareholders. It is found that the cost of capital is lower when trading costs are lower; this is to be expected because many investors prefer to hold securities which are easy to trade and they are therefore willing to accept slightly lower returns on more tradable shares.
- This second relationship is used to estimate how much the cost of capital would fall in consequence of the total integration postulated above.
- This reduction in capital costs is plugged into a complex macroeconomic model, to see how much investment, and consequently production, would rise in the event of full financial integration.

The methods used in this study are open to the following objections:

- The capitalization data used to predict future trading costs in Europe come from the period 2000–01, that is the high point of the stock market bubble. If later figures were used the effect would be much less.
- An implausible degree of integration is predicted which would mean a downward convergence in dealing costs for shares all over Europe. It is not clear how competition among different stock markets could be combined with such a high degree of integration.

- In any case not all share trading is necessarily desirable – over-liquid markets can lead to volatility; if corporations then focus on short-run changes in their share price, their strategies may become distorted.
- The link between the postulated fall in capital costs and investment may be exaggerated. The London Economics model involves an unusually large response of investment to a small reduction in the cost of capital; in other models this parameter is much lower.

The London Economics study, like the Cecchini studies in the past, illustrates one of the pitfalls of buying research on the market, which is that the buyers may get what they want. The existence of independent research institutes, committed to the critical study of public policy, may be threatened by the commercialization of research.

6.10   THE GYLLENHAMMAR REPORT

A report to the European Financial Services Round Table (Heinemann and Jopp, 2002, known as the Gyllenhammar Report) contains another extravagant estimate of the benefits of financial integration. This is derived quite uncritically from a previous study by De Gregorio (1999) which found a large effect of financial integration on growth.

However, De Gregorio's study does not estimate a direct relationship between financial *integration* and economic growth – in fact he fails to find any such relationship. Like many other researchers he does find a positive association between financial *development* and growth and he also finds an association between financial *openness* and financial development and he then puts these two associations together, even though he has no empirical justification for so doing, to deduce a relationship between openness and growth.[10]

The Gyllenhammar Report then makes an estimate of the growth impact of financial integration in Europe. This is done by assuming that an arbitrary (but supposedly 'plausible') increase in integration will take place and then using De Gregorio's estimates of the impact on financial development and then onto economic growth. This gives the enormous figure of a €42 billion annual bonus for the EU economy. A further difficulty of this procedure is that the De Gregorio study included many developing countries, where financial development, starting from a very primitive financial system, is likely to have a big impact. There is no reason to believe that the further expansion of Europe's much more developed systems would lead to outcomes on the same scale.[11]

6.11   A SECTORAL STUDY

Another study, commissioned by the EU and frequently used to support current strategies for financial integration, is that of Giannetti et al. (2002). This uses an approach pioneered by Rajan and Zingales (1998) who explored the effect of financial development on growth, sector by sector, on the basis that companies in different sectors had different needs for external finance. In the Giannetti study it is again the case that the empirical estimates refer to the relationship between financial *development* and economic growth, not to financial integration as such.

To simulate the effect of financial *integration*, these authors *assume* that it translates into development. They have identified the US as having the most developed financial system; they *assume* that EU integration measures suffice to raise all member countries to the same level. On this basis, impressive gains result – the growth rate in many countries increases by over 1 per cent per year!

Gains of this magnitude arise as countries with less developed financial systems are assumed to converge rapidly on the highest standards. The authors recognize that in practice integration may well take the form of penetration of foreign banks and financial corporations and that this would skew the distribution of benefits towards the financial sectors of the stronger economies. However, they argue that such a development would still be desirable because households and non-financial companies in the weaker economies would still gain from better and cheaper financial services. This proposition, however, is simply stated, not demonstrated.

A second simulation attempts to measure the potential impact of legal and regulatory harmonization on economic growth. For this, numerical indicators have to be found for such intangibles as the 'rule of law' or 'creditor rights'. In fact the most important such variable turns out to be 'accounting standards'. These are specified as: Sweden, 84; UK, 78; Finland, 77; France, 69; Netherlands, 64; Spain, 64; Germany, 62; Denmark, 62; Italy, 62; Belgium 61; Greece, 55; Austria 54; Portugal, 36; Ireland and Luxembourg, no data. It is doubtful whether such numbers signify anything more than a typical vote in the Eurovision song contest; they are obviously exposed to many challenges. Accounting standards in the US are put at 71, that is as superior to those in France, Germany and the Netherlands, but in the wake of recent revelations in the US that figure may seem a little high.

In any case an association is found between these indicators and financial development and this permits a simulation in which 'integration' is assumed to raise these institutional factors to the highest level in Europe (thus, in the case of accounting standards, to Sweden's 84). The benefits from so doing are again massive – but this is only to say that a completely successful modernization of Europe's financial systems would produce large benefits.[12] So also would, for example, a convergence of industrial productivity throughout the EU on the existing levels in France and Germany. What remains to be shown is how specific policy moves, such as those in the Financial Services Action Plan (FSAP), will have concrete effects on the functioning of European financial systems.

6.12   CONCLUSION

The economic studies used by the Commission to support its case for financial integration are very sophisticated in technical terms – they deploy state-of-the-art modelling techniques and statistical procedures. But their strength in technical terms does not in itself justify their extremely optimistic conclusions which rest, in every case, on heroic assumptions – for example, when it is assumed, without any empirical evidence at all, that the limited harmonization and liberalization measures in the FSAP could miraculously bring about full financial integration and a level of financial efficiency equal to that in Germany or the US.[13]

Indeed, the very technical sophistication of these studies becomes dangerous in such circumstances, since it may seem to endow their conclusions with a scientific status they do not, in fact, possess. Public discussion and scrutiny of EU policies are not furthered, but are in fact distorted, by such procedures.

The European Commission frequently resorts to the purchase of technically sophisticated but basically tendentious studies from commercial research organizations who seem to know very well what their paymaster wants to hear. Over time, this practice can only serve to further undermine public confidence in, and public respect for, the European project.

NOTES

1. This was officially recognized. The Cecchini Report in 1988 had projected that the 'single market' would add 4.5 per cent to the GDP of the 12-nation EU, adding 1.8 million jobs. Four years later, the EU released a report on the impact of the single market and it estimated that the GDP of the now 15-nation EU was 1.1 to 1.5 per cent higher than it would have been without the removal of market barriers and that a net 300 000 to 900 000 new jobs were created (European Commission, 1996). These much more modest claims themselves are open to question. The Cecchini Report itself is a massive multi-volume work; its key arguments can be found in Emerson et al. (1988).
2. This argument, although it is based on the strength of the market economy, is often embarrassing to neoliberals, who want to argue that every single control or regulation is a costly impairment of free exchange.

3. For the new international trade theory see Krugman and Obstfeld (2007).
4. Thus, this kind of situation may justify industrial policies designed to change a country's pattern of specialization.
5. Even in a perfectly integrated market local financial services might still play an important role in providing finance to small-scale borrowers. Small business lending involves the production of soft information that cannot be easily collected by loan officers external to the local community. This type of information is also not easily shared with outsiders. This implies that in specific segments of the credit market integration would be less relevant (Guiso et al., 2002).
6. Thus by 2004, foreign banks accounted for almost all banking assets in the ex-Soviet transition economies of the EU: 92 per cent in the Czech Republic; 98 per cent in Estonia; 77 per cent in Hungary; 58 per cent in Latvia; 93 per cent in Lithuania; 68 per cent in Poland; and 97 per cent in Slovakia. See Allen, et al. (2005).
7. These studies adopt an orthodox view of finance, as facilitating transactions over time. From the heterodox position discussed in the introduction, the role of finance may be even more important in that financial mechanisms are needed to handle the huge imbalances and disequilibria which arise in the course of economic development.
8. EU leaders persistently refuse to acknowledge that the higher employment levels and more rapid economic growth achieved in the US are due to a more expansionary macroeconomic regime.
9. Greenspan had actually used this term some years earlier, but had then retreated somewhat from his critical view of behaviour in the stock market.
10. In fact, the correlations found by De Gregorio suggest the following: that financial development is associated with economic growth, *to the extent that it is indigenous financial development and not simply induced by the entry of foreign financial corporations following capital market liberalization.*
11. The report makes no use of the study by Neimke et al. (2002) even though this study was specially commissioned for it. Neimke actually defines integration as the penetration of foreign banks and suggests that countries where penetration is high display more rapid gains in economic efficiency. The statistical basis of these claims is weak, however, because there are only 13 observations, and the estimated relationship is a poor fit to the data. It is probably because of these statistical weaknesses that Gyllenhammar does not cite the study.
12. Sweden also has a highly concentrated banking sector and very concentrated family-based ownership structure of firms. This fact obviously influences the role of good information availability for the functioning of the stock market in comparison, for example, with the United States.
13. Thus the Commission (2003a) is hardly justified in characterizing such assumptions as 'conservative'.

7. International finance and instability in the EU

Jan Toporowski

7.1 INTRODUCTION

Within the financial sector itself, financial instability tends to be defined in a very narrow way. The mainstream view of the International Monetary Fund, central banks and commercial financial institutions associates financial instability with excessive volatility in asset prices, unstable equilibrium in an otherwise stable general equilibrium, or the discontinuities that may arise in the financial system with the failure of a significant bank or financial institution. Instability outside the financial system (failure of non-financial firms, or volatility in markets for current production) tends therefore to be treated as a kind of Schumpeterian 'creative destruction', a natural condition in which markets are continually adapting to changes in competition, tastes, or technology, changes which are best left for markets to deal with.

This narrowing of the scope, if not the effects, of financial instability reflects in part the regulatory capture of central banking institutions by commercial banking and financial interests. As central banks have been made increasingly independent of governments they have been more and more exposed to pressures from the financial corporations they are supposed to be regulating. Commercial banking and financial institutions have an interest in ensuring that the financial authorities do not allow those institutions to become subject to the 'natural' disciplines that markets impose on non-financial firms.

More critical economists (for example, Minsky, 2004; Wolfson, 1994) have traditionally taken a much broader view that financial crises are features of a particular kind of capitalism that emerges with the development of the financial system. In their view financial crises cannot just be reduced either to 'natural' market adjustments, or to an incorrect equilibrium in the financial markets. What they regard as financial crisis arises out of firms' inability to settle financial liabilities. Such crises therefore arise out of the normal functioning of the financial system, rather than from any abnormality in that system.

The question of the scope of financial instability is more than just a conceptual one. A policy focus on maintaining the functioning and liquidity of existing banks and financial institutions has a tendency to maintain existing structures of indebtedness in the real economy. A situation of over-indebtedness in the real economy is then left to work itself out through a process of debt deflation (reduced corporate expenditure in order to pay off excessive debts) (Lavoie and Godley, 2001; see also section 7.4 below). In effect, an apparent stability of the financial system is purchased at the cost of prolonged financial crisis in the rest of the economy.

A key example is given by the crisis of Third World debt which broke out in 1982 with the near bankruptcy of Mexico and then other developing countries. The big Western banks which had lent money to Third World governments were rescued by the intervention of the IMF and the central banks of their home countries. But the overhang of unpayable debt remained and held back many developing countries for the next two decades.

7.2 ATTEMPTS TO MODEL EXPOSURE TO FINANCIAL CRISIS

Following the emerging market crises of the 1990s, and the banking crises that have affected European economies during and since that decade, issues of financial stability have come to the fore in policy-making and institutional design. The International Monetary Fund now requires member governments to provide Financial Sector Assessment Programmes showing how they have subjected models of their financial systems to stress tests, in order to reveal those systems' vulnerability to financial crisis. This modelling is also encouraged for individual banks and financial institutions by bank regulators under the Basel Accord. However, there are several problems with this kind of examination.

The first is a policy and methodological problem that arises with modelling disasters such as financial crises. Financial crises appear in models as discontinuities in certain variables or the impact of identifiable shocks when such shocks exceed certain thresholds. Commercial banks or central banks modelling instability in this way are thereby able to determine a range of balance sheet positions that may make those firms, or the financial system as a whole, vulnerable to financial instability. If such balance sheet positions are avoided, then policy measures to deal with financial instability (for example, a lender of last resort facility) become redundant. This is not a valid conclusion because financial instability may still arise from 'shocks' not previously identified. The recent 'sub-prime' crisis illustrates the point exactly – the commercial banks and other financial corporations involved had not understood that mortgage assets would be subject to the drastic losses which were actually experienced.

Moreover, financial institutions using this type of model may come to believe that they are invulnerable to financial instability. As the 'sub-prime' crisis again shows, this may have moral hazard consequences in making firms, central banks and financial institutions more careless about transactions which their models tell them are unlikely to cause financial instability.

Further difficulties arise from the application of economically simplistic (although mathematically sophisticated) techniques to the assessment of financial risks. The models used to assess sub-prime mortgages assumed that default risks on these mortgages were largely independent; this may have been a valid assumption for relatively prosperous periods with high levels of employment; at such times the main factors leading to default may be individual misfortunes of various kinds. When the economic cycle turns down, however, the pressures leading to defaults cease to be individual and become system-wide – general reductions in employment and incomes result in widespread financial distress and waves of mortgage defaults and the disturbances in the model suddenly become highly interdependent. (See Mandelbrot and Hudson, 2004, for a mathematician's critique of these procedures.)

To the extent that the majority of financial institutions adopt very similar methods of assessing risk, they are likely to make very similar investment decisions and this itself will increase the vulnerability of the financial system as a whole by first bidding up the price of the assets concerned and then multiplying the problems of a price collapse.

The role of credit rating agencies in the risk assessment process also raises serious problems. The use of these agencies by banks and other financial corporations is increasing but there are serious conflicts of interest as the agencies are paid by the corporations which are raising money and may therefore be tempted to downplay the risks to the creditors. By the time the boom in sub-prime mortgages reached its peak these agencies were making half of their profits by rating mortgage-backed securities. They managed somehow to rate some 80 to 90 per cent of the securities backed by sub-prime mortgages as 'triple A', that is, as being as safe as the securities issued by governments in wealthy and stable countries. (For a detailed account of this process see IMF, 2008a, p. 59).

In view of the many problems arising from these risk assessment procedures, it is worrying that recent reforms of international banking regulation, based on the Basel II accords within the Bank for International Settlements, increase the reliance of the financial system as a whole on the relatively free use of these procedures by the big banks.

7.3   INSTABILITY AND FINANCIAL INTEGRATION

Problems of financial instability are exacerbated by international financial integration, whether in regions, such as Europe, or globally, for example through the increasing financial integration of key regional financial centres around the US financial system. Among the most often-cited arguments advanced in favour of financial integration is the scope that it affords for money capital ('savings') to move to where the returns from productive use of that money capital are highest, thereby concentrating finance on sectors and regions of the economy where it is most needed. This has been foremost among the arguments for European financial integration since its earliest discussions in the 1980s. However, a corollary of financial integration is that it also propagates crises and financial instability much more widely than when financial markets are small and weakly integrated (Rybczynski, 1997). The nation states making up the European Union each have institutions such as inter-bank markets and supervisory regimes that are intended to deal with financial instability, including lender of last resort facilities. But the growth of cross-border exposures (or commitments to make payments in another country) that occurs with financial integration makes it much more difficult to deal with instability when it arises. There is an obvious reluctance on the part of national central banks to take responsibility for foreign payments. Such exposures also make a national economy much more vulnerable to shocks that are outside the control of national policy and national institutions for stabilizing the economy.

Furthermore, whereas in fragmented markets the geographic and economic location of a crisis are easy to identify, in integrated markets it becomes necessary to untangle often complex systems of financial liabilities to identify liquidity bottlenecks that may be causing a credit crunch (Wojnilower, 1980). The allocation of capital in such a way that private or social returns are maximized may be an *eventual* outcome of financial integration. But by increasing the scope for capital mobility, raising the amounts of capital turned over in markets, and concentrating and centralizing that capital through mergers and takeovers, the process of financial integration expands the mechanisms for propagating crises in various markets and inflates the costs of coping with crises well before that optimal allocation of capital is ever achieved (if at all). The prospect of ultimate financial efficiency then serves to justify the reality of financial crisis and instability that is the characteristic of a market economy increasingly dominated by financial obligations and banking relations.

Within Europe, two processes of financial integration have been identified. The first and oldest is the process of integrating Europe's financial

and banking markets with markets outside Europe, principally those in
the United States but also what came later to be described as 'emerging
markets' in the developing countries and Eastern Europe. These exposed
European banks and markets to financial crises and instability outside
Europe, and outside the formal, nationally-regulated markets. The second
process is the process of integrating European financial markets, and
integrating the monetary system around the euro. This integration process
is described in two chapters preceding this one (Chapters 3 and 4). The
effect of such internal integration is to create endogenous mechanisms for
propagating instability in Europe.

We can distinguish two very different approaches to financial instability
within the institutions of the European Union. Within the Commission,
the Directorate-General for the Internal Market has direct responsibility
for the integration of member states' financial systems. We have the tes-
timony of no less a figure than Alexandre Lamfalussy, chair of the 'Wise
Men' brought in to reorganize the Financial Services Action Programme
(FSAP) when it seemed about to fail, that the Internal Market DG's atti-
tude to possible instability problems was strikingly insouciant. The Wise
Men had argued that

> greater efficiency does not necessarily go hand in hand with enhanced stability
> ... Increased integration of securities markets entails more interconnection
> between financial intermediaries on a cross-border basis, increasing their expo-
> sure to common shocks ... there is an urgent need to strengthen cooperation at
> the European level between financial market regulators and the institutions in
> charge of micro and macro prudential regulation. (cited in Lamfalussy, 2003)

This was not the sort of thing the promoters of the FSAP wanted
to hear: 'It was politely but firmly suggested that we drop the subject'.
(Lamfalussy, 2003).

As opposed to the Commission's single-minded drive for market integration at any price, central banks, including the European Central Bank,
have to be concerned about financial instability since monetary policy is
implemented through the banks and financial markets.

7.4   CAUSES OF FINANCIAL CRISIS

Participants in financial markets are inclined to be collectively self-
regarding and, where financial developments offer business opportunities,
prone to histrionic pronouncements as a way of generating business, or
inducing support from the financial authorities. This has effects on the

way in which financial crises are perceived. Not all incidents that are called crises actually involve the kind of macroeconomic disturbances that cause significant unemployment and falling living standards. Equally, because of the general impact of difficulties in financial intermediation, failure in the financial sector is frequently avoided at the cost of more widespread economic failure outside the financial sector. Typically, banks and financial institutions respond to higher perceptions of risk by restricting new lending, or charging higher margins over central bank interest rates. This reduces the liquidity of small and medium-sized non-financial businesses which find themselves unexpectedly unable to roll over debts, or having to pay prohibitive interest in order to avoid default. Reduced liquidity then has adverse effects on employment. In the EU countries, most private sector employment is in small and medium-sized enterprises. Larger companies, even though they can maintain their liquidity through hedging and diversified sources of financing, tend to respond to reduced liquidity in markets by reducing their productive capital investments. This in turn causes a reduction in industrial production and employment.

Financial crisis, in a broad sense, therefore occurs when firms are unable to settle financial obligations. Isolated incidents of such failure are common, every-day occurrences. Financial crisis occurs more generally when crisis transmission mechanisms drive companies into failure in a systematic way. A widely cited account of these mechanisms is the debt deflation theory of Irving Fisher (Fisher, 1933). Fisher supposed that some incident would cause firms to take a more pessimistic view of investment prospects. They would then reduce their investment. The effect of this would be to reduce economic activity and prices. A fall in prices would cause the real value of debts (denominated in money terms) to rise. This rising indebtedness would cause a further fall in investment, in turn reducing economic activity and prices. In this way, the more firms try to pay off their excessive debts, the more the real value of those debts rises. The modern example of such a financial crisis is the case of Japan in the 1990s, and during the early years of the twenty-first century.

However, in recent times, with the exception of Japan in the 1990s, prices have not shown any tendency to fall. Indeed, the fixing of inflation targets by central banks at a positive figure (2 per cent in the case of the European Central Bank) rather than zero, as would be implied by absolute price stability, is intended to avoid precisely that kind of debt deflation.

The more common mechanism for transmitting financial crisis is through the fringe of companies that are net borrowers in the economy, that is, their financial liabilities exceed the value of the assets that they can dispose of (cf. Stockhammer, 2004). This fringe of companies is found in virtually any economy, below the stratum of the largest companies that can maintain and adjust their liquidity through the sales of assets or the issue of financial liabilities, as well as through the accumulation of retained profits. The fringe of net borrowing companies are therefore found among small and medium-sized enterprises, in between large business, and the smallest businesses and households that are excluded from the credit system. Unable to adjust their liquidity freely through the financial markets, they are correspondingly more dependent on sales revenue for the operating profits out of which they service their debts (Steindl, 1990, chapters 2 and 24).

The dynamic effects of monetary policy and business cycles are obtained through expanding the activity and borrowing of this fringe of net borrowers. The mechanism of financial crisis comes into play when the companies in that fringe find that their sales revenues are insufficient to service their financial liabilities, and the companies collapse (Kalecki, 1968). The large companies, however, that can maintain their liquidity, also undertake the vast bulk of fixed capital investment that still largely determines the progress of the business cycle. In this situation, any given effect on economic growth can only be obtained by a correspondingly larger impact of monetary policy or the business cycle on the fringe of net borrowers.

In Europe, the common instrument for regulating the business cycle is the rate of interest. An increase in interest rates affects the rate of economic growth and inflation through its impact upon the fringe of net borrowing companies in the economy. Because such an increase has minimal impact upon larger companies, which can easily adjust their liquidity through various financial markets, a disproportionately larger number of companies in the fringe of net borrowers must be driven into financial crisis (inability to service their financial liabilities) for that increase in interest rates to have a given effect on economic growth and inflation. In this way, financial crisis becomes the transmission mechanism of restrictive monetary policy and the business cycle. Expansionary monetary policy in turn has a much weaker effect on companies in this sector because they have much more limited ability, because of inadequate financial reserves, to operate their balance sheets to raise borrowing.

It follows that the absorption of smaller companies into larger companies, the concentration and centralization of capital, increases the preponderance of companies in the economy that are not subject to this financial crisis mechanism. As a result, companies remaining in that fringe of net borrowers of the economy have to suffer even greater crisis in order to obtain a given effect of restrictive monetary policy. European financial integration, by expanding the facilities to enable firms to combine (or be taken over) and move out of the fringe of net borrowers, in this way makes counter-cyclical policy less effective, or requires more financial crisis for the policy to be effective.

7.5 THE EVOLUTION OF FINANCIAL INSTABILITY

The next sections examine episodes of instability generated from outside Europe, and affecting Europe because of its global financial integration.

In these sections, financial crisis is considered from the narrower perspective that is common among banking and financial institutions, their regulators, and central banks (see section 7.1 above). These financial crises may be divided into currency, banking and stock market crises.

Currency crises usually involve a sudden and substantial devaluation of a currency in the foreign exchange markets. This will hit badly businesses engaged in foreign trade with foreign currency liabilities, whose value will increase in proportion to the devaluation. Large companies in financially advanced countries can usually avoid the consequences of such crises by diversifying their sources of finance and hedging them with foreign currency income or deposits. However, small and medium-sized companies and companies in less financially advanced countries cannot do this, and may find themselves facing large increases in foreign currency costs.

Banking crises involve the failure of banks, usually because they have tied up too much of their assets in illiquid loans, which they may be unable to realize when depositors wish to withdraw their deposits or, more commonly today, if they are unable to obtain cash in inter-bank markets. Loans frequently become illiquid after periods of speculative activity in real estate markets, for example, when property collateral, which previously sold for a good price, cannot be sold for cash except at a price that will not cover outstanding debts against the property.

Finally, stock market crises are usually characterized by a fall in liquidity in securities markets, with the result that securities cannot be sold in them except at very low prices. Like banking crises, stock market crises make it difficult for firms to roll over or refinance existing financial obligations. Speculative booms in stock markets tend to encourage companies to take speculative positions in them, very often under the guise of merger and takeover activity. A stock market crisis may then leave companies with serious refinancing problems.

The US has the largest financial markets in the world and plays a key role in the functioning of the international financial system. As a consequence of this, European markets tend to respond to developments in US markets, (for example, the collapse of stock market activity after 2000), while US markets tend to be rather less responsive to developments in markets outside the US. Emerging markets apart from Eastern Europe have not yet had much impact on the developed European markets.

As defined above, financial crises are more than just a collapse of one or more financial institutions, in the usual Schumpeterian 'creative destruction' in which financial firms replace each other in continually functioning markets. Here, however, crisis is defined in the way commonly accepted by central banks, namely any incident that may make activity in one or more financial markets break down. Because the operation of financial markets is threatened, financial crises require the intervention of the financial and monetary authorities to ensure that markets can continue to function.

7.6   POST-BRETTON WOODS CRISES IN EUROPE

In fact, the 1950s and 1960s, characterized by strong government intervention, stable exchange rates and restrictions on international capital flows, were a time of exceptional financial stability. The break-up of the Bretton Woods agreement, however, signalled the beginning of a new era, marked by frequent financial crises (see Table 7.1). Just because they wished to preserve macroeconomic stability, the first reaction of European governments to the collapse of the Bretton Woods system of fixed exchange rates was to attempt to recreate within Europe a fixed exchange rate zone. The reason for this was the relative openness of the smaller and medium-sized European economies, which meant that exchange rate instability had a much more immediate effect on prices and costs than such instability has in larger, relatively more closed economies such as that of the United States. However, attempts to re-establish fixed exchange rates were structurally flawed because of the particular status of the West German economy, which had a very big balance of payments surplus and a long record of low inflation rates. Because Deutschmarks were seen by wealth-holders around the world as exceptionally stable, any doubts about the value of the dollar or concern about inflation in the US resulted in huge purchases of Deutschmarks. Since other European currencies (except for the Swiss Franc) were not affected in the same way, it was difficult for them to hold their own currencies stable against the Deutschmark during such episodes. When they did so their currencies appreciated so much against the dollar that they suffered from a loss of competitiveness. Thus periodic realignments of European exchange rates during the 1970s and 1980s usually followed a depreciation of the US dollar against the Deutschmark.

The 'snake', a voluntary agreement between governments to hold exchange rates stable against the Deutschmark, failed repeatedly during the 1970s. A more formal system of exchange rate stabilization, the

Table 7.1   Financial crises in the US and Europe since 1971

Year	Currency	Banking	Stock market
1971	US Sweden Netherlands Belgium Spain Denmark		
1974	Germany UK	UK US	
1976	UK Italy Spain Portugal Denmark Ireland		
1977	Spain		
1979	US		
1982	UK Belgium Spain France		
1983	Portugal		
1984	US		
1985	US		
1986	Finland Ireland		
1987	Denmark Norway	US, UK, Ireland Norway	
1990	Italy		
1991	Finland Sweden	Finland Sweden	Finland
1992	UK, Sweden, Italy, Spain Denmark Ireland		

Table 7.1   (continued)

Year	Currency	Banking	Stock market
1993	Finland, France Denmark		
1994	France	France	
1995	Italy, Spain		
1998	Russia	Russia	Russia, US
2000			US, UK, Greece
2001	Turkey		Turkey
2003			Germany (Neue Markt)
2007–8		US, UK, Germany	

Sources: Various, and author's own researches.

European Monetary System (EMS), kept going until 1992, when it too succumbed to major speculation against the exchange rate bands. Significantly, the collapse of the (EMS) Exchange Rate Mechanism, formally disguised as a widening of exchange rate bands, in 1992–3 followed the elimination of controls on foreign capital movements between member states in Europe. Germany had eliminated foreign exchange controls in 1982, France in 1989. (Portugal would do so in 1993, and Greece in 1994). The Maastricht Treaty in 1991 explicitly envisaged the abolition of foreign exchange controls as part of the movement to European Monetary Union. It was in any case increasingly difficult, and in many cases impossible, to enforce foreign exchange controls. This regulatory failure, and the exposure, increased by international merger and acquisition activity, of industrial and commercial firms to adverse exchange rate fluctuations, gave a major impetus to the movement for European Monetary Union during the 1990s. But the financial crises of the 1980s were also political crises that exposed the inability of governments to regulate the activity of financial markets. An equally strong impetus was given towards allowing banks and financial institutions to be constrained by market forces alone, with central banks only acting to maintain their liquidity and their ability to maintain payments.

The elimination at the start of the 1990s of capital controls on international portfolio and banking capital movements in Europe, had three consequences. The first was a large increase in mergers and acquisitions between companies in individual European countries, encouraged by governments that wanted to have 'national champions' to ensure that businesses did not leave their territory with the advent of the single European capital market. The rapid increase in the balance sheets of banks and financial institutions required expanded cash flows, lending and stock issuance to maintain the liquidity and profits of the larger financial service conglomerates now operating. However, the rapid expansion of credit is usually incompatible with the maintenance of credit quality. It is significant that the major financial crises of the 1990s in Europe occurred in Scandinavia, a region arguably already over-banked before the 1990s, and with heavily cartelized banking markets. The introduction of competition into financial markets that had previously concentrated on routine financial business gave rise to a boom in lending into speculative financial and property markets. The priority given to exchange rate stability meant that central banks were unable to use interest rates to moderate the growth of credit going into speculation. More importantly, when asset values fell in Sweden and Finland in 1992, and in France in 1993, central banks were unable to relieve financial pressure by lowering interest rates, because the Bundesbank was raising interest rates to head off post-unification inflation in Germany. The result was a major financial crisis that pushed Finland into a recession from which, even ten years later, the country had barely recovered. Gross Domestic Product in France fell in 1994 for the first time since the Second World War (Boyer et al., 2004).

The second effect of the elimination of controls on international capital movements was the increased exposure of European securities markets to US stock market movements. This arises out of two structural features of international securities trading. The first is the listing of securities issued by multinational companies in various financial centres where capital is raised. A fall in prices in the New York or Chicago markets tends to cause arbitrage trades in the form of a sell-off in European markets of securities listed on both sides of the Atlantic, and buying of those securities in US markets. The sell-off in the relatively less liquid European markets depresses prices in Europe on a much bigger scale than buying in the more liquid US markets raises prices there. In 2000, securities prices in the New York Stock Exchange fell by 40 per cent. In Frankfurt, they fell by 70 per cent. The second structural feature is the domination of international financial markets by large US institutional investors, whose response to financial crises inside and outside the US is to switch into US government securities, often selling assets abroad that may not have been affected by crisis at all. These two structural features mean that far from making international markets more liquid and more efficient (in the sense of ensuring similar and stable prices everywhere), international financial integration causes greater instability outside the US in response to financial crisis anywhere in the world. In other words, international financial integration is asymmetrical. This too adds a further rationale for developing strong and stable financial markets in Europe.

The third effect of deregulating cross-border capital transactions was a boom in cross-border mergers and acquisitions in banking and financial services. This increased the difficulties of financial regulation, which remains still largely at a national level. International regulations, such as Brussels Directives and the Basel Accord, still require national regulators to enforce them. In turn national regulators do not have the same access to information on bank activities abroad that they have on banks' activities within their national jurisdiction. This remains a major cause of concern among financial authorities

As a consequence of the growing integration of securities markets, the sell-off in the US stock market after the bursting of the 'new economy' bubble in 2000 caused a major failure in markets for smaller company stocks in Europe after 2000. Europe also remains vulnerable to financial instability in the emerging markets to its East, where Western European banking groups have expanded their interests in recent years and where, as a response to the financial weakness of institutions in new member countries of the European Union in Eastern Europe, many of these institutions have been transferred to the ownership of Western European banks. Since these new member countries do not yet belong to the European Monetary Union, Western European banks may have significant exposures in countries subject to currency risk. The most recent Russian and Turkish crises have no particular common features – the Russian collapse was caused by the default on its obligations of the Russian government, while the Turkish debacle is much more like an emerging market crisis, precipitated by private sector default. However, the extension of Western European banks' activities into their 'natural' foreign markets to the East, brings exposure to less stable economies in that region.

7.7   THE PURSUIT OF FINANCIAL STABILITY

The official response to such problems is not encouraging. As was pointed out at the beginning of this chapter, the greater emphasis on 'financial stability' following the crises of the 1990s, is generally interpreted by the International Monetary Fund, the European Central Bank and financial regulators as avoiding failure of banks and financial institutions. In the first place, all of the members of the European System of Central Banks, together with the European Central Bank hope to assure this by monitoring financial stability. This means evaluating financial markets' vulnerability to events that might cause a breakdown in those markets. All the central banks in Europe simulate 'scenarios' of possible 'shocks' to their systems that might cause such a breakdown. This is done with a view to having market procedures that will be less vulnerable. One problem with simulations like this is that the choice of 'shocks' to which models of the financial system are treated, is heavily dependent on what shocks financial and central bank analysts believe are probable. The probability of shocks, in turn, is usually measured by their incidence in recent years. The result is that central banks and financial institutions have a strong tendency to prepare themselves for the last crisis that happened, rather than anticipating the next crisis. The real difficulty is that effective anticipation of crisis requires a more nuanced understanding of financial market processes than is afforded by time series analysis and probabilistic calculations (see also 7.2 above).

A second line of defence is the possibility of lending to banks or financial institutions that might be affected by such a crisis. This was done on a very big scale in the 'sub-prime' crisis in both Europe and the US in spite of the danger ('moral hazard') of indemnifying banks and other financial corporations against the consequences of their own mistakes. A third defence is the possibility of a reduction in interest rates, to ease interest costs for affected institutions. However, this last is a relatively blunt instrument: interest rates are now set centrally for the whole of the eurozone, and reducing interest rates throughout the monetary union may be a rather inefficient and undiscriminating way of assisting a specific market in a particular country. In any case, interest rates are supposed to be used to keep general price inflation under control, rather than to ease difficulties in financial markets. This implies that in a period when output prices were rising, the ECB might be extremely reluctant to cut interest rates to limit instability.

More recently the Bank for International Settlements has criticized this system of regulation. Low inflation in its view has resulted in low interest rates, and these in turn tend to encourage speculation in financial asset and real estate markets. The result is that the main threat to financial stability, in the view of BIS economists, comes not so much from a payments failure, as from the possibility of an asset bubble. The way to prevent this, in their view, is to raise interest rates (BIS, 2005). The problem with this analysis is not so much its criticism of the narrow perception of financial crisis that is considered possible in central bank policy circles. It is more that its suggested policy of higher interest rates is a very blunt instrument. Where it does stop asset bubbles, it tends to do so catastrophically, as happened in Japan in 1991, bringing on the wider economic crisis that the higher interest rates were supposed to prevent.

In the BIS and the Bundesbank the remaining monetarists (that is, those economists who retain a belief in some version of the quantity theory of money) who have not gone over to the 'New Consensus on Monetary Policy' that favours regulation by interest rates alone, have sought to give a contemporary significance to measures of the money supply or credit stock by arguing that excessive monetary expansion is responsible for financial bubbles and instability. Central bankers are increasingly arguing that asset bubbles are caused by excessive liquidity in the financial markets. For example, booming financial markets in the United States are supposed to be caused by excessive East Asian purchases of US financial assets ('The great thrift shift', *The Economist*, 24 September 2005). At the very least, changes in broad measures of the money supply (M3) are supposed to provide 'information' about likely asset bubbles in the future. But the policy implication is vague and impractical as long as the rate of interest is the key instrument of monetary policy. It is not possible, for example, to keep interest rates low if, say, consumer prices show signs of falling, while restricting the money supply to prevent an asset bubble. Moreover, the evidence provided for using the money supply to regulate asset prices tends to be highly selective. It ignores the Japanese experience of 'quantitative easing' since the 1990s: the flooding of Japanese financial markets with liquidity had minimal impact, until recently, upon Japanese financial asset prices.

No one doubts the ability of central banks to ensure the integrity and functioning of banking and financial markets. This was demonstrated during the 1930s when, with the exception of the Kreditanstalt collapse in 1931, banks and financial institutions did not fail in Europe as they did in the United States. The much more important issue is the part played by firms in the rest of the economy in assuring such stability. If market mechanisms play a more central role in policing prudent lending, this means that banks will be even more inclined to pass financial risks onto their industrial, commercial and household customers. Withdrawal of lending facilities at times of economic slow-down means that the stability of the financial system is purchased at the cost of instability in the real economy. There is a strong case for preventing this transmission of financial crisis by having effective public sector institutions operating in financial systems, and effective counter-cyclical policies in general.

7.8   THE CREDIT TURMOIL IN 2007–08

As this chapter was prepared for publication, a major financial crisis (the 'sub-prime mortgage crisis') had impaired credit markets in both North

America and Europe. In the background were both a long period of low interest rates which led financial corporations to adopt increasingly risky, leveraged (that is, debt-financed) positions and a chronic external payments deficit of the US economy which made for increasingly reckless attempts to induce capital flows into the US.

The main source of losses were securities backed by 'sub-prime' mortgages, that is mortgage loans to customers with chequered credit records. In some cases these customers seem to have been bound to default since they were almost without financial resources. Only a period of artificially low repayments induced them to take out loans and they ceased to service their debts as soon as normal interest payments and principal repayments were required.

These risky loans were securitized and repackaged into apparently less risky Collateralized Debt Obligations, that is, bonds on which payments are the principal and interest paid on the mortgage loans packaged up into such bonds. The buying of such bonds by banks and financial institutions throughout the world has made a localized US banking problem into a global financial crisis. The unknown extent of banks' holding of such loans made banks reluctant to lend to each other, causing a breakdown in European and North American inter-bank money markets. Banks have responded to this by raising interest rate margins to discourage new borrowing and to persuade existing borrowers to repay their loans by refinancing existing loans with other banks.

In several respects the resulting crisis calls key aspects of the current financial system into question. Firstly, the major banks of Western countries have been in the centre of these developments: these banks are the most important actors in the global financial system (Plihon et al., 2006); it is now clear that ill-judged strategies have resulted in very big losses for them and that the regulatory systems designed to avoid such disruption have completely failed. Secondly, the credit markets most affected are those linked to real estate in the US – these are the biggest credit markets in the world, central to the investment strategies of virtually all financial corporations. Thirdly, the disturbance to credit markets has been so severe as to impair the ability of central banks to guide the movement of short-run interest rates – the key instrument of monetary policy. In the US, in the eurozone and in Britain, actual credit market interest rates have been well above (and have sometimes failed to respond to) the rates promulgated by the authorities.

In this situation, the major central banks have, quite correctly, been very active, prepared to lend on an immense scale and to relax their usual credit conditions concerning collateral and counterparties, in order to avoid disruption of the banking system or the security markets.

However, as has been argued throughout this chapter, in itself this central bank intervention may tend to damage the non-financial economy by preventing the elimination or the devaluation of the debt structures built up in the previous sub-prime bubble and by requiring households and non-financial businesses to contribute to the restoration of the financial sector. Thus the major banks are stabilizing their balance sheets by increasing their margins and restricting their lending. Even if this strategy successfully refinances the banks themselves, this may be at the cost of a prolonged slowdown in productive activity and of a rise in unemployment, especially in the sector of small and medium-sized enterprises that are dependent upon bank borrowing.

8. The transformation of corporate Europe

Photis Lysandrou

8.1 INTRODUCTION

A distinguishing trait of the European corporate governance model is its balanced reconciliation of differing, and potentially conflicting, stakeholder priorities. This feature, however, has been disappearing fast as the leading European corporations declare their commitment to shareholder value, a position usually associated with American or British firms. Nevertheless, there is still evidence of continuity with past traditions. Although many continental European companies now claim to give overriding priority to shareholders' interests, most of them still try to meet a broader range of social and economic objectives than is generally the case in the US or Britain. And although some of the distinctive institutions giving employees a say in the running of European corporations are under pressure to change, these institutions are still in place. In short, what seems to exist in continental Europe at present is a peculiar version of a capital market-oriented model of corporate governance that is at once more socially focused and more democratic than its Anglo-Saxon counterpart.

One body of opinion holds that this situation is unsustainable on the grounds that adoption of any one part of the Anglo-Saxon model must inevitably lead to the adoption of the model as a whole.[1] Thus to accept that shareholders' interests take precedence over those of other stakeholders is to accept that corporations must be run in a more authoritarian style, that corporate managers must be given generous stock options, that free play must be given to hostile takeovers and so on. This construction of the Anglo-Saxon model as an inviolable totality explains why some commentators argue that the current European fascination with shareholder value principles has to be reversed if the social and democratic aspects of European corporate practice are to be protected.[2] This same construction explains why there are other commentators on the opposite end of the political spectrum who maintain that European corporations must abandon or at least dilute their commitment to corporate democracy and social responsibility if they are to successfully embrace 'shareholder value' principles and thereby remain globally competitive.[3]

There is another body of opinion that views the current position in Europe as perfectly viable and thus sustainable in the long run on the grounds that the re-ordering of corporate priorities made necessary by the expansion and integration of the global financial markets need not entail a complete overhaul of existing European institutions. Some authors talk of an emerging 'hybrid' model of European corporate governance, one that fuses elements of the traditionally contrasted 'stakeholder' and 'shareholder' models.[4] Other authors talk of an 'enlightened' or 'negotiated' version of a shareholder model in Europe.[5] The language may differ, but the common underlying idea is that it is possible for European corporations to combine a much higher priority for shareholder interests with continued commitment to a broad range of social and democratic objectives and to the institutions and procedures necessary to the realization of these objectives.

This chapter seeks to add weight to this latter position. The argument divides as follows. Section 2 identifies the major driving forces behind the emergence of the shareholder paradigm in the US and its subsequent spread in continental Europe. Section 3 discusses the major changes to European corporate practice that are necessary to accommodate this paradigm. Section 4 discusses the changes that are not required for such an accommodation to be made. Section 5 explains why the current social and democratic features of European corporate governance are entirely compatible with the re-ordering of corporate priorities in line with shareholder value. Section 6 gives some conclusions.

8.2   SHAREHOLDER VALUE

To understand the reasons behind the ongoing consolidation of the shareholder value model of corporate governance in continental Europe it is first necessary to look at the reasons for its ascendancy in the US. That ascendancy dates from the 1980s, which was also the time when pension funds and other institutional investors became the dominant force in the US equity markets. This close correlation between the emergence of shareholder value and the rise of the institutional investors can be explained as follows:

(i)   *Changes in US household savings patterns.* As households have been made to take more responsibility for retirement arrangements they have had to take a keener interest in the returns on their assets, a fact which helps to explain the shift in the composition of household assets away from bank deposits towards capital market securities including equities. At the same time households have had to manage the higher risks associated with a yield-enhancing savings strategy, a fact which helps to explain the strong trend away from direct equity holdings towards institutional asset management.

(ii) *Changes in the structure of the US asset management industry*. Faced with the rising demands on their traditional role, namely to exploit advantages of size and expertise to generate higher returns subject to a given level of risk than is possible for the average individual investor, institutional investors have had to radically alter their organizational and control structures to accommodate these demands while containing the costs of that accommodation. The most striking feature of this reorganization is the separation between 'core' and 'satellite' investment strategies (core portfolios simply attempt to replicate a broad market index, while satellite portfolios concentrate on a sub-section of the market and are managed according to a particular investment style) coupled with a further separation between 'passive' and 'active' strategies (passive portfolios stay very close to their benchmarks while active portfolios accept limited departures from their benchmarks). The huge growth of institutional investors' funds has meant that they cannot continue to operate purely discretionary investment policies – to a greater or lesser extent they must try to follow general market trends.

(iii) *The use of shareholder value as a portfolio management tool*. The process of selecting the appropriate corporate securities for inclusion in tightly specified institutional portfolios can be a time-consuming and potentially error-strewn process if portfolio managers are forced to rely on firms' own criteria for weighing the costs of, and evaluating the returns on, investments. By contrast, the process is rendered more simple and efficient if portfolio managers have at their disposal a common benchmark for measuring underlying company performance. The shareholder value paradigm, in so far as it embodies a view of how the costs and profitability of investments are measured which is oriented towards the capital market rather than the corporation, provides just such a benchmark.[6] A further point is that since the general return–risk profile of a given portfolio depends to a considerable extent on the characteristics of the individual securities comprising it, and since these characteristics depend crucially on how corporations are managed and their cash distribution policy is determined, it follows that portfolio managers struggling to stay close to their benchmarks cannot afford to be indifferent to these issues. To safeguard the integrity of the portfolio in question, institutional investors demand from corporate managers a firm guarantee of consistency in behaviour. A declaration of commitment to shareholder value provides just such a guarantee.

(iv) *Equity market pressure on US corporations.* As US institutional investors began to deploy portfolios to the same core-satellite patterns, they began to use the same shareholder value metrics for judging the quality of securities to be included in portfolios; and as the users of these metrics became the majority holders of equity, and responsible for the majority of equity trading volume, the metrics themselves came to be generalized as market standards. This explains why the constraints on firms as suppliers of equity increasingly resemble the constraints on them as suppliers of goods. Providing they rest content with a private client base for their equity, managers can still independently set the terms for the distribution of cash to shareholders, and for other actions that potentially impact on their equity, just as they can continue to set their own production standards providing they maintain private markets for their goods. However, just as firms have to abide by competitively set production standards when choosing to participate in the broader market, so also must they comply with shareholder-oriented governance standards when seeking access to the broader equity market on advantageous terms.

There have certainly been cyclical factors at work also – the very high interest rates of the 1980s made debt finance very expensive and this encouraged firms to attach greater importance to shareholders. However, the main factors were long-term rather than cyclical.

Allowing for differences in style and tempo, the same pattern of development is currently unfolding in continental Europe as has unfolded in the US:

(i)   with the tightening of constraints on government finances, increasing numbers of households are having to take greater responsibility for their welfare, and, as a result, households are increasingly looking towards the capital markets for better returns on their savings while also seeking to contain the risks of this savings strategy by relying on the intermediary role of professional asset managers;[7]

(ii) faced with this expansion in the demand for their services, asset management firms are increasingly relying on a rule-based approach to portfolio management to contain the costs of accommodating that expanding demand;

(iii) as in the US, so also in continental Europe, fund managers charged with running portfolios to pre-determined constraints need to use shareholder value metrics in their stock selection and trading decisions to keep within these constraints;

(iv) as in the US case, all large European corporations are under increasing pressure to give priority to shareholder value maximization. A further factor in the European situation has been demand for shares by US fund managers seeking to diversify their portfolios on an international basis.

In elaborating on each of these claims, we begin with the question of the equity markets. The development of the European equity markets has until recently lagged far behind those in the US due to a combination of supply and demand side factors. On the supply side, the relatively high cost of equity, due to the fragmented and illiquid nature of the European financial markets, deterred all but the very largest corporations from issuing publicly tradable stock. However, the fall in the cost of capital made possible by the gradual integration of the European capital markets culminating with EMU has encouraged larger numbers of European firms to place greater reliance on equity funding. On the demand side, the prevalence of unfunded government and corporate pension systems was an important contributory factor serving to keep national equity markets small and illiquid. However, this is now changing as the restructuring of these systems is leading to an increased demand for equity. Rising levels of income and savings are increasing demand for the products of the institutional investors; many governments have encouraged this trend by seeking to transfer some of the responsibility for pension provision from the state to the household; in the context of demographic pressures and constraints on government budgets, the quality of public provision has frequently been reduced and this has led higher-income groups to make increasing use of market provision. In parallel with this, while unfunded company pension schemes are still the norm in many European countries, an increasing number of corporations are seeking to shift to fully funded schemes in order to avoid the negative impact on their credit ratings of book-reserve pension liabilities (now transparent with the shift to market value accounting).

As in the case of the equity markets, the growth of the role of institutional investors in continental Europe has lagged behind that in the US or the UK, a fact which is in large part due to the more conservative, risk-averse saving habits of European households. However, increasing disappointment with the falling real rates of return on traditional bank savings, which reflect the low inflation environment of the late 1990s and the advent of EMU, has resulted in more savings being diverted into higher yielding investment fund instruments. European commercial banks continue to be larger than the investment institutions, essentially because they still retain a substantial loyal customer base. However, the reduced interest rate margins on their traditional lending business – a reflection as much of the increasingly competitive environment of EMU as of its low inflation environment – has forced them to significantly expand their asset management activities to maintain profitability. Thus to obtain a more accurate picture of the size and importance of the European asset management industry one has to include the institutional investment role of 'universal' banks alongside pension funds, mutual funds and insurance companies.

As in the US, so in Europe, the deployment of shareholder value as a performance metric and control tool has less to do with resolving asymmetric information and incentive problems than with overcoming the difficulties of portfolio construction and maintenance. If the European situation is to be differentiated in any way, it is that in Europe shareholder value has *even less* to do with agency problems and *even more* to do with those of portfolio management. That the difficulties surrounding stock selection and portfolio construction are of an even greater dimension in Europe became readily apparent with the advent of the euro. Prior to the introduction of the euro, European institutional investment funds exhibited a strong home bias, with other European country securities occupying separate and marginal roles in portfolios; in other words, diversification according to country (or currency) dominated diversification according to sector. With the establishment of a single currency, and with the continued lifting of the various legal and political constraints on institutional equity holdings, portfolio diversification across euro-member country securities is based solely on sector. However, the very removal of the currency and legal impediments to the diversification of institutional portfolios served to throw into bold relief the more severe obstacles created by the different procedures and conventions for the evaluation of profitability and of the returns on equity. A key motivation behind the promotion of shareholder value as a performance metric is that only with the substitution of a single, capital-market-based view of corporate profitability for the different national- and firm-specific views can institutional investors be in a position to make speedy and efficient comparisons of individual securities against their peer groups on a Europe-wide basis.

Slightly more problematic is the question of whether European-based institutional investors need to use the shareholder value framework not only to measure companies' performance but also to guarantee their consistency and thus that of the reward–risk characteristics of their securities. At first glance it may appear that this particular use of shareholder value as a means of keeping a given portfolio close to its market benchmark is not as important in Europe as in the US because of the comparatively small scale of indexing: approximately 10 per cent of European institutionally managed equity funds are currently in index-linked portfolios, compared to 35 per cent in the US. This observation, that the overwhelming bulk of funds are in actively managed portfolios, might be taken to imply that portfolio managers have huge scope for discretion which in turn ought to imply that they can afford to give company managers equal scope for discretionary behaviour. These implications are in fact wrong because 'active' portfolio management cannot be simply identified with 'discretionary' portfolio management. All portfolios that form part of a core-satellite structure are subject to investment mandate constraints to one degree or another, from which it follows that it is not the 'passive'/'active' ratio so much as the core-satellite/non core-satellite ratio that one must look at in order to judge the importance of shareholder value as a performance maintenance tool. In this respect, the situation in continental Europe is more akin to that in the US: core-satellite portfolios account for approximately 80 per cent of institutionally managed funds in the US compared to approximately 65 per cent in Europe.[8] What this means is that the tiering and narrowing of portfolios is as much a feature of European as of US institutional investment management, from which it follows that here also there is just as great a need to deploy shareholder value in a portfolio protection capacity.[9]

As already stated, the pressure on corporations to increase shareholder value signifies a certain loss of managerial discretion regarding corporate objectives. The large corporations can continue to pursue a range of objectives that meet the needs of various stakeholders, but only to the extent that these are broadly compatible with the shareholder value objective. This constraint on firms' room for manoeuvre explains why the diffusion of shareholder value through continental European corporations is viewed in certain quarters with alarm and is resisted every step of the way. This resistance is understandable, but whether it is correct is another matter. The fundamental question here is whether continental Europe as a whole is in need of deep capital markets. If it were assumed that it can do without such markets – in other words, if it were assumed, on the one hand, that European households can rely exclusively on unfunded public and corporate pension systems, and, on the other hand, that the large corporations can rely exclusively on banks for their external funding needs – then of course it can be claimed that corporations alone should not have to account for their priorities to the capital markets. If, however, it is accepted that continental Europe does need deep capital markets, then acceptance of the shareholder value constraint on corporations must follow as a matter of course. The logic is remorseless. The existence of deep capital markets presupposes mass participation in them on the part of European households as the chief suppliers of finance; such participation in turn presupposes the marketing of standardized products and processes by institutional investors, and finally the ability to market such products presupposes that corporate managers show themselves willing to be monitored and measured against market benchmarks.

To summarize, the continuing diffusion of shareholder value metrics and procedures in continental Europe is a necessary and irreversible development in so far as it is endogenous to the development of the European equity markets. Foreign influences continue to be instrumental in this diffusion, as is the ideology which supplies it with its rhetoric and intellectual gloss. However, the major forces behind the spread of shareholder value in Europe are domestic and economic in nature. As the equity markets and the role of institutional investors expand in scale in continental Europe, this expansion is bound to mean intensified pressure on corporate managers to demonstrate commitment to shareholder value. Continental Europeans can continue to differ from their Anglo-Saxon counterparts as regards their range of objectives, but have to move towards the Anglo-Saxon model in according a higher priority to capital market constraints in general and shareholder interests in particular. As institutional investors come to dominate the European equity markets, the commitment to shareholder value becomes a condition for corporate participation in those markets. And as the appeal of equity financing rises with the increasing depth and liquidity of the equity markets, developments to which institutional investors make a key contribution, then the large corporations become increasingly willing to meet the conditions for participation.

8.3   WHAT MUST CHANGE IN EUROPEAN CORPORATE GOVERNANCE

The recognition of shareholder priorities in European corporate governance systems does not necessarily imply the convergence of these systems on Anglo-Saxon governance models. To leap to such a conclusion would be to ignore the implications for corporate governance arising out of the expansion of the asset management industry. Chief amongst these is the shift in the focus of shareholders away from the control of corporate managers as such towards the control of corporate equity. This shift in focus makes possible a distinctive European version of the shareholder value model. While some changes to past European practices are necessary to the accommodation of shareholder value principles, other proposed changes are entirely unnecessary. In this section we concentrate on the necessary changes, leaving discussion of the unnecessary changes to the next sections.

Recent crises and scandals have also made it clear that there are serious flaws in the working of market-based corporate finance in the US. Although it seems extremely unlikely that the trend towards greater use of capital markets will be halted, there is a new awareness of the risks and instabilities which are associated with it. This awareness may represent an opportunity for the European economies if they can develop a more effective financial system. It is pointed out in other chapters that European policy-makers have, so far, tended merely to imitate US practice. The argument here is that they can respond to the new role of security markets in ways which provide superior outcomes than are obtained in the US.

The rise of shareholder value in Europe closely correlates with the growth and integration of the European equity markets and with the expansion of the institutional asset management industry. The difficulties facing institutional investors in an age when there are mass demands on their services can be subdivided into those connected with stock assessment and selection (portfolio construction) and those connected with the guarantee of stock quality (portfolio maintenance). Likewise, the necessary changes to current European corporate practice can be looked at in terms of the same division. The changes pertaining to portfolio construction have primarily to do with issues of information, while those pertaining to portfolio maintenance have primarily to do with issues of corporate strategy. The new informational requirements can be broken down into three categories: the transparency and disclosure of information, the comparability of information, and the authenticity of information.

Transparency and Disclosure

An integral feature of the close relationships between stakeholders traditionally characterizing European corporate systems as 'insider' systems was the opacity of these relationships to outsiders. While the expansion in the role of the equity markets and of the institutional investors does not presuppose the elimination of these stakeholder relationships as such, it certainly requires them to become much more transparent. If institutional investors are to be in a position to assess the particular characteristics of securities considered for purchase in the primary or secondary markets, they need prompt access to all information about internal company activities and procedures which might impact on company performance. An example of initiatives to improve the level and quality of information in the primary market is the new Prospectus Directive that standardizes disclosure requirements for issuers.[10] An example of initiatives to improve information provision in the secondary markets is the new Transparency Directive which substantially tightens the periodic information requirements for issuers.[11]

Comparability

It is largely because bank credit constituted the main source of external corporate financing in European stakeholder systems that these systems could traditionally afford to give scope to the heterogeneity of national- and firm-specific (creditor-friendly) accounting systems. However, with the expansion and integration of the European equity markets and the corresponding diversification of institutional portfolios on a European-wide basis, this scope is being narrowed. Investors do not just need company information relevant to the quality of its shares, they need it in a form that facilitates comparison with the shares of other companies. This need is a major force behind the ongoing convergence of European accounting systems towards a single, market-based (shareholder-friendly) system. The recent regulation requiring all listed companies to prepare their consolidated financial statements in accordance with International Accounting Standards by 2005 is representative of this trend.[12]

Authenticity

If investors are to make informed decisions about company securities they need to be sure that the integrity of the information provided by companies is beyond reproach. This presupposes the integrity of the external audit mechanisms. The Commission communication issued in May 2003 (European Union, 2003d), was an initiative specifically targeted at strengthening the external audit function in the EU. This it sought to do by laying down new requirements for auditor independence, external quality assurance and disciplinary sanctioning, and by requiring the use of International Standards on Auditing (ISA) by 2005. The Commission presented its proposal for the new Directive on Statutory Audit in March 2004 and this was enacted by the European Union in 2006 (European Union, 2006).

Turning to the question of institutional portfolio maintenance, we find that the changes in European corporate practice that are necessary here relate primarily to the ability of shareholding institutions to exert influence over corporate managers. The question of information disclosure is not irrelevant here, as adequate and timely access to company information is a precondition for enabling shareholders to intervene in defence of their interests. However, beside these communication channels, the methods by which investors can exert a reverse pressure on managers to maintain the consistency in quality of the equity are also important. These channels, generally referred to as internal corporate governance mechanisms, include the adequate organization of the board of directors and the voting rights attached to ordinary shares.

Board of Directors

As regards the monitoring and control function of the board, the ability to exercise this in a way that fully meets the needs of outside investors depends crucially on the existence of an independent body within the board and on the degree of professionalism of that body. We thus find that, while the present differences between two-tier and one-tier board systems continue to remain in place in Europe, the general trend common to both systems is towards strengthening the size and power of the independent body, and the criteria for appointments to that body. In two-board systems, this takes the form of increasing the power of the supervisory board to appoint, supervise and dismiss members of the management board responsible for the company's day-to-day operation, while in one-tier board systems this takes the form of increasing the power of non-executive directors (for example through separating the positions of board chairman and chief executive officer).

Voting Rights

The ability of institutional investors to make their voice heard on company matters that are likely to affect the quality of the shares in their possession depends ultimately on their right to vote. We accordingly find that it is the institutional investors, notably the American and British investors but also including continental European investors, who are behind the pressures on corporations to ensure that ordinary shares exhibit one vote for each share, and on regulators to amend the law to facilitate voting rights for all shareholders. While we are not yet at the point of full harmonization of European practices and laws around the 'one share, one vote' principle, an increasing number of corporations are eliminating differences in voting rights and the laws guaranteeing equal rights for minority shareholders are being strengthened.

To summarize this section, the changes in European corporate governance necessary to the accommodation of shareholder value principles are those forcing corporations to become transparent and accountable to the equity markets and to the institutional investors who are the dominant players in these markets. Only if it were thought possible to contain or reverse the growth of the equity markets in Europe, and thus that of the fund management industry, would it make sense to resist these changes. If, on the other hand, the growth of the equity markets and of the role of delegated asset management are accepted as necessary developments, then it makes sense to accept many of the demands requiring corporate practices to be more open and accountable to outsiders. The same cannot be said of hostile takeovers and stock options, issues to which we now turn.

8.4   WHERE EUROPEAN GOVERNANCE CAN REMAIN DISTINCT

The rapid diffusion of shareholder value principles across continental Europe has not been matched by a similar spread of hostile takeovers or of the use of stock options. Hostile takeovers are still an extremely rare event. The much publicized takeover of Mannesmann by Vodafone in 2000 proved to be an isolated case, not the harbinger of a general trend. And while the use of stock options in the large European corporations is more conspicuous today than a decade ago, their contribution to total European CEO pay packages remains small by comparison to their contribution to American executive remuneration. This current state of affairs can be interpreted in different ways. One line of argument (which appears to have informed the thinking of the European Commission when trying to push through the 13th Directive on Takeover Bids in 2001) is that hostile takeovers and stock options represent essential constituent parts of the shareholder model of corporate governance but are difficult to introduce into Europe because of the various material and psychological barriers associated with past practices and traditions. In this view, the gradual erosion of these barriers will lead to an acceleration in the use of these capital-market-based instruments. An alternative argument, which is supported here, is that the rapid adoption of shareholder principles together with this marked reluctance to contemplate hostile takeovers and stock options suggests that these instruments are not necessary to the shareholder value paradigm. In expanding on this latter argument, we first look at the question of hostile takeovers.

Hostile Takeovers

The idea behind the role of hostile takeovers in corporate governance is simple: if sufficient numbers of disaffected shareholders sell their shares this will have a detrimental impact on the market valuation of the firm, and the threat of a hostile takeover triggered by the decline in share price can have a sobering effect on the firm's management. The problem with this formulation is that it dates back to a period when small investors were dominant on the US equity markets and when, therefore, the balance of forces was very favourable to corporate managements. With the rise of large investors and the redirection of the corporate governance function towards sustaining the value of equity, the use of these instruments has become problematic. Hostile takeovers are supposed to provide investors with a means of disciplining managers, but any beneficial long-term effects on a company's management are likely to be outweighed by the short-term negative effects on a company's equity arising out of the disruption to the company's production activity. This is no small matter for institutional investors trying to manage portfolios to specified targets and it helps to explain why hostile takeovers remain an extremely small proportion of total US merger and acquisition activity.[13]

Given the more close-knit nature of relationships between the different stakeholders in European corporations, hostile takeovers are likely to have an even more costly and disruptive effect on corporate activities than is the case in Anglo-Saxon countries. It follows that any potential long-term effects of a successful hostile takeover would tend to be outweighed, even more than in the US, by the negative short-term effects on corporate equity and thus on institutional portfolios. Against this backdrop it is difficult to understand the European Commission's attempt to push through legislation that would have deprived corporations of any effective means of defence against hostile takeover bids. That decision may have reflected an uncritical acceptance of neoliberal ideology, but it made no sense at all when judged against the economic conditions existing in Europe. While there is general agreement that the rules governing takeover bids need to be improved and harmonized, a more sensible and balanced approach to achieving this is one that enables boards to take measures to defend the companies' long-term interests. This approach has been incorporated in the national legislation passed by some governments soon after the rejection of the 13th Directive by the European Parliament.

Stock Options

In the wake of the recent corporate scandals in the US, the use of stock options in that country has come under close scrutiny and been subjected to severe criticism. The basic rationale for stock options – the right to buy shares at a future date at a pre-set price – is that by using the capital market to give incentives to, rather than to discipline corporate leaderships, agency problems could be resolved in a more efficient, because less disruptive, manner. In reality, stock options have proved to be either ineffective as incentives, or effective in a negative way that causes more agency problems than are resolved. The tendency on the part of US executives to exercise options well before their expiry date and then sell their shares on the open market; the use of derivatives to hedge positions should the share price fall below the agreed strike price; the writing of contracts for managers that fail to differentiate industry or broad market effects on the share price from managerial performance effects – these are some examples of practices that are entirely inconsistent with the incentivizing thesis. Stock options have a negative effect in so far as they encourage 'earnings management', the manipulation or glossing over of profit and balance sheet figures to provide an optimistic outlook that keeps investors happy even though the true prospects of the firm are more bleak.[14] An additional, more general, point is that stock options have caused widespread resentment in the US as it became clear that the very top managers at the largest corporations have used these instruments to enrich themselves on an enormous scale at the expense of all other stake-holders in firms.[15]

Clearly, to advocate the wider use of stock options in continental Europe is to help promote the same type of problems as outlined above. The only difference would be that, given the circumstances currently prevailing in Europe, these problems would be on an even greater scale than in the US. One notable example concerns the question of over-valuation. Stock options were introduced to deal with the problem of under-valued equity; they are in no way designed to deal with the opposite problem of over-valued equity. On the contrary, as recent experience in the US shows, over-valued equity can lead managers whose compensation packages are tied to the share price to engage in actions that, while aimed at shoring up the price, do long-term damage to the firm and thus ultimately to the quality of its equity.[16] In continental Europe, where the equity markets are not yet as deep and liquid as those in the US, although the presence of large institutional investors is just as dominant, the problem of overvalued equity – particularly in regard to the large cap securities that dominate the European indexes – is likely to be more acute.

To summarize, there is no valid case for European corporate governance to incorporate hostile takeovers and stock options as part of its accommodation of the shareholder value paradigm. The extreme rarity of hostile takeovers in the US is ample proof that they are not essential to this paradigm. The same holds for stock options as is attested by the increasing disenchantment with, and severe criticism of, these instruments in the US. While there is little likelihood that stock options will be discontinued in that country, it is clear that the conditions of their use there are being considerably tightened. In continental Europe, where the practice of stock options has yet to be established on anything like the scale in the US, there is an opportunity for reversing this practice altogether.

8.5   CONTINUITY IN THE EUROPEAN CORPORATION

The changes to European corporate governance that are deemed unnecessary to the accommodation of shareholder value can be sub-divided into two categories: those that involve the introduction of entirely new practices or instruments such as hostile takeovers and stock options that were discussed above, and those that involve the reduction or elimination of existing practices. In regard to the latter, it has been suggested that the new shareholder value orientation of European corporations is not compatible with the continued maintenance of a broad array of social objectives or with the continued institutional provision for employee involvement in key areas of corporate decision making.[17] Both of these propositions are highly questionable.

The 'Social' Dimension of European Corporate Governance

It is true that in contrast to the past when corporations could frequently prioritize employment or social objectives, over equity returns, they must now consistently give a high priority to the latter. However, this proposition does not mean that corporations must give 'sole' priority to the profit objective, that, in other words, they must relinquish or downplay other broader objectives. To give priority only to profits may be in the immediate interests of certain types of investors, but this is the exception rather than the rule. From the standpoint of institutional investors taken as a whole, corporate commitment to social objectives is not only compatible with, but also complementary to, the commitment to shareholder value maximization. Although the quality of the equity included in portfolios is dependent on a consistent dividend policy, it is also dependent on the long-term stability of the firm, a stability which presupposes a degree of sensitivity and commitment not only to the interests of other stakeholders in firms but also to the interests of the wider community and environment within which firms operate. It is a measure of how some institutional investors in the US, most notably the public pension funds, see corporate social objectives as complementary to the more narrow profit targets, that they have been instrumental in pressuring US corporations to show greater commitment to these objectives.[18] It would be ironic if European corporations were to become less socially responsible in their pursuit of shareholder value at the very time that US corporations are moving in the opposite direction towards the European social model of corporate governance.

The 'Democratic' Dimension of European Corporate Governance

Turning to the question of industrial relations in continental Europe, we find that the major institutions that have traditionally given these a relatively more democratic orientation essentially remain intact. Systems of co-determination, although diverse in character and operating in different ways, continue to be deeply rooted in many countries.[19] In 12 out of 28 EU and EEA member states, workers have a mandatory and legally binding right to representation on company boards and to be heard on important management decisions. In contrast to the divisions that were manifest over takeover policy, national government initiatives guaranteeing labour participation in corporate governance have been given support at EU level. The European Works Councils Directive, for example, emphasizes that 'sound corporate governance' requires labour relations in which workers' participation in decision-making is statutorily recognized and guaranteed. Similarly, the European Company Statute allows for staff representatives to be assigned a seat on the board on a cross-border basis.

The fact that the diffusion of shareholder value in Europe has not undermined co-determination, taken in combination with the reverse observation that the persistence of co-determination has not prevented the diffusion of shareholder value, would indicate that there are key areas where the economic interests of workers and institutional investors coincide. Consider this coincidence of interests from the workers' standpoint. There have been many reported cases, among which the Vodafone takeover of Mannesman is most notable, where the works councils have sided with shareholders in their demands for greater transparency and accountability, in their opposition to prestige- or power-building investments, and in their insistence on corporate restructurings which enable a more focused attention on core capabilities. These cases demonstrate an awareness on the part of the works councils that the fight for greater managerial accountability is as important in defending the quality of labour conditions in corporations as it is in defending the quality of corporate equity held by investors. Consider next the coincidence of interests from the investors' standpoint. Their readiness to hold shares in many large European corporations that remain committed to co-determination demonstrates an awareness that giving employees a voice in the running of corporations is to their advantage, both in terms of labour productivity and in terms of managerial accountability. Going by the experience of many of the major European economies, it has been clear that the greater the provision for some form of employee involvement in corporate decision making, the higher the corresponding level of worker commitment and productivity. This evidence has to carry some weight with institutional investors because the quality of the equity they hold principally depends on the performance of corporations in their respective industries, and because corporate performance depends crucially on how skilled, motivated and productive is the labour force. Although it is important not to exaggerate the possibilities, there are certain issues where employees and shareholders may have interests in common as against the interests of top corporate managements. One example is a common interest in transparency – in being fully and promptly informed about a company's situation and about changes in its strategy. Another concerns the remuneration of the executives – both investors and employees want to prevent the resources of the company being wasted by excessive rewards to top managers.

It should not be inferred from the above that the diffusion of shareholder value in continental Europe has had no impact on employment and industrial relations in general. On the contrary, the expansion of the European capital markets and of the role of institutional investors, which form the principal source of pressures on corporations to adopt a shareholder value orientation, are also leading to changes towards what some commentators have termed the 'marketization' of employment relations.[20] The shrinking numbers of 'core' workers in favour of an expanding 'periphery' and the shift away from egalitarian and solidaristic wages towards decentralized wage-setting and variable pay are among the important manifestations of this marketization. The main institutions of industrial relations are also changing in response to this trend. Collective bargaining is increasingly taking on a more defensive role as it moves away from solidaristic wage-setting towards managing the process of decentralization. At the same time, co-determination is taking on a more micro-oriented focus as it becomes less an instrument for promoting class solidarity and more a tool for the co-management of corporate restructuring and organizational change. These changes in the realm of industrial relations mirror, and interlock with, those in the realm of corporate management. Just as managers are under pressure from the capital markets to concentrate their attention on a firm's core operations, so are labour organizations under pressure to concentrate their efforts on defending the interests of a firm's core workforce. And just as labour organizations are today instrumental in the channelling of capital market pressures on managers to be more transparent, accountable and focused, so do managers represent a key conduit through which flow the same pressures on labour organizations to become more firm- and insider-oriented.

To the extent that workers have to be more committed to the competitive strength of individual enterprises, other means must be found to defend the more general interests of workers across the economy. The pressure of social movements based outside the workplace may be one such means but the most important defence of the general interests of employees must necessarily be government regulation of business and employment.

To summarize, the expansion of the European equity markets and the diffusion of shareholder value are key factors in the tightening of the conditions under which the European corporate governance systems function. These systems, however, can retain their social and democratic features if the political pressure for them to do so is sufficiently strong. European corporations must be more transparent in their pursuit of broader social objectives and must demonstrate the compatibility of these objectives with equity return targets. Labour organizations also face new constraints: their ability to continue to exercise voice in the management of corporations is contingent on the subordination of any wider class-oriented aspirations they may have to their more concrete, firm-centred responsibilities. Therefore, wider objectives going beyond the enterprise will have to be pursued by other means.

These propositions should not be conflated with, or used to support, the much stronger and erroneous claim that the growth of the equity markets and shareholder value spell the end of the European social democratic model of corporate governance. On the contrary, the very fact that this model is changing in a way that can accommodate shareholder value while retaining its social and democratic characteristics is putting it in a position where it can seriously challenge, and surpass, its Anglo-Saxon rival.

8.6 CONCLUSION

This chapter has outlined the economic pressures behind the transformation of corporate Europe towards a more shareholder-friendly position. As institutional investors take a more central role in the European capital markets, and these markets take a more central role in corporate financing, so must the leading European corporations, like their counterparts in other parts of the world, recognize the promotion of shareholder value as an unavoidable constraint. This convergence in the ordering of corporate priorities has not been, and does not need to be, accompanied by a convergence in the institutional forms of corporate governance. The European 'stakeholder' model will need to make greater provision for transparency and accountability as it takes on a 'shareholder' orientation, but it will otherwise remain intact. This new hybrid model of corporate governance will endure in continental Europe only partly because of the persistence of historically and culturally conditioned institutions and practices. The more fundamental reason is that the rise of institutional investors as the dominant players on the capital markets has brought with it a substantive shift in the strategic function of corporate governance. If there had been no change in function, and shareholder value remained purely a matter of how investors can get managers to give them back their money, then we would likely see the eventual erosion of the stakeholder character of European firms. But there has been a change in function. Because shareholder interests now centre on the equity contained in institutional portfolios, and because the coalitional nature of European firms can materially contribute to the performance of this new corporate governance function, we are likely to see a retention of many of the social and democratic features that have traditionally distinguished the European corporate governance model.

NOTES

1. See Lane (2003).
2. See Dore (2000); Aglietta and Rebérioux (2005)
3. See Hansmann and Kraakman (2001)
4. See Plihon et al. (2003); Thomsen (2003)
5. See Vitols (2003); Jackson et. al. (2004)
6. Broadly defined, shareholder value is corporate value minus debt, where corporate value is the future stream of cash flow discounted by the weighted average cost of capital. Different consultancy firms market different versions of the shareholder value metric, but what all these versions have in common is their use of capital market measures of return (free cash flow) and risk (beta).
7. For data see Davis and Steil (2001).
8. See BIS (2003); Edhec (2005).
9. 'Tiering' and 'narrowing' refer to the practice of constructing rather narrow, somewhat more specialized, portfolios (for example, specialized in smaller companies, or tracking a particular index) within a general strategy of diversification.
10. Directive 2003/71/EC of the European Parliament and of the Council of 28 January 2003 on the prospectus to be published when securities are offered to the public or admitted to trading and amending Directive 2001/34/EC (European Union, 2003).
11. Directive 2004/09/EC of the European Parliament and of the Council of 15 December 2004 on the harmonization of transparency requirements in relation to information about issuers whose securities are admitted to trading on a regulated market and amending Directive 2001/34 EC (European Union, 2004).
12. Regulation (EC) No 1606/2002 of the European Parliament and of the Council of 19 July on the application of international accounting standards is representative of this trend (European Union, 2002).
13. Goergen et al. write: 'hostile acquisitions tend to be more disruptive than friendly ones. Therefore, even in the US and UK where widely-held firms prevail, hostile takeovers are relatively rarely used. Over the 1990s, 239 hostile takeovers were announced in the US and 158 in the UK. This constitutes 2.3 and 6.5 per cent of the total number of

announced tender offers respectively' (2005, pp. 6–7). See also Becht et al. who present a similar argument (2002, p. 24).
14. See Holstrom and Kaplan (2003).
15. See Krugman (2003b); Brenner (2003b).
16. See Jensen (2005).
17. See Roe (1999); Rebérioux (2003); Aglietta and Rebérioux (2005).
18. Plihon et al. (2003) in particular stress this point. See also Thomsen (2003).
19. See European Trade Union Confederation (2006).
20. See Jackson et al. (2004).

9. Financial markets and social security

John Grahl

9.1 INTRODUCTION

The increasing salience of financial markets and the rapid growth in many countries of institutional investors channelling household savings onto these markets have been pointed out in earlier chapters. These developments form the background to a political project to transfer responsibility for important welfare functions from the state to the market. The two most important examples are probably health care and retirement pensions. In both cases, throughout Europe, provision today is very largely a public function. But there is a strong drive to limit or reduce public responsibility both for health care and for pensions, and to make households, using private insurance companies and privately managed pension funds, take over a large part of the responsibility. The argument for this kind of change is one aspect of a general assault on public services and social security which tries to call many public goods and social services into question and to privatize broad areas of the public sector.

The present chapter concentrates on the pensions issue. It makes a critical assessment of the moves towards market-based provision in the European Union and of the arguments on which these moves are based. It is suggested that these arguments fail in three key respects: firstly, they are conceptually incoherent in that they do not address the resource issues involved; secondly, they fail to recognize the efficiency of public provision and the inefficiency of most private provision in the field of pensions; thirdly, they promote changes which must aggravate social inequalities and divert resources away from those pensioners most in need.

9.2 THE CASE FOR MARKET PENSIONS

A very significant document in the present debate was a report from the World Bank (1994), which has been very influential in policy debates. The argument was that ageing populations would make the present reliance of most Western countries on public 'pay-as-you-go' (PAYGO) systems unsustainable. The ratio of inactive pensioners to the employed population whose contributions provided their pensions was going to deteriorate. The recommended solution was to move responsibility away from the state towards the market: funded pensions, based on the marketable assets accumulated by households through the institutional investors, would compensate for the predicted inadequacy of public provision in the future.

The entire argument rests on a massive *petitio principii*: that the accumulation of marketable financial claims will produce resources which cannot be mobilized through existing public PAYGO pension schemes. As has been frequently pointed out, a financial claim (on the state, on an enterprise or, usually via a financial intermediary, on households) and a public pension entitlement are two logically equivalent devices for transferring current output to the holder of the claim: neither of them as such generates the output in question.

The proponents of pension privatization thus have to suggest that, in some way, the accumulation of claims in private pension funds will promote the availability of real resources from which tomorrow's more numerous pensions can be paid. Two arguments are made to support such a suggestion, both equally specious.

Firstly, it is argued that the current savings made today by people contributing to funded pensions will raise the rate of investment and thus render the economy more productive in the future. In fact it is impossible to establish any positive relationship between the role of private funded pensions and the level of savings in an economy. Two countries which depend to a very great extent on market-based pensions, Britain and the US, have notoriously low, sometimes negative, rates of household savings (together with serious problems of indebtedness for many households) while in Germany, for example, where pensions are still largely provided through a public PAYGO scheme, household savings are very high – indeed in recent years perhaps too high in that private consumption expenditures have been so low as to restrict employment in the domestic economy.

Of course, the management of savings and investment is a key concern of macroeconomic policy and it may at times be important to stimulate household savings (indeed it would be desirable to do so in Britain to limit the importation of consumer goods and to contain problems of over-indebtedness for low-income consumers). However, there is no evidence whatsoever that the promotion of market-based pensions acts as such a stimulus. In fact, the tax breaks used to encourage people to take out such schemes, although they are very expensive and a serious burden on public budgets, seem to have the principal effect of merely diverting the savings stream of high-income households from one channel to another.

The second argument from 'demographic crisis' to the need for market-based pensions simply depends on the notion that there are clear limits to public spending on pensions. It is not clear what these limits would be: no evidence exists that higher social security contributions to cover higher numbers of pensioners would be a disincentive either to employment or to savings. From the point of view of the neoliberal project there is, or should be, a maximum level of public spending which it is imperative not to transgress. In reality it is normal, when the proportion of older people in the population rises, to increase the proportion of GDP which goes to older people.[1]

9.3   DEMOGRAPHIC CRISIS AND MORAL PANIC

It has been pointed out that an increase in the proportion of older people in the population raises a question of resources, not a question of financial techniques. But this resource question has been grossly exaggerated. Between the present and 2050, the time horizon in many studies of population ageing, there is enormous scope firstly for a big reduction in unemployment, which would substantially improve the balance between contributions and payments in public systems, and for economic development, which would provide additional income out of which the increased needs of an older population could be met.

According to EU data, on present policies public pension expenditure will increase by more than 5 per cent of GDP between now and 2050 in the following countries: Belgium (5.1 per cent) the Czech Republic (5.6 per cent), Cyprus (12.1 per cent), Luxembourg (7.4 per cent), Hungary (9.9 per cent), the Netherlands (7.6 per cent), Portugal (9.7 per cent), Spain (7.1 per cent), and Slovenia (8.3 per cent) (see Table 9.1).

In the cases of Cyprus and Spain, actual levels of expenditure are well below the EU average and most of what will be taking place is simply a movement towards European norms. Luxembourg has such a small and wealthy population that there cannot be any reason for concern. In the Netherlands, the public sector provides a universal flat rate pension at some 70 per cent of the minimum wage (a pension based on years of residence rather than employment). This is a very successful strategy against poverty in old age and there is a political will to maintain the scheme even though its costs will rise with demographic change. On the other hand, the Netherlands already has bigger private pension funds than any country in Europe except Switzerland (in 2001, pension fund assets amounted to 105

Table 9.1   Predicted pension expenditure as a percentage of GDP

Country	Public pensions, gross as % of GDP								Change 2004–30	Change 2030–50	Change 2004–50
	2004	2010	2015	2020	2025	2030	2040	2050			
BE	10.4	10.4	11.0	12.1	13.4	14.7	15.7	15.5	4.3	0.8	5.1
CZ	8.5	8.2	8.2	8.4	8.9	9.6	12.2	14.0	1.1	4.5	5.6
DK	9.5	10.1	10.8	11.3	12.0	12.8	13.5	12.8	3.3	0.0	3.3
DE	11.4	10.5	10.5	11.0	11.6	12.3	12.8	13.1	0.9	0.8	1.7
EE	6.7	6.8	6.0	5.4	5.1	4.7	4.4	4.2	−1.9	−0.5	−2.5
GR											
ES	8.6	8.9	8.8	9.3	10.4	11.8	15.2	15.7	3.3	3.9	7.1
FR	12.8	12.9	13.2	13.7	14.0	14.3	15.0	14.8	1.5	0.5	2.0
IE	4.7	5.2	5.9	6.5	7.2	7.9	9.3	11.1	3.1	3.2	6.4
IT	14.2	14.0	13.8	14.0	14.4	15.0	15.9	14.7	0.8	−0.4	0.4
CY	6.9	8.0	8.8	9.9	10.8	12.2	15.0	19.8	5.3	7.6	12.9
LV	6.8	4.9	4.6	4.9	5.3	5.6	5.9	5.6	−1.2	−0.1	−1.2
LT	6.7	6.6	6.6	7.0	7.6	7.9	8.2	8.6	1.2	0.7	1.8
LU	10.0	9.8	10.9	11.9	13.7	15.0	17.0	17.4	5.0	2.4	7.4
HU	10.4	11.1	11.6	12.5	13.0	13.5	16.0	17.1	3.1	3.7	6.7
MT	7.4	8.8	9.8	10.2	10.0	9.1	7.9	7.0	1.7	2.1	−0.4
NL	7.7	7.6	8.3	9.0	9.7	10.7	11.7	11.2	2.9	0.6	3.5
AT	13.4	12.8	12.7	12.8	13.5	14.0	13.47	12.2	0.6	−1.7	−1.2
PL	13.9	11.3	9.8	9.7	9.5	9.2	8.6	8.0	−4.7	−1.2	−5.9
PT	11.1	11.9	12.6	14.1	15.0	16.0	18.8	20.8	4.9	4.8	9.7
SI	11.0	11.1	11.6	12.3	13.3	14.4	16.8	18.3	3.4	3.9	7.3
SK	7.2	6.7	6.6	7.0	7.3	7.7	8.2	9.0	0.5	1.3	1.8
FI	10.7	11.2	12.0	12.9	13.5	14.0	13.8	13.7	3.3	−0.3	3.1
SE	10.6	10.1	10.3	10.4	10.7	11.1	11.6	11.2	0.4	0.2	0.6
UK	6.6	6.6	6.7	6.9	7.3	7.9	8.4	8.6	1.3	0.7	2.0
EU-15[1]	10.6	10.4	10.5	10.8	11.4	12.1	12.9	12.9	1.5	0.8	2.3
EU-10	10.9	9.8	9.2	9.5	9.7	9.8	10.6	11.1	−1.0	1.3	0.3
EU-12[1]	11.5	11.3	11.4	11.8	12.5	13.2	14.2	14.1	1.6	0.9	2.6
EU-25[1]	10.6	10.3	10.4	10.7	11.3	11.9	12.8	12.8	1.3	0.8	2.2

Note: [1] Excluding Greece.

Source: European Commission (2006b).

per cent of GDP in the Netherlands as against 66 per cent in the UK and 63 per cent in the US, according to OECD 2005b, p. 24) and so it is difficult to see what a further development of market-based funded pensions could contribute. Portugal does seem to be one case where ageing will give rise to tight constraints. The Portuguese situation is marked by very high degrees of inequality both among pensioners and for the population as a whole; increased spending per head of the older population will be necessary to relieve poverty.

In general, however, it is clear that there is no emergency. Relatively small increases in public spending on pensions as a fraction of GDP are required, on average from 11.0 per cent to 14.6 per cent over more than 40 years; there is no reason, apart from neoliberal ideology, why these increases cannot be made.

9.4 ADMINISTRATION COSTS

There are big economies of scale in pension provision, whether or not this provision involves funding.[2] Governmental schemes, involving the whole employed population and not allowing individuals to opt out, tend to have the lowest costs per euro of pension finally delivered. Occupational schemes, organized on a sectoral basis or by very large employers, have significantly higher costs; schemes sold by institutional investors directly to individuals have the highest costs, and these costs are the higher, the wider is the choice of schemes open to the individual.

From the point of view of an individual customer, the costs of a funded occupational pension scheme can be divided into: accumulation costs (the difference between the returns on the securities underlying the scheme and the returns credited to the individual's account); alteration costs (which must often be met when the individual's circumstances change – for example, a change of employer); and annuitization costs which occur when the individual retires and has to turn the funds accumulated in their account into a regular payment (Herbertsson and Orszag, 2001).

The alteration costs are often very high, representing a distribution away from contributors who change their occupation or employer towards those in more stable circumstances. Although this has been an embarrassing problem for the advocates of 'flexible' labour markets, their preferred solution, to replace occupational by 'personal' pensions chosen by the individual, fails because of the very high marketing costs of the latter. From the point of view of the institutional investor as pension provider, costs can be divided into: acquisition costs (costs of acquiring new business, essentially marketing costs); administration costs (costs of administering individual accounts); and asset management costs as such (portfolio purchase and alteration). It is the first two of these which dominate the supplier's costs, with 'acquisition' or marketing costs being particularly onerous for 'personal' schemes.

A typical personal pension in the UK absorbed 40 per cent of the individual's contributions (Murthi et al, 1999, cited by Herbertsson and Orszag, 2001).[3] It is for this reason that most of the personal pensions marketed in the UK in the 1980s were later declared to have been mis-sold and the institutional investors who were responsible were made to compensate their customers.

9.5   WEALTH INEQUALITIES

There are three broad principles according to which pension income can be distributed. There can be, firstly, distribution according to *citizenship* or, in practice, *residence*. This is the most egalitarian approach, and the most developed example is perhaps the basic component of the public pension in Denmark. Although at present only relatively limited schemes, of course in the public sector, function in this way, there are strong arguments for a move in this direction to reduce inequalities and simplify the working of social security systems.

The second distributional principle, which has been predominant in continental European countries up to the present, is *earnings-related*. Pensions calculated in this way depend on wages while in work (and often on years of employment). These systems aim to maintain the broad pattern of wage distribution among the employed population into retirement. They are obviously considerably less egalitarian than flat-rate pensions and may tend to perpetuate the injustices of working life into the years of retirement, in particular as regards women's pensions. For this reason earnings-related systems can be modified in favour of lower earners or to take child care and care of the elderly into account as well as employment records. Most such systems work on a public sector PAYGO basis, which facilitates this redistributional objective, but many pre-funded occupational schemes also correspond essentially to the 'earnings-related' principle, especially where they are 'defined benefit' schemes, that is where they guarantee a certain pension in function of years of contribution; the guarantee is usually expressed as a fraction of earnings in employment.

The third possible principle characterizes 'personal' pensions but also, to an increasing extent, other private-sector pensions, such as the defined contribution schemes operated by many employers. This is simply to pay pensions in function of the accumulation achieved by the individual, that is, in accordance with their *wealth*. This is a radically inegalitarian approach since, in all countries, the distribution of wealth is extremely unequal, much more so than the distribution of earnings. One's ability to acquire wealth depends on how much wealth one already has and on the amount of savings one can devote to further accumulation – those with high incomes can save many times more than those with average incomes while, for the lowest income groups, saving may be practically impossible

Table 9.2   Distribution of wealth in selected countries (c. 2000)

	Share of wealth of richest 1%	Share of wealth of richest 10%	Percentage of households with zero/ negative net worth
Canada	15%	53%	20%
Finland	13%	45%	15%
Germany	14%	54%	19%
Italy	11%	42%	3%
Sweden	18%	58%	27%
UK	10%	45%	11%
US	29%	67%	17%

Source: Luxembourg Wealth Study (Sierminska et al., 2006).

and no wealth at all can be accumulated. This is certainly the case today as regards market-based pensions.

All studies of wealth distribution testify to massive inequalities. For example, a very recent study (Sierminska et al., 2006) attempts to produce comparable measures for seven countries (see Table 9.2).

The data in Table 9.2 specifically exclude pension entitlements, but this only reinforces the point. Even social-democratic Sweden is characterized by extreme inequality in the distribution of wealth. In Europe, especially in Scandinavia, these inequalities are mitigated by pension entitlements based on residence, on earnings and, for those without resources, on need. To the extent, however, that market-based pensions displace public PAYGO schemes while collective provision gives way to purely individual responsibility, pensions will become a simple corollary of personal wealth – inadequate except for a privileged minority.[4]

9.6   RISK AND THE MOVE TO DEFINED CONTRIBUTION

The social security systems which were built up over the twentieth century are not only effective systems for the redistribution of income. Quite apart from their redistributive aspects they are extremely efficient systems for insurance against risk. Many of the risks which can be routinely covered by public social security systems are either impossible or very expensive to insure via financial markets (Barr, 2001). This is true, for example, for such risks as unemployment, chronic sickness or the need for intensive care in old age. Information problems, non-diversifiable risks, externalities and other difficulties frequently obstruct market-based approaches to many of the risks which confront people in their everyday lives.[5]

Market-based pensions, pre-funded from the accumulation of securities, are subject to two main risks. Firstly, there is the danger that the pension provider – whether an employer sponsoring a pension scheme for their workers, or an institutional investor selling pension schemes to individuals – might become insolvent: there have been numerous recent cases in Britain and the US. It is interesting that the response of the authorities has been to intervene and to regulate, in Britain for example by compelling providers to contribute to a state-run system to refinance insolvent pension schemes.

The second risk is that the assets accumulated in the fund will prove inadequate to pay the pensions required, either because the net return on the investments is too low, or because very low interest rates make it costly to turn an accumulated pension account into a regular ('annuitized') pension. In principle this risk can be insured against on the market – insurance companies in particular may offer long-term savings plans with a guaranteed pay-out. These tend, however, to be very expensive so that most individuals buying pension products opt for 'defined contribution' rather than 'defined benefit' schemes, meaning that it is the contributions rather than the final pension pay-out which is fixed.

Until recently, however, private pensions with a somewhat more collective character – those organized on a sectoral basis or by large employers – tended to be on a defined benefit basis, where members of the scheme were guaranteed a certain pension, usually in function of their earnings at work. Thus the risk that pension funds' assets would not cover liabilities was assumed by the sponsor of the fund, whether an employer or an institutional investor. This corresponded to a situation where occupational pensions were essentially perceived as deferred wages – as arising from the employment contract (often subject to collective bargaining).

In recent years there has been a wholesale flight from 'defined benefit' pension provision. Particularly in the US and in Britain, where employer-provided pensions were of great significance, employers began to close defined benefit pension schemes and replace them with defined contribution schemes. The employees concerned usually lost out in two ways: firstly, they had henceforth to carry all the risks of the security markets in which their pension funds were invested; secondly, they usually faced a straightforward decline in provision since employers cut back their payments into the new funds.

This was essentially equivalent to a cut in wages – the rewards offered to employees were reduced. Clearly these moves by employers were made possible by a decline in the strength of organized labour. At the same time, however, the widespread refusal by employers to accept pension fund risks demonstrated how important the risks were that could not simply be diversified away across security markets; to the extent that diversification can eliminate risk any sizeable pension portfolio can do so. But, after diversification, systemic risk (that affecting all securities) remains, and it is clear that this risk was substantial. To cope with systemic risk is a public function since only governments are in a position to defend pension entitlements in the face of a generalized decline in investment returns.

9.7 EU PENSION POLICY AND THE OCCUPATIONAL PENSION DIRECTIVE

Although EU leaders were clearly dazzled by the rapid rise of equity prices (especially for high-tech stocks) when the Lisbon agenda was being defined in 2000, it has not been possible for them to promote pre-funded pensions, based on the security markets and delivered by the institutional investors, as a plausible response to pension problems in the EU. The difficulties with such an approach were too great: even if a switch to pre-funded pensions were brought about, no resources would thereby become available to meet future pension needs; the costs of market-based pensions might well be prohibitive, especially for low-income groups; reliance on such pensions would clearly have extremely adverse distributional consequences, incompatible with the European Social Models; and the risks involved for those with limited resources were obviously excessive.

Nevertheless some significant moves have been made in that direction. In Germany the Schröder government introduced a market-based, funded element into the state system, but this remains predominantly a PAYGO scheme. A very small funded element has recently been introduced into the Swedish scheme. In Britain, where many pensions are very inadequate, a new funded scheme, based on employers' and employees' contributions is planned. Originally this was to be operated by a new central agency but pressure from the institutional investors prevented this. However, the most important reform in Britain was the recent decision to strengthen the basic state pension by linking it to the growth of incomes, not just the rise in prices.

In practice, the main reforms taking place are *parametric* changes within public PAYGO systems rather than moves away from these systems. The key parameters here are: the age at which pensions become payable (or the number of years of labour market participation required for eligibility); the contribution rates levied on employers and employees; the level of pension subsidy from general taxation (or the level of pension surplus appropriated by the government); and the generosity or otherwise of pension provision. It is very important that the parametric changes which are used do in fact improve the position of the disadvantaged pensioners. This is not in general the case for increases in the age at which pensions become payable except perhaps in some southern European countries where the age of retirement has been very low for specific occupational groups. This is firstly because the life expectancy of the poor is often much lower than that of the rich and so even this apparently technical adjustment may aggravate social injustice. Secondly, the activity rates of older workers, especially the lower paid and more disadvantaged ones, are very low and if their pensions are delayed many of them will be unemployed or compelled to remain in very poor jobs. An important 'parametric' resource which is insufficiently used would be to reduce the tax breaks given to high-income groups with private pension schemes.

Thus, although many EU leaders might well have desired a thorough-going market approach, they realized that this was impractical. They did try to develop a European pensions market in the Directive on Occupational Pensions which was adopted in 2003. However, it was never very likely that this market would grow rapidly to any significant scale. At the same time therefore the European Commission developed a somewhat different approach, which might be regarded as a surrogate form of pre-funding. The main emphasis today is less on replacing public by private provision, but rather more on 'strengthening' the public finances so that higher rates of public expenditure in the future can be accommodated without a big increase in tax revenues. To this end, member state governments are urged to run budget surpluses, so that it will be easier to run deficits to cover the future peak in age-related spending. The Commission (2006b) now writes:

> The Stockholm European Council outlined a three-pronged strategy to tackle the budgetary implications of ageing populations:
> – Member States should reduce public debt levels at a faster pace;
> – Member States should undertake comprehensive labour market reforms, including tax and benefit systems, in order to achieve higher employment rates, in particular among older workers and women;
> – Member States should undertake appropriate reforms of pension systems in order to contain pressures on public finances, to place pension systems on a sound financial footing and ensure a fair intergenerational balance.

This approach has at least the merit of recognizing that pension provision is and must remain essentially a public responsibility. It has, however, several demerits.

Firstly, public finance objectives are laid down with no consideration of their macroeconomic consequences. Any large or rapid tightening of budgetary policy is likely to have a negative effect on employment and thus undermine the attempt to increase the ratio of the active to the inactive population. Secondly, the dogmatic repetition of the demand for 'comprehensive labour market reforms' ignores the tendency of these 'flexibility' measures to increase inequalities. As has been suggested throughout the present discussion, the real problem of pensions in Europe is basically one of inequality rather than demographics: pensioners in general are not a disadvantaged group, but there are very many poor pensioners. Measures designed to increase employment by imposing lower wages and economic insecurity on the most vulnerable sections of the workforce will make this situation worse. Thirdly, to the extent that there is a demographic problem, it is quite logical to finance the associated expenditures in part by government deficits and thus avoid a sharp fluctuation in the total tax burden. Only if a problem continuing over a very long period were anticipated would it be necessary to make a fundamental shift in the budgetary stance, and even then, it would be desirable to make the shift gradually.

9.8 PENSIONS IN THE NEW MEMBER STATES

In many of the new member states of the EU, previously within the Soviet sphere, there have been rapid and dramatic changes in the pension system in recent years. In the Baltic states, in Hungary, Poland and the Slovak Republic very similar market-oriented reforms have been implemented. These involve adding to the existing public PAYGO systems, a second *mandatory* scheme, which is to be fully funded and to operate on a defined contribution basis.[6] The population which is compulsorily insured in this way usually consists of all members of the workforce below a certain age; since older workers have no hope of accumulating significant entitlements they are not required to make contributions.

So far, there are numerous restrictions on the institutions which manage the funds collected by these schemes – their fund management has not yet been opened up to external penetration although this is certainly in the logic of the Occupational Pension Directive. The fact that these new member states retain, for the time being, their own currencies makes it possible for their governments to restrict investment in foreign assets to 30 per cent of the total value of the funds. Initially at least, these pension funds have invested very heavily in the bonds issued by their own governments – which calls their rationale into question: if the assets accumulated are merely claims on the government why not simply record claims (also on the government) within a PAYGO system? The administrative costs of the second option would be much lower.[7] It is far too soon to evaluate the performance of these new funded schemes, which will not mature and start to pay out significant numbers of pensions for several decades. However, it is possible to point to characteristics of these societies which lead to specific problems for their pension systems.

The structures inherited from the state socialist era, although far from adequate, scored rather high in terms of both coverage and distribution: EU indicators for income equality among pensioners, for replacement ratios and for poverty 'risks' among pensioners have rather favourable values in these countries. These data, however, must be interpreted in light of the low levels of income of the population and the drastic disruption of economic and social life during the 1990s.[8]

Financial problems for social security systems in these countries are very immediate. Although the population is certainly ageing in some of them, the real constraint on their social security systems arises from low employment rates, especially among workers aged over 55 (see Table 9.3). These low rates, in turn, reflect the massive process of deindustrialization which followed the collapse of the centrally planned economy and the virtual impossibility of reintegrating all those who lost their jobs at that time.

In these circumstances, the move to 'funded' provision, a long time into the future, reflects less a response to long-run demographic problems than an inability to respond to current pressures with systems which historically depended on high levels of employment.

The nearly uniform imposition of radical, market-oriented change by most of these countries perhaps indicates weaknesses in civil society. The

Table 9.3   Employment rate in selected new member states (ex-Soviet bloc)

Employment rate (%) 55–64 years	
Czech Republic	43
Estonia	52
Hungary	31
Latvia	48
Lithuania	47
Poland	26
Slovak Republic	27
EU25	**41**

Source: European Commission (2006b), Technical Annexe p. 33.

representation of domestic interest groups is weak; the influence of foreign agencies and their 'experts' is more powerful and direct than it would be in Western Europe.

The Czech Republic represents an interesting contrast to the other post-Soviet economies. Its institutional development has clearly been more influenced than that of Poland, for example, by social-democratic experience in Western Europe, and its pension system has been redesigned more along Western European lines than according to the blueprints of the neoliberal advisors whose handiwork is seen across most of the other new member states. Currently the Czech Republic has one of the most effective pension systems in the EU: over 65s at risk of poverty number only 4 per cent; the incomes of over 65s are 83 per cent of those of younger people; and the distribution of pensioner incomes is both more equal than among the Czech population at large and more equal than in most other EU countries. This is not a cheap system – it requires contributions of 28 per cent of payroll – and this has been made possible by an overall economic performance somewhat better than that in other new member states.

9.9 A QUESTIONABLE 'MODERNIZATION'

Many statements of the EU's Lisbon Agenda call for a modernization of the European Social Model. It is impossible to object to modernization in the abstract, but in concrete terms one central meaning of the modernization is usually a shift from public to market-based pension provision. This would not in reality be a modernization of the European social models but an abandonment of one of their defining goals, the security of the European populations in their old age.

It is noteworthy that in the member state where reliance on market provision has gone furthest, the UK, the functioning of the pension system is, by the EU's own reckoning, very weak (see Chapter 10). It is irresponsible, given such results, to promote pension strategies which, in effect, take the UK as a model.

Change in the direction which is advocated by many European leaderships would do nothing to provide more resources for the retired; it would aggravate social inequalities; and it would undermine the economic security of European populations. To the extent that such policies are motivated by a desire to expand the role of security markets in contemporary economic life, they display a confusion of ends and means and a misunderstanding of the role that market finance can play in economic development.

NOTES

1. The dimensions of the 'ageing' problem are frequently expressed in terms of a 'dependency ratio', that is the ratio of the retired to the employed population. The underlying notion here is some kind of labour theory of value according to which the entire social product would accrue to employees. In fact the share of wages in GDP has been falling for two decades in most EU countries and is now around 60 per cent, with around 40 per cent representing various forms of property income. Obviously this last is in potential an important source of revenue for governments. It must also be recognized that the economically non-active population includes children as well as retired people. The ratio of the active to the non-active population as a whole is much more stable than the ratio of the active population to the retired.
2. It is also true, of course, that PAYGO schemes are cheaper to administer than prefunded ones, because they do not have to bear the costs of asset management.
3. The Labour administration elected in 1997 attempted to reduce these costs by promoting 'cheap and cheerful' standardized pension schemes, known as 'stakeholder' pensions. They have been successful neither with the public, to whom they offer minimal benefits, nor with the institutional investors, who cannot make much profit out of them.
4. No argument will be made against the accumulation of market-based pensions by the wealthy, as a *supplement* to public schemes. And the role of market-based savings schemes will tend to expand as societies become richer. However, it is neither necessary nor just to subsidize such accumulation out of public funds.
5. Shiller (2003) argues that innovation and technical change in securities markets may make them able to handle more of the risks of ordinary life. But it is significant that many of his examples of successful innovation in covering risks relate in fact to public systems of social insurance, not to the financial markets.
6. The Lithuanian funded scheme is in principle voluntary, but once someone has joined it they cannot leave.
7. No custody costs, very few regulatory or legal costs, no transactions costs, and so on.
8. In Poland, the incomes of people above 65 years are higher (113 per cent) than those of younger people – this is a unique situation in Europe but it relates to widespread poverty among the younger population.

10. Finance and the household

John Grahl

10.1 INTRODUCTION

Most discussion of regulation in the financial sector identifies two broad motives: stability and consumer protection.[1] The issue of financial stability is dealt with in Chapter 7 above and again in chapter 14; thus the present chapter concerns only consumer protection.[2] It should be noted, however, that sometimes the actual regulatory measures which might be adopted on grounds of stability coincide with those taken to protect the consumer of financial services; for example, measures to maintain confidence in the banking system can serve both purposes.

Information Asymmetries

Much of the mainstream literature on regulation runs in terms of information asymmetries between the suppliers and the users of financial services. The basic notion is that retail consumers, whether individuals, households or small businesses, have much less information about the efficiency, quality and honesty of specific financial service providers than do the providers themselves. If then consumers are unable to discriminate between good and bad services, they may simply distrust all suppliers rather than choosing the best. This limits the market for the service in question; indeed it may, in the limit, prevent any transactions at all. Honest and efficient suppliers are penalized by the activities of dishonest and inefficient ones.

Among the factors leading to information asymmetries is the fact that households may transact much less frequently than the financial companies with which they are dealing – for example, someone may only ever need to arrange one or two mortgages – and this means they are bound to lack the detailed knowledge which will be available to a financial company specialized in the provision of mortgages. The same may well apply to a pension or a long-term savings plan.[3]

Market Power

Market power may be a further motive for consumer protection measures. Some financial sectors are highly concentrated and this can lead to the exploitation of consumers. And effective market power may result also from information problems when consumers are unaware of the full range of suppliers of a particular product.[4]

Social Inequalities

Both information asymmetries and market power can result in market failure. In terms of mainstream economic analysis they may justify regulation or other forms of intervention to increase the efficiency of the market economy.

However, these narrowly economic motives are not in practice the only reasons for regulation to protect consumers – broad considerations of social justice and equality are also at work. Banks, insurance companies and other financial institutions are often among the richest and most powerful structures in contemporary society and those who own and control them among the richest and most powerful individuals. Limits on the ability of these institutions to profit at the expense of ordinary people and, especially, of the most vulnerable, are therefore seen as necessary in terms of social justice and the legitimacy of the economic system.

Market Regulation versus Public Provision

The view taken throughout this book is that many household needs are better met through public than through market provision. This is, for example, the case for most health insurance. It is also true for most pension needs – the public sector can provide pensions at lower cost, with greater security and in a much fairer way than can the private sector (see Chapter 9). For example, actual pensions outcomes are much less satisfactory in Britain, where there has recently been a substantial move away from state provision, than in France or Germany where the state continues to play a larger role.[5] Thus the arguments below for stronger regulation of market finance are not meant to imply that even well regulated financial markets are superior to state provision – on the contrary.

However, even where the state retains a major role in such fields as pension provision, the market demand for financial services is likely to grow as a result of rising levels of income and the increasing complexity of economic relations. And where private sector provision is extensive it is important that it works as well as possible, even though more public provision might be desirable.

10.2   METHODS OF CONSUMER PROTECTION

As for financial regulation in general, consumer protection systems exhibit a great deal of diversity across Europe, as a consequence of differences in needs and in types of provision. In recent years, however, regulatory systems have tended to converge to a certain extent. One trend has been a move to cross-sectoral regulatory institutions and away from sector-specific institutions; this might be seen as a response to the increased ability of financial companies to enter different sectors – as when British banks became big players in the mortgage market. A second trend has been a move to more formal rules and procedures; this can be related to the increased openness of some financial activities to competitive entry so that the population of enterprises supplying a given service might be less stable and less susceptible to informal controls.

Both trends can be seen as moving towards the US model of a dominant single regulator in the financial sphere – the Securities Exchange Commission (SEC). In fact, there has been some pressure from the US to converge on this model, at least as far as security markets were concerned, in order to avoid a competitive disadvantage for US security markets (Lütz, 2002). However that may be, unitary regulators have been introduced in Germany, for example, by bringing banking, insurance and security trading regulators under one roof (Fröhlich and Huffschmid, 2004, chapter II, section 1.1), and in Britain where legislation in 2000 replaced a series of sectoral regulators by the unitary Financial Services Authority.

In retail sectors, regulatory change has tended to involve more precise rules governing the description and marketing of financial products (as with the introduction of statutory 'cooling-off periods' during which a customer might cancel a financial agreement without penalty) and the treatment of customer complaints, with a widespread use of ombudsmen to reduce the cost of disputes. But this kind of formalization has tended to focus on procedures rather than on the substantive nature of the financial services which are being sold to the public. The prevalent view has been that substantive restrictions are an obstacle to competition and innovation and a number of such restrictions have been removed – most importantly restrictions on the portfolios of institutional investors such as limits to their placements in certain assets or abroad. Thus stricter control over procedures has accompanied some substantive liberalization and deregulation. Once again, US practice has often been influential – for example in relaxing specific controls over many of the portfolios managed by institutional investors and substituting some version of the 'prudent man' approach used in the US which simply requires that portfolio decisions are reasonable given the interests of the consumer.

10.3   THE FAILURE OF INTEGRATION IN THE RETAIL SPHERE

The Commission itself has had to acknowledge that the Financial Services Action Plan has not yet brought about much integration in retail finance. Retail markets for banking services, institutional investment, consumption and housing credit and so on are characterized by considerable national variations; branch networks, representing huge investments, are still very important in some of these markets and constitute barriers to the entry of suppliers from other countries. The local knowledge which domestic suppliers possess about customers, about their requirements and preferences and about the risks in extending credit to households and small businesses may be very important and may also represent obstacles to market penetration by foreign financial enterprises.

Thus a Commission report in 2004 finds the highest level of integration among financial institutions themselves, considerable integration in the provision of financial services to non-financial companies, but very little in the retail sphere: some convergence in prices is claimed and the emergence of some new transnational infrastructures (mostly, one expects, in the provision of payment services) but virtually no cross-border establishments by providers of retail services (Frangakis, 2005).

These obstacles to direct market entry mean that financial companies wishing to penetrate retail markets in other European countries may often seek to do so by mergers and acquisitions, by purchasing existing companies. Here again, however, less integration is observed than might have been expected – there are in fact fewer cross-border mergers in retail finance than in most other sectors of the economy, a fact which the Commission deplores and which it brought to the attention of the ECOFIN council in 2004.[6]

A final factor depressing international markets for retail finance may be the recent crises on the stock market and in the banking system and the associated corporate and financial scandals. Many retail investors were inveigled into schemes promising big returns from international placements and may now feel inclined to distrust similar adventures.

However, there may also be some long-run tendencies towards greater integration: the introduction of the euro must itself facilitate cross-border transactions, and the growing use of the Internet may give rise to new forms of service provision which are less tied to specific countries or localities (for this reason the Commission takes a great deal of interest in e-commerce). There are also, at least in principle, benefits from further international portfolio diversification[7] which can be expected to improve the risk/return characteristics of the investment products offered to households provided that external investors are not systematically disadvantaged by their lack of knowledge or of influence.[8]

The point here is that these are long-run tendencies which may lead to greater integration if countervailing forces do not prove to be stronger. The voluntarism of the EU, which sees integration as the outcome of legislative and administrative commitment has, as so often in the past, clearly shown its limits in the field of retail finance.

10.4   INTEGRATION OF MORTGAGE MARKETS

In 2007, the European Commission's Directorate-General for the Internal Market, which has been responsible for some of the most extreme free market projects launched by the EU, started to push for a full integration of European mortgage markets (European Commission, 2007b). This is a particularly fatuous proposal. It is based on the usual one-sided and exaggerated estimate of the benefits of integration. In fact, since the financial corporations which make home loans already have full access to wholesale credit markets in each other's countries, there is no great need to integrate the retail side of the market. The Commission claims that integration would widen the range of mortgage products available to consumers but such widening might well work to the disadvantage of consumers because it could make for spurious product differentiation and render price comparisons more difficult.

At the same time, integration of mortgage markets would require a convergence of regulatory systems and in practice this would mean a levelling down of standards. Regulation in housing markets, developed over generations in response to the specific social priorities of different member states, would be crudely levelled downwards to permit the interpenetration of markets by the biggest corporate players.

As usual with the D-G for the Internal Market, a simplistic view of US practices inspires ill-thought-out proposals for Europe. Until recently, American mortgage markets were strongly influenced by big quasi-official institutions ('Freddie Mac' and 'Fannie Mae') which allocated mortgage credit with a concern for stability in housing finance and with the social objective of facilitating access to property ownership for middle-income groups. Naturally no suggestion of similar strong institutions to influence European markets comes from the Commission. Rather, the Commission admires the recent deregulation of US housing finance and proposes to imitate it.

But this deregulated mortgage market, with an unrestricted secondary market in mortgages and mortgage-backed securities was a major factor in the 'sub-prime' financial crisis which has led to the disruption of banking and credit markets around the world. In the housing sector itself, the specific consequences of the crisis include drastic declines in house prices, a collapse of house-building and the subjection of thousands of low-income households to the distress of repossession. In the UK, which has one of the most deregulated mortgage markets, many of the same phenomena can be seen.

The Commission had rapidly to change its tune on these stability issues. In the expert report which was used to prepare the way for the launch of the mortgage market integration drive (European Commission, 2006d, p. 9) it was argued that a strong secondary market in mortgages would necessarily contribute to stability by spreading risk. By the end of 2007 it had to be acknowledged, in the *White Paper* itself, that things were not as simple and that the secondary market in mortgages could involve problems in monitoring debtors. The *White Paper* recognizes that the fact that

> many of the rules which restrict the offering of certain products on a cross-border basis have been designed to protect consumers and/or preserve financial stability. The problems which occurred recently on the US sub-prime market serve as useful reminders of the importance of not taking undue risks with these crucial public policy objectives (European Commission, 2007b, p. 4).

In practice, however, close and detailed regulation of secondary markets would block the move to market integration since it would deter many financial corporations from moving into other member states.

10.5   THE FIN-USE CRITIQUE

It is a sign of the distortion of political processes in the EU that it was only when the FSAP was virtually finished that any systematic attempt was made to consult with the retail users of financial services (households and small businesses) as to the validity of the strategy. One aspect of this belated integration of consumers was the creation of FIN-NET. This establishes communications among the various member state systems for dealing with customer complaints and if possible resolving disputes between providers and consumers without court action.[9] The objective is to encourage cross-border transactions by making it easier for dissatisfied customers to complain and to seek compensation. The premise of the system is what is usually called 'home country control', that is, each financial institution is regulated in the country in which it is based and this regulation is recognized as valid in each member state in which it operates.

The second aspect of consultation with consumers, the establishment of FIN-USE, a forum of experts representing user interests called exactly this premise into question. What is needed, claimed these experts is 'user home country control', that is a general requirement of a financial institution operating in another country to meet all the regulatory requirements of that country (FIN-USE Forum, 2004). These requirements are not arbitrary but reflect specific user needs, rooted in history, culture and social norms. Such a view leads the users to come close to seeing the FSAP as a whole as a case of regulatory capture, as a series of policies whose essence is to promote the interests of the powerful suppliers of financial services. The four reports on which FIN-USE was asked to comment are seen in virtually these terms, as representing compromises between suppliers and regulators to the detriment of users:

> It is a common feature of the four reports that they fail to discuss the possibility that the creation of pan-European markets in financial services could have negative effects on some users. Yet it is well-known that economic integration has winners and losers even if the overall impact is positive. FIN-USE is concerned that no thought seems to be given to compensating the 'losers' (p. 4).

> FIN-USE is of the opinion that these [national] laws, developed over many years and reflective of the diverse cultures that make up the EU, should not be lightly dismissed. Instead, an empirical case must be made for why the potential benefits of a bigger market outweigh the costs of doing away with existing consumer protection laws (p. 5).

From this position a comprehensive critique of the FSAP is developed. This may leave intact the case for integrating wholesale markets where powerful and knowledgeable actors confront each other, but it completely undermines, on both social and economic grounds, the basic thrust of the FSAP towards regime competition, self-regulation of finance by the financial companies themselves, and the removal of strict rules in the interests of market integration. The box (10.1) of counter-examples offered by FIN-USE is worth reproducing as a whole.

BOX 10.1 BENEFITS OF STRICT PROTECTION LAWS

In order to prevent the sale of 'false' or unnecessary insurance – sometimes combined or 'packed' with legitimate insurance products – consumer protection legislation and case law often guarantees that insurance must provide coverage of risks that the target group actually faces. These same laws specify 'cooling off' periods (i.e., periods during which the purchase of insurance products can be cancelled without penalty) and set maxima for the length of time that buyers must pay insurance premiums.

- In payment systems, some countries have created a right to a basic bank account for all citizens (including over-indebted individuals and those with very low income). In addition, some countries have placed restrictions on the ability of service providers to terminate payment services. These laws presumably reflect a societal belief that access to financial services should not depend only on the ability of suppliers to profit from service provision.
- In securities markets, an increasing body of national law concerns the allocation of risk in particular investment vehicles. The idea is that adequate advice, informed by the individual financial situation of the investor, must be provided.
- Laws against excessive pricing (including, for example, usorious interest rates, excessive fees for unwanted services and excessive penalties for exiting long-term contracts), predatory lending, fraudulent investments have a long history especially on the continent.
- Laws that protect the elderly against fraudulent investment products.

Source: FIN-USE Forum (2004).

10.6 SYSTEM-WIDE PROBLEMS

One point made strongly by FIN-USE is that the massive failures of the US financial system from the dotcom bubble and consequent stock market collapse through such corporate scandals as Worldcom and Enron and the revelation of widespread fraud and malpractice by institutional investors, financial advisers and security dealers, have not elicited any adequate response from the Commission. It has imitated the US government in calling for more effective auditing and financial reporting by enterprises but has not called into question either the overall working of the financial system or the direction of change towards a wider role for security markets.

However, there is a lot of evidence to indicate that financial problems today are indeed system-wide, and cannot be reduced to the misconduct of individuals or to localized malfunctions. The security-based financial system can be viewed as a series of links, connecting the households which are the ultimate suppliers of financial resources with the corporations which are major users of these resources. Households, often through the activities of advisers or other agents, supply savings to insurance companies and other institutional investors who, in turn, place these funds on secondary financial markets. A host of agents – analysts, credit ratings agencies, stock traders and fund managers, clearance and settlement agencies – are involved in their so doing. Through the interconnection of secondary and primary markets, the valuations established on the secondary markets control the allocation of capital among the corporations in general. A continuous flow of accurate information to the security markets is one necessary condition for these valuations to be meaningful and another host of agents, inside and outside the corporations, are involved in acquiring and transmitting this information – such as financial managers, auditors and accountants. The distributed profits of the corporations then return via the institutional investors to repay and reward the households as providers of funds. The structures of corporate governance, such as boards of directors and management incentive systems, have, as at least one of their functions, the alignment of corporate behaviour with investor interests.

Now, every link in these complex chains has been called into question by the recent development of financial systems. The institutional investors have sold inappropriate savings products to households, often using unscrupulous sales forces whose commissions push up the costs of the products and lower the returns to customers. The same institutional investors have often carried out transactions on security markets which are contrary to the interests of their customers – firstly by failing to make the best possible assessments of the securities they are trading and then by incurring excessive transactions costs which have benefited a range of security market professionals – in both cases to the detriment of their customers. The corporations which were supposed to function in the interests of investors have rather been guided by the priorities of their top managements who have creamed off an ever-growing share of company revenues. The professionals – outside directors, accountants, auditors and the rest – who were supposed to control management have failed to do so and have instead been induced by easy money to give free rein to excessive managerial rewards and to the deception of investors.

These considerations apply in general not just to households as investors but also to the other main interactions between households and the financial system, where households are borrowers or users of the payments infrastructure. According to free market doctrines the interests of the households should predominate; in reality their interests are often subordinated to those of the enterprises which supply financial services.

The main response to the scandals and crises of recent years, both by the US authorities and the European Commission, has been to call for more *transparency*, for fuller and more accurate flows of information. In general, this proposal is justified, although a move to very frequent reporting periods may not be an advantage if it encourages a preoccupation with short-run variations in company performance.

More fundamental flaws in the financial structure have to be acknowledged. Firstly, there are many grounds to question the power and autonomy of the modern corporation. Those who promote the drive to enhance the economic role of security markets take it for granted that the markets in which an enterprise functions, together with minimal legal safeguards, constitute an adequate system of social control. Many corporations themselves are starting to recognize the implausibility of such claims, as the increasing discussion of 'corporate social responsibility' makes clear. But the rhetorical tribute paid to social responsibility does not alter the profound gaps in the social control of large businesses, endowed with legal personality; when the maximization of investor returns becomes the only legitimate objective for corporate leaderships then they are sanctioned to disregard or circumvent every social constraint without being effectively subordinated even to the interests of shareholders.

In fact, it has been realized since the 1930s that the emergence of giant corporations brings about a separation of ownership and control which compromises the position of outside investors. (The classic thesis of Berle and Means, the separation of ownership and control, has recently been re-examined and updated by several writers; see in particular, Aglietta and Rebérioux, 2005). Some wish to see in the growth of institutional investors a strong countervailing force to that of corporate leaderships, but the actual functioning of these financial institutions is, perhaps necessarily, centred on the security markets and on the construction and maintenance of portfolios rather than on the monitoring and control of individual corporations. Although pension funds, investment trusts and insurance companies will certainly press for transparency from the corporations in which they invest, they are not in a position to exercise close and continuous supervision of the corporations – indeed they would be reluctant to develop close relations with any specific company because this would compromise their ability to trade the securities concerned.

The problematic role of the corporation, then, is one deep factor determining the malfunctions of the financial system. A second is the intrinsic susceptibility of security markets to cumulative waves of rising or falling prices, related to imitative behaviour among the traders active on these markets. Once again, the fact that, today, institutional investors play a very big role on these markets does not change the basic nature of the difficulty – indeed, the competition among institutional investors may promote imitative behaviour as each of them tries to avoid being left behind by the portfolio shifts of the others. These speculative swings on security markets cannot be eliminated simply by improving information flows if the division of the market into individual actors with separate interests is maintained. It is the emergence of certain common views of future developments which can limit these waves of pessimism and optimism, but such shared opinions emerge from a discursive process with a political and social content – which has to be regarded as a public good.[10]

Thus, the problems of retail finance should not be seen as limited failures of a financial structure which is fundamentally sound; rather, these problems result from basic weaknesses in the corporation as an institution and in the functioning of the securities markets.

10.7 THE BRITISH CASE

To present the problems of retail finance in a more concrete manner, it is useful to examine some of the many failures in the British system. Britain is a lot closer to the market-dominated financial structures which are found in the US than are other European countries. The British case can therefore be taken to represent the kind of financial system which the EU's financial integration strategy is trying to bring about by its promotion of the role of security markets. There is a lot of evidence that the British system serves the interests of households very badly.

Households as Savers

This negative view of the British system has been reinforced by a number of authoritative reports into various aspects of retail finance. The Myners (2001) review of institutional investment, although very much written from the point of view of the financial sector itself, identified serious 'distortions' in the activities of pension funds, including a tendency to 'herd' in their investment decisions. The critical relationship between fund managers and the brokers who dealt on their behalf in the stock market was opaque, so that there was a tendency for transactions costs to be excessive. The review identified even more serious failings with the individual savings products sold by insurance companies (in Britain, most of these are what is known as 'with profits' schemes). The fierce competition in this sector was all about marketing the products and had little or no impact on the net returns received by savers.

The Sandler report (2002) examined the products of the insurance companies in more detail and also considered the functioning of investment companies. The role of so-called 'Independent Financial Advisers' was looked at in more detail. These enterprises are not in any true sense independent – they derive their income not in the form of fees from those they advise but as commissions from the institutional investors whose products they sell. Governments have repeatedly retreated from radical reform of the IFAs because the necessary reform – to eliminate the IFAs' interest in distorting consumer choice by forbidding them to accept commissions, or at least to make this interest clear to the consumer by strict disclosure requirements – would put much of the parasitic IFA structure out of business. Sandler comments that 'the focus of competition for providers is on winning distribution rather than on providing simple, good value products to the end consumer.' The latest attempt at reform, in 2005, changed the rules governing the range of products to be distributed but again shied away from tackling the deep conflict of interest which prevents IFAs giving impartial advice.

British commentators often refer to a 'savings gap', meaning by this that many households are not acquiring sufficient assets for a decent retirement. There are various measures of the 'gap'; Sandler refers to an estimate that personal savings are 20 per cent below the required level. In fact the whole notion of a savings gap is tendentious because it rules out reinforced public provision as the best way to improve pensions and because it neglects the fact that many pensioners are very well off so that the distribution of income among pensioners is just as important an issue as the total amount of income going to pensions. Nevertheless, those who accept the notion of a gap just because they wish to exclude redistribution and public provision face the difficulty that public distrust of the financial sector is such as to discourage many people from increasing their savings. It was this perspective which informed the enquiry of the Treasury Select Committee (2004) of the House of Commons. The Select Committee endorses and strengthens the Sandler critique of commission-driven sales in the retail financial sector. It emphasizes that the information failures in the sector include a failure to give consumers an accurate account of the risks of many products. The overall judgement is harsh:

> Presently, many areas of the long-term savings industry are struggling to offer returns that can realistically be expected to be much better than those available from a good deposit account, especially when allowance is made for the risks involved in most forms of long-term savings. This suggests that one of the main priorities for the long-term savings industry is to work out how it can deliver competitive returns to the saver. This is likely to require both the development of lower cost distribution mechanisms and a much greater emphasis on investment performance and asset allocation.
>
> [Nevertheless] the industry currently fails to engage in serious dialogue on a regular basis with consumer bodies and other interested parties on issues such as pension reform, access for the less affluent or, indeed, general consumer confidence. This may well partly explain why the industry in recent years has seemed to limp from crisis to crisis (p. 69).

Households as Borrowers

British households as investors, then, are not well served. In many ways their treatment as borrowers, as users of finance, is even more alarming. Long-term borrowing for house purchase does not in itself raise particular difficulties, although the provision of mortgages in Britain was for a long time linked to the sale of certain savings products ('endowments') which were subject to all the problems referred to above. Mortgage endowments were eventually treated as a case of mass 'mis-selling', and the financial sector is still involved in the slow and often reluctant compensation of some of the victims.

However, it is the provision of shorter-term credit, to support consumption expenditures, where the most serious problems arise. Two illustrations can be given. Banks and other providers of unsecured loans often try to sell to the borrower at the same time an insurance policy known as 'payment protection insurance'. These policies are supplied to banks and other lenders by insurance companies and then sold on, at the same time as a loan is agreed, to households at horrific mark-ups. Further, they are often sold to people to whom they are valueless – for example, the self-employed who are not covered against unemployment. Even when the policy is of some value, it clearly benefits the lender as well as, or even more than, the borrower because it greatly reduces the chances of default; it is in particular less sophisticated customers, and those most in need of credit, who are persuaded to purchase these over-priced and deceptive products. Although the FSA (2005) has been trying to limit the scale of abuse, lenders make enormous sums from payment protection which is said to account for 10 per cent of the profits of major commercial banks. A report from the Office of Fair Trading (2006) recently concludes that, in the market for payment protection, some £5.5 billion annually, 'consumer detriment appears to be a significant fraction of the total market value'. The matter has been referred to the Competition Commission (2008), whose first report begins by estimating 'that the 12 largest distributors of PPI made profits in excess of the cost of capital of £1.4 billion in 2006, on their combined Gross Written Premium (GWP) of £3.5 billion'. This is attributed to inadequate competition, although it is as much a question of simple dishonesty as of market power.

In a similar way, other malfunctions in the provision of credit to households affect above all those on inadequate incomes or facing economic insecurity. Many British households are in debt difficulties, as is signalled by the rapidly rising number of personal bankruptcies. 'Some 8% of individuals have monthly repayments on unsecured borrowing in excess of 25% of their income'. Yet financial corporations market all forms of consumer credit in the most ferocious way. 'County court judgements against personal debtors in the first half of 2005 rose by 15% to 290,643'. Between September and November of 2005, credit card issuers sent over 100 million unsolicited offers of credit cards to British households (Credit Action, 2006).

As in much of the financial sector, competition is focused on marketing and product discrimination rather than price, so that competition does not effectively reduce the cost of credit to households. The Treasury Select Committee, which issued a damning report on credit cards in 2003, noted certain improvements in industry practice in 2005, but added: 'The industry as a whole has further to go if the goal is to be achieved of ensuring that customers can understand clearly what they are being charged for in their use of their credit cards and, for some, avoid arriving almost unknowingly at a point where they have built up dangerous levels of personal debts'. (Treasury Select Committee, 2005).

The poorest and most vulnerable individuals tend not to deal with established banks or financial corporations but become the prey of loan sharks and 'doorstep' lenders. Here, three-digit interest rates are the rule rather than the exception: the Housing Corporation (2005) reports that

> financially excluded families with no access to affordable credit will have to borrow money from doorstep lenders at rates of up to 600%. For those forced to turn to illegal loan sharks, the prospects are even worse. In July 2005, a loan shark in Birmingham was convicted having charged interest rates of up to 8,000%.

There are no adequate systems or structures in Britain to protect the poor from this ruthless exploitation.

Households and the Payments System

In an economy which makes less and less use of cash, individuals without access to the payments system face immense difficulties in their daily lives. For most of the population, the necessary transactions services are provided in the form of current accounts with commercial banks. Households in general are not well served by the banks. The Cruikshank (2000) report, commissioned by the then British Chancellor of the Exchequer, Gordon Brown, told what is now a familiar story of overpriced products and poor services. One can take as typical the judgement on money transmission:

> Money transmission services are supplied in the UK through a series of unregulated networks, mostly controlled by the same few large banks who in turn dominate the markets for services to SMEs and personal customers. This market structure results in the creation of artificial barriers to entry, high costs to retailers for accepting credit and debit cards, charges for cash withdrawals up to six times their cost, and a cumbersome and inflexible payment system that is only slowly adapting to the demands of e-commerce.'

All other aspects of Bank services are criticized in similar term – the commercial banks meanwhile make profits which dwarf those of most other enterprises.

Once again the worst difficulties are faced by the weakest and most vulnerable. In some other European countries, notably France, individuals have the right to a basic bank account which permits them to receive wages or social security benefits, to make a certain number of electronic payments free of charge and also to make a certain number of free cash withdrawals each month. In Britain, however, reluctance to constrain the activities of the financial corporations means that no such right has been established. The Treasury (HM Treasury, 2004) report on the issue begins by recognizing that

> One in twelve households in the UK lacks access to a bank account of any kind. For them the costs of transactions as simple as cashing cheques or paying bills are high, and services such as hiring videos and contract mobile telephones are unavailable. Whilst lacking a bank account has costs in itself, the implications of financial exclusion can be much broader. Families can be locked in a cycle of poverty and exclusion, or turn to high cost credit or even illegal lenders, resulting in greater financial strain and unmanageable debt.

In Britain the term, 'exclusion' is used too much, a weasel word for poverty. People with decent jobs, homes and incomes will often be able to include themselves in social life. Nevertheless, in the context of payments services it is valid to speak of exclusion, in a concrete sense.

The critique of British retail finance is of general significance because the whole thrust of the EU's financial strategy is towards exactly this kind of system: British finance is characterized by powerful financial corporations, by huge security markets, by the prevalence of 'arm's-length', market-based corporate finance over the socially embedded investors often found in continental Europe. The regulatory constraints on British financial companies are minimal in order to give as much scope as possible to market forces. It is just such a system, on a Europe-wide basis, that is aimed at by the FSAP and the Lisbon agenda in general, while EU competition rules for the service sector threaten to undermine existing structures of social control and intervention at member state level. But the most elementary examination of the retail finance in Britain, drawing on documents from the most orthodox establishment sources can show that the financial model which is aimed at by the EU may have a very negative impact on the welfare of the households which make use of it.

10.8　DISMANTLING SOCIAL CONTROL

At the retail, as at the wholesale level, financial services are increasingly important and an essential aspect of contemporary economic life. Many retail services work well for many people much of the time. But when they fail to do so, as happens sometimes for most consumers and very frequently for the poorest and most vulnerable, the results are distressing and in complete conflict with the values of the European social models.

In this sphere as in others, the European social models require effective systems of social control. Yet the main tendency in recent decades has been to dismantle such systems. This process has many aspects, only some of which have been discussed here.

- Established barriers between particular sectors of retail finance have been removed in order to stimulate competition; in any case, technological change was making it difficult to maintain these barriers.
- Public sector provision has been reduced, both to control public spending and as part of the broad privatization drive. Particularly important here has been a general reduction, across Europe, in the provision of financial services through post offices. These services were often used most by low-income groups. There have been threats also to the public sector banks (Sparkassen) in Germany, whose position has been challenged as contrary to European competition rules.

- Along with the reduction in public provision there has also been a move away from non-profit provision – the role of cooperative and mutual financial institutions has been reduced, again often in order to enforce competition rules. There is evidence, however, that the transformation of mutuals into profit-making corporations, for example in the case of British building societies, has worked against the interests of consumers.

- There has been a switch in regulation away from the substantive control of financial services and products to a focus on procedures – on information disclosure, for example, or marketing practices. It has been argued, to justify this switch, that substantive controls block innovation. In practice, however, many innovations are spurious – a question of marketing rather than genuinely new services and the abolition of controls on pricing and quality standards may have damaged consumers – especially low-income consumers.

- Growing international trade in retail financial services and the increasing use of the Internet to sell and deliver financial services, although both trends are slower than is sometimes thought, raise a whole series of new problems for effective social control.

In principle, the EU is very well placed to act as a vector of renewed social control, through its transnational reach and its ability to promulgate and police high minimum standards in service provision. There are some signs that EU institutions are becoming more aware of these responsibilities.[11] But to discharge them in an adequate way will require a shift away from the current insistence on market-led integration as the overriding priority of EU policy in retail finance.

NOTES

1. See Goodhart et al. (1998) chapter 1, 'The rationale for regulation'.
2. The term 'consumer protection' is used here to emphasize that the household, whether it is saving, borrowing or using other financial services, stands in a relation to the company providing the service which is analogous to that of a retail customer to a corporation providing consumer goods or services. Much of what follows, however, also applies to small businesses as users of financial services since the imbalances in power and information between small businesses and financial corporations can be as great as for households. The term 'investor protection' is also often used in the literature when the service involves the use of household savings.
3. Thus, detailed protection regulation is usually thought to be less necessary in wholesale financial markets where all participants can be assumed to be experts and to have a good understanding of the product and services which are traded. But note that even in wholesale markets, investors are not always as informed as they should be.
4. For example, many British people were unaware that they were entitled to use certain

pension savings to buy an annuity from any supplier and simply bought it from the company providing the pension savings plan. Regulation was used to try to ensure that companies made customers aware of the 'market option'.

5. If the poverty threshold is set at 50 per cent of median income, then the percentage of old (over 65 years) people in poverty is as follows: France, 7.8; Germany, 9.8; Sweden, 7.7; United Kingdom, 20.9, United States, 24.7 (Wu, 2005).

6. See European Commission (2005c), annex I, section IV. The Commission seemed to suspect that member state competition regimes were being used as protective devices to block cross-border mergers, although it offered no evidence of this. Some conceivable types of integration do not take place because there is little or no need for them but it is always difficult for the Commission, usually so committed to market principles, to understand this elementary aspect of market economics.

7. Davis and Steil (2001, p. 33) give the following figures for the percentage of pension fund portfolios held in foreign assets: United Kingdom, 18; United States, 11; Germany, 7; Japan, 18; Canada, 15; France, 5; Italy, 0. There would appear to be considerable scope for more diversification to take advantage of the variation in the macroeconomic cycle across countries as well as of differences in economic structure and thus in exposure to economic risks.

8. Such disadvantages, however, have certainly marked many of the first steps towards the internationalization of asset management: when it becomes difficult to find a domestic purchaser for a dubious asset then attempts are made to find a sufficiently naive foreigner. The external adventures of Britain's Midland Bank and Abbey National, the huge foreign losses of the Credit Lyonnais, the problems met by Deutsche Bank in its drive for global supremacy all supply chastening illustrations.

9. It is rather difficult to assess the value of the FIN-NET system. It is reported that some 400 consumer complaints were dealt with in its first year of operation (2002) but no full evaluation seems as yet to be available.

10. Both the sub-prime crisis and the preceding dotcom bubble and collapse were conditioned by the attempt of wealth-holders – individuals but also and especially banks and other financial corporations – to obtain rates of return which simply could not be delivered on a continuing basis by the economy. Establishing more realistic conventions regarding the yield on investments is a key condition for more efficient financial markets, but such conventions cannot be produced by market processes themselves.

11. Besides the FIN-USE network, referred to above, one can mention the recent study, by the European Economic and Social Committee (2007), of the social consequences of recent financial developments, although there were clearly divisions within the committee on the need for stronger measures of social control. However, recent developments in EU policy have been rather negative in this respect. The influence of financial service users on policy formulation seems to have been attenuated.

11. The impact of financial change on European employment relations

John Grahl

11.1 ECONOMIC AND IDEOLOGICAL FACTORS AND STANDARDS

In attempting to assess the impact of financial change on employment relations in Europe, it is necessary to recognize that this change has more than one dimension: clearly there are both economic and ideological aspects to the new salience of security markets and shareholders. Also of great importance is the issue of standards of practice where economic and ideological forces are combined.

Finance and Corporate Behaviour

The direct economic aspects are related to the constraints and opportunities in the financial environment of an enterprise. From the late 1950s, many mainstream economists thought that financial mechanisms would have little or no impact on corporate behaviour or corporate strategies. This was the implication of the Miller–Modigliani theorem which states that the value of an investment (and by extension, of an enterprise as an assembly of investment projects) is unaffected by the way in which it is financed.[1] Were this the case, changes in the system of corporate finance would have no economic impact on employment relations.

However, the Miller–Modigliani theorem depends on the absence of asymmetric information. Information may be incomplete without being asymmetric so that investments involve risks but, by assumption, both the suppliers and users of finance assess these risks in the same way. When this assumption is not made, that is, when it is recognized that the enterprise as a user of funds will probably have more information than the suppliers of finance, the result no longer holds. Financial institutions and financial practices can now affect the value of potential investments, and thus corporate behaviour, by their impact on the information flows from the enterprise to its creditors and investors.[2] The theme of asymmetric information permeates finance theory today and supports the view that changing structures of corporate finance might well alter corporate strategies, including approaches to employment relations.

The Shareholder Ideology

But ideological aspects must also be recognized. The increased scale and importance of equity markets, in particular, is not simply an economic development: the notion of *shareholder value* provides one view of the meaning and purpose of the modern corporation, a view that has been widely propagated in recent years. It is not, however, the only such view – at the same time a different, even to some extent opposed, corporate ideology has developed, that of 'corporate social responsibility'. Both types of thinking can be related to the separation of ownership from managerial control in the giant modern enterprise: shareholder value denies the separation by suggesting that the proprietors (the 'principals') are still essentially in control through the management (their 'agents'); on the other hand, corporate social responsibility acknowledges that managerial autonomy is a reality but claims that it is exercised in socially legitimate ways.

Codes of Practice

However, it is also necessary to see the ways in which financial change *combines economic pressures with the development of norms of conduct*. Both equity and bond markets today depend on the standardization of the financial claims which are traded on them and this standardization of securities implies the imposition of common standards of practice among the firms which issue these securities. This is true immediately of the essential flows of information from a corporation back to the markets on which it is financed, that is the requirements on reporting corporate performance and on the accounting conventions to be used when doing so. But the standards of practice linked to these markets go beyond information flows in this narrow sense to embrace corporate governance as a whole: the way decision making in the firm is organized and the forms of accountability which are established. One aspect of the increased salience of security markets and dispersed ownership of equity is that formal codes of governance tend to become more important; when there are only a few large investors closely tied to the company, it is less important to codify procedures in this way because the allocation of responsibilities can be directly apprehended by those involved.

Thus a comparative study of European corporate governance codes finds that they have proliferated in recent years, the majority (25 out of 35) having been issued since 1997, and that there are strong trends towards convergence in the practices and structures which are recommended in individual countries and, increasingly, on an international basis.[3] Even though the legal position of shareholders is very different across member states, this convergence of norms signals the increased weight of the capital markets in corporate life because it establishes benchmarks of practice which make it easier to relate company performance to the measures of risk and return used by dispersed investors.

11.2   SHAREHOLDERS AND CORPORATE STRATEGIES

Managerial Predation

In reality, shareholders have generally failed to impose their priorities on corporate managements. Brenner (2003b) documents this for the central case of a market-based financial system, the US. In 1992, the Chief Executive Officers of US corporations owned about 2 per cent of their outstanding equity; by 2002 this had become 12 per cent, perhaps the biggest expropriation of wealth in human history, and essentially at the shareholders' expense.

A necessary condition of this vast failure of market-based control was consistent and dramatic overvaluation of companies on the equity markets. Michael Jensen, one of the leading academic advocates of shareholder value, now accepts that things went badly wrong and points to overvaluation as one of the key factors.[4]

However, in the aftermath of the world-wide stock market crash of 2000 and 2001 and with institutional investors attempting to rehabilitate themselves among their customers, equity markets may regain some of their disciplinary role. Just as important is the wide range of issues over which corporate leaderships themselves endorse a shareholder orientation of their strategies, a process of internalization of norms which, in Europe, has tended to run ahead of actual changes in financial constraints although these also have been accelerating.

Thus in his survey of changes in European corporate organization, Streeck (2001) observes that:

> In recent years, European large firms have come under pressure to extend similar attention to shareholders, especially minority shareholders, as Anglo-American firms; this is reflected in the debate on 'shareholder value' . . . as well as in ongoing changes in European regimes of corporate governance. Anglo-American arm's-length financial relations mediated through a

developed capital market are increasingly beginning to invade and replace traditional European systems of *national insider finance*. In the process, the behaviour of Continental-European companies is changing as they find themselves forced to address many of the issues emphasized by the standard corporate governance literature: e.g., how to ensure that minority shareholders are given reliable information; how to prevent 'insider trading' at the expense of outsiders; and how to hold management accountable to the interests of minority investors.

(It is pointed out that this reorientation does not stem from immediate financial pressures as most large European corporations could rely upon internally generated funds to meet most of their investment needs.)[5]

What strategies would a shareholder orientation suggest? As far as employment relations are concerned the general answer is straightforward: a relegation of the interests of labour, in so far as these are in conflict with profitability. In the abstract, there might be issues on which shareholders and employees could find common ground as against corporate managements; both groups might have an interest in making management more accountable, in limiting managerial predation and in extracting more information about the activities and plans of the management.[6] However, in practice, decision-making power in the company usually remains with senior management, and strategies continue to reflect the interests of these elites. Shareholder interests, as interpreted by the managerial leadership, seem likely to sharpen antagonisms between employees and employers in so far as they imply pressure for higher profits.

If we look at how more specific aspects of corporate strategy might, under shareholder pressure, impact on employees then there are several examples, all of which seem to be adverse to employee interests. Firstly, there might be pressure to curtail investment and to distribute a higher fraction of profits to shareholders; the retention of earnings inside the firm and the adoption of investment projects aimed at growth more than profitability are classical sources of friction between management and dispersed shareholders; employees would normally favour more investment at the price of lower dividends.

A related example concerns company structure. On grounds of transparency dispersed shareholders dislike conglomerate companies; they prefer to control risks by diversifying their portfolios rather than by diversification of activities at the level of the individual enterprise. This preference may become more marked as institutional investors come to the fore because they, unlike all but the wealthiest individual investors, can carry out effective portfolio diversification and therefore have little interest in reducing the risks carried by single companies for a given expected rate of return.[7] This investor preference, however, directly increases the job insecurity of the employees by reducing the scope for redeployment within the firm.

On similar grounds, shareholders might press for the outsourcing of any activities which are not central to the production and sales strategies of the corporation. In this case, the transparency of company performance may not be the only motive: investors may also wish to dispose of assets which have lower rates of return than the targets they try to set for the enterprise.

Associated with such targets are various performance metrics, such as 'economic value added' which are intended to correspond to the shareholders' interests. These differ from each other in some respects but tend to have in common that they focus on profitability while seeking to limit managerial discretion in reporting performance. They tend therefore to emphasize cash flows as an indicator of the resources which might become available to shareholders. The result may be a general pressure to reduce expenses which could impact adversely on working conditions. From the point of view of shareholder value, the very notion of 'retained earnings' is suspect. Everything, in this perspective, belongs to the shareholders and must be distributed to them unless retention serves their interests.

Mergers and Restructuring

A key aspect of the shareholder value movement is its approach to company restructuring, mergers and so on. On the one hand, mergers often present an opportunity for the extraction of large amounts of cash from the corporate sector; on the other, they are typically seen, from a shareholder point of view, as a means of bringing inefficient or spendthrift managements to account. The productive logic of many mergers, however, is unclear while employee interests tend to be relegated to the extent that financial motives are determinant. Clearly there may be occasions when a merger or takeover rescues jobs in an enterprise which would otherwise fail. However, the reverse is even more frequent – the restructuring is the occasion for job-shedding and wage-cutting.

Even when European elites were rushing to embrace virtually every aspect of the US shareholder model, there remained considerable reticence on the question of takeovers. The Commission officials responsible for the internal market had no doubts – their aim was to facilitate hostile takeovers by outlawing most of the measures by which an incumbent management might fight off an unwelcome bid. From their point of view the interests of the (dispersed) shareholders of the target firm should be paramount. The Takeover Directive was seen as central to financial integration: the key consideration was that shares issued anywhere in Europe should have the same characteristics, including the same possibility of being purchased in the course of a takeover.

However, in July 2001 the European Parliament, in a dramatic tied vote, rejected the Commission's proposals for a Takeover Directive. A very diluted version was passed by the EP in December 2003, but this did not establish the 'level playing field' desired by the Commission because the legal framework for (especially hostile) takeover bids remained very different in different member states. The outcome was not particularly logical in that no clear or agreed view emerged as to the reasons which would justify blocking a takeover; in that sense, the compromise Directive reflected the uneasy conscience of the EP. However, the extreme view of the Commission, that the only thing that mattered was the right of the holders of shares to dispose of them as they pleased, was certainly rejected and behind this rejection lay a concern for the social implications of restructuring.[8]

Incentives and Inequalities

Finally, it can be pointed out that the shareholder value drive is associated with sharply unequal rewards within the corporation. The activities of both management and employees are interpreted in a 'principal–agent' framework according to which the principals (the shareholders) have the problem of constraining their agents (corporate managements in the first instance) to subordinate their own interests to those on whose behalf they are supposed to be working. The solution proposed was to reward corporate leaderships in function of the returns they generated for shareholders in dividend payouts or rising share prices. In practice this led simply to an enormous inflation of rewards for corporate leaders, with no corresponding benefits to the so-called principals.[9]

At the same time, the focus on shareholder interests means that there will be an attempt to compress the incomes of those employees whose performance is most easily monitored or who are most easily subjected to market disciplines.[10] The outcome is a widening of income inequalities within the corporation. In contrast, where corporate strategy relates to a coalition of stakeholder interests, these inequalities will be smaller.

Corporate Bonds

It should be added that, in quantitative terms, the bond market is much more important in corporate finance in Europe than is the equity market. Further, there are clear signs of a recent increase in its importance. Banks and other financial institutions have always made considerable use of the

Financial corporations other than MFIs (dotted line)
Non-financial corporations (solid line)

Note: Gross Issues, all maturities, all currencies (by sector of the issuer; EUR billions; transactions during the month; nominal values) January 1990 to January 2006.

Source: ECB securities issues statistics.

Figure 11.1   Debt securities issued by euro area residents

bond market, but now non-financial corporations appear to be doing so. The big expansion of these issues around the turn of the century was linked to the auction of third generation mobile phone frequencies, and the subsequent decline in issues suggested that the corporate bond market might return to the levels of the mid-1990s. This does not appear to be the case, however, and the new, much higher level of activity seems to have been established (Figure 11.1).

However, the greater prominence of bond markets does not have the same implications for the corporation as an increased dependence on equity markets. Bondholders resemble shareholders in that they both require 'transparency' and a full flow of information to the security markets. But there the resemblance ends. To the holders of bonds and other fixed-income securities, the value of their holdings depends on the extent to which risk can be reduced. For this reason they prefer corporate issuers to possess wide margins of safety, in terms of both revenues and assets. The first of these reduces the probability of default on debt service, the second reduces the probability of loss following default. In both cases shareholder interests are opposed to those of the bondholders because the former are seeking to reduce asset holdings and direct all revenue flows not needed for profitable investments back to themselves. Thus the switch of many large European corporations away from bank loans and towards the bond market does not seem likely to have major implications for corporate strategy.

11.3   THE SHAREHOLDER DRIVE IN GERMANY

The impact of the shareholder movement in Germany is of particular interest because Germany is often seen as the most important example of a form of financial organization which puts much less emphasis on security markets than does the US, since the typical large corporation has tended to rely for equity capital on a small number of 'inside' investors with close links to and expert knowledge of its activities. To the extent that the wider public has contributed to corporate finance, it has been indirectly, through the banks, which have been by far the biggest suppliers of credit to the corporate sector.

The German financial system was, until recently, regarded as particularly efficient in view of the rapid development and strong competitiveness of the German economy over several decades. However, like other features of the German system, it has been called into question in the context of the slow growth and high unemployment rates seen in Germany since the early 1990s.

It is important to recognize that employment relations in Germany are also under enormous pressure for reasons other than financial change. Since the 1980s neoliberal projects have sought to lower labour standards, to encourage more inequalities in the distribution of income and to compress both direct labour costs and the social wage. The specific rationale for this project has sometimes changed; what began as, above all, a strategy against inflation is continued as a strategy to promote low-cost service employment and to respond to the supposed challenges of globalization. Most recently a series of reforms to the social security system has drastically reduced indemnities for the long-run unemployed and tightened up eligibility criteria with a view to promoting low-paid and part-time employment as well as self-employment by the unemployed.

Thus the shareholder value drive takes its place among an array of forces working to destabilize German employment relations and to intensify both administrative and market constraints on workers. Nevertheless, it may be possible to link certain developments more closely to financial change.

Recent Changes in Financial Structures in Germany

Compared with other continental economies, in particular that of France, patterns of corporate finance were relatively stable in Germany until very recently. Ownership of the larger enterprises was highly concentrated and often involved either a single dominant investor or a small group with effective control. There was an extensive network of cross-holdings among the larger enterprises, with the big banks in particular holding substantial stakes in industrial companies. This structure, sometimes known as *Deutschland AG* or 'Germany Incorporated', was seen as the support for close linkages among the biggest firms. The general public held relatively few shares and participated in the finance of industry indirectly, through the banks. The stock market was relatively undeveloped in terms of both the number of firms listed on it and its overall capitalization. Foreign ownership was very limited except for a few foreign, mostly American, companies which had established a presence in Germany.

This situation now seems to be changing fast, especially as concerns the very biggest firms. The structure of industrial cross-holdings is now considerably attenuated, as is the role of the banks as a shareholder in other companies. The German Monopoly Commission reports that whereas in 1996 the six biggest private sector banks held stakes in 75 of the largest 100 companies, by 2004 this had been reduced to 30. Over the same period the total number of cross-holdings among the 100 largest companies fell from 51 to 28 and the number of enterprises (including the banks) possessing such stakes from 39 to 17 (Deutscher Bundestag, 2006). These developments have been analysed by Streeck and Höpner (2003) as the dissolution of *Deutschland AG*, in a process which is redefining German corporate interests and transforming corporate practice.

There is only a slow decline in the role of bank finance in the German economy. However, financial change in Germany is reflected less by quantitative change in the financial activities of the banks as in a change in their role. The banks themselves are increasingly active in fund management and now tend to regard their shareholdings in other German companies as essentially portfolios of securities rather than as the support for industrial collaborations.

Stock market data are hard to interpret because the stock market crash of 2001–02 was particularly severe in Germany. Capitalization fell from $1432 billion at the end of 1999 to $686 billion at the end of 2002. Since then, however, it has grown at an accelerating rate to reach $2105 billion in 2007. The number of companies quoted on the Deutsche Börse on the other hand has not recovered its peak of 983 in 2001 but has grown fast from a low of 764 in 2005 to reach 866 in 2007.[11]

*Table 11.1	Distribution of German financial system liabilities by type of financial institution*

	1991	1992	1993	1994	1995	1996	1997	1998	1999	2000	2001	2002
Banking sector	76.9	77.1	76.0	75.4	75.4	74.8	72.9	72.1	69.9	70.4	71.3	72.9
Insurance sector	18.2	18.0	18.3	18.6	18.3	18.1	18.8	18.6	18.9	18.2	17.8	16.9
Other financial services	4.9	4.9	5.7	6.0	6.2	7.0	8.3	9.3	11.2	11.4	10.8	10.2

Source:	Vitols (2003).

These changes appear to be less rapid among smaller companies, where cross-holdings remain common and foreign ownership is growing less rapidly.

The stock market crash of 2001–02 and in particular the failure of the Neue Markt, a secondary stock market specializing in innovative companies and start-ups, may also have delayed the pace of change in German finance. However, there has been a shared determination among business and political elites in Germany to reorient the corporate sector towards market-based finance. A most important step in this direction was a tax reform by the Schröder government which allowed banks and other companies to sell off their accumulated holdings of shares free of capital gains tax.

Shareholder Orientation in Germany

Although these changes in financial practice are often very recent, the orientation of German companies has shifted rapidly. For example, Lane (2003) writes that

> the German system of corporate governance . . . is in the process of converging towards the Anglo-American system and . . . this has fundamentally affected the way strategic decisions are made in firms. Large, internationally oriented companies are particularly affected. But the notion of shareholder value and its many behavioural effects are gradually spreading also to other parts of the economy. Consequently, the distinctive logic, which had underpinned the German variety of capitalism during most of the post-war period, is eroding. This transformation is affecting also labour and industrial relations in negative ways.

Lane sees the sources of this reorientation not only in international capital markets (potential access to which may affect corporate behaviour even though actual financial practice is relatively stable) but also in the pressures of product market competition and

> new cultural and/or ideological orientations ... the reference is to the concept of shareholder value and associated motivations, cognitions and scenarios for action. These have been widely propagated by consultancy firms which often are of Anglo-American origin. They also have been absorbed through participation in new programmes of management education, particularly the MBA, and, last, during extended spells of direct exposure to Anglo-American business environments when managing German subsidiaries in these two countries. The management practice of measuring performance through application of precise financial indicators, fundamental to the concept of shareholder value, has become widely adopted by and legitimate among higher German managers.

This transformation in corporate behaviour, then, involves both specific changes in company ownership and corporate finance and a more general reorientation towards the global economy. Factors at work include the increasing autonomy of large enterprises in all countries with respect to national regulatory regimes and their increasing use of financial market conditions as a reference point. But ideological influences have also been important.

11.4 CAPITAL MARKETS AND SHAREHOLDER POWER

For a balanced assessment of contemporary financial change it is necessary to distinguish the expanding role of internationalized security markets from the ideology of shareholder value. The first of these is an essentially economic development which adapts financial relations to the internationalization of production and exchange. Until now, in fact, it is more obvious in European bond markets than equity markets, although the internationalization of debt markets makes the internationalization of equity markets feasible, because the pricing of equities relates them to the return on a very low-risk security such as a government bond.

The problems arising from these developments are discussed throughout this book. They include the intrinsic instability of deregulated equity markets, the tendency of *all* markets not subject to effective social control to generate inequalities and the weight of established interests (those of powerful financial actors in Europe and, especially, the US) in the design and construction of the new international market regimes.

In principle, these problems of regulation and control are best addressed at a European level. However, at present EU leaderships remain wedded to simple market-based integration, divorced from any social project and threatening to undermine existing forms of social control in member states, without building European structures to replace them.[12] In these circumstances, it can be important to defend social objectives at member state level, even if this retards the development of certain international economic relations.

However, it should be remembered that there is nothing sacred about the financial *status quo ante* in Europe. It is true that the 'inside' investors who control the big corporations have been constrained, in different ways in different countries and regions, to recognize the validity of other interests, including those of the employees. However, these groups still constituted privileged elites which sought to defend their own concentrated economic power. Indeed, it is often established industrial elites who are leading the drive towards an internationalized economic and financial system, partly at least because these developments can free them from the social compromises of the past.[13]

In the German case, for example, the structure of interlocking ownership and control which characterized large-scale industry in Germany (and, as has been seen, continues to do so) was not seen as desirable by the trade unions because it meant that, in any conflict, they were confronted not by separate employers but by a closely integrated grouping mobilized to defend the collective interests of big capital. Thus the social advances made within the 'stakeholder model' of German capitalism should not be identified with that model itself which is open to many objections.

On the other hand, the ideology of 'shareholder value' cannot be validated by the new salience of equity markets at an international level, even though some financial developments lent a certain plausibility to some of the claims which it makes. This ideology seeks to deny that large corporations today represent concentrations of unaccountable power, by claiming that the interests of shareholders remain predominant, actually or potentially, in corporate decision making.

The empirical falsification of the shareholder story (most obvious in the predation of corporate leaderships and related scandals) has been referred to above. The logical weaknesses of the shareholder value position have been well expressed by Aglietta and Rebérioux (2005). Dispersed shareholders have, in reality, traded in the possibility of corporate control against the *liquidity* of their holdings. Their own interests mean that they value the ability to exit from their investment more highly than a decisive voice in corporate strategy. Indeed, were a shareholder to develop a privileged, 'insider', position in a corporation, the very knowledge so acquired would become an obstacle to dealing in the shares concerned as it would give rise to an information asymmetry with other investors.

Contrary to a fashionable view, the recent rise of the institutional investors does nothing to mitigate the divorce of ownership and control. Essentially, it intensifies it because the institutions are even more focused on portfolio liquidity and market trading than are individual investors (for a survey, see Grahl and Lysandrou, 2006). These investors will certainly exercise significant influence on aspects of corporate governance which might affect their ability to trade equity. But they have no ambition to control the companies concerned and will avoid any relationship to a corporation which might give them the status of insiders because this would inhibit their trading.[14]

11.5 SHAREHOLDERS AND CAPITAL MARKETS

It may be necessary to distinguish more clearly than is often done between the following trends. On the one hand is the broad rise of security markets, including equity markets, to become much more important aspects of the corporate environment than in the past. This is true especially, but by no means only, in countries such as Germany where they were previously of very limited importance. On the other hand are the specific claims and ambitions which are articulated in terms of shareholder interests. The first shift seems to be systemic and irreversible, a function of the changing global economy and the new financial linkages which sustain it. The second only coincides with the first in some respects, that is in terms of those shareholder interests which can be met through market pressure on the issuing enterprise, while the nostalgic view, which would restore shareholders to the status of sovereign proprietors, will eventually fade because of its irrealism (Aglietta and Rebérioux, 2005). But even though the shareholder doctrine may prove to be a simplistic and idealized account of the new role of financial markets, this will not free large corporations from the much tighter constraints which capital markets exercise today.

NOTES

1. According to the theorem, the balance between equity and debt in the finance of an investment makes no difference to its value because it is always open to the creditors and shareholders to reallocate risks among themselves if they see an advantage in so doing. Miller and Modigliani give as an analogy a dairy farm: the value of its milk is not affected by whether it is sold as whole milk or separated into cream and skim.
2. One example of this kind of reasoning is the argument that the dominance of a few large 'inside' investors in German corporations has made it easier to transmit information to them and thus to finance corporate expansion. On the other hand, it is sometimes

suggested that it is more difficult to finance business start-ups in Germany than in the US because of the absence of a venture capital system.

3. 'Notwithstanding legal differences among EU member states, the trends toward convergence in corporate governance practices in EU member states appear to be both more numerous and more powerful than any trends toward differentiation. In this regard, the codes – together with market pressures – appear to serve as a converging force, by focusing attention and discussion on governance issues, articulating best practice recommendations and encouraging companies to adopt them.' (Weil, Gotshal and Manges, LLP, 2002, p. 3).

4. See Jensen (2004): 'When a firm's equity becomes substantially overvalued it sets in motion a set of organizational forces that are extremely difficult to manage, forces that almost inevitably lead to destruction of part or all of the core value of the firm'. He adds that 'equity-based compensation cannot solve the problem because it makes the problem worse, not better'. See also Jensen and Murphy (2004). Jensen now often appeals to ethical forces ('integrity') as the basis for a solution to problems of corporate control but it is hard to see how a world of corporate rivalry, enormous individual enrichment and a focus on profit maximization could be consistent with high ethical standards.

5. Note, however, that the statistics of equity issues need to be handled with care. The fact that *net* issues of equity are low over the economy as a whole does not mean that the equity market is unimportant to individual corporations. If some companies are retiring equity (often in the context of mergers and acquisitions) while others are issuing new shares then the stock market can be an important financial constraint on the companies concerned even though the corporate sector in aggregate is not drawing new funds from the household sector. Over the period January 1999 to January 2006, net issues of shares by non-financial corporations in the eurozone amounted to €367.5 billion; gross issues over the same period were €623.9 billion. It is the latter figure which indicates the importance of the stock market to the finance of individual corporations.

6. On this question see Jackson (2005) and Rehder (2003), both of whom argue, correctly, that of the three groups, managers, employees and shareholders, any two might combine against the third (note as well that only under certain conditions will these groups themselves be able to aggregate the interests of the individuals who compose them). Jackson calls these possibilities 'class coalitions' (workers against managers and shareholders); 'insider–outsider coalitions' (workers and managers against shareholders); and 'transparency coalitions' (workers and shareholders against management). Insider–outsider or 'productivist coalitions' – have often been observed and are particularly probable at division-level in multi-divisional companies when divisions are competing for investment. But alliances between shareholders and employees are *oppositional* in nature – they cannot make corporate decisions but must aim to constrain the decisions taken by senior management.

7. Most of the *customers* of the institutional investors are extremely risk-averse, but would still tend to endorse the diversification strategies of the latter, to the extent that they are effective.

8. See also Chapter 4 above. The position of the Commission no longer corresponded to the situation in the US, usually taken as the model for financial reform. Although the US Supreme Court had in 1982 struck down state legislation to restrict hostile takeovers, concern over the consequences of a wave of very ruthless takeovers in the 1980s led it to change its position and, in 1987, to endorse a restrictive statute in Indiana. 'State legislators were not concerned that stock ownership was changing hands, rather, it was the aftermath that was disturbing. In many cases, the goal of acquirers was not to simply control the stock, but to control the assets. In these instances, bidders would acquire controlling interest in a target company and then *profit* from the large-scale liquidation of assets or the corporate restructurings that resulted in plant closings, layoffs, or out-of-state relocations. Takeovers motivated by such objectives were believed to threaten jobs, tax revenues, existing interdependent business relationships,

community stability, and corporate contributions to socially responsible causes. . . . As of March 1992, over 40 states had passed or strengthened statutes regulating hostile takeovers'. Mallette and Spagnola (1994).

9. Thus in the largest 350 US corporations, the shareholder drive carried CEO compensation from 50 times the average wage of employees in 1982 to 525 times the average wage in 2000. The collapse of the stock market bubble brought this down to a mere 281 times average wages in 2002 (the mean CEO compensation standing then at $7 400 000 (Erturk et al., 2005).

10. Thus the same era which saw the explosion of CEO rewards in the US was also marked by a slow decline in real wages for most workers.

11. Data from the World Federation of Exchanges.

12. The most obvious recent example of this approach is the notorious Bolkestein Directive, which sought directly to undermine and even to suppress a wide range of regulatory measures at member state level. See Dräger and Wagenknecht (2005).

13. The Swedish economy is a good example of this process. Swedish corporations are the most multinational in Europe, at least in part because of their desire to free themselves from the constraints imposed upon their activities in Sweden itself.

14. Today it is usually a legal requirement that trades must not be made on privileged information; but it is also an economic necessity. Institutional investors are able to trade with each other on a routine basis only because they can plausibly claim *not* to be trading on private information.

12. Inclusion: universal access, consumer and workers' protection

Jörg Huffschmid

12.1 INTRODUCTION

Experience has shown (see Chapter 10) that the potential benefits of large integrated financial markets do not automatically occur and that where they do occur they often do not reach society as a whole but only specific privileged groups. Enlargement of European markets for retail finance could lead to selective supply and cherry-picking of attractive cross-country business opportunities and the neglect of those areas which were – although less profitable – previously covered in a domestic framework. Opening up of markets could also trigger more concentration and centralization to cope with more intense competition and to establish stronger market positions of national champions, which could exploit such positions against weak and vulnerable customers such as individuals and small businesses and farmers. Full liberalization of capital markets will also facilitate capital flows to the most profitable locations without concern for the consequences of job losses, deterioration of work conditions or of closures and relocations for the workers, communities and regions concerned. For all these reasons, political measures are needed to ensure comprehensive instead of selective positive effects of financial integration.

Financial institutions and their associations on the national and European level often argue that instead of legislative measures (the implementation of which requires a great amount of bureaucracy) self-regulation should be preferred, which would lead to simpler and more efficient solutions for everyone. But where self-regulation includes all the stakeholders, including consumers, communities and workers, it is often very general and inefficient. The kind of self-regulation which can be done on the cheap is regulation by suppliers and biased towards suppliers' interests. Binding legislative measures are therefore preferable and indeed necessary to ensure the public good character of financial integration.

As in the single market strategy the liberalization of financial services is also a prominent issue on the GATS agenda of liberalization of trade in services on a world scale. In the financial sphere as elsewhere, such liberalization can threaten important aspects of social cohesion. The EU is the best placed trading bloc to resist the introduction of liberalization rules which compromise consumer and worker protection and to ensure that financial companies entering the European market are constrained to observe the highest possible standards. Such conditionality for the liberalization of the financial sector would in the long run reinforce European competitiveness and attract customers for European financial services.

The EU members have different traditions and cultures concerning how the financial sector is integrated into the social and economic fabric. Such differences should not be regarded as obstacles to integration but as an asset and a potential factor of financial and social stability. Legislation relating to financial inclusion should therefore remain primarily national legislation. Full harmonization on the European level is probably impossible to achieve and it seems also not desirable. However, what is conceivable and desirable is the introduction of minimum standards with an envisaged built-in dynamics of upwards convergence. Such minimum standards should not serve as a justification for reduction of standards where they are already higher. They relate to access to financial services, to protection of non-commercial users or consumers and to protection of workers affected by takeovers as a consequence of the single European market.

12.2   UNIVERSAL ACCESS TO BASIC FINANCIAL SERVICES

In modern societies access to basic financial services is vital for participation in social life and must therefore be treated as a democratic right and a public good. The provision of this good is a social and political responsibility even where financial services are completely or mostly supplied by private firms. Access to financial services in this sense includes at least two dimensions and could be extended to a third area.

The first dimension is the right of every *individual* to have access to basic financial services regardless of the income or social status of that individual. This is by no means the case in the EU. A report on financial exclusion published by the European Commission in May 2008 revealed that in 2003 7 per cent of the adult population in the EU-15 and 34 per cent of adults in the EU-10 countries were financially excluded in so far as they had neither a bank account, nor financial savings nor access to revolving credit. These averages ranged from 1 per cent in Belgium, Denmark, Netherlands and Luxembourg to 48 per cent in Latvia, 41 per cent in Lithuania and 40 per cent in Poland, 34 per cent in Hungary and 28 per cent in Greece (European Commission, 2008, pp. 18, 20). Regulations to enhance financial inclusion exist in different member countries, but they are often rather vague and not very efficient and differ substantially from each other. The European approach should consist of two steps. In the first step the EU should oblige member countries to establish legal rights and standards ensuring the individual access to basic financial services. In a second step rules as to the minimum content of basic financial services should be elaborated and adopted on the EU level through directives. They should include the right to a bank account, to a bank card, to withdraw money from ATMs at least of a certain network, to make and receive payments, and to a number of free money transfers per month. For welfare recipients and other low-income individuals these services should be granted without charge by all credit institutions.

The second dimension of the universal access to financial services is the *regional* one. Credit institutions must be within a reasonable regional reach of users to give real effect to the right of access for everyone. Traditionally this function was fulfilled by the national postal services. However, these are increasingly being transformed into legal corporate entities, and subsequently deregulated and privatized. During this process the financial services branch is downsized, and often outsourced and sometimes sold to private banks without any infrastructural mandate (see de Lima et al., 2002, pp. 22–4). The process of concentration and centralization was accompanied by a wave of closures in regions where the provision of services was seen as too costly. It is therefore necessary to counter the tendency to regional desertification with regard to the territorial availability of financial services. One way of ensuring this is the preservation of public savings banks which play an outstanding role in Germany. Where such banks do not exist, private commercial banks should be obliged to set up a minimum number of service points in every region. They could consist of networks of different density for ATMs (high density) and other financial services (lower density).

The third dimension of universal access is that of the non-discriminatory availability of money and credit for *small enterprises*, workshops and small farmers. Under the new regime of Basel II the tendency to exclude these from loans either directly or indirectly through high interest rates and tight credit conditions will be exacerbated and exert additional pressure on these sectors. To avoid further polarization between national champions and large players on the one side and the great majority of small and medium enterprises on the other side, measures must be introduced to offset the structural disadvantage of SMEs with regard to external finance.

There are different options regarding organizing and financing the implementation of rules to ensure universal access to financial services in these three dimensions. One way would be to maintain a network of public banks which would offer services to every individual, operate in every region, and grant special conditions to SMEs, farmers and so on. They would operate on a not-for-profit basis, and where costs cannot be covered they would be subsidized through public expenditure. Another way would be to subsidize private institutions which undertake to provide social accounts or other activities to maintain or create universal access. A third and more radical option would be to impose both the finance and the performance of the universal access function entirely upon the private sector: a fund would be created to which all financial institutions would contribute according to their financial assets and from which they would receive compensation for the maintenance of the universal access function. Large banks which are not active in remote areas and only slightly interested in the retail business would have to pay large amounts into the funds and receive little or nothing from them, while small banks with social and/ or regional commitments would receive considerable support from the funds. Such a solution would probably diminish the incentive for large banks to withdraw from social commitments and from business in small towns or villages.

12.3   CONSUMER PROTECTION

In spite of official rhetoric consumer protection is presently still a subordinated and widely neglected aspect of the EU's policies for financial markets (see FIN-USE, 2004). Financial liberalization and deregulation have not always brought economic benefits, and in some cases have caused considerable damage to households (particularly those with modest incomes), to small firms, and to the social fabric. The most recent demonstration of this is the turmoil and damage caused by the current sub-prime crisis. Therefore the EU should concentrate its priorities on enhancing the legitimacy of EU actions in financial services policy, thereby restoring public confidence in this field. Such a reorientation would not have a negative impact on growth and investment. In the present context of financial disorder, the subordination of consumer interests to 'market-creating' integration may even be self-defeating because consumer suspicion will hold back financial development and deprive many financial companies of new resources. On the other hand, the gradual restoration of confidence in financial institutions would tend to support a socially responsible integration project and to make for a wider and more stable supply of financial resources. To this end, consumer protection must regain greater weight than it currently has. It must go beyond the setting up of a European network 'FIN-NET' which deals with complaints with regard to cross-border financial services but has neither formal competence nor power.[1]

Self-regulation, although it is often recommended by financial firms as an appropriate instrument to safeguard consumer interests, has not prevented many cases of mis-selling and unfair dealing by financial services providers with their customers (see Chapter 10 above). The strong asymmetry of information and power between large providers and small users of financial services makes the latter – individuals and small enterprises – vulnerable with regard to misbehaviour of the former. This asymmetry will not disappear with financial liberalization, even if liberalization results in stronger competition – which is not self-evident. Against the common interests of providers in maintaining this asymmetry, stronger statutory regulations are necessary to protect consumers. It is necessary to introduce high, Europe-wide, legal minimum standards of consumer protection, summed up by the rule, *caveat venditor*: the seller is responsible. Provisions for such protection are missing in the 'Directive on credit agreements for consumers and repealing Council directive 87/102/EC' which was finally adopted by the Council and European Parliament in April 2008 (OJ, 2008). In retail markets where individuals confront large and sophisticated companies, and where a single decision – on borrowing and lending especially in the areas of mortgages and life insurance – can have enormous implications for long-run welfare, the most effective regulatory principle is to oblige the providers of financial services to investigate thoroughly the interests (and not only the ability to pay) of their customers. Credit advanced to households without such investigation should be irrecoverable; savers should be indemnified if a failure to consult their interests leads to losses. Regulations to this effect should be introduced into the rules of corporate governance for the financial industry.

A more recent policy statement, the Green Paper on retail financial services (European Commission, 2007a) may indicate a certain shift in approach. This document signals a new sensitivity to consumer needs which, it is declared, are now central to policy formulation. In particular there is now a recognition that financial corporations may provide information in a confusing way and that not all new financial products benefit consumers. However, the Green Paper repeats the previous statements of the Commission to the effect that more cross-border service provision and more competition are the best ways to enhance consumer welfare, while it fails to support these dogmatic assertions with evidence. A major weakness in the document relates to financial advice – it is recognized that advice to consumers should be 'objective, based on the profile of the customer, and commensurate with the complexity of the products and the risks involved'.

The enormous difficulties involved in obtaining such advice on a commercial basis, and the consequent need for public actions and interventions to provide it are, however, unrecognized by the Commission.

European legislation on minimum standards of consumer protection in financial services should not be developed using the Lamfalussy procedure but with the full participation of consumer groups and other stakeholders such as welfare organizations, churches and so on. It may be desirable to leave much of the detailed regulation of financial products and practices to national authorities. On the EU-level the adoption of minimum standards is preferable to full harmonization, because it allows countries with higher standards to maintain these.[2] At the same time a process and timetable for upward convergence should be envisaged.

One of the most important cornerstones for European consumer protection is the rejection of the principle of home country control and its replacement by the principle of *consumer country control*. This would avoid the – unmanageable – effort for the users of financial services to obtain and correctly evaluate information about many different legislations and give them the safety of the national legal framework in which the user lives. It would also take into account the different financial structures, habits and cultures which have developed in different countries and should be taken as an asset and not as an obstacle to financial stability. The recent directive is a combination of two undesirable principles: general maximum harmonization (prohibiting better standards) and occasional home country control provisions.

Following a proposal of the Institute for Financial Services in Hamburg a 'European Coalition for Responsible Credit' has adopted in 2005 seven principles that should be brought forward for a directive on consumer credit (European Coalition for Responsible Credit, 2005).

1. Responsible and affordable credit must be provided for all.
2. Credit relations have to be transparent and understandable.
3. Lending has at all times to be cautious, responsible and fair.
4. Adaptation should be preferred to credit cancellation and destruction.
5. Protective legislation has to be effective.
6. Over-indebtedness should be a public concern.
7. Borrowers must have adequate means to defend their rights and be free to voice their concerns. (ECRC, 2006).

More concretely European consumer protection in financial services should include the following:

● *Standardization of certain retail services.* Frequently, enterprises in the financial sector engage in excessive and spurious product differentiation. This is made possible by the marked information asymmetries between suppliers and customers. The outcome corresponds to the classical analysis of monopolistic competition: excess capacity; wide margins between costs and prices; a loss of scale economies; heavy and dysfunctional marketing expenditures. In such situations the authorities should be empowered to require a simplification of product descriptions. This again implies that regulators should have power over *products*, not just over marketing *procedures*. The financial enterprises argue that such regulation threatens innovation, but this is unconvincing because many of the financial 'innovations' which are introduced in this sector are without value and serve only to confuse.

- *Enforcement of socially responsible behaviour by commercial enterprises.* Similarly, profit-making financial actors themselves should be constrained to respect social objectives in their commercial activities, for example to avoid discrimination against lower-income customers. German and French enterprises which close production facilities are required to draw up 'social plans' in the interests of their employees. Similar rules should apply, on a Europe-wide basis, to the withdrawal of financial services from communities with inadequate alternative provision. It is interesting that this kind of constraint can be found in the US, although this is not an aspect of the US system which attracts the attention of EU elites. The Community Reinvestment Act (CRA), enacted in 1977, aims to ensure a flow of credit to low-income communities, and all banks above a certain size are required to participate. Although the CRA was something of a dead letter under the Reagan administration, it was reinforced in the 1990s, and there is now an effective if imperfect monitoring system to ensure compliance (see www.ffiec.gov/cra/default.htm).

- *Protection of non-profit and publicly owned enterprises.* In many countries, mutual and other non-profit enterprises in the retail financial sector, and the provision of financial services by publicly owned enterprises have come under pressure – from deregulation and liberalization (the British Building Societies) and from the European competition regime (the public Sparkassen and Landesbanken in Germany). But such institutions provide important public goods such as financial services for low-income households and communities, micro-credit to start-up enterprises, the support of local initiatives and certain forms of redistribution and collective insurance which would not be provided by purely commercial enterprises. There is also a general interest in the development of the 'social sector' of European economies. In consequence, the competition regime for European retail financial services must permit national, regional and local governments to subsidize the provision of such services, or themselves to provide them.

12.4   WORKERS' PROTECTION

Workers are often the victims of increasingly deregulated financial markets. On the one hand they feel the pressure which a new shareholder value orientation introduces into all aspects of industrial relations, especially on work conditions, working time and wages and salaries. On the other hand financial takeovers of firms by institutional investors – some with long-term strategic objectives, but others, including private equity houses or even hedge funds, with only short-term raider's or speculator's interest – often are followed by closures and/or relocations of plants, with severe consequences for workers.

A particularly worrying development, in recent years, has been the very rapid growth of 'private equity' in Europe. Private equity investment groups buy up companies in order to undertake financial or productive reorganizations, or both, and then to exit from the position by reselling the companies. Although not all these restructuring exercises are harmful, they often sacrifice the interests of employees and other stakeholders to those of the investors by asset-stripping the companies concerned or by burdening them with very high levels of debt. Such investment groups are a long-established feature of the European economy, but the very low yields on many financial assets in recent years have encouraged many wealth-holders to turn to private equity where very high leverage (high levels of borrowing relative to the use of the groups' own funds) is used to boost profits. Here as elsewhere this leverage involves serious risks not only for the investors but for the companies in which they trade (for critical assessments see Froud et al., 2007 and PSE, 2007).

Remedies against harmful consequences for workers through the activities of financial market agents should consist in strengthening the right of workers to participate in the control of the firm with a veto right in matters of employment and work conditions. This is of course difficult to implement because structures and provisions in Europe are very different amongst member countries and because the resistance of management and owners against such introduction of elements of democracy into the organization and management will be strong and adamant.

In relation to takeovers, specific rules for the protection of workers' interests should be developed. As discussed above (Chapters 8 and 11), a takeover directive was recently adopted (Directive 2004/25/EC of 21 April 2004), which leaves it to member states to decide how far companies are allowed to protect themselves against hostile takeovers. In this area the effort of the Commission to create an area of financial expansion without any constraint was not successful and there remains room to shape conditions for takeovers which take account of interests and concerns of the target firm. The main concern in the discussion preceding this directive has been the protection of the interests of minority shareholders. The interests of workers which are at least as much affected by takeovers have been given very little attention and at present the protection of their interests goes no further than the information of employees and their representatives and their right to formulate a separate opinion on the effects of the takeover on employment. It is reasonable to strengthen substantially this protection of the interests of workers. This could be done by imposing social obligations upon the buyer, above all to guarantee – at least for a certain time – the number of jobs and refrain from tightening pay and work conditions. There should be strong veto powers against closures and relocations of plants after a takeover. Where they are clearly shown to be unavoidable – in the context of a corporate strategy about which workers' representatives must be fully informed – there should be adequate compensation to dismissed workers and to the region affected by the measure. Again it is necessary to give these rules concrete expression in each national legal system, and this should be facilitated by article 14 of the takeover directive requesting respect for the relevant national provisions. The EU should adopt a directive with three clear mandates for workers' protection in the case of cross-country takeovers: first it should oblige the parties concerned to elaborate and take the measures mentioned above. Second, it should define certain minimum standards for workers' protection. Third, European minimum standards should not lead to the reduction of standards where they are already higher than the required minimum.

NOTES

1. FIN-NET was set up by the European Commission in 2001 as a European network of national out-of-court complaints bodies for financial services. It was designed to facilitate the out-of-court resolution of consumer disputes when the service provider is established in an EU member state other than that where the consumer lives. According to the yearly reports between 2001 and 2007, 4883 cases were referred to the members of FIN-NET. See http://ec.europa.eu/internal_market/finservices-retail/finnet/index_de.htm#guide.
2. It has always been a principle of EU regulation that individual member states, although they could not adopt lower standards than those of the relevant directives, were fully

entitled to enforce higher standards, whether these related to consumer protection, to the rights of employees or to the preservation of the environment. It is a cause for concern that this principle has been called into question in the sphere of financial services, on the grounds that 'excessively' high standards (so-called 'gold-plating') were an obstacle to integration. In some cases high standards may indeed slow down the integration process, but member states have a right to limit integration in this way. By doing so they ensure that when integration does proceed it will be at a high level of public welfare. Service providers, if they are determined to penetrate the markets of such member states, can always do so by achieving the standards required.

13. Protection of the elderly against the risks of capital markets: the advantages of public PAYGO pension systems

Jörg Huffschmid

13.1 PRINCIPLES UNDER PRESSURE

It has been one of the major historic achievements of the European welfare states that they regard – notwithstanding their many differences – a decent living for the elderly as a public good and a matter of social responsibility, which can be complemented and enhanced but not replaced by individual responsibility. People who have worked for decades should be entitled not only to be protected from old age poverty but to roughly maintain their living standards during their period of retirement. For the large majority of EU member countries this responsibility has led to mandatory public Pay-As-You-Go-systems (PAYGO), which represented 83.5 per cent of all pension payouts in the EU at the end of the 1990s.[1] These systems reflect an intergenerational contract through which the working population pays – via taxes or contributions on their incomes – the pensions for the retired part of the population. The pension of the now active population will in turn be paid by the following generation and so on. In such a system of direct and immediate transfer of money from one part to another part of the population, financial markets do not play a relevant role (except as a medium for this transfer or for short-term cash management). Even in countries where large parts of the pension systems were organized via collective pension funds and individual savings and are therefore dependent on performing financial markets – the UK, Sweden and the Netherlands – they were regulated in a way which made them fairly reliable with regard to the objective of guaranteeing a continuity of living standards for the elderly.

This overall principal perspective has also been underlined in an official joint report of the Social Protection Committee and the Economic Policy

Committee of the European Council which was transmitted to and adopted by the European Council summit in Laeken in December 2001. There it was declared:

> Member states should safeguard the capacity of pensions systems to meet their social objectives. To this end, against the background of their specific national circumstances, they should:
> 1. Ensure that older people are not placed at risk of poverty and can enjoy a decent standard of living; that they share in the economic well-being of their country and can accordingly participate actively in public, social and cultural life;
> 2. Provide access for all individuals to appropriate pension arrangements, public and/or private, which allow them to earn the pension entitlements enabling them to maintain, to a reasonable degree, their living standard after retirement; and
> 3. Promote solidarity within and between generations. (European Council, 2001, p. 6)

However, during the last decade the stable traditional systems of pensions in Europe have come under increasing pressure and attack, and the call for thorough reform is mounting. One of the spearheads of this call is the European Commission (EC) although formally the competence for pensions is a purely national matter. To overcome this lack of formal competence the EC has developed the 'Open Method of Co-ordination' (OMC) as an instrument to develop comparisons and benchmarks and generate common orientations in areas for which the EU has no formal competence, such as social and labour market policies. This method which could be helpful for the development of more social cohesion has instead been used for a strong attack on the traditional pension system by the European institutions. There are a number of economic and political reasons for this.

- The persistently high level of unemployment in most countries of the EU undermines the financial basis for pensions in so far as it leads to a fall in taxes and social security contributions. The current financial problems of national pension systems are caused by this unemployment and by the accompanying fall in wages and the increase in precarious work without social security contributions. Under conditions of full employment in Europe there would for the present and near future be no financial problems and bottlenecks for the pension systems. Therefore the main political focus should be put on an efficient employment policy and reasonable remuneration and work protection instead of cuts in the public pension systems.

- Under the influence of new technologies and new social attitudes professional careers have become less steady and continuous and more flexible and patchy, with times of self-employment, parental leave or unemployment; this requires adjustments to the pension systems.
- The age structure of the population is changing towards a larger proportion of older and retired people which must be financed by the taxes/contributions of the actively employed population. The interpretation of this fact as an argument of a 'demographic time bomb' was originally developed and broadly publicized by the World Bank in its famous 1994 publication *Averting the Old Age Crisis*, which triggered a worldwide stampede for pension reform. The general direction of the World Bank recommendations included the promotion of a second and third pillar for national pension systems to complement (and one could add: gradually replace) the public systems. These two additional pillars should be funded through private savings of the individuals during their working lives and these savings should be invested in collective occupational pension funds (second pillar) or individually on the financial markets (third pillar). The capital stock formed in this way would generate additional income at the time of retirement. This recommendation has been embraced by the EU, and since the summits of Lisbon (March 2000) and particularly Laeken (December 2001) a European-wide pension reform has become one of the main features on the European agenda.
- A persistent redistribution of wealth and income towards the top of the income pyramid has taken place in recent decades, reinforced both by policies favouring the rich and by the pressure of unemployment on many working people. This accumulation of wealth has given new importance to a group of financial agents, institutional investors, who aggregate household savings and search for profitable investment opportunities. The privatization of hitherto public social security systems, particularly pensions, is undoubtedly a very attractive option for the financial industry.

The critique of these developments has been developed in Chapter 9 of this book. In the present chapter we discuss the alternatives: the most important of these is to maintain and strengthen existing PAYGO systems and give them a European dimension (section 13.2). Where capital funded systems exist they need stronger national and European frameworks to ensure safety, more consumer protection and democratization of management (section 13.3).

13.2   MAINTAIN, STRENGTHEN AND RESHAPE PUBLIC PAYGO SYSTEMS IN A EUROPEAN DIMENSION

The existing PAYGO systems should be maintained and strengthened wherever they exist, and shifts to capital funded systems should be avoided and where they have been undertaken, reversed, if this is possible. Firstly, the arguments in favour of capital funded systems are not tenable. Secondly there are a number of decisive economic and social advantages of traditional PAYGO systems. Thirdly the problem of financing public systems under conditions of demographic changes can be solved within the framework of PAYGO systems. Fourthly public PAYGO can and should be made more attractive also in a European perspective.

Untenable Arguments for a Shift Towards Capital Funded Pension Systems

There are basically two groups of arguments against the claim that demographic changes require the set-up of capital funded pension schemes as complements and partial replacements of public PAYGO systems.

Firstly the scope and intensity of demographic changes has been greatly exaggerated in an alarmist way. Capitalist countries have continually experienced demographic changes since the start of industrialization and in spite of this they have been able to set up and improve stable pension systems. In Germany for instance, which is regarded as one of the most vulnerable countries in demographic terms, the share of people over 60 years rose between 1950 and 2001 from 14.6 to 24.1 per cent of the population and is expected to rise further to 36.7 per cent by 2050 (Statistisches Bundesamt, 2003, p. 31). The basis for the success in establishing a stable pension system was that employment and productivity rose more than the population. There is no reason to assume that this will not be possible in the future. Much more important than the demographic dependency rate is the economic dependency rate, that is the ratio between inactive and active parts of the population. The current financial problems of pension schemes are due to unemployment and low wages and must be dealt with through employment and incomes policies.

Secondly, even if there were a financing problem caused by demographic changes up to 2040 it could not be resolved through the recommended restructuring of the present systems towards more individual savings (see Etxezarreta, 2005, pp. 70–81). The arguments in this direction seem plausible from an individual perspective, but they are untenable from a macroeconomic view which is the only view appropriate to pensions as a social institution. The argument goes as follows: more individual savings for future pensions raise the national savings rate, and this leads to higher investment, hence to an increase in the productive capacity and hence to higher production in the future. This increase in production is the basis on which the retired population can draw with their additional pension income from their individual capital stock. But there are various flaws in the argument:

(a) Higher individual savings for retirement do not necessarily lead to higher aggregate savings. They can also lead to a shift in the structure of personal savings from more short-term to more long-term savings. This will probably be the case for persons who cannot afford to save more from their current incomes than they already do.

(b) Even if aggregate savings rose as a consequence of pension reform, this might not automatically lead to higher investment but in all probability to lower investment. For a rise in savings means at the same time a fall in private consumption as by far the largest part of aggregate demand in the economy. This fall might well dampen the sales perspectives for firms and enterprises and thus trigger the (from a microeconomic view: rational) response of a reduction in investment. As a consequence, the productive capacities of the economy would not be enhanced but reduced through a pension reform leading to higher current savings. The relatively low levels of private investment in recent decades in many Western countries are not to be explained by a lack of savings but by a lack of profitable investment opportunities and by the inadequacy and instability of aggregate demand.

(c) If in the future the retiring part of the population uses the income from their individual capital stock for consumption purposes they would be drawing on a weakened productive potential and a smaller than possible production. This could then result in an inflationary push which would provoke deflationary counter-measures on the part of the Central Bank.

Advantages of PAYGO over Capital Funded Systems

In addition to the errors of the macroeconomic arguments for capital funded systems there are a number of decisive advantages of PAYGO over capital funded systems.

(a) Public PAYGO systems are much more stable and reliable than capital funded ones, although they also experience periods of more and of less progress or even stagnation in the course of the business cycle. But the performance of capital funded systems depends strongly on the performance of the financial markets which often do not follow the general performance of the economy, and the amplitudes in the cycles in financial markets are much sharper than those of the economy, GDP or wages in general. On the one hand, pensioners can be better off than recipients of PAYGO systems, but there is also the danger that they are much worse off and that in the worst case their schemes collapse and they fall into poverty and become dependent on social welfare. That this is not a purely theoretical possibility has been impressively demonstrated in the financial crisis of the beginning of the 2000s in the US and in Britain.

(b) Public PAYGO systems regularly cover periods of interruption of paid employment for reasons of sickness, parental leave, unemployment and so on. These elements of social solidarity are missing in capital funded systems and this increases the risks and costs for the members of these schemes.

(c) Public PAYGO systems reflect the relative income positions that the current pensioners had during their active working lives. Most such schemes also have a redistributive element (of greater or lesser importance depending on the country concerned) which improves the retirement position of those with the lowest earnings during their working lives. Under conditions of capital funded systems disparities in the current income hierarchy are not only reflected but exacerbated in the hierarchy of future pension income – at least when the system is voluntary. The reason for this is that income earners in the lower part of the income pyramid are often not able to set aside an additional amount of their low incomes for pension-oriented savings. When they retire the gap between their pension and those of persons who have made additional savings becomes even greater than it was during their active working lives.

(d) Finally the costs of centralized public PAYGO systems are substantially lower than those of decentralized private systems. They use regularly less than 1 per cent of tax/contribution revenue for administrative purposes while in the private schemes the administrative and other costs together with the profits of the scheme owners generally amount to more than 15 per cent of revenues. As Dean Baker writes:

> It is clearly far more efficient to administer a single, centralized, defined benefit system than a system of individual accounts, especially a decentralised system of accounts. At this point there is now a considerable amount of data on the administrative costs of these accounts, much of it from the World Bank (e.g. James, E., J. Smalhout and D. Vittas, 1999). It shows that administrative costs are generally more than twenty times as large with individual accounts as with a centralized defined benefit system. While the administrative costs of running the

Social Security system in the United States are less than 0.5% of annual contributions, the administrative costs of the privatized systems in Latin America are generally more than 15% of contributions, and in some cases more than 20% (Baker and Kar, 2002). In fact, in several countries, including Mexico, Bolivia, and Peru, the cost of operating the supervisory body that regulates the financial institutions that offer individual accounts exceeds the total administrative costs of operating the Social Security system in the United States (measured relative to contributions). (Baker, 2003, p. 12)

The Financing of PAYGO Systems under Conditions of Demographic Change

Ongoing and future demographic changes in the age structure of the population – even if they are much less dramatic than usually asserted – require adjustments in the financial structure of the pension systems. The basic question is of course the political decision regarding whether or not pensioners as a generation should enjoy approximately the same position relative to the rest of society as they had during their economically active lives. We hold that this position is one of the main achievements of the European social models in all their varieties. Therefore, if the proportion of the pensioners to the active population rises, the share in national production (and therefore also in income) which goes to the pensioners must also rise. This is an unavoidable necessity following from the basic welfare-orientated decision. From this perspective it does not make any difference whether this redistribution of income is organized via the introduction of capital funded systems or via adjustments of taxes or contributions in PAYGO systems. But given the considerable advantages of the latter, the preferable solution is to raise taxes or contributions to finance a transfer from the working population to the pensioners which safeguards the relative position of the latter.

Theoretically there are three different options to achieve this: The first option is to increase the *aggregate amount of working hours* through enhancing employment participation rates, the reduction of unemployment or the extension of individual working times, either as lifetime extension (going from 65 to 67 or 70 years as retirement threshold) or as an increase in the working time per week (day, month). In this case the absolute amount of taxes or social security contributions would rise without an increase in tax or contribution rates for the active population. Whereas the increase of participation rates and the reduction of unemployment are certainly to be welcomed, the extension of individual working times is not a reasonable option, because it tends to increase unemployment and to reduce participation rates.

The second option is to *raise the productivity of work* to finance the increased monetary transfers from the active population towards pensioners without imposing an increasing absolute burden upon the former. Productivity increases make the financing of both rising pensions and wages/salaries compatible with a larger proportion of pensioners in the population. A 1.5 per cent growth in productivity over 40 years would generate an increase in real income per worker of 81 per cent, which can be divided amongst workers and pensioners. (Note also that even if the productivity performance of the economy turns out to be disappointing this creates as many problems for funded private pension schemes as for public PAYGO ones.)

The third option is to broaden the basis for contributions for the pension system from wages and salaries to all forms of individual incomes including interest and dividend incomes, rent income and others. The argument for the collection of pension contributions from all incomes is that these cannot be generated and appropriated outside the social system and therefore all incomes should participate in the financing of this social system which includes PAYGO pension schemes. This option would to a certain effect neutralize the harmful effects of the redistribution of incomes from wages to capital income upon the financial resources of the pension system.

Reform and Europeanization of PAYGO Systems

The plea to maintain and strengthen the PAYGO systems currently in force in most members of the EU does not mean that there is no need for reform. The most obvious is the need for more transparency and democratic structures. Centralized national systems tend to develop bureaucratic structures which are very opaque and inaccessible for the citizens.

Although pension systems have developed historically under different circumstances and take different shapes in different countries, there is room for a more European perspective and coherence. In the implementation of such perspectives the European institutions could in a first phase have recourse to a progressive application of the OMC, although in a later stage more binding provisions should be envisaged. This could be achieved in two areas: firstly, there is a perspective for European minimum standards for public PAYGO pension systems. These standards could, in the first instance, relate to matters of transparency and access referred to above. In a further step minimum standards could also be introduced with regard to minimum replacement rates or – in the not-so-rare cases where income from work is already very low – a guaranteed minimum pension for every retired person.

Secondly, a decisive further step would be the introduction of a small

European pension paid out of the EU budget as a complement to the respective national pensions. This would be expensive but possibly also very useful for the future of European cohesion. If for instance the EU were to pay a pension of €50 a month (€600 per year) to about 100 million persons over 65 years old this would cost €60 billion. Obviously this could not be financed out of a total European budget of €100 billion, but would require a considerable increase in this budget. If this were to be accepted and it were decided that the EU budget should rise in several steps to 5 per cent of EU-GDP instead of staying at the current 1 per cent, the pension would be feasible and cost about 12 per cent of the budget. The advantages could be considerable: on the one hand a European pension would enhance the visibility and tangibility of Europe for the people. On the other hand it would contribute to social cohesion and upwards convergence, because a flat amount of €50 for every pensioner would have a much higher impact in poorer countries than in richer ones.

13.3 CAPITAL FUNDED SYSTEMS: MORE SECURITY, CONSUMER PROTECTION AND MANAGEMENT DEMOCRATIZATION

Even if public PAYGO systems are superior to private capital funded schemes (CFS), the latter have a long tradition and now dominate the social security systems in some countries such as the UK, Sweden and the Netherlands.[2] They will therefore in all probability be preserved and expand further. In the majority of the new members from Eastern Europe the privatization of pension systems has been undertaken with the explicit purpose of promoting the emergence of financial markets. It is therefore necessary to set up a system of supervision and control to protect savers and future pensioners against the risks of financial markets in general and against misbehaviour by the suppliers of private pension schemes in particular. Furthermore, as a result of financial liberalization, private pension funds and other institutional investors are now tending to expand in the EU. It is therefore necessary and reasonable to establish a European regulatory framework of minimum standards for capital funded pension schemes, even though it would for many reasons be preferable to maintain and strengthen public PAYGO systems. The framework which has been put in force via the Financial Services Action Plan (FSAP) – in the first place the directive on Occupational Pension Schemes (Directive 2003/71/EC) – is rather one-sided in so far as it is mostly concerned with European mobility, low transaction costs and transparency rules for such schemes. Although the latter is a positive element, to benefit from this presupposes a well informed citizen who can judge the pros and cons of specific offers on the part of the pension fund industry. For a large number of persons this condition is not fulfilled.

A framework for European cooperation in the area of capital funded pension schemes could be agreement of the following principles:

1. Where CFS play a relevant role in the pension system they should be required to guarantee the participation of everyone. For low-income recipients the payments to the pension funds should be publicly subsidized or taken over by the public budget altogether. The basic principle – as an essential pillar of the European Social Model – should be that CFS – like PAYGO systems – must lead not only to the prevention of poverty, but to the approximate preservation of the living standards of pensioners when they retire. The reference basis for such schemes should therefore be a defined future income or benefit (in relation to present income), not a defined present contribution which leaves the future benefit open. This requires the reversal of the current trend to shift from defined benefit to defined contribution systems which transfer the risk connected with financial markets completely to the employee.

2. Pension funds should preferably be public and democratically controlled funds rather than employers' funds or those of private institutional investors. Their management and/or supervisory body should include stakeholders such as active employees, pensioners and regional or central governments. The investment policies of such funds should in the first place ensure a safe income for the future pensioners; in addition they should take into account general public purposes such as environmental protection, regional development, and the suppression of arms trade. Although the conception of a pension-fund democracy (Aglietta, 1998, for example or Sjöberg, 2004) exaggerates the potentials of such institutions, democratically controlled funds can at certain times exert some positive influence.

3. Where individual savings are invested in private pension funds or similar institutions these should be exposed to strict supervision and regulation. These should cover their marketing and their investment strategies alike: On the *marketing side* it is necessary to enhance consumer protection and protect individuals not only from fraudulent behaviour but also from very complicated and misleading marketing strategies (mis-selling) by the financial institutions which compete for these savings. Three measures are conceivable to this end:
    –   The first is tight public market supervision and co-operation among national supervisory authorities.

– The second is a certain standardization of basic capital funded pension schemes, on a national and, with full liberalization, also on the European level.
– The third measure is the participation of current and future pensioners (that is employees) in the management and administration of all pension funds.

On the *investment strategies* side – in the case of both individual employers' funds and those of institutional investors – strict regulation should exclude any engagement in offshore or other speculative activities such as hedge funds. Also, the fraction of the fund's assets which is invested in equities should be more limited than it is presently in most countries and in the EU directive. Investment in government bonds should be the favoured strategy. On the other hand there should be an insurance fund to cover losses from failure of pension funds. This insurance fund should be financed by the pension funds industry which makes big profits from capital funded systems.

These proposals should not only relate to national legislation and implementation but also play a role on the European level. But the actual emphasis of the European institutions is not on protection of consumers and future pensioners but mostly on cost-cutting and facilitation of cross-border investments for financial institutions. It is interesting and depressing at the same time to note that the key directive on pension funds in Europe starts not with a declaration that safe pensions in the EU are its main purpose but with the sentence 'A genuine internal market for financial services is crucial for economic growth and job creation in the Community'. In this directive no concrete limits are set for investment in derivatives (including hedge funds) and only very lax limits are set to investment in shares (70 per cent) and in foreign currency paper (30 per cent).

A correction of this directive is necessary. It should limit the range of investment options (that is exclude hedge funds and other derivatives) and broaden safety, consumer protection and democratic management of occupational funds.

13.4   CONCLUSION

The main message of this chapter is: keep financial markets away from pension systems. It has been argued that pension systems in the EU should best be organized on a public PAYGO basis, as is still the case in many countries. Current financial problems of these schemes are mostly due to high unemployment, low wages and slow growth and should be resolved through appropriate macroeconomic policies for full employment with decent wages. Long-term problems to finance PAYGO pension systems under conditions of demographic changes can be managed through parametric changes like an increase of contribution rates or the broadening of the basis for contributions to all kinds of incomes, and – most importantly – to restore and maintain a highly productive economy. Where capital funded schemes exist and play a relevant role they should be compulsory public institutions. Where private funds – mostly big institutional investors – are involved, public regulation should guarantee the income of pensioners (principle of preservation of living standards), impose investment restraints, and ensure appropriate participation by employees and pensioners in the administration of their money.

NOTES

1. See Pragma Consulting (1999), quoted in Klaus Dräger (2003)
2. Note, however, that the situation in the Netherlands and Sweden is very different from that in Britain. In both Sweden and the Netherlands there are relatively strong public PAYGO systems, which deliver flat rate pensions to virtually all residents. In the Netherlands for example they replace about 70 per cent of the minimum wage, roughly 30 per cent of average earnings. The basic state pension in Britain replaces only 17 per cent of average earnings or less than 40 per cent of the (low) minimum wage. The funded schemes in Sweden and the Netherlands are predominantly occupational schemes, covering 90 per cent of the working population in each case and subject to both significant public regulation and strong trade union influence. In Britain, less than half the working population have occupational pensions and these are often very low.

14.   Financial stability

Dominique Plihon

14.1   INTRODUCTION

Financial stability is a public good – in the same way as health, education, knowledge, environment and peace – because it is indivisible and non-exclusive, that is it benefits all players and all countries. In a symmetrical way, financial instability is an international public bad because it creates important negative externalities: the bankruptcy of individual banks or investors can lead to crises at the national and international levels. This is known as 'systemic risk', a well-known phenomenon in international finance. The cost of resolving such global crises is paid by taxpayers, although of course the total social costs may be much higher than these expenditures.

The international financial stability which characterized the first decades after World War II disappeared in the 1970s with the generalization of flexible exchange rate regimes caused by the breakdown of the Bretton Woods monetary system. Financial instability increased sharply in the 1990s due to the globalization process, which led to a very high mobility of capital, to very much larger international capital flows and to the explosive growth of financial markets in the world economy. Many empirical studies have shown the high correlation between financial instability and the accelerated process of financial deregulation which was decided by major industrial countries and imposed on developing countries during the last two decades.[1]

The demand for international public goods, such as financial stability, has grown along with globalization. But their supply remains restricted because governments, central banks and businesses are acting in isolation; they do not take into consideration the benefits or the costs of their actions for other peoples or countries. Besides, the benefits of financial stability are not the same for all players. This makes coordination difficult and explains why financial stability is undersupplied as an international public good.[2]

In the 1990s, a consensus emerged as to the necessity of preventing future crises, but the measures proposed by leading countries and international organizations have been unsuccessful, as is illustrated by the dramatic crises in the so-called 'emerging markets' in East-Asia (1997–8) and Argentina (2001). The main reason for this failure is that most proposed measures are only aiming at increasing market discipline and information transparency. There is no real political will on the part of the official community to take drastic measures to curb speculation and to control capital flows. There is a need for more coercive forms of regulation and for institutional reforms designed to build a more stable international financial system.

The existing European institutions[3] have not been organized to tackle financial instability. The ECB has a very narrow mandate and only recognizes price stability as its central objective. There is no European agency with clear responsibility for banking supervision and financial stability at the regional level. In fact, banking supervision and financial stability policies are still defined and implemented at the national level.[4] The European Union as such does not play a significant role on the international scene as regards financial stability issues.

14.2 ALTERNATIVES TO BASEL II

One of the major lessons of recent experience is that bank failures are one of the major mechanisms leading to financial crises. During the last decades, most crises have been 'twin crises', involving system-wide banking crises along with crises in asset markets (foreign exchange market, stock market, real estate market . . .).[5] On the other hand, financial crises tend to have limited consequences if the banking system is secure and unaffected. This is why banking supervision should be one of the major weapons against financial instability.

The first measures towards coordinated supervision in international banking, the Basel Agreements, were taken in response to the new risks to banking systems that emerged with the move from fixed to floating exchange rates in the 1970s and the increasing liberalization of international capital movements.

The first Basel guidelines implemented from 1988 contributed to improving the stability of the banking systems in major industrial countries (with the important exception of Japan).[6] The major rule implemented by the Basel I guidelines is the capital adequacy ratio (also called the Cooke ratio) which led international banks to cover up to 8 per cent of their risk-weighted loans and investments with their own funds. This usually required banks to raise more capital from shareholders and other investors and thus to reduce the risks run by their depositors. The fact that the same ratios apply to all internationally active banks, regardless of the country where they are based, limits regime competition: individual countries cannot promote their own banks by less restrictive capital requirements, which would make the entire system more fragile.

A similar rule has also been enforced in the European Union through the capital adequacy Directive (1993). The new Basel II guidelines, implemented in the EU by the Capital Requirements Directive of 2006, correct certain lacunae of the previous Basel agreement thanks to much more elaborate methods of evaluating and measuring risk according to the type of credit and financial asset. Such measures are meant to reinforce the robustness of banking systems in the context of globalization. Basel II introduces three innovations: (1) it creates a closer link between capital requirements and underlying risks; (2) it relies to a greater extent on internal risk management practices by sophisticated institutions; and (3) it puts emphasis on market discipline by improving public disclosure, especially of banks' risk exposure. At the European Union level, a new capital adequacy directive (2003) takes into account the major changes introduced by the Basel II reform.

While these new guidelines introduce some positive changes (such as a better measure of risks), they are not acceptable as they stand because they are subject to important limits and will have perverse effects. Six main criticisms should be addressed to Basel II:

1. Basel II is designed for large banks which are able to implement sophisticated and costly risk management instruments; the capital charges will be higher for small banks which will not be able to use these new instruments. Small banks will be under pressure to merge with large banks to comply with the new rules. The new guidelines also propose to use external credit ratings to assess the risk faced by small lending institutions. But most small business firms do not have credit ratings. Hence, Basel II will put these firms in a difficult situation.

2. Basel II allows banks to calculate themselves the risk of their exposures and thus the capital needed to cover these risks. Supervisors will no longer examine the banks' portfolios directly. They will only examine the internal control procedures of banks. This is a real problem, as we know that banks may be inclined to use this greater freedom to take excessive risks.

3. Basel II is not adapted to developing countries. Firstly, banks in these countries are not generally in a position to build sophisticated risk management systems. They may be forced to merge with large banks

in developing countries to comply with Basel II. Secondly, ratings by private rating agencies do not exist for many developing countries and private sector borrowers in these countries.

4. There is a strong risk that the new guidelines will have pro-cyclical effects, due to the fact that ratings are often downgraded during a slowdown or a crisis. Hence Basel II is likely to have perverse effects on some firms and on developing countries if the availability of credit is reduced when they are facing difficulties.

5. Basel II implicitly presupposes market efficiency because it is assumed that micro-prudential legislation (that is prudential rules implemented by individual banks) is a sufficient condition for stability; for this reason Basel II does not deal adequately with the threat of systemic crises.

6. Basel II deals only with banks and bank-related institutions; no specific rules are designed for other financial institutions such as pension funds, mutual funds and hedge funds. Hence Basel II does not deal with financial conglomerates which operate in banking, financial investment and insurance markets.[7]

In view of the above drawbacks of Basel II which are widely recognized, one must propose an alternative approach to the regulation of financial institutions[8]. First, there is a need for a unified and comprehensive framework for the control of all (bank and non-bank) financial institutions. All investment funds (including especially hedge funds) have to be subjected to strict regulation with a view to reducing speculative operations and to limiting their exposure to risks. This implies that there should be a single supervisory authority in charge of all financial institutions and all financial operations (banking, investment, insurance). In the context of the Single Market, the single national authorities should cooperate very closely on the basis of common rules. In a long-term perspective a comprehensive supervisory agency should operate at the European level.

Secondly, the instruments of supervision should be adapted to the type of players and to the size of banks. The sophisticated Basel II risk management system should be used only by large banks and for large borrowers operating on international markets. A specific, and more simple, framework must be designed for small banks, small and medium sized borrowers, and for developing countries. There is a need for the creation of specialized financial intermediaries, some of them funded by public resources, which are able to deal with the different types of risk (developing countries, small business). There is also a need for *public agencies* performing credit rating functions for agents and institutions which are neglected by private ratings agencies. One solution would be to create such a public rating agency at the international level, which could be related to the Bank of International Settlements.

Thirdly, one must question the emphasis put on market discipline and internal control by the Basel II reform. Banks, like other financial actors, are prone to short-sightedness and cannot be relied upon to exercise self-discipline with respect to risk management.[9] Furthermore, as indicated, most financial actors have no interest in refraining from speculation and risk-taking transactions. Hence, there is a need for a more coercive regulatory framework, defined and implemented by European public supervisory authorities. Among measures to be taken, one should think of instruments, such as taxation, designed to make financial players internalize the negative externalities caused by excessive risk-taking.

Fourthly, *macro-prudential policies* must be implemented with a view to preventing systemic risks. It has been shown that the depth of financial crises, in developed as well as in developing countries, is related to 'reverberation effects'[10] and 'contagion effects' across the different asset markets (forex, credit market, security and real estate markets), among which the credit market plays a crucial role.[11]

The authorities must develop tools for analysing the resistance of financial systems to the synchronization of failures and accidents, or to the occurrence of macroeconomic shocks affecting all banks simultaneously (exchange rate crisis, drastic rise in interest rates, start of a recession).

14.3   FINANCIAL STABILITY SHOULD BECOME AN OBJECTIVE OF CENTRAL BANKS

Financial globalization has led to a new situation, which calls for a renewal of the goals and instruments of monetary policy. In the 1960s, the objective of the *Keynesian central bank* was to establish the best trade-off between inflation and *full employment*, often favouring the latter to the detriment of the former. The 1980s marked the triumph of *conservative* central banks, almost exclusively dedicated to fighting inflation and preserving nominal *monetary stability*. But the victory over inflation has resulted in a sharp decrease of interest rates which is stimulating bank credit and the ballooning of stock market prices and real estate prices, whether commercial or residential. Thus, whether or not central banks realize it, they themselves encourage the emergence of speculative bubbles, as suggested by the experiences of Japan and the United States in the 1990s. Indeed, one is entitled to think that these speculative bubbles were only made possible by the sharp decline in interest rates decided on by central banks in the two countries mentioned. In the context of developed financial markets, changes in interest rates decided by monetary authorities are not only an instrument to manage the demand for goods and services, but also, and perhaps even primarily, a signal to the financial community. In fact, the most important way in which central bank decisions on interest rates affect aggregate demand may be through their effect on financial markets.

It follows that *financial stability* should be added to the central banks' existing role of preserving monetary stability (apart from the necessity also to give them responsibility for the promotion of growth and employment). There is a need for a third generation of central banks dedicated both to monetary stability and financial stability. In the context of global finance, monetary stability and financial stability are two inseparable missions. Of course, central banks need additional instruments to achieve this additional target. To start with, central banks must learn to communicate with operators on financial markets, in particular when a surge in credit and in asset prices heralds the start of a phase of speculation. Secondly, there should be interventions in security markets and real estate markets by central banks and/or by public agencies. In France, the *Caisse des Dépôts et Consignations* played this role of stabilizing stock market rates in the past. Real estate institutions can play the same role for land prices, and by extension, real estate prices. One of the major arguments against interventions on markets by public authorities is that the latter are not in a position to do so efficiently. This argument does not hold for two reasons: first, central banks already intervene efficiently in one market, that is, the money market; second, central banks have a longer memory than private traders; and they are in a position to collect information which supports a broader view of financial market disequilibria. Since the 1980s, conservative central banks have been supposed to evaluate the natural rate of unemployment (or the NAIRU) in order to define their policy stances. Why shouldn't they now be in a position to estimate long-term prices for financial assets and real estate?

14.4 EFFICIENT AND STABLE PAYMENT SYSTEMS

The existence of efficient and robust payment systems is certainly one of the basic conditions for the stability of financial systems. Indeed, one of the major functions of banking and financial systems is to provide efficient and safe payment mechanisms for households, firms, banks, central banks and other policy makers.

There are three categories of payment systems: (1) large-value payment systems; (2) retail payment systems; and (3) securities settlement systems. The problems raised by these three payment systems are quite different in most countries. The role of a large-value payment system is to ensure the efficient execution of money market transactions and thus the uniform distribution of liquidity and a homogeneous level of short-term interest rates across a monetary area. This is a prerequisite for the efficient conduct of monetary policy operations. A large-value payment system should also be robust in order to cushion systemic risk and to contribute to financial stability. In the European Union, important and rapid progress in the integration of large-value payment systems has been achieved by countries in the European Union. One of the main functions of the Eurosystem is to manage the Trans-European Automated Real-time Gross Settlement Express Transfer (TARGET) system which contributed to the rapid integration of the euro money market.

By contrast, retail payments systems and securities settlement systems are still largely fragmented today in the EU, as in most parts of the world. National retail payments systems are not interlinked, meaning that they cannot be used for processing cross-border or EU payments. Cross-border credit transfers in euros are not efficient. There is a clear difference between national and cross-border credit transfers, the latter being much more costly and lengthy. The main reasons for the difference in service for cross-border retail payments and national payments are a failure to use agreed pan-European standards and the low level of automation. However, since July 2004 a European Directive has been enforced which requires that an intra-EU transfer should not cost more than a national transfer, provided the forms are correctly filled out with BIC and IBAN (that is, numbers identifying the bank and the account concerned in a standardized way).

European authorities and banks decided to implement an ambitious programme towards the establishment of the Single Euro Payments Area (SEPA) in 2010. The ultimate objective is to transform the euro area into a fully integrated payments area.

Although investor demand for foreign securities has increased sharply within the EU since the introduction of the euro, the EU infrastructure for clearing and settling cross-border transactions remains highly fragmented. Pan-European investors are required to access many national systems that provide very different types of services, have different technical requirements/market practices, and operate within different tax and legal frameworks. Using the per-transaction income of intermediaries as a proxy for cost, it appears that cross-border transactions costs on the securities market are about 11 times higher than domestic transactions.

The additional cost represents a major limitation on the scope for cross-border securities trading in the EU. It reflects the existence of barriers to efficient cross-border clearing and settlement within a fragmented EU infrastructure.

The European Central Bank (ECB) and the Committee of European Securities Regulators (CESR), which is an independent body, appointed a joint working group which issued a report entitled 'Standards for securities clearing and settlement in the European Union'. The report contains 19 standards that aim at increasing the safety, soundness and efficiency of securities clearing and settlement systems in the EU. The standards are based on the *Recommendations* for securities settlement systems issued jointly by the Technical Committee of the International Organization of Securities Commissions (IOSCO) and the Committee on Payment and Settlement Systems (CPSS) in November 2001, adapting them to the European context. This set of standards will come into force when an 'assessment methodology' has been developed and after an analysis of the impact of the standards has been undertaken.

The impact on financial stability of the lack of integration in securities settlement systems can run in both directions. On the one hand, inefficient systems create distortions which may exert destabilizing effects on markets and individual investors. But, on the other hand, highly integrated security markets in Europe may facilitate contagion effects among European countries, and contribute to systemic risk.

14.5 EXTERNAL DIMENSION OF FINANCIAL STABILITY

There is an important external dimension to the issue of stability. At present, major central banks have no clear responsibility for the evolution of global financial relations. This applies to international monetary relations. Indeed, the American Federal Reserve and the ECB have no declared exchange rate policies. The market is supposed to determine equilibrium exchange rates. This neoliberal vision is largely contradicted by existing evidence as shown by persistent and large misalignments of the major currencies. Since the creation of the euro, international monetary relations have been dominated by an asymmetrical and unstable relationship between the dollar and the euro.

Although financial globalization limits the powers of national central banks acting in isolation, mechanisms for international cooperation are extremely weak. Cooperation about exchange rate management takes place only in the event of an emergency, and cooperation tends to be limited because, although central banks sometimes cooperate on foreign exchange market interventions, they are not prepared to coordinate their monetary policies. There is a need for systematic cooperation. Furthermore, major central banks are not very active with respect to the issue of the reform of international financial institutions. This is surprising because the need for such a reform has been widely recognized since the East Asian crises in the late 1990s.

14.6　CAPITAL CONTROLS AND TAXATION

Excessive capital mobility is one the major drawbacks of financial globalization. It limits the effectiveness of national monetary and fiscal policies. It is a major cause of financial instability. Hence, there is a need to 'throw sand in the wheels' as James Tobin put it 30 years ago, at the outset of financial globalization. Prudential supervision instruments, such as the Basel guidelines, are not sufficient to reduce financial instability as they only concern banking institutions. Additional instruments are necessary, such as capital controls and taxation. Four series of reasons may be invoked in favour of such controls.

1. Financial stability is a public good. But it is not a 'common good', in the sense that all actors are not interested in promoting financial stability. Today, a large share of profits of banks, investors and multinational firms comes from speculative operations. In other words, in the eyes of dominant actors in the world economy, the cost of financial stability would be very high. The pursuit of international financial stability not only raises the problem of how to coordinate private choices so as to counteract the short-sightedness of markets and private players; it must also be the subject of deliberate political choice at the expense of actors who take advantage of the existing instability. Achieving financial stability is not a question of market efficiency; it is a matter of implementing coercive policies, such as taxation of speculative transactions or control of capital flows.
2. The international mobility of capital hinders the implementation of economic policy in developed countries, as well as in developing countries. Central banks, as well as budget and fiscal authorities, are dominated by financial markets which are quick to sanction with speculative attack policies they judge to be contrary to their interests. A country cannot maintain the stability of its own currency and the autonomy of its economic policy simultaneously in a context of perfect mobility of capital (Mundell's impossible trilogy). In order to regain some room for manoeuvre, countries, especially the weaker ones, must be able to protect themselves against destabilizing effects of short-term capital flows.
3. Capital inflows cause major macroeconomic imbalances (surges in credit, consumption, and non-productive investments), creating

inflationary tendencies and giving rise to speculative bubbles. Preventing such imbalances requires controlling or sterilizing capital flows. This applies particularly to the so-called 'emerging markets'.

4. Since international financial instability is directly linked to the deregulation policies implemented since the early 1980s, one important channel for restoring financial stability is to give every country that so wishes the possibility to introduce capital flows controls, at the national or regional (European) levels, through regulation and taxation. In other words, there is a need for re-regulation, in developed and, even more, in developing countries.

Several types of capital controls and taxation can be implemented, depending on the situation of the country.

1. The best-known tax is that proposed by Tobin, which is intended to reduce speculation and is applied to all transactions on the foreign exchange market. There is a debate nowadays about efficiency of the Tobin tax which was proposed in the 1970s.[12] While it is necessary to adapt this instrument to the new context of global finance, there is no reason to abandon Keynes's intuition that taxation is a useful instrument to fight speculation. There have been several proposals to improve the Tobin tax. The Spahn double tax system, which envisages a very low tax rate in normal conditions, is one of the most interesting proposals. Indeed, this tax system makes it possible to achieve two goals (fighting speculation and collecting funds), and its efficiency against speculation is enhanced by the fact that one of the two tax rates can increase in connection with the intensity of speculation.[13]

2. The introduction of *obligatory reserves* has shown its effectiveness in limiting the scope of destabilizing *capital inflows* without leading to serious productive inefficiency in emerging countries, as is shown by the Chilean example in the 1990s. The rules of the game are announced to the financial community and the reserve ratio or tax rate is fixed in function of the internal macroeconomic situation. This rate can even be reduced to zero, while keeping in place the general measure, as is currently the case with the *encaje* measure in Chile. These measures discourage banks from building up foreign currency exposures. Taxation of such exposures may also be a useful measure.

3. When it has not been possible to avoid a balance of payments crisis, and/or an exchange rate crisis, the advantage of a *control over capital outflows* must be recognized. This type of control proved its efficiency in Malaysia in the late 1990s.

The different experiences of capital taxation and exchange controls just mentioned show that capital control policies may be efficient even when they are implemented by individual countries, sometimes against the will of the financial community and the IMF, as was the case of Malaysia in 1998. But the ultimate goal should be to put into force global taxation among all countries, as was initially proposed by Tobin. It will be difficult to achieve this goal in the short term because of the opposition of countries, such as the United States and the United Kingdom, which protect their financial industry. In the meantime, as an intermediate stage, capital taxation should be implemented on a regional scale by the eurozone, or by the European Union. In some European countries (Belgium, France), the Parliament has already voted in favour of such measures. The vote in the European Parliament for a Tobin tax failed by a small margin. New member states (such as Poland and Hungary) should be permitted to operate exchange controls since they are required to stabilize their own currency without any support from the Western member states or the ECB.

14.7   THE 'SUB-PRIME' CRISIS

The vulnerability of the global financial system was dramatically revealed by the serious crisis that broke out in the summer of 2007. In the background was a general decline in interest rates. Many banks and other financial corporations, unwilling to accept these lower rates, began to adopt highly leveraged positions, incurring large debts and investing this borrowed money in an attempt to obtain higher returns from their positions.

Increased leverage throughout the financial system greatly increased the risks both to individual financial companies and to the system as a whole. Very large sums of money flowed into the hedge funds which adopt highly speculative positions. In Europe, there were also very large placements with the venture capital companies which undertake speculative corporate takeovers and restructurings. But the main object of speculation was a range of mortgage-backed securities issued in the US. These were called 'sub-prime' because the borrowers had low incomes or bad credit records and were therefore much more likely to default than is usually the case. For the same reason the interest rates were high and this attracted the attention of banks and wealth-holders around the world.

Both American and European banks started to purchase immense amounts of securities based on these mortgages. As they did so the agents arranging the mortgages became more and more heedless of the dangers of default. Big loans were made to 'NINJA' borrowers, that is to individuals with No Income, No Job and no Assets. Since the mortgage was not held by the agents arranging it but immediately sold, at a premium, to the banks, there was a big incentive to lend as much money as possible.

The banks purchasing these very dubious assets were in principle repackaging them as standardized securities and reselling them on the security markets, thus dispersing the risks through the financial system. In practice, however, sales to the wider public were limited. The banks moved the mortgage-backed assets and other claims such as credit card debts off their balance sheets into legally separate companies which they themselves established and controlled (called 'conduits' or SIVs, that is 'structured investment vehicles') but this accounting device, although it meant that the banks avoided holding capital against the risk of loss, did nothing to disperse that risk.

The SIVs and conduits obtained very high credit ratings from the rating agencies who were by this time getting most of their profits from certifying this kind of financial instrument. In spite of these high ratings the mortgage-backed securities which they issued (CDOs or 'collateralized debt obligations') were not widely distributed outside the banking system which therefore retained much of the risk. To finance themselves the conduits had to rely on rolling over very short-run borrowing and on guarantees from the banks themselves.

From the start of 2007 defaults on sub-prime mortgages became more and more frequent. Many of these defaults were inevitable, but a slowdown in the US economy increased the number of borrowers in difficulties. The dwellings which supposedly acted as collateral for these loans had been overvalued and house prices in the US started to fall, further reducing the money which could be recovered.

Major banks across the US and Europe, together with financial companies such as hedge funds owned by the banks, were facing very big losses, totalling hundreds of billions of dollars, on their own holdings of CDOs and in keeping afloat the conduits and SIVs which they had guaranteed. It was impossible to calculate either the exact scale of these losses or the size and timing of the payments the banks would have to make. This impaired the liquidity of the global banking system as a whole. Interest rates on inter-bank credit markets shot up. The central banks which are normally able to control these interest rates pumped huge sums into these markets without, however, being able to re-establish control. In a chaotic climate some important financial corporations, such as the British bank Northern Rock and the US investment bank, Lehman Brothers, had to be rescued by the authorities.

Most major banks were compelled to strengthen their positions by raising more capital. One way they did this was by attracting big investments from 'sovereign wealth funds', that is state-owned institutional investors from such countries as Saudi Arabia, Singapore or the United Arab Emirates.

The turmoil in the banking system had serious consequences for production and employment as it provoked a drastic slowdown in economic activity in the US and the UK. It is too soon to measure all these effects but it is clear that there has been a major failure in the regulation of financial systems. Central banks responded more or less effectively as lenders of last resort after the crisis broke out, but they did little or nothing to prevent it. Specific regulatory reforms will no doubt be needed to deal with such problems as the credit rating agencies and the accounting systems which allow banks to move exposures off their balance sheets, but much wider issues are raised about the functioning of the global banking system and the need for social control.[14]

14.8   REFORM OF THE EUROPEAN INSTITUTIONS

If financial stability is to become an important objective of the European Union, and of the eurozone, then important institutional changes should take place. Firstly, a fundamental reform of the statutes, objectives and practices of the ECB is necessary. The ECB mandate needs to be broadened so as to include financial stability, both at the regional (eurozone) level and at the international level. This means, in particular, that the ECB would have to implement active policies both on financial markets and on foreign exchange markets. Such policies could be threefold: (1) surveillance of financial institutions which can go as far as implementing prompt corrective actions in order to prevent failures of individual actors which could lead to systemic risks; (2) intervention on the markets; and (3) coordination with other central banks.

Such a change in the ECB mandate implies that the latter is submitted to democratic control, a necessary reform to permit a wider conception of general interests. With respect to foreign exchange policy, the situation is peculiar since it is a competence shared by the ECB and the EMU governments. The latter could regain control over foreign exchange policy, if they had the political will to do so. The division of labour should be clarified and give the governments (that is the Council) competence over the setting (and readjusting) of target rates and fluctuation bands while assigning the implementation and day-to-day business to the ECB.

Reforms also have to be undertaken with a view to reinforcing the EU's central capacity to confront issues of systemic stability and to undertake active, macro-prudential, measures in response to malfunctions in the increasingly integrated European financial sector. The gradual integration of the European financial sector requires reinforced coordination of the public authorities in charge of financial and banking stability. Progress needs to be made in two directions. First, increased coordination is needed among individual countries. In particular, clear contingency plans are necessary to deal with possible banking crises when measures to be taken exceed the intervention capacities of individual countries and there is a threat of an EU-wide process of contagion. Second, reinforced coordination is needed among the authorities in charge of the different financial – banking and non-banking – actors. The large number of these authorities in the EU, which was pinpointed by the Lamfalussy Report,[15] creates confusion as to responsibilities for preventive policies and for intervention, and makes for delay in taking emergency measures in the case of crises. Broader, multi-sectoral supervision is a necessity since today the dominant financial actors are multi-specialized conglomerates.

The need for stronger coordination both at the pan-European level, and among bank and non-bank supervisors, calls for institutional innovations at the EU level. Different solutions are possible. At the minimum, mechanisms for the collective supervision of financial actors and markets – such as the European Committee on Banking Supervision – should cease to be purely consultative and be accorded full responsibility for system-wide stabilization. The most ambitious solution would be to create a European Financial Service Authority, which could operate in connection with national bodies so as to evolve into a federal institution.

NOTES

1. This neoliberal doctrine is often known as the 'Washington Consensus'.
2. In general, markets without specific controls will fail to provide an appropriate amount of public goods because individuals who benefit from these goods cannot be charged for them. The failure to supplement markets with such public provision is a pervasive problem in the international economy.
3. For an account of existing arrangements see ECB (2006b).
4. One important result of this state of affairs was seen during the 'sub-prime' crisis which broke out in 2007. The Bank of England, responsible for most of the largest financial markets in the EU, and the European Central Bank, responsible for monetary policy in the eurozone, adopted different policies in response to the crisis. These policies worked against each other at least to some extent.
5. For a comprehensive analysis see Boyer et al. (2004).
6. Among large advanced industrial countries, Japan is the only country which experienced a deep economic and financial crisis which lasted for more than a decade (1993–2005). One of the major causes of this crisis has been the vulnerability of the Japanese banking system.
7. Many traditional institutional investors are 100 per cent capitalized and do not take

up positions with borrowed funds. The same is not true, however, for hedge funds and private equity companies which frequently adopt highly leveraged positions but are not subject to Basel II rules.

8. In the wake of the credit crisis of 2007–08, the Commission itself recognized some of these drawbacks and launched an urgent consultation on the need for 'refinements' to the Capital Requirements Directive.

9. An important factor in the financial turbulence which affected the world banking system from 2007 was the complete inadequacy of the risk assessment systems used by the big banks.

10. Reverberation effects correspond to the destabilizing influence exerted by the interactions of the different asset markets. A good example is provided by 'twin crises' (banking crisis and FX crisis) in emerging markets.

11. Boyer et al. (2004).

12. For a sceptical view see Grahl and Lysandrou (2003).

13. See Spahn (1995).

14. For accounts of the crisis see Artus (2008), Blackburn (2008) and Evans (2008). For an official view and a large amount of statistical information see IMF (2008a).

15. See Lamfalussy (2001).

15. Financing social protection and social equity in Europe

Dominique Plihon

15.1 INTRODUCTION

Social protection is one of the building blocks of European democracies. A significant measure of social equity has been achieved through a high level of public spending and taxation within quite different national institutional frameworks (section 2). But globalization is threatening European social models through competition among national social and fiscal systems (section 3). Today, there is a need to meet this threat by preventing tax competition, by the harmonization of fiscal policies through cooperation and through new forms of taxation (section 4). In the context of a globalized world dominated by transnational corporations, 'corporate social responsibility' can be a way to improve social equity and environmental outcomes provided international standards are binding (section 5).

15.2 SOCIAL EQUITY, PUBLIC SPENDING AND TAXATION IN EUROPEAN COUNTRIES

The level of public spending and taxation is much higher on average in European countries than in other industrial countries, such as Japan and the US. One of the major reasons for these differences between European countries and other major industrial countries is the importance of public social expenditure which is higher, on average, in Europe. However one must note that, in the context of globalization, there has been a recent trend towards a narrower gap between European countries and other OECD members, as shown by Table 15.1.

Furthermore, as seen in Table 15.2, ratios of social protection expenditures to GDP are, on the average, significantly lower among some of the most recent members of the European Union, the countries previously in the Soviet bloc, than for those whose membership dates back to 1995 or earlier.[1]

Table 15.1   Public social expenditures* to GDP ratios, percentage points

	1990	1997	2003	Change 1997–2003
EU-15	**21.9**	**23.2**	**23.9**	**+ 0.7**
Japan	11.2	14.2	17.7	+ 3.4
US	13.4	15.4	16.3	+ 0.9
OECD	**17.9**	**19.6**	**20.7**	**+ 1.1**

Note: * All public expenditures for social purposes, including tax expenditures.

Source: OECD, Factbook 2008, Economic, Environmental and Social Statistics.

Table 15.2   Social protection expenditures to GDP ratios in the EU, 2005, percentage points

Social protection expenditure to GDP ratio, 2005, %	
Belgium	27.2
Denmark	30.1
France	31.5
Germany	29.4
Greece	24.2
Ireland	18.2
Netherlands	28.2
Spain	20.8
Portugal	24.7
United Kingdom	26.8
New members:	
Hungary	21.9
Lithuania	13.2
Poland	19.6
Slovenia	23.4
Czech Republic	19.1

Source: Eurostat, ESSPROS Database.

Tax to GDP ratios were rising until 2000 on the average in the EU-25 zone, as shown by Table 15.3. There is a general declining trend from 2000 to 2004. There are, however, important differences among EU-25 countries. Tax to GDP ratios are significantly lower in Ireland and among new members (EU-10). Besides, the reduction in the tax burden took place earlier in the 1990s and was more drastic in the latter countries than in most EU-15 countries.

Table 15.3   Tax to GDP ratios, percentage points

	Tax to GDP ratio (%)		
	1995	2000	2004
Denmark	48.8	49.4	48.8
France	42.7	44.1	43.4
Germany	39.8	41.9	38.7
Ireland	33.1	31.6	30.2
Italy	40.1	41.8	40.6
Netherlands	40.5	41.5	37.8
United Kingdom	35.4	37.4	36.0
Poland	38.5	34.2	32.9
Hungary	41.6	39.2	39.1
EU-25*	**39.7**	**41.0**	**39.3**
EU-15*	**39.8**	**41.3**	**39.6**
EU-10*	**38.0**	**34.7**	**34.5**
Japan	29.1	–	25.6
US	27.3	–	25.4

Note: * Simple averages.

Source: European Commission, 'Structures of the taxation systems in the European Union: 1995–2004', 2006.

In fact, there have been very aggressive and non-cooperative tax policies on the part of some of the small EU countries. The case of Ireland is very illustrative (see Box 15.1).

Social protection systems and their financing in industrialized countries exhibit important differences reflecting different levels of 'socialization'. Public funding of pension, health, social assistance and education spending is much higher in continental Europe than in Anglo-Saxon countries. (For these purposes at least, Ireland is to be regarded as an 'Anglo-Saxon' country.) On the average, public spending amounts to 45 per cent of GDP in continental European countries, of which 11 percentage points go to pensions, 8 to health, 3 to unemployment allowances, 3 to family/ housing/poverty relief, 3 to economic subsidies, 8 to collective spending, 3 to capital spending.

Three types of social protection system which shape public expenditures and taxation are often distinguished. The Bismarkian system (Austria, France, Germany, Netherlands) with high public spending funded by contributions from wages; the Scandinavian system (high public spending funded by income taxes); and the Anglo-Saxon system (low public spending funded by taxation).

BOX 15.1   THE NEGATIVE EFFECTS OF IRISH FISCAL POLICIES

Low taxation is the centrepiece of the Irish strategy to become a 'Celtic tiger economy'.[2] Just as Ireland's corporate tax rate of 12.5 per cent is the lowest in Europe, so also is its tax take as a percentage of GDP: 30.2 per cent as compared with an average EU-25 of 39.3 in 2004. This tax policy raises serious problems. On the one hand, Ireland is playing a non-cooperative game in the EU, based on very aggressive tax competition with other EU members. On the other hand, this policy exerts a profoundly negative impact on large sections of the Irish population for three reasons. First, the policies for cutting taxes on income and corporate profits rather than taxes on expenditure have contributed to an increase in inequality in people's disposable income. Second, the reduction in revenues has been detrimental to the distributional function of fiscal policies. Third, lower tax income translates into lower government spending on welfare and social provision. In 1990, Irish government public social expenditure amounted to 18.7 per cent of GDP. This ratio dropped to 13.8 per cent in 2001. It is the lowest ratio in Europe and compares with an EU-15 average of 23.9 per cent (cf Table 15.1).

15.3   GLOBALIZATION IS THREATENING EUROPEAN SOCIAL MODELS

The European social model is threatened by globalization processes which put tax and social systems into competition. This process is reinforced by the fact that treaties establishing the European Community and the European Union stress four 'fundamental freedoms': free movement of persons, services, goods and capital. The free mobility of capital and products enables companies to choose to locate their production among industrial countries, or between industrial and emerging economies. Taxing the more mobile factors (large companies, financial capital, highly skilled workers and wealthy people) is more and more difficult; this undermines domestic redistributive policies aiming at social equity. Some countries choose to offer low public spending and hence low tax revenues. These countries may thus attract wealthy foreigners and large companies, as is the case with the UK and with some small countries such as Ireland. Very small countries such as Luxembourg may offer low tax rates on property income to attract savings from abroad. Older people may leave the country where they built up their wealth and retire to a country where property and inheritance are tax exempt. Companies may decide to locate their profits in a country other than those where their production is located.

Competition obliges European countries to cut their public spending and to tax mainly immobile factors such as labour and dwellings. Countries gradually lose their ability to implement the redistribution policies decided upon by voters. Lower taxation is used more and more to achieve competitiveness at the expense of social goals. European policies have encouraged a rise in multinationalization of firms leading to fiscal arbitrage.

As a result of globalization and tax competition, most countries have implemented fiscal reforms which alter their tax structure by cutting taxes on mobile factors, such as company profits and high incomes.

Recent Trends in Fiscal and Social Policies

The evolution of tax structures is shaped by globalization and tax competition. The tax burden on capital and high incomes (mobile factors) is declining while remaining stable on labour and consumption (see Table 15.4):

- There is a downward trend in corporate taxation rates and in the taxation of dividends (Table 15.4).
- Income tax becoming less progressive (Table 15.5).
- In Europe, the tax burden on capital is declining, particularly in the new member states, while the tax burden on labour and consumption remains stable (Table 15.6).

Table 15.4 Lower taxes on capital

	Corporate income tax rates		Top marginal tax rates on dividend incomes	
	2000	2003	2000	20003
EU-15	35.1	31.7	51.7	47.9
OECD average	33.6	30.8	50.1	46.4
United States	39.4	39.4	59.3	51.3

Source: OECD (2004).

Table 15.5   Less progressive income tax

	Marginal tax rates for high-income employees	
	2000	20003
EU-15	51.52	49.20
OECD average	48.95	46.75
United States	47.96	42.87

Source: OECD (2004).

Table 15.6   Taxation of capital, labour and consumption

Implicit tax rates on:	1995	1999	2003
Capital			
EU-25	23.1	27.6	25.8
EU-15	24.4	31.1	29.9
EU-10	17.0	17.2	14.0
Labour			
EU-25	35.7	36.1	35.9
EU-15	36.1	36.7	36.5
EU-10	35.2	35.2	34.7
Consumption			
EU-25	21.1	21.3	21.9
EU-15	21.5	22.5	22.6
EU-10	20.5	19.3	20.8

Source: European Commission (2006).

According to Vito Tanzi (2000), 'the most direct and powerful impact [of globalization] will probably come through its effect on tax systems . . . One can visualize many fiscal termites that are busily gnawing at the foundations of the fiscal house'. These include:

- the growing inability of countries to tax, especially with high rates, financial capital and also incomes of individuals with high mobility and highly tradable skills.
- a growing use of electronic trade.
- the growth of new financial instruments and agents for channelling savings, such as derivatives and hedge funds.

The growing importance of offshore financial centres and tax havens constitutes the dark side of financial globalization. As John Christensen

(2006) puts it, calling into question the conventional wisdom about corruption:

> Most reasonable observers might expect that government of onshore States would act collectively to prevent tax and regulatory degradation, but in practice key actors, notably Switzerland, the UK and the USA, act to restrain efforts at achieving global cooperation ... Around 40 per cent of the countries identified as least corrupt are offshore tax havens; including Switzerland, UK, Luxemburg, Germany, USA, Belgium and Ireland.

15.4 THE NEED FOR COOPERATION AND INSTITUTIONAL INNOVATIONS TO PREVENT THE COLLAPSE OF THE EUROPEAN SOCIAL MODEL

Europe has to choose between two strategies. The first strategy consists in moving towards a liberal model, based on tax competition leading to tax cuts and the privatization of welfare. This strategy supposes that Europeans agree to forgo their social models and to live in a society with greater inequalities. This strategy must be rejected because it is contrary to European values, such as social equity, and to the interest of most European citizens. The second strategy consists in maintaining the European social model, characterized by a significant level of social transfers and public expenditures, and thus of taxation. The social systems will have to be protected from tax competition by the introduction of minimum tax rates in some cases, and by tough measures against tax havens on a worldwide scale. The European social model will have to rely on its comparative advantages (free education and health for all, public infrastructures, social security benefits) to remain competitive in the face of globalization.

In most European countries, the high level of unemployment, the ageing of populations, and the rising trend of health spending are likely to lead to an increase in social contributions. This rise in social contributions could be avoided if people resorted more to private insurance, as in the United States. But the US experience does not give any evidence that private health insurance or pensions are more efficient and cheaper than public social insurance (see Chapter 9).

Reforms are necessary to adapt the European social model to new needs of the populations and to new constraints related to globalization. European countries have to set new forms of cooperation, and to invent new forms of taxation.

Towards Minimum Social Standards

It does not seem possible, in the current state of European integration, to unify or even to bring about a convergence of national social protection systems, even though market unification in Europe makes it more and more difficult for different social systems to coexist. Social protection is bound to remain largely national as long as social institutions, trade unions and negotiations are domestic. European social systems are extremely heterogeneous in terms of pensions, unemployment and health benefits. Hence, each country should remain responsible for implementing social policies according to its citizens' political choices. But, at the same time, EU members must define common principles and standards. The open method of coordination should be a useful tool in this respect. First, EU members ought to state clearly that the principle of free competition should not apply to social insurance regimes, with a view to protecting their social and redistributive goals. Second, EU members should reduce the risk of competition by defining common social standards at the European level: minimum wage, old age income, universal health insurance, family benefits, minimum pension income.

Coordination of Capital Income Taxation

One of the major consequences of tax competition is to bring about a sharp decline in capital income taxation because capital is mobile and can take advantage of low tax locations. Coordination needs to be substituted for competition. Company taxation certainly is one of the most sensitive tax issues although this tax amounts to a small share of tax revenues. According to a standard, and arbitrary, definition, company taxation is the sum of corporate taxation, wages tax, tax on company capital, company property tax and local taxes. The level and the structure of company taxation differs sharply from one European country to another. It varies from 1.7 per cent of GDP (Germany) to more than 5 per cent (France, Italy and Sweden), as shown in Table 15.7.

It would be difficult to harmonize the different components of company taxation so as to have similar taxation structures. Local taxes, for instance, are typically linked to domestic factors. The major goal for harmonization should be corporation tax. In the 1990s most European countries cut their corporate tax rates, while widening their tax base, in response to tax competition. This competition has recently been enhanced since new member states generally have lower rates than 'old' member states. In the ten years from 1995 to 2005, the average statutory rate in the 'old' member states fell by 8.1 percentage points whilst falling by

Table 15.7   Company taxes as a percentage of GDP in 2003

	Corporate tax	Tax on wages	Others	Total	Employers' social contributions
Denmark	3.0	0.2	0.5	3.7	0
France	2.5	1.1	2.1	5.7	11.1
Germany	1.3	0.0	0.4	1.7	7.1
Italy	2.9	0.0	2.6	5.5	8.9
UK	2.8	0.0	1.7	4.5	3.7
Poland	1.8	0.2	0.4	2.4	8.8
Sweden	2.5	2.5	0.6	5.6	11.8
USA	2.1	0.0	1.5	3.6	3.4

Source: OECD (2005a).

10.8 percentage points in the 'new' ones. And, as the 'new' members of the union started out with lower rates than the 'old' ones, by 2005 their average nominal tax rate was 10 percentage points lower than in the 'old' member states.

The irony is that the 'new' member states that have participated most actively in this downward tax competition have not even had the short-term gains in the form of increased foreign direct investment from the 'old' Member states that they could have expected.

Corporations increasingly base their success on institutional and societal competitiveness, in short on the qualities of the societies they are part of, typically financed by public funds, rather than qualities they have built and developed independently. As a result, more and more government spending is used to enhance just such competitiveness. Not just equity but efficiency considerations would suggest that corporations, not just their workers, should contribute substantially to the investments that make them flourish.[2]

Thus new rules should be implemented to stop the erosion of EU members' tax revenues. First, minimum rates should be imposed on corporate tax rates, which means that some states (such as Ireland or Estonia, which have tax rates equal to 10 per cent and 0 per cent, respectively) should increase their tax rates. Second, tax bases should be harmonized. Third, the *source principle* should be applied, rather than the *residence principle* for corporate taxation. The *residence principle* allows firms to escape taxation if they locate in a tax haven. Convergence in corporate taxation will certainly be painful and will require some political courage on the part of governments. But this harmonization is necessary for reasons of equity and fair competition. A good principle could be to trade corporate taxation convergence against more freedom for member states to subsidize their companies.

Tax Reforms Aiming at Financing Social Security

Different tax reforms have been implemented in European countries with a view to financing social security systems. Some countries (Germany) are in the process of transferring to VAT a part of the burden of social contributions previously paid by firms. But while this policy is good for competitiveness, because VAT, unlike social security contributions, is levied on imports but not on exports, this tax measure is not fair on social grounds because it reduces employees' purchasing power.

A more satisfactory way to cope with this situation, implemented by Sweden, is to raise environmental taxation in order to cut personal income taxation and employers' contributions. These measures are interesting because they follow the 'double dividend' logic. Indeed, implementing environmental taxation has two potential advantages: firstly, this tax would be an incentive to reduce the use of polluting products; secondly, it would permit lower labour taxation, which is supposed to create employment. In other words, the combination of environmental taxation and of cuts in employers' social contributions may generate, at no net cost to the public finances, both lower pollution and less unemployment.

Common European Taxes

There are good reasons to introduce common taxes in the EU. Firstly, common taxes would represent a significant step towards the building of European citizenship. Secondly, there is a need to finance common goods with a European dimension, such as education, health, equity, a cleaner environment and financial stability. Such common goods are best financed by common taxes. Several types of European taxes can be proposed. Two taxes would be particularly well adapted in today's Europe. First, environmental taxation is a natural candidate since environmental problems cannot generally be solved efficiently at the national level. Revenues from this tax could be used both at the European level to finance environmental investments (research, alternative sources of energy, public infrastructures), and at the national level to reduce social security contributions and to support employment. Second, common financial taxes could be implemented, such as taxes on foreign exchange transactions and on stock market transactions (see Chapter 14). Revenues derived from these common financial taxes could be used to finance the common

European budget which needs to be increased well above its actual level (1 per cent of European GDP). The increase in the EU budget could be used to finance European public goods such as education, and to finance redistributive policies, particularly in the direction of new EU members, to help them to catch up with old EU members in both technology and social welfare.

15.5 'CORPORATE SOCIAL RESPONSIBILITY' AS A METHOD OF SOCIAL REGULATION?

Transnational companies are major actors in globalization. They play an important role in social regulation in Europe. Recent years have been marked by fights against the subcontracting practices of Nike or Reebok, against the irresponsible negligence of TotalFinaElf, against layoffs, by Danone or Marks & Spencer, which were not required for the survival of the corporation but were carried out just in order to boost shareholder returns, against 'macdonaldization' and the marketization of the world, for the respect of the International Conventions of ILO and the workers' rights. . . . These struggles pose, in an increasingly acute way, the question of the democratic control of the major decisions of the transnational corporations, each one of which affects thousands, even millions of people over vast areas of the planet.

'Corporate social responsibility'(CSR) appears to be one of the answers from leading elites to the social movements which are increasingly challenging the exorbitant powers of the multinationals, which have been strengthened over a period now of 20 years by political decisions to privatize and deregulate.

Two tendencies can be recognized in 'corporate social responsibility'. First, 'corporate social responsibility' can be viewed as falling under the more global trend towards the privatization[4] of law. The field of 'social responsibility' is thus that of 'soft law', non-constraining, freely chosen, made from an engagement with moral values, but not judicially punishable, in contrast to state legal regulations. It is a matter of promoting self-regulation, in cooperation with chosen partners, instead of the collective bargaining with compulsory partners. In this view, CSR could be a way to short-circuit the trade unions. The majority of corporations see CSR in this way. The response of the multinationals to the Green Book of the European Commission often insists on the necessarily voluntary and non-constraining character of CSR initiatives. The companies are often ready to devote some resources to the creation of a specific directive ('business ethics' or 'sustainable development'), to the drafting of charters and the diffusion of 'good practices'. Much rarer are those which would readily agree to work out a public' social assessment', based on objective, measurable criteria, defined outside the company.

According to a second view, the emergence of corporate social responsibility testifies to the weakening of the hegemony of the neoliberal doctrine of 'corporate governance' exclusively in terms of 'shareholder value' and of the growing interest for the reformist approach known as the 'stakeholder' enterprise, which recognizes the legitimacy of the interests of all the 'stakeholders' of the company. Deep down and to a large extent, the rise of the 'social responsibility' theme is linked to the crippling illegitimacy of the pure neoliberal doctrine which considers that the exclusive mission of the corporation is to maximize the income of shareholders. In this view, CSR can prove beneficial for all partners of corporations, besides shareholders. CSR can be a way to increase the room for manoeuvre of the labour unions, independent NGOs, and international organizations such as the ILO. CSR should be used to take the multinational companies and their managers 'at their word'.[5]

If one takes this second view seriously, which considers that CSR matters, binding standards are needed to take CSR beyond voluntarism. Actual experience shows that the voluntary commitment of business is insufficient to guarantee good practice.[6] For instance, Coca-Cola subscribes to high principles of ethical behaviour and stresses the importance of 'using natural resources responsibly'. Yet thousands of miles from the company's headquarters, its subsidiary in India stands accused of depleting village wells in areas where water is notoriously scarce.

Today, there are no mechanisms to make ethical and human rights standards binding on business. International procedures are lacking and resorting to national laws is not efficient for the regulation of transnational corporations. Parent companies establish separate entities to operate in different countries. It is then difficult to hold transnational corporations responsible for the misconduct of their subsidiaries. Among NGOs and the UN administrations, such as the UN sub-commission on the promotion of human rights, there is an emerging consensus for the promulgation of binding international standards.

To summarize, there are good reasons why multinationals should be brought under international law:[7]

- human rights and the environment need protection,
- national legislation and regulation are insufficient,
- wholly voluntary approaches are totally inadequate,
- companies have rights but few obligations,

- the growing power of multinationals needs to be checked,
- the risk of legal action would influence markets and motivate companies to comply.

Besides binding international standards, NGOs such as Christian Aid advocate complementary regulatory mechanisms, such as the introduction of penalties for failure to meet new standards, as well as improved access to redress for individuals and communities harmed by corporate activities.

The European Union has a critical role to play in developing new international standards for business because some of its member states are home to some of the largest and more influential transnational corporations. Moreover, company and commercial law is increasingly formulated within a Europe-wide context.

Unfortunately, the European Commission's view on CSR is very conservative because it only seeks to encourage 'best practices' as can be seen in its Green Book on 'Promoting a European framework for corporate social responsibility' (2001).

Regrettably, it seems that the European Commission prefers the neo-liberal view, that SCR means the privatization of corporate law. On the key issues of governance, takeovers and rewards to senior management, it has adopted an ultra-liberal position, ignoring the obvious social consequences of executive greed (which is seen merely as an issue for investors, not for society as a whole) and it pushes for unrestricted mergers and takeovers even though, in the US itself, most states have legislated to constrain mergers and takeovers in order to stabilize employment.

15.6 CONCLUSION

This book is devoted to the emergence of a global financial system, to its consequences especially in Europe and to the necessity of social control over the powerful forces which have been released in the financial sphere. A wide range of policy measures – including new forms of regulation, reinforced interventions, fiscal initiatives, legislative reforms and so on – have been recommended to limit the threats to economic stability, to employment security and to social justice which current financial developments bring with them and to impose wider and more positive goals on the global financial system.

The present chapter responds to the fact that these financial forces are not operating in isolation. They have been released in a context in which many governments and international agencies are reluctant to interfere with the activities of powerful corporations or to assert social objectives against market forces. The use of off-shore centres by corporations and wealthy individuals to escape from both financial regulation and the tax regimes of the countries in which their income is generated is one key example of this continuity between the financial aspects of globalization and its more general features. The phenomenon of regime competition, promoted by transnational corporations especially in the field of taxation, is another such example.

Thus the need for more effective control over financial functions is part of the more general need to assert social control over the emerging global system and to subject that system to the need for greater equality both within individual countries and at the international level. It has only been possible to consider some possible strategies and some possible instruments to achieve these goals; no doubt other possibilities will arise as social movements of many kinds endeavour to counter, and to correct, the social and environmental damage done through unchecked market activities in the emerging global systems.

NOTES

1. Indicators in Table 15.2, which were prepared by Eurostat, are different from indicators in Table 15.1, which were prepared with OECD methodology.
2. See Lysandrou (2006).
3. International Confederation of Free Trade Unions (2006)
4. Or of 're-feudalization' according to the expression of the lawyer Alain Supiot (2001) on 'the employers' self-regulation'.
5. On Corporate Social Responsibility see Attac, Conseil Scientifique (2003).
6. Christian Aid (2005).
7. See Christian Aid (2004).

References

Adam, K., T. Jappelli, A. Menichini, M. Padula and M. Pagamo (2002), 'Analyse, compare and apply alternative indicators and monitoring methodologies to measure the evolution of capital market integration in the EU', CSEF, University of Salerno.

Aglietta, M. (1998), 'Capitalism at the turn of the century: regulation theory and the challenge of social change', *New Left Review*, I(232) (November–December).

Aglietta, M. and A. Rebérioux (2005), *Corporate Governance Adrift*, Cheltenham, UK and Northampton, MA, USA: Edward Elgar.

Albert, M. (1993), *Capitalism against Capitalism*, London: Whurr Publishers.

Aliber, R.Z. (2005), 'The 35 most tumultuous years in monetary history: shocks, the transfer problem and financial trauma', *IMF Staff Papers*, **52**, (special issue).

Allen, F., L. Bartiloro and O. Kowalewski (2005), 'The financial system of the EU 25'; accessed at: http://ssrn.com/abstract=871454.

Anderson, J., J. Grahl, S. Jefferys and A. Tasiran (2006), 'Labour market flexibility and sectoral productivity: a comparative study', Department of Trade and Industry employment relations research series no. 66.

APACS and British Bankers Association (2006), *Financial Inclusion*, November, London: British Bankers' Association.

Artus, Patrick (ed.) (2008), *La Crise Financière: Causes, Effects et Réformes Necessaries*, Paris: PUF.

Attac, Conseil Scientifique (2003), 'Responsabilité sociale des entreprises ou contrôle démocratique des décisions économiques?' accessed at www.france.attac.org.

Baele, L., A. Ferrando, P. Hördahl, E. Krylova and C. Monnet (2004), 'Measuring financial integration in the Euro area', European Central Bank occasional paper series no. 14, April.

Baker, D. (2003), 'The Battle over restructuring social security in the United States', paper presented to the Conference on the Privatization of Public Pension Systems: Forces, Experiences, Systems, Vienna, accessed at www.epoc.uni-bremen.de.

Bank for International Settlements (BIS) (1983), 'The international inter-bank market: a descriptive study', BIS economic papers no. 8, Geneva.

BIS (2003), 'Incentive structures in institutional asset management and their implications for financial markets', report submitted by a working group of the Committee on The Global Financial System, Geneva.

BIS (2004), 'Triennial and semi-annual surveys on positions in global over-the-counter (OTC), derivatives markets at end-June 2004', December, Geneva.

BIS (2005), 'Annual report', Geneva: BIS.

BIS (2007), 'Triennial Central Bank survey of foreign exchange and derivatives market activity in 2007', December, Geneva: BIS.

Barr, N. (2001), *The Welfare State as Piggy Bank: Information, Risk, Uncertainty, and the Role of the State*, Oxford: Oxford University Press.

Barros P.P., E. Berglöf, P. Fulghieri, J. Gual, C. Mayer and X. Vives (2005), 'Integration of European banking: the way forward', *Monitoring European Deregulation*, 3, CEPR and Fundacion BBVA.

Barroso, J.M. (2005), 'Working together for growth and jobs: a new start to the Lisbon Strategy', communication to the Spring European Council, COM (2005) 24, Brussels.

Becht, M., P. Bolton and A. Roell (2002), 'Corporate governance and control', in G. Constandinides, M. Harris and R. Stulz (eds), *Handbook of the Economics of Finance*, Amsterdam: North Holland.

Begg, I. (2007), 'Lisbon II, two years on: an assessment of the partnership for growth and jobs', special Centre for European Policy Studies report, Brussels, July.

Belaisch, A., L. Kodres, J. Levy and A. Ubide (2001) 'Euro-area banking at the crossroads', International Monetary Ford working paper series WP/01/28.

Berle, A. and G. Means (1932), *The Modern Corporation and Private Property*, Macmillan, republished 1991, New Brunswick, NJ: Transaction Publishers.

Blackburn, R. (2006), 'Finance and the fourth dimension', *New Left Review*, **39** (May–June), pp. 39–70.

Blackburn, R. (2008), 'The subprime crisis', *New Left Review*, **50** (March–April).

Bloomfield, A. (1959), *Monetary Policy under the International Gold Standard, 1890–1914*, New York: Federal Reserve Bank of New York.

Bloomfield, A. (1968), 'Patterns of fluctuation in international finance before 1914', Princeton studies in international finance no. 21, Princeton University.

Borio, C. (2005), 'The search for the elusive twin goals of monetary and financial stability', paper presented at the 2005 DG ECFIN Annual Research Conference, Brussels, 7 October.

Boyer, R., M. Dehove and D. Plihon (2004), *Les Crises Financières*, Paris: Conseil d'Analyse Economique, Documentation Française.

Brenner, R. (2003a), *The Boom and the Bubble*, London: Verso.

Brenner, R. (2003b), 'Towards the precipice', *London Review of Books*, **25**(3), 6 February.

Cabral, I., Frank Dierick and Jukka Vesala (2002), 'Banking integration in the Euro area', European Central Bank occasional paper Series no. 6, December.

Callaghan and M. Höpner (2005), 'European integration and the clash of capitalism: political cleavages over takeover liberalization', *Comparative European Politics*, **3**(3), pp. 307–32.

Cameron, R. and L. Neal (2003), *A Concise Economic History of the World*, Oxford: Oxford University Press.

Caprio, G. and D. Klingebiel (2003), 'Episodes of systemic and borderline financial crises', mimeo, World Bank, Washington, DC, January.

Casey, J-P. and K. Lannoo (2005), *Europe's Hidden Capital Markets*, Brussels: Centre for European Policy Studies.

Christensen, J. (2006), 'Follow the money – how tax havens facilitate dirty money flows and distort global markets', Tax Justice Network, accessed September, 2006 at. www.taxjustice.net.

Christian Aid (2005), 'Behind the mask – the real face of corporate responsibility', London: Christian Aid.

City of London (2008), 'Global Financial Centres Index', accessed at www.cityoflondon.gov.uk.

Competition Commission (2008), 'Market investigation into payment protection insurance', provisional findings report, June, accessed at www.competition-commission.org.uk.

Corbett, J. and T. Jenkinson (1996), 'The financing of industry 1970–89', *Journal of Japanese and International Economics*, **10**(1).

Council of the European Union (2001), 'Quality and viability of pensions: joint report on objectives and working methods in the area of pensions', SOC 469, ECOFIN 334, Brussels.

Credit Action (2006), 'Debt facts and figures', compiled 6 January, accessed at www.creditaction.org.uk.

Cruikshank, D. (2000), 'Competition in UK Banking: a report to the Chancellor of the Exchequer', HMSO, London.

Danthine, J.P., Francesco Giavazzi and Ernst-Ludvig Von Thadden (2000), 'European financial markets after EMU: a first assessment', Centre for Economic Policy Research, discussion paper series, no. 2413, Brussels.

Davis, P. (2002), 'Institutional investors, corporate governance and the performance of the corporate sector', *Economic Systems*, **26**(3), 203–29.

Davis, P. and B. Steil (2001), *Institutional Investors*, Cambridge, MA: MIT.

De Boissieu, C. (2003), 'Financial supervision, banking stability and the ECB', evidence to the Committee on Monetary and Economic Affairs of the European Parliament, Brussels, 12 June.

De Cecco, M. (1974), *Money and Empire: The International Gold Standard, 1890–1914*, Oxford: Blackwell.

De Grauwe, P. (1994), *The Economics of Monetary Integration*, Oxford: Oxford University Press.

De Gregorio, Jose (1999), 'Financial integration, financial development and economic growth', *Estudios de Economia*, **26**(2), pp. 137–61.

De Lima, P., R. Hugounenq and B. Ventelou (2002), 'Public services and European Integration', in EuroMemorandum Group (ed.), 'Better institutions, rules and tools for full employment and social welfare in Europe', EuroMemorandum 2002, accessed at www.memo-Europe. uni-bremen.de.

Dermine, J. (2003), 'Banking in Europe: past, present and future, in V. Gaspar, Philipp Hartmann and Olaf Sleijpen (eds), *The Transformation of the European Financial System: Second ECB Central Banking Conference*, Frankfurt: European Central Bank.

Deutscher Bundestag (2006),'Sechzehntes Hauptgutachten der Monopolkommission 2004–2005, issue 16/2460, 25 August.

Dickson, Martin (2006), 'Capital gain: how London is thriving as it takes on the global competition', *Financial Times*, 27 March.

Dore, R. (2000), *Stock Market Capitalism-Welfare Capitalism: Japan and Germany versus the Anglo-Saxons*, Oxford: Oxford University Press.

Dräger, Klaus (2003), '"Pension reform" in the European Union', background dossier for the meeting of the Forum Social Europe and the GUE/NGL Group in the European Parliament, Brussels, 3 April 2003; accessed at www.epoc.uni-bremen.de.

Dräger, K. and S. Wagenknecht (2005), 'Der Bolkesteinhammer muss weg!', Brussels: GUE/NGL.

European Bank for Reconstruction and Development (EBRD) (2007), *Transition Report 2007*, London: EBRD.

European Central Bank (ECB) (2003), 'Developments in the debt financing of the Euro area private sector', *European Central Bank, Monthly Bulletin*, (November), Frankfurt.

ECB (2004), 'Report on EU banking structure', European Central Bank, Frankfurt, November.

ECB (2005), 'Banking structures in the new EU member states', European Central Bank, Frankfurt, January.

ECB (2006a), 'EU banking structures', European Central Bank, Frankfurt, October.

ECB (2006b), 'The EU arrangements for financial crisis management', Financial Stability Review, European Central Bank, Frankfurt, December.

ECB (2006c), 'Financial stability report', European Central Bank, Frankfurt, May.

ECB (2007a) 'The EU arrangements for financial crisis management', *European Central Bank, Monthly Bulletin*, (February), Frankfurt.

ECB (2007b), 'EU banking structures', European Central Bank, Frankfurt, October.

ECB (2007c), 'Financial integration in Europe', European Central Bank, Frankfurt, March.

ECB (2008), European Central Bank: the first 10 years', *European Central Bank Monthly Bulletin*, special issue, (May), Frankfurt.

European Coalition for Responsible Credit (ECRC) (2006), 'Principles for responsible credit', 24 July 2008, accessed at www.responsible-credit. net.

EDHEC (2005), *European Asset Management Practices Survey*, Lille-Nice: Edhec Business School.

Eichengreen, B. (1996), *Globalizing Capital: A History of the International Monetary System*, Princeton, NJ: Princeton University Press

Emerson, M., M. Aujean, M. Catinat, P. Goubet and A Jacquemin (1988), 'The economics of 1992', *European Economy*, **35**, (March).

Erturk, I., J. Froud, S. Johal and K. Williams (2005), 'Pay for corporate performance or pay as social division: rethinking the problem of top management pay in giant Corporations', *Competition and Change*, **9**(1), 49–75.

Etxezarreta, Miren (2005), 'The "modernization" of social policy: a critique of pension reforms', in Jörg Huffschmid (ed.), *Economic Policy for a Social Europe: A Critique of Neo-liberalism and Proposals for Alternatives*, London: Palgrave.

European Coalition for Responsible Credit (2005), 'Ensuring a responsible credit market, principles for responsible credit', accessed at www. responsible-credit.net/media.php?id=1651.

European Commission (1983), 'Financial integration: communication from the Commission to the Council', COM (83) 207 final, 20 April, Brussels.

European Commission (1985), 'Completing the internal market', white paper from the Commission to the European Council, COM (1985) 310 final, Brussels.

European Commission (1996), 'The impact and effectiveness of the single market: communication to the European Parliament and Council', 30 October, Brussels.

European Commission (1999), 'Financial services: implementing the framework for financial markets – action plan', COM (1999) 232, Brussels.

European Commission (2000a), 'The Lisbon European Council – an agenda of economic and social renewal for Europe', contribution of the European Commission to the special European Council in Lisbon, 23-24 March 2000, DOC/00/7, Brussels.

European Commission (2000b), 'The social policy agenda', COM (2000) 379 final, Brussels.

European Commission (2000c), 'Realising the European Union's potential: consolidating and extending the Lisbon Strategy', contribution of the European Commission to the Spring European Council, Stockholm, 23-24 March, 2001, Brussels.

European Commission (2001), 'Promoting a European framework for corporate social responsibility, COM (2001) 366 final, July, Brussels.

European Commission (2002) 'Report by the Economic and Financial Committee (EFC) on EU financial integration', European economy, economic papers no. 171, May, Brussels.

European Commission (2003a), 'Tracking EU financial integration', Commission staff working paper 26 SEC(2003) 628, May, Brussels.

European Commission (2003b), 'Report on the implementation of the 2002 broad economic policy guidelines', COM (2003) 4 final, Brussels.

European Commission (2003c) 'Draft joint exclusion report: statistical annexe', Commission working paper, COM (2003) 773 final, Brussels.

European Commission (2003d), 'Reinforcing the statutory audit in the EU', COM (2003) 286 final, Brussels.

European Commission (2004a), 'Financial integration monitor', SEC (2004) 559, April, Brussels.

European Commission (2004b), 'D.-G. for employment and social affairs', report of the High Level Group on the Future of Social Policy in an Enlarged European Union, Brussels.

European Commission (2004c), 'Amended proposal for a directive of the European Parliament and of the Council on the harmonisation of the laws, regulations and administrative provisions of the member states concerning credit for consumers repealing Directive 87/102/EC and modifying Directive 93/13/EC', COM (2004) 747 final of 28 October 2004.

European Commission (2005a), 'White paper on financial services policy 2005–2010', COM(2005) 629, Brussels.

European Commission (2005b), 'On the social agenda', COM (2005) 33 final, February, Brussels.

European Commission (2005c), 'Green paper on financial services policy 2005–2010', COM (2005) 177, Brussels.

European Commission (2005d), 'Modified proposal for a directive of the European Parliament and of the Council on credit agreements for consumers amending Council Directive 93/13/EC', COM (2005) 483 final of 7 October 2005, Brussels.

European Commission (2006a), 'Single market in financial services progress report 2004-2005', SEC (2006) 17, Brussels.

European Commission (2006b), 'Synthesis report on adequate and sustainable pensions' with 'technical annexe', COM (2006) 62 final, Brussels.

European Commission (2006c), 'Green paper: modernising labour law to meet the challenges of the 21st century', COM (2006) 708 final, Brussels.

European Commission (2006d), 'Report of the Mortgage Funding Expert Group', December, Brussels.

European Commission (2006e), 'Directive 2006/43/EC on statutory audits of annual and consolidated accounts (8th Company Law Directive)', Brussels.

European Commission (2007a), 'Green paper on retail financial services in the single market', COM (2007) 226 final of 30 April 2007, Brussels.

European Commission (2007b), 'White paper on the integration of EU mortgage credit markets', COM (2007) 807 final, Brussels.

European Commission (2007c), 'Report on the implementation of the directive on takeover bids', SEC (2007) 268, Brussels.

European Commission (2007d), 'European financial integration report 2007', SEC (2007) 1696/10 December 2007

European Commission (2008), 'Financial services provision and prevention of financial exclusion', Brussels.

European Council (2000), 'Presidency conclusions', Lisbon European Council, 23–24 March 2000.

European Council (2001), 'Quality and viability of pensions', joint report on objectives and working methods in the area of pensions, SOC 469 ECOFIN 334 of 24 November, Brussels.

European Trade Union Confederation (ETUC) (2006), 'Corporate governance at European level', resolution adopted by the ETUC Executive Committee, March.

European Union (2003), Directive on the activities and supervision of institutions for occupational retirement provision, Directive 2003/71/EC, Official Journal of 31 December, L 235, p. 10.

European Union (2004), Directive on takeover bids, Directive 2004/25/EC, Official Journal of 30 April, p. 12.

European Union (2006), Directive on statutory audits of annual and consolidated accounts (8th company law directive), Directive 2006/43/EC Official Journal of 9 June, 2006, L157, p. 87.

European Union (2002), Regulation on the application of international accounting standards, Regulation (EC) no. 1606/2002, Official Journal of 11 September, 2002, L243, p. 1.

Evans, T. (2008), 'Die internationalen finanzielen Turbulenzen', in *Euromemo 2007,* VSA Verlag, English version accessed at, www.memo-europe.uni-bremen.de/euromemo/indexmem.htm.

Financial Services Authority (FSA) (2005), 'The sale of payment protection insurance – the results of thematic work', London: FSA.

FIN-USE Forum (2004), 'Financial services, consumers and small businesses: a user perspective on the reports on banking, asset management, securities and insurance of the post FSAP stocktaking groups', European Commission DG Internal Market, Brussels.

Fisher, I. (1933), 'The debt deflation theory of great depressions', *Econometrica,* **1**(1), 337–57.

Frangakis, M. (2005), 'Green paper on financial policy in the EU 2005-2010', note prepared for the FISC Network Workshop, Berlin, 24–25 June.

Friedman, M. (1953), 'The case for flexible exchange rates', in *Essays in Positive Economics,* Chicago: University of Chicago Press.

Frölich, Nils and Jörg Huffschmid (2004), *Der Finanzdienstleistungsektor in Deutschland, Entwicklung, Politik, Strategien,* Dusseldorf: Boeckler.

Froud, J., C. Haslam, S. Johal and K. Williams (2000), 'Restructuring for shareholder value and its implications for labour', *Cambridge Journal of Economics,* **24**, 771–97.

Froud, J., S. Johal, A. Leaver and K. Williams (2007), 'Private equity, intermediary capitalism and the agent problem: written submission on private equity for the Treasury Select Committee', mimeo, Centre for Research on Socio-Cultural Change, University of Manchester.

Gershenkron, A. (1962), *Economic Backwardness in Historical Development,* Cambridge, MA: Harvard University Press.

Giannetti, M., L. Guiso, T. Jappelli, M. Padula and M. Pagano (2002), 'Financial market integration, corporate financing and economic growth: final report,' 22 November, *European Economy,* economic papers no.179.

Glyn, A.J. (2001), 'Inequalities of employment and wages in OECD Countries,' *Oxford Bulletin of Economics and Statistics,* **63**, (special issue: The Labour Market Consequences of Technical and Structural Change).

Goergen, M., M. Martynova and L. Renneboog (2005), 'Corporate governance convergence: evidence from takeover regulation reforms in Europe', Tjalling C. Koopmans Research Institute discussion paper 05-19.

Goodhart, C. et al. (1998) *Financial Regulation: Why, How and Where Now?*, London: Routledge.

Grahl, J (2001), 'Globalised finance and the challenge to the euro', *New Left Review*, (March/April).

Grahl, J. (2007), 'The microfoundations debate and the strange death of Keynesian Europe', in G. Krause (ed.), *Is Keynes an Alternative?*, Berlin: Dietz Verlag.

Grahl, J. and P. Lysandrou (2003), 'Sand in the wheels or spanner in the works? The Tobin tax and global finance', *Cambridge Journal of Economics*, **27**(4) (July), pp. 23–46, 597–621.

Grahl, J. and P. Lysandrou (2006), 'Capital market trading volume: an overview and some preliminary conclusions', *Cambridge Journal of Economics*, **30**, 955–79.

Grahl, J. and P. Teague (2003), 'Problems of financial integration in the EU', *European Journal of Public Policy*, **12**(6), pp 1005–21.

Gnerrera, F. (2006), 'The wrong focus? How the race to meet targets can throw corporate America off course', *Financial Times*, 24 July.

Guerrera, F. and J. Politi (2007), 'Moody's slams private equity', *Financial Times*, 9 July.

Guiso, L., P. Sapienza. and L. Zingales (2002), 'Does local financial development matter?', CEPR working paper DP3307.

Hall, P. and D. Soskice (2001), *Varieties of Capitalism: The Institutional Foundations of Comparative Advantage*, Oxford: Oxford University Press.

Hansmann, H. and R. Kraakman (2001), 'The end of history for corporate law', *Georgetown Law Journal,* **89**, pp. 439–68.

Heinemann, F. and M. Jopp (2002), 'Gyllenhammer Report, The benefits of a working European retail market for financial services', report to the European Financial Services Round Table, Europa-Union Verlag.

Henning, C.R. (1985), *Currencies and Politics in the United States, Germany and Japan*, Washington, DC: Institute for International Economics.

Herbertsson, T. and J. Orszag (2001), 'Policy options and issues in reforming European supplementary pension systems', SSRN working paper.

Holland, S. (ed.) (1972), *The State as Entrepreneur*, London: Weidenfeld and Nicolson.

HM Treasury (2004), *Promoting Financial Inclusion*, foreword, London: HMSO.

Holmstrom, B. and S. Kaplan (2003), 'The state of US corporate governance: what's right and what's wrong', National Bureau for Economic Research working paper no. 9613.

Huffschmid, J. (2002), 'Financial markets in Europe', unpublished paper.

Huffschmid, J. (ed.) (2005), *Economic Policy for a Social Europe: A Critique of Neo-liberalism and Proposals for Alternatives*, London: Palgrave.

Hutton, W. (1996), *The State We're in: Why Britain is in Crisis and How to Overcome It*, London: Vintage.

International Financial Services (IFSL) Research (2008a), *Securitisation*, March, London: IFSL.

IFSL Research (2008b), *Sovereign Wealth Funds*, April, London: IFSL.

IFSL Research (2008c), *International Financial Markets in the UK*, May, London: IFSL.

International Monetary Fund (IMF) (2008a) *Global Financial Stability Report 2008*, Washington, DC: IMF.

IMF (2008b), *Coordinated Portfolio Investment Survey*, Table 11, July, Washington, DC: IMF.

Institut für Finanzdienstleistungen (2005), *EU-Verbraucherkreditrichtlinienentwurf 2005: Kritische Einführung und Ausgewählte Auszüge*, Hamburg

Inter-Institutional Monitoring Group (2004), 'Second interim report monitoring the Lamfalussy Process'.

International Confederation of Free Trade Unions (2006), 'Having their cake and eating it too – the big corporate tax break', accessed at www.icftu.org/www/pdf/taxbreak/tax_break_EN.pdf.

Jackson, G. (2005), 'Stakeholders under pressure: corporate governance and labour management in Germany and Japan', *Corporate Governance*, **13**(3), May.

Jackson, G., M. Höpner and A. Kurdelbusch (2004), 'Corporate governance and employees in Germany: changing linkages, complementarities and tensions', RIETI discussion paper series 04-E-008.

James, Estelle, James Smalhout and Dimitri Vitlas (1999), *Administrative Costs and the Organization of Individual Account Systems: a Comparative Perspective*, World Bank pension primer, Washington, DC: World Bank Institute.

Jensen, M. (2004), 'Agency costs of overvalued equity', Harvard NOM research paper no. 04-26

Jensen, M. (2005), 'Agency costs of overrated equity', *Financial Management*, **34**(1) (Spring).

Jensen, M. and K. Murphy (2004), 'Remuneration: where we've been, how we got to here, what are the problems and how to fix them', ECGI working paper 44.

Kalecki, M. (1968) 'Trend and business cycles reconsidered', *Economic Journal*, **78**(2), (June), 263–76.

Keune, M. and M. Jepsen (2007), 'Not balanced and hardly new: the European Commission's quest for flexicurity', in H. Jørgensen and P.K. Madsen (eds), *Flexicurity and Beyond*, Copenhagen: DJØF Publishing.

Keynes, J.M. (1936), *The General Theory of Employment, Interest and Money*, London: Macmillan.

Kindleberger, C.P. (1973) *The World in Depression, 1929–1939*, Berkeley, CA: University of California Press.

Kindleberger, C.P. (2005), *Panics, Manias and Crashes. A History of Financial Crises*, 5th edn, London: Palgrave Macmillan.

Kleinknecht, A. (1998), 'Is labour market flexibility harmful to innovation?', *Cambridge Journal of Economics*, **22**(3), 387–96.

Kok, W. (2004), *Report from the High Level Group: Facing the Challenge – the Lisbon Strategy for Growth and Employment*, Brussels: European Communities.

Kremers J.M., D. Schoenmaker and P.J. Wierts (eds) (2003), *Financial Supervision in Europe*, Cheltenham, UK and Northampton, MA, USA: Edward Elgar.

Krugman, P. (2002), 'American's poor standards: Standard and Poor's does what our government refuses to do', *New York Times*, 17 May.

Krugman, P. and M. Obstfeld (2007), *International Economics*, 8th edn, Boston: Addison-Wesley.

Lamfalussy, A. (ed.) (2001), *Final Report of the Committee of Wise Men on the Regulation of European Securities Markets*, 15 February, Brussels: European Commission.

Lamfalussy, A. (2003), 'Creating an integrated European market for financial services', in P. Booth and D. Currie (eds), *The Regulation of Financial Markets*, London: IEA.

Lane, C. (2003), 'Changes in the corporate governance of German corporations: convergence to the Anglo-American model?', *Competition and Change*, **7**, (2–3).

Lannoo, K. and M. Levin (2004), 'Securities market regulation in the EU', Centre for European Policy Studies research report in finance and banking no. 33, May.

Lannoo, K. (2007), 'The future of Europe's financial centres', ECMI Policy brief no. 10, December.

Larsen, Peter Thal (2006), 'From pit to pinnacle: why traders are calling the shots on Wall Street', *Financial Times*, 15 June.

Lastra, R.M. (2003), 'The governance structure for financial regulation and supervision in Europe', *Columbia Journal of European Law*, **10**(1) (Fall).

Lavoie, M. (2001), 'Pricing', in Richard Hold and Steven Pressman (eds), *A New Guide to Post-Keynesian Economics*, London: Routledge.

Lavoie, M. and W. Godley (2001), 'Kaleckian models of growth in a coherent stock-flow monetary framework: a Kaldorian view', *Journal of Post-Keynesian Economics*, **24**(2), 277–312.

Lazonick, W. and M. O'Sullivan (2000), 'Maximising shareholder value: a new ideology of corporate governance', *Economy and Society*, **29**(1).

Levine, R. (2005), 'Finance and growth: theory and evidence', in P. Aghion and N. Durlauf (eds), *Handbook of Economic Growth*, Amsterdam: Elsevier.

Lim, E.-G. (2006), 'The euro's challenge to the dollar: different views from economists and evidence from COFER and other data', International Monetary Fund working paper, WP/06/154, June.

London Economics (in association with PricewaterhouseCoopers and Oxford Economic Forecasting) (2002), 'Quantification of the macro-economic impact of integration of EU financial markets', London, November 2002.

London Economics (2008), 'The importance of wholesale financial services to the EU economy 2008', London, July.

Lütz, S. (2002), *Der Staat und die Globalisierung von Finanzmärkten: Regulative Politik in Deutschland, Grossbritannien und den USA*, Cologne: Campus.

Lysandrou, Y. (2006), 'Hugh O'Neil as "Hamlet-plus": (post)colonialism and dynamic stasis in Brian Friel's *Making History*', *Irish Studies Review*, **14**(1), 91–106.

Mallette, P. and R. Spagnola (1994), 'State takeover legislation: the political defense', *SAM Advanced Management Journal*, **59**(3), 15–23.

Mandelbrot, B. and R.L Hudson (2004), *The (Mis)behaviour of Markets: a Fractal View of Risk, Ruin and Reward*, London: Profile Books.

McKean, L., S. Lessem and E. Bax (2006), *Money Management by Low-Income Households: Earnings, Spending, Saving, and Accessing Financial Services*, August, Chicago: Centre for Impact Research.

McKinsey Global Institute (2005), *Taking Stock of the World's Capital Markets*, McKinsey & Co.

McKinsey Global Institute (2007), *Mapping the Global Capital Market – Third Annual Report*, McKinsey & Co.

McKinsey Global Institute (2008), *Mapping Global Capital Markets – Fourth Annual Report*, McKinsey & Co.

Minsky, H.P. (1993), 'The financial instability hypothesis', in P. Arestis and M. Sawyer (eds), *Handbook of Radical Political Economy*, Aldershot, UK and Brookfield, US: Edward Elgar.

Minsky, H.P. (2004), *Induced Investment and Business Cycles*, Cheltenham, UK and Northampton, MA, USA: Edward Elgar.

Mizruchi, M. and G. Davis (2003), 'The globalization of American banking, 1962 to 1981', in Frank Dobbin (ed.), *The Sociology of the Economy*, New York: Russell Sage Foundation.

Morgenstern, O. (1959), *International Financial Transactions and Business Cycles*, Princeton, NJ: Princeton University Press.

Myners, P. (2001) *Institutional Investment in the United Kingdom: A Review*, London: HM Treasury.

Neimke, Markus et al. (2002), 'Deepening European financial integration: theoretical considerations and empirical evaluation of growth and employment benefits', background paper for the Gyllenhammer Report.

Norman, P. (2007), *Plumbers and Visionaries*, Chichester: Wiley.

Organisation for Economic Co-operation and Development (OECD) (2004), *Recent Tax Policy Trends and Reforms in OCED Countries*, Paris: OECD.

OECD (2005a), *Bank Profitability, Financial Statements of Banks*, Paris: OECD.

OECD (2005b), 'Ageing and pension system reform: implications for financial markets and economic policies', *Financial Market Trends*, (supplement), November.

Office of Fair Trading (OFT) (2006), 'Payment protection insurance: report on the market study and proposed decision to make a market investigation reference', OFT report 869, October.

OJ Official Journal (2008), 'Directive 2008/48/EC on credit agreements for consumers and repealing Council Directive 87/102/EC', OJ L133/66.

O'Mahony, M. and B. van Ark (2003), *EU Productivity and Competitiveness: an Industry Perspective*, Luxembourg: European Communities.

Padoa-Schioppa, T. and G. Saccomanni (1994), 'Managing a market-led global financial system', in P. Kenen (ed.), *Managing the World Economy: Fifty Years After Bretton Woods*, Washington, DC: IIE, pp. 235–68.

Parboni, R. (1981), *The Dollar and Its Rivals*, London: Verso.

Partnoy, F. (1997), *F.I.A.S.C.O. Blood in the Water in Wall Street*, London: Profile Books.

Petschnigg, R. (2005), 'The institutional framework for financial market policy in the USA seen from an EU perspective', European Central Bank occasional paper series no. 35, September.

Plihon, D., J. Couppey-Soubeyran and D. Saïdane (2006), *Les Banques: Acteurs de la Globalisation Financière*, Paris: Documentation Française.

Plihon, D., J.-P. Ponssard and P. Zarlowski (2003), 'Towards a convergence of the shareholder and stakeholder models, École Polytechnique, cahier no. 2003-011.

Pollin, R. (1995), 'Financial structures and egalitarian economic policy', *New Left Review*, **I**(214) (November/December).

Pragma Consulting (1999), *Rebuilding Pensions*, study for the European Commission on the prudential regulation of occupational pension funds, Brussels: European Commission.

PricewaterhouseCoopers (2008), 'From uncertainty to opportunity: FS M&A in Europe's developed and developing markets', March, London.

Socialist Group in the European Parliament (PSE) (2007), *Hedge Funds and Private Equity: A Critical Analysis*, Brussels.

Rajan, R. and L. Zingales (1998), 'Financial dependence and growth', *American Economic Review*, **88**, pp. 537–58.

Rajan, R. and L. Zingales (2003), 'Banks and markets: the changing character of European finance', in V. Gaspar, Philipp Hartmann and Olaf Sleijpen (eds), *The Transformation of the European Financial System: Second ECB Central Banking Conference*, Frankfurt: European Central Bank.

Rawls, J. (1971), *A Theory of Justice*, Cambridge, MA: Harvard University Press.

Rebérioux, A. (2002), 'European style of corporate governance at the crossroads: the role of worker involvement', *Journal of Common Market Studies*, **40**(1).

Rehder, B. (2003), 'Corporate governance in Mehrebenen System: Konfliktkonstellationen im Investitionswettbewerb', in W. Streeck and M. Höpner (eds), *Alle Macht dem Markt? Fallstundien zur Abwicklung der Deutschland AG*, Cologne: Campus.

Reszat, B. (2005), *European Financial Systems in the Global Economy*, London: John Wiley.

Roe, M.J. (1999), 'Codetermination and German securities markets', in M.M. Blair and M.J. Roe, *Employees and Corporate Governance*, Washington, DC: Brookings Institution.

Rybczynski, T.M. (1997), 'A new look at the evolution of the financial system', in J. Revell (ed.), *The Recent Evolution of Financial Systems*, Basingstoke: Macmillan.

Sandler, R. (2002), *Medium and Long-Term Retail Savings in the UK*, London: HM Treasury.

Sapir, A. (2003), *An Agenda for a Growing Europe*, report of an independent high-level study group established on the initiative of the President of the European Commission, July, Brussels: European Commission.

Scharpf, F. (1999), *Governing in Europe, Effective and Democratic?*, Oxford: Oxford University Press.

Schinasi, G.J. and P.G. Teixeira (2006), 'The lender of last resort in the European single financial market', International Monetary Fund working paper WP/06/127.

Schleifer, A. (2000), *Inefficient Markets. An Introduction to Behavioural Finance*, Oxford: Oxford University Press.

Shiller, R. (2003), *The New Financial Order: Risk in the Twenty-first Century*, Princeton, NJ: Princeton University Press.

Sierminska, E., A. Brandolini and T. Smeeding (2006), 'Comparing wealth distribution across rich countries', Luxembourg Wealth Study working paper no. 1.

Sjöberg, S. (2004), 'Economic democracy: a core issue for the European Left of the 21st century?', Initiative on Economic Democracy, organized by Transform, GUE/NGL and European Research Network on Economic Democracy (EURED), Brussels, 7–8 December, accessed at www.transform-network.org/fileadmin/user_upload/pdf/ED_Brussels_04.pdf.

Skidelsky, R. (2000), *John Maynard Keynes, vol. 3, Fighting For Britain*, London: Macmillan.

Smith, I.C. and I. Walter (2000), 'Global wholesale finance: structure, conduct, performance', paper presented at the 22nd Annual Colloquium of the Société Universitaire Europeenne de Recherches Financières (SUERF), Vienna, 27–29 April.

Spahn, P. (1995), 'International financial flows and transaction taxes: survey and options', International Monetary Fund working paper series no. WP/95/60, Washington, DC, June, accessed at www.wiwi.uni-frankfurt.de/fessoren/spahn/Spahn_010618.pdf.

Spiro, D.E. (1999), *The Hidden Hand of American Hegemony*, Ithaca, NY: Cornell University Press.

Statistisches Bundesamt (2003), *Bevölkerungsentwicklung bis 2050*, Wiesbaden.

Steindl, J. (1990), *Economic Papers 1941–1988*, Basingstoke: Macmillan.

Stiglitz, J. (1992), 'Banks versus markets as mechanisms for allocating and coordinating investment', in J.A. Roumasset and S. Barr (eds), *The Economics of Cooperation: East Asian Development and the Case for Pro-Market Intervention*, Boulder, CO: Westview Press.

Stiglitz, J. and B. Greenwald (2003), *Towards a New Paradigm in Monetary Economics*, Cambridge: Cambridge University Press.

Stockhammer, E. (2004), 'Financialization and the slowdown of accumulation', *Cambridge Journal of Economics,* **28**(5), 719–42.

Streeck, W. (2001), 'The transformation of corporate organisation in Europe: an overview', Max-Planck-Institut für Gesellschaftsforschung, working paper 01/8, Cologne.

Streeck, W. and M. Höpner (eds) (2003), *Alle Macht dem Markt?: Fallstudien zur Abwicklung der Deutschland AG*, Cologne: Campus.

Supiot, A. (2001), *Beyond Employment: Changes in Work and the Future of Labour Law in Europe*, Oxford: Oxford University Press.

Tanzi, V. (2000), 'Globalization and the future of social protection', International Monetary Fund working paper, January.

Theobald, T. (2006), 'Hostile takeovers and hostile defences: a comparative look at US board deference and the European effort at harmonization' (16 October), Bepress legal series working paper 1838, accessed at http://law.bepress.com/expresso/eps/1838.

Thiel, Michael (2001), 'Finance and economic growth – a review of theory and the available evidence', *European Economy*, economic papers no. 158.

Thomsen, S. (2003), 'The convergence of corporate governance systems to European and Anglo-American standards', *European Business Organisation Law Review*, **4**(1).

Toporowski, Jan (2005), *Theories of Financial Disturbance*, Cheltenham, UK and Northampton, MA, USA: Edward Elgar.

Treasury Select Committee (2004), 'Restoring confidence in long-term savings', London: House of Commons.

Treasury Select Committee (2005), 'Credit card charges and marketing', London: House of Commons.

Treasury Select Committee (2007), 'Private Equity', 24 July, London: House of Commons.

Triffin, R. (1960), *Gold and the Dollar Crisis: The Future of Convertibility*, New Haven, CT: Yale University Press.

US Bureau of Economic Affairs (n.d.), 'National income and production accounts', table 1.14, accessed at www.bea.gov.

US Treasury Department, Federal Reserve Bank of New York and Board of Governors of the Federal Reserve System (2008), 'Report on Foreign Portfolio Holdings of US Securities as of June 30, 2007', April.

Van Duyn, A. and P. Munter (2004), 'How Citigroup shook Europe's bond markets with two minutes of trading', *Financial Times*, 10 September.

Vitols, S. (2003) 'Negotiated shareholder value: the german version of an Anglo-American Practice', SP II 2003-25, Berlin: WZB.

Walkner, C. and J.P. Raes (2005), 'Integration and consolidation in EU banking – an unfinished business', European Commission D.G. for Economic and Financial Affairs economic papers no. 226, April.

Walter, I. (2003), 'Financial integration across borders and across sectors: implications for regulatory structures', in J.M. Kremers, D. Schoenmaker and P.J. Wierts (eds), *Financial Supervision in Europe*, Cheltenham, UK and Northampton, MA, USA: Edward Elgar.

Weil, Gotshal and Manges, LLP (2002), 'Comparative study of European Governance Codes relevant to the European Union and its member states', European Commission, Brussels.

Willman, J. (2007), 'Big spenders. How sovereign funds are stirring up protectionism', *Financial Times*, 30 July.

Wojnilower, A.M. (1980), 'The central role of credit crunches in recent financial history', *Brookings Papers on Economic Activity*, **2**, pp. 277–339.

Wolfson, M.H. (1994), *Financial Crises: Understanding the Post-War U.S. Experience*, Armonk, NY: M.E. Sharpe.

World Bank (1994), *Averting the Old Age Crisis*, New York: Oxford University Press.

World Trade Organization (2008), *World Trade 2007*, 17 April, Geneva, WTO.

Wu, K. (2005) 'The material consequences of how social security keeps older persons out of poverty across developed countries', Luxembourg income study working paper 410, May.

Index

NEW DIRECTIONS IN MODERN ECONOMICS

Modern State Intervention in the Era of Globalisation
Nikolaos Karagiannis and Zagros Madjd-Sadjadi

Financialization and the US Economy
Özgür Orhangazi

Monetary Policy and Financial Stability
A Post-Keynesian Agenda
Edited by Claude Gnos and Louis-Philippe Rochon

Inequality, Consumer Credit and the Saving Puzzle
Christopher Brown

Global Finance and Social Europe
Edited by John Grahl